Shojo Beat

OTOMEN

Story & Art by
Aya Kanno

Volume
EIGHT

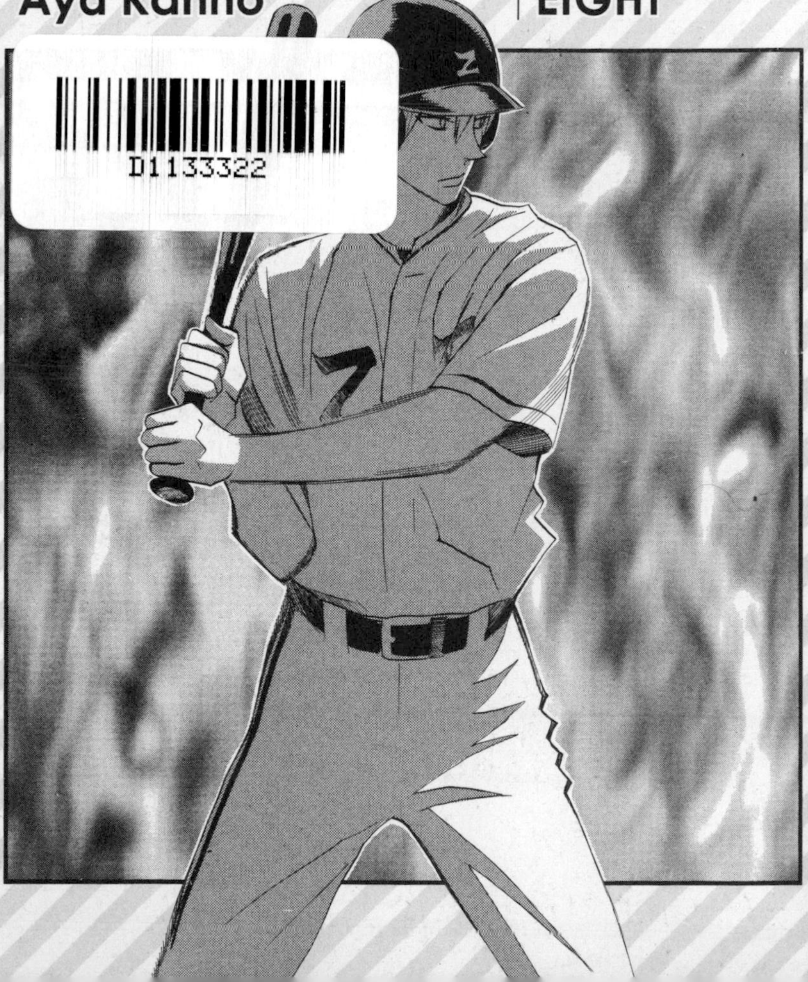

OTOMEN CHARACTERS & STORY

What is an OTOMEN?

O•to•men *[OH-toe-men]*

1) A young man with girlish interests and thoughts.

2) A young man who has talent for cooking, needlework and general housework.

3) A manly young man with a girlish heart.

Asuka Masamune

The captain of Ginyuri Academy High School's kendo team. He is handsome, studious and (to the casual observer) the perfect high school student. But he is actually an *otomen*, a man with a girlish heart. He loves cute things ♥, and he has a natural talent for cooking, needlework and general housekeeping. He's even a big fan of the shojo manga *Love Chick*.

STORY

Asuka Masamune, the kendo captain, is actually an *otomen* (a girlish guy)—a man who likes cute things, housework and shojo manga. When he was young, his father left home to become a woman. His mother was traumatized, and ever since then, he has kept his girlish interests a secret. However, things change when he meets Juta, a guy who is using Asuka as the basis for the female character in the shojo manga he is writing (←top secret). Asuka also starts having feelings for a tomboy girl who is good at martial arts. Because of this, he's slowly reverting to his true *otomen* self!

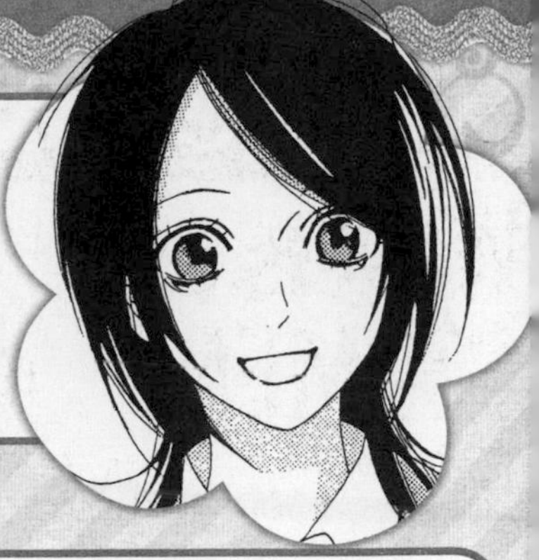

Ryo Miyakozuka

Asuka's classmate for whom he has feelings. She has studied martial arts under her father ever since she was little, and she is very good at it. On the other hand, her housekeeping skills are disastrous. She's a very eccentric beauty.

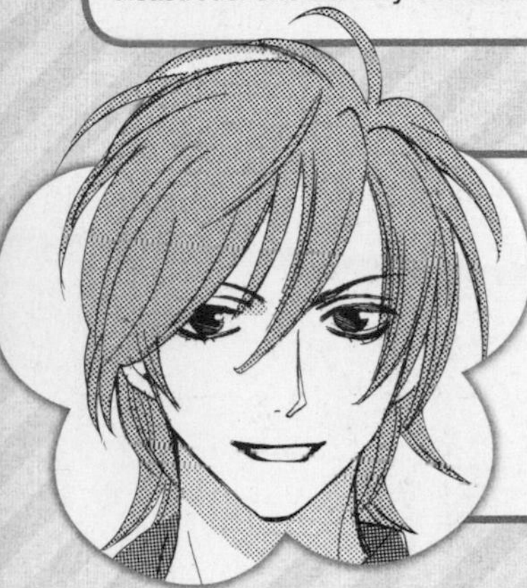

Juta Tachibana

Asuka's classmate. He's flirtatious, but he's actually the popular shojo manga artist Jewel Sachihana. He is using Asuka and Ryo as character concepts in his manga *Love Chick*, which is being published in the shojo magazine *Hana to Mame*. His personal life is a mystery! He has ten younger sisters!!

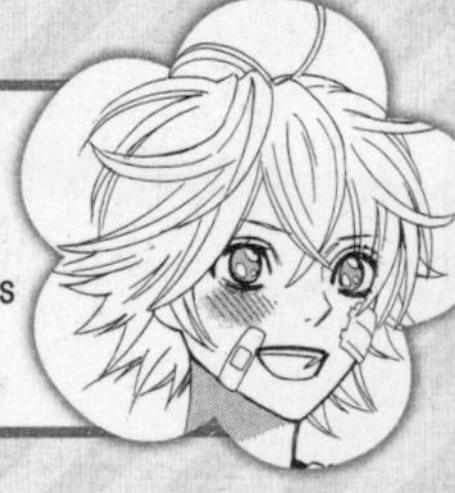

Yamato Ariake

Underclassman at Asuka's school. He looks like a girl, but he admires manliness and has long, delusional fantasies about being manly…

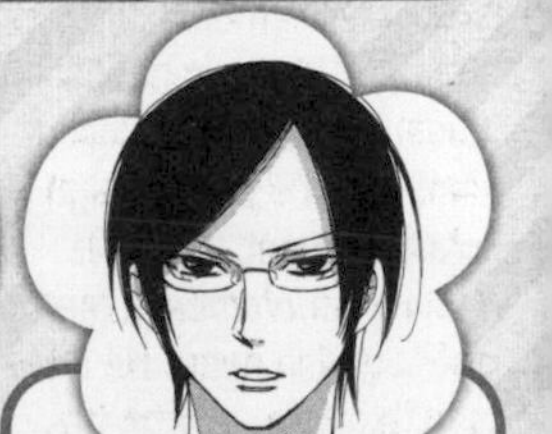

Hajime Tonomine

The captain of Kinbara High School's kendo team, he sees Asuka as his lifelong rival. He is the strong and silent type but is actually an *otomen* who is good with makeup. A *Tsun-sama*.

("Tsun-sama" © Juta Tachibana.)

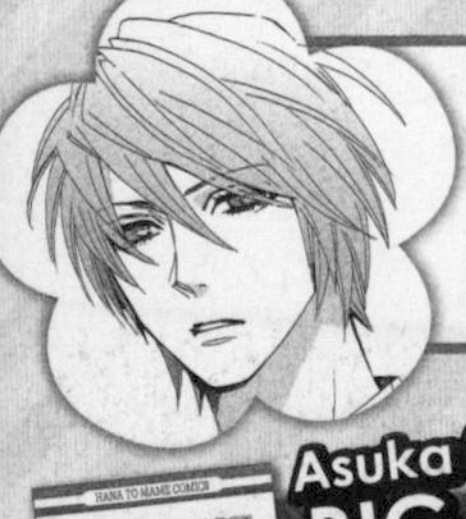

Kitora Kurokawa

Asuka's classmate. He is obsessed with the beauty of flowers. He is an *otomen* who refers to himself as the Flower Evangelist.

Asuka is also a BIG FAN!

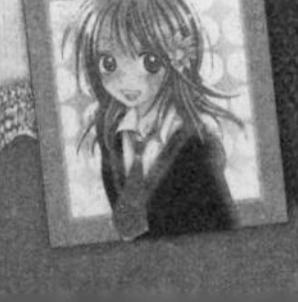
HANA TO MAME COMICS
LOVE CHICK
Jewel Sachihana 1

Hana to Mame Comics

LOVE CHICK by Jewel Sachihana

(Now serialized in *Hana to Mame*)

The very popular shojo comic that Juta writes (under the pen name Jewel Sachihana).

OTOMEN

volume 8
CONTENTS

OTOMEN 05

GLOSSARY 192

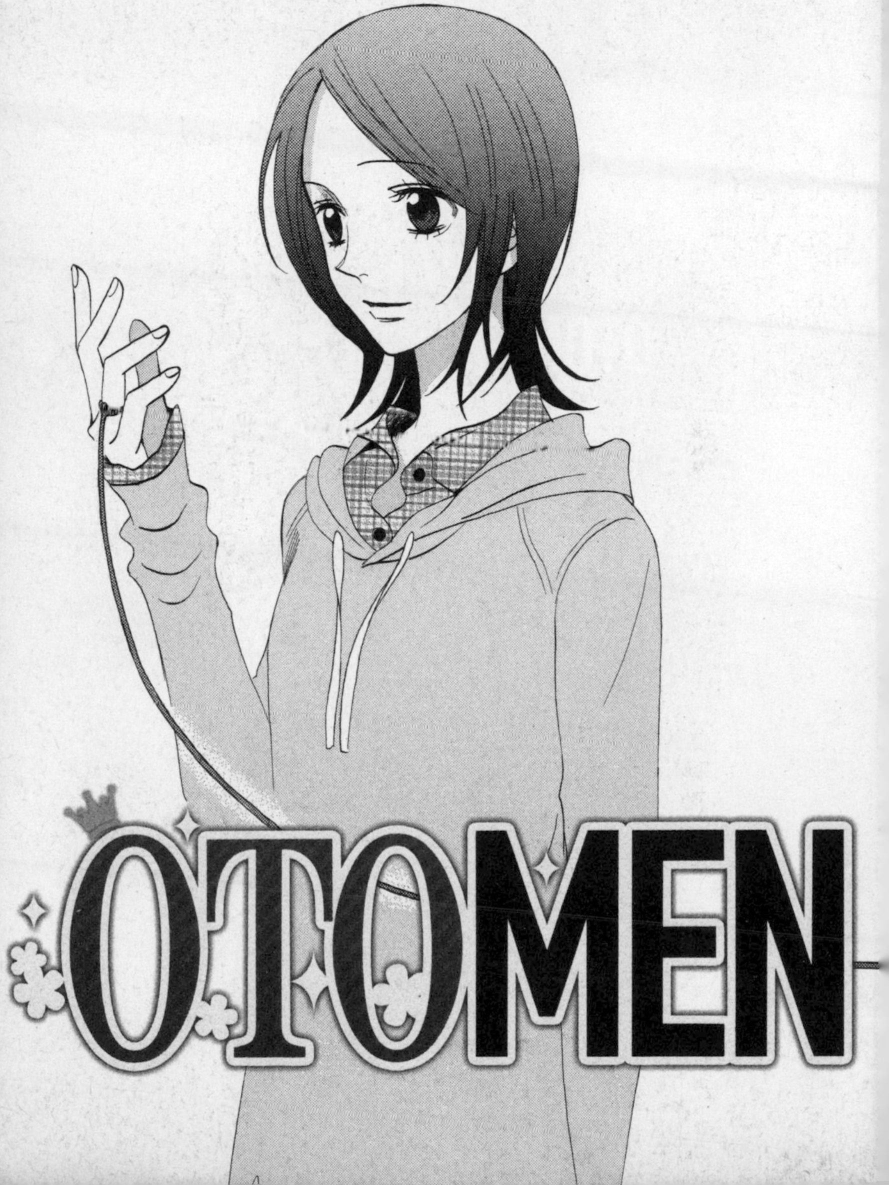
OTOMEN

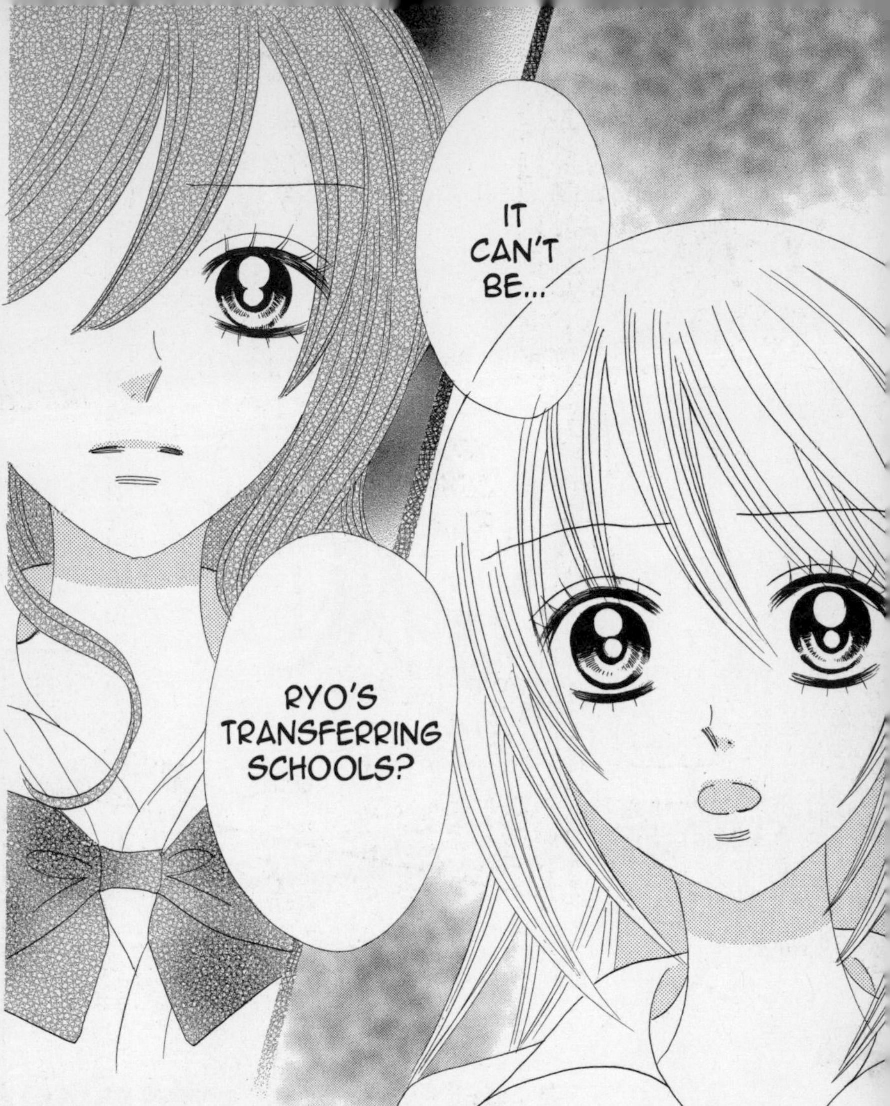
IT CAN'T BE...
RYO'S TRANSFERRING SCHOOLS?

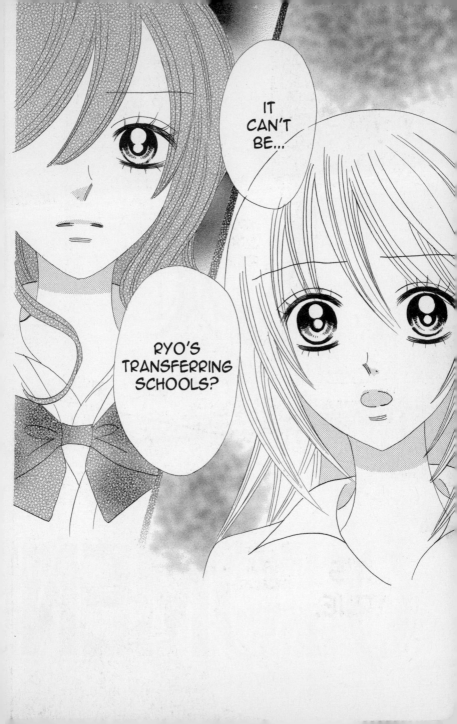

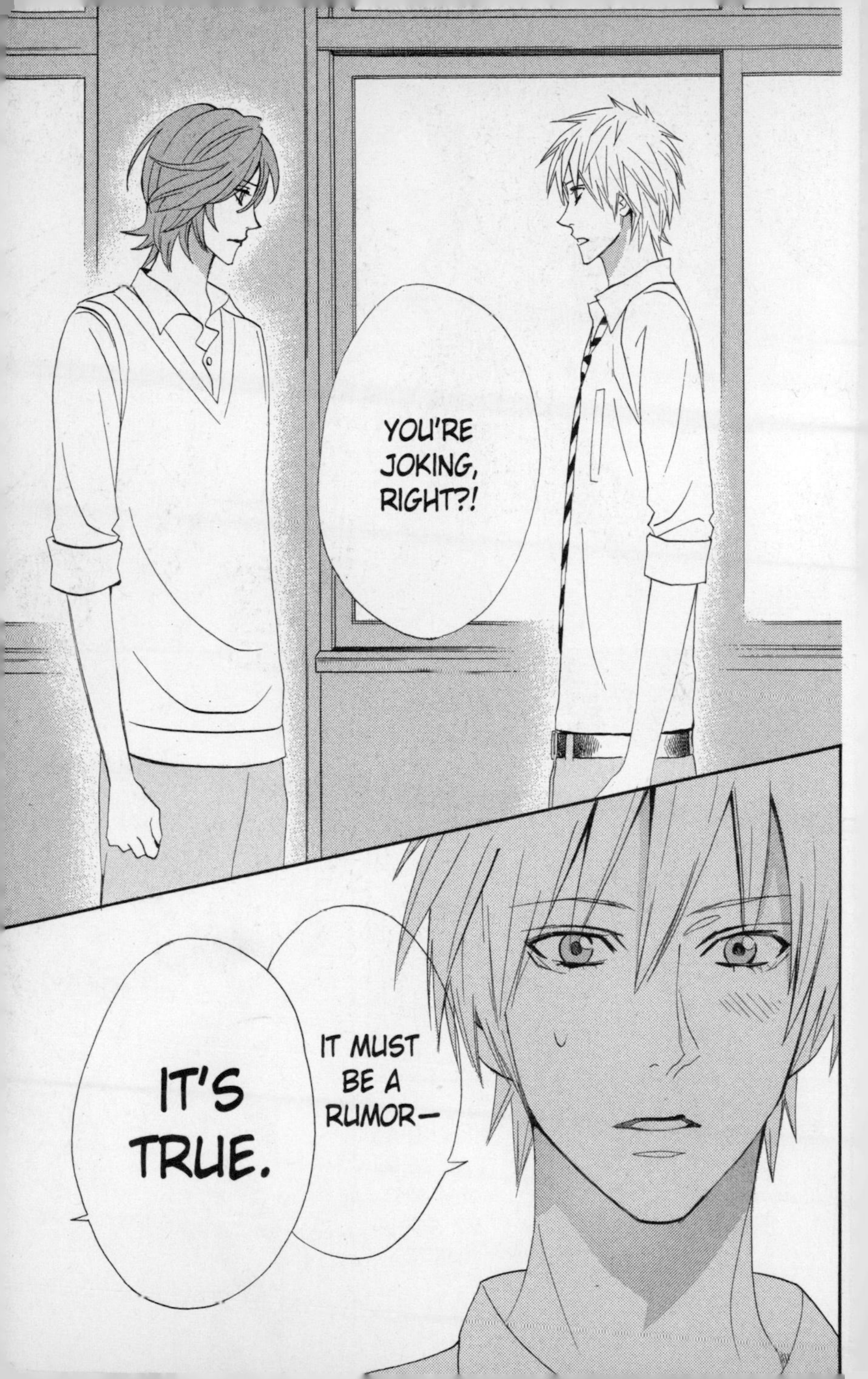
YOU'RE JOKING, RIGHT?!
IT MUST BE A RUMOR—
IT'S TRUE.

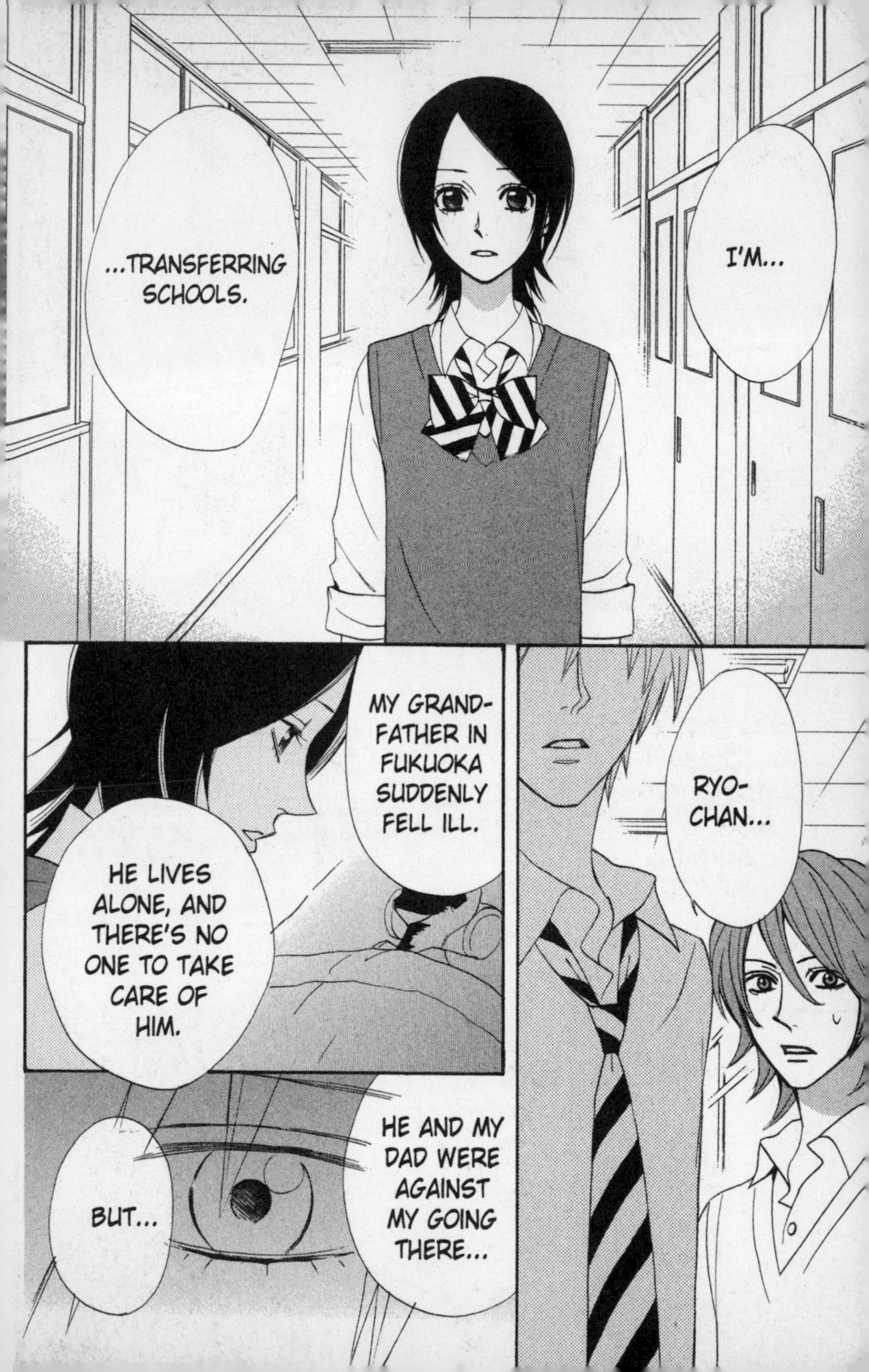
I'M...
...TRANSFERRING SCHOOLS.
RYO-CHAN...
MY GRAND-FATHER IN FUKUOKA SUDDENLY FELL ILL.
HE LIVES ALONE, AND THERE'S NO ONE TO TAKE CARE OF HIM.
HE AND MY DAD WERE AGAINST MY GOING THERE...
BUT...

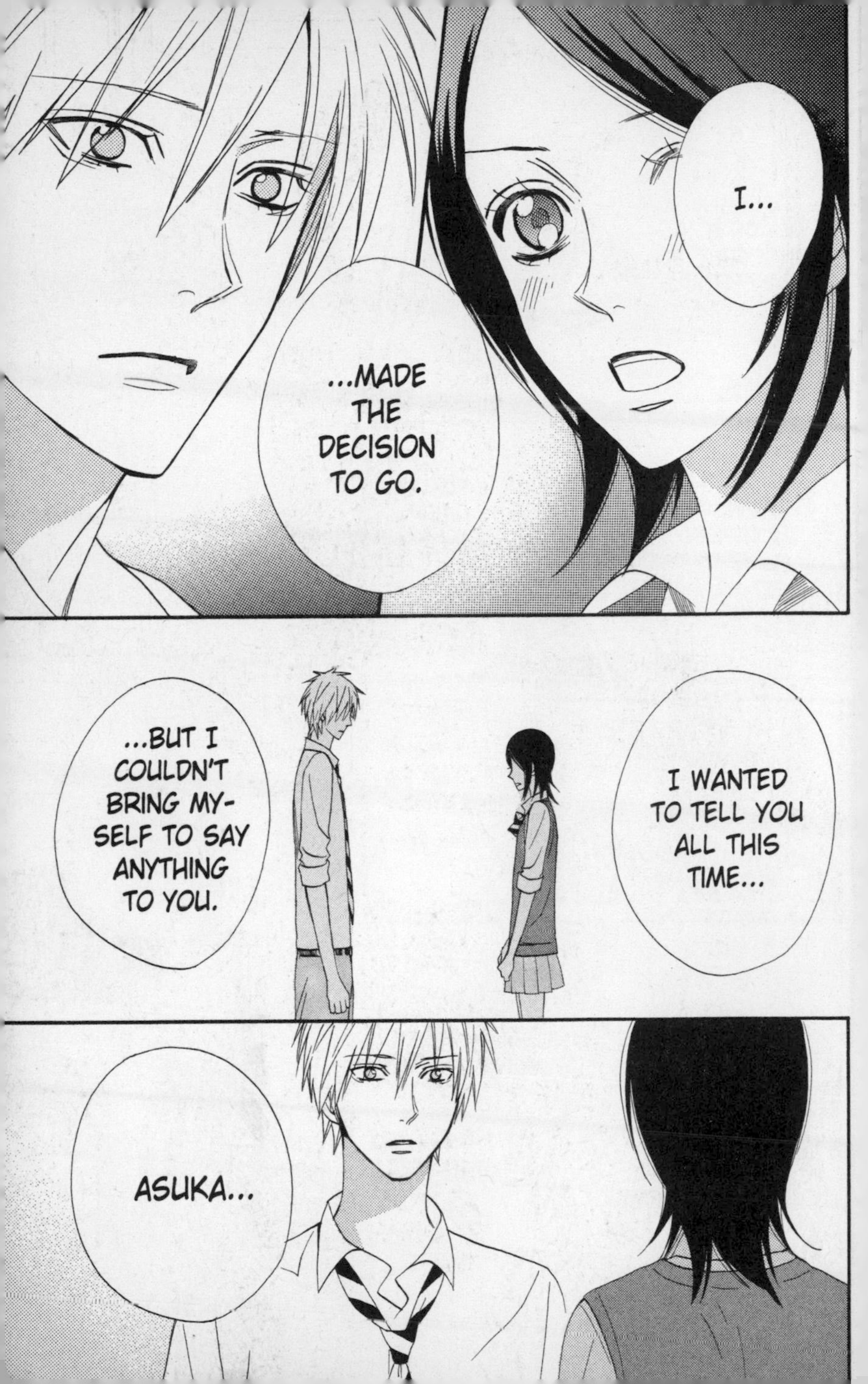
I...
...MADE THE DECISION TO GO.
I WANTED TO TELL YOU ALL THIS TIME...
...BUT I COULDN'T BRING MY-SELF TO SAY ANYTHING TO YOU.
ASUKA...

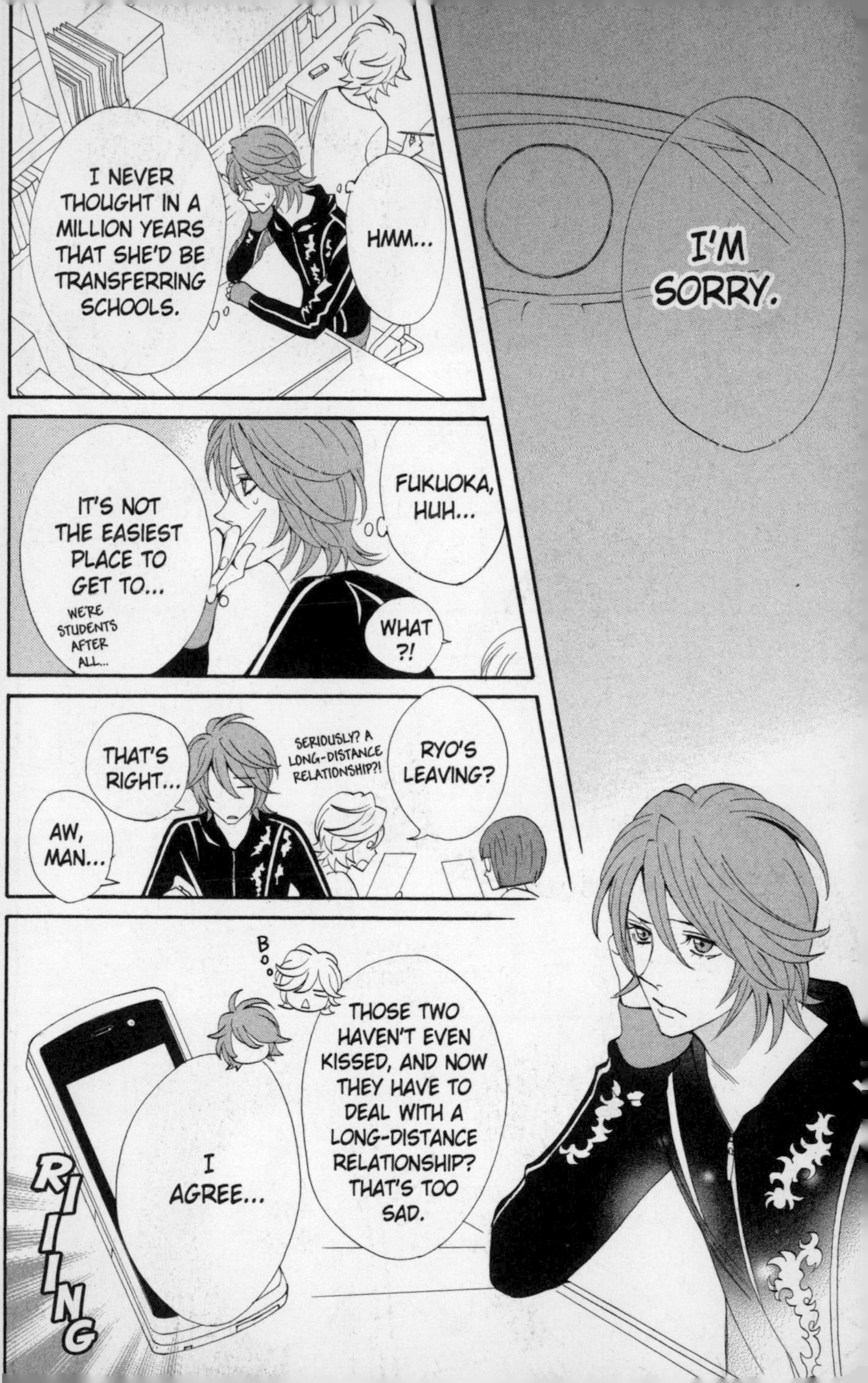
I'M SORRY.
HMM...
I NEVER THOUGHT IN A MILLION YEARS THAT SHE'D BE TRANSFERRING SCHOOLS.
FUKUOKA, HUH...
WHAT ?!
IT'S NOT THE EASIEST PLACE TO GET TO...
WE'RE STUDENTS AFTER ALL...
RYO'S LEAVING?
SERIOUSLY? A LONG-DISTANCE RELATIONSHIP?!
THAT'S RIGHT...
AW, MAN...
B
THOSE TWO HAVEN'T EVEN KISSED, AND NOW THEY HAVE TO DEAL WITH A LONG-DISTANCE RELATIONSHIP? THAT'S TOO SAD.
I AGREE...
RIIING

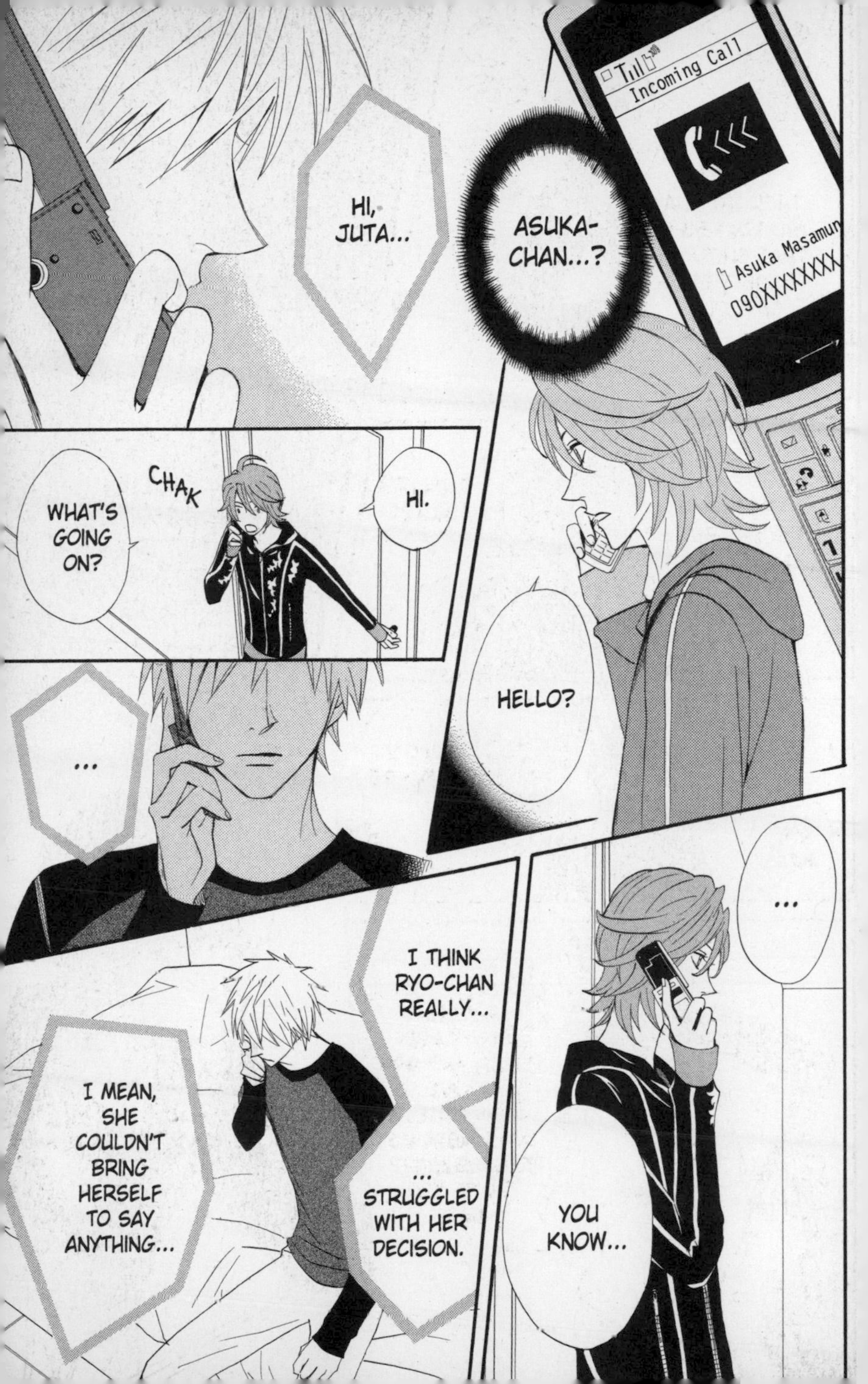
Incoming Call
Asuka Masamun
090XXXXXXXX
ASUKA-CHAN...?
HELLO?
HI, JUTA...
HI.
CHAK
WHAT'S GOING ON?
...
...
YOU KNOW...
I THINK RYO-CHAN REALLY...
... STRUGGLED WITH HER DECISION.
I MEAN, SHE COULDN'T BRING HERSELF TO SAY ANYTHING...

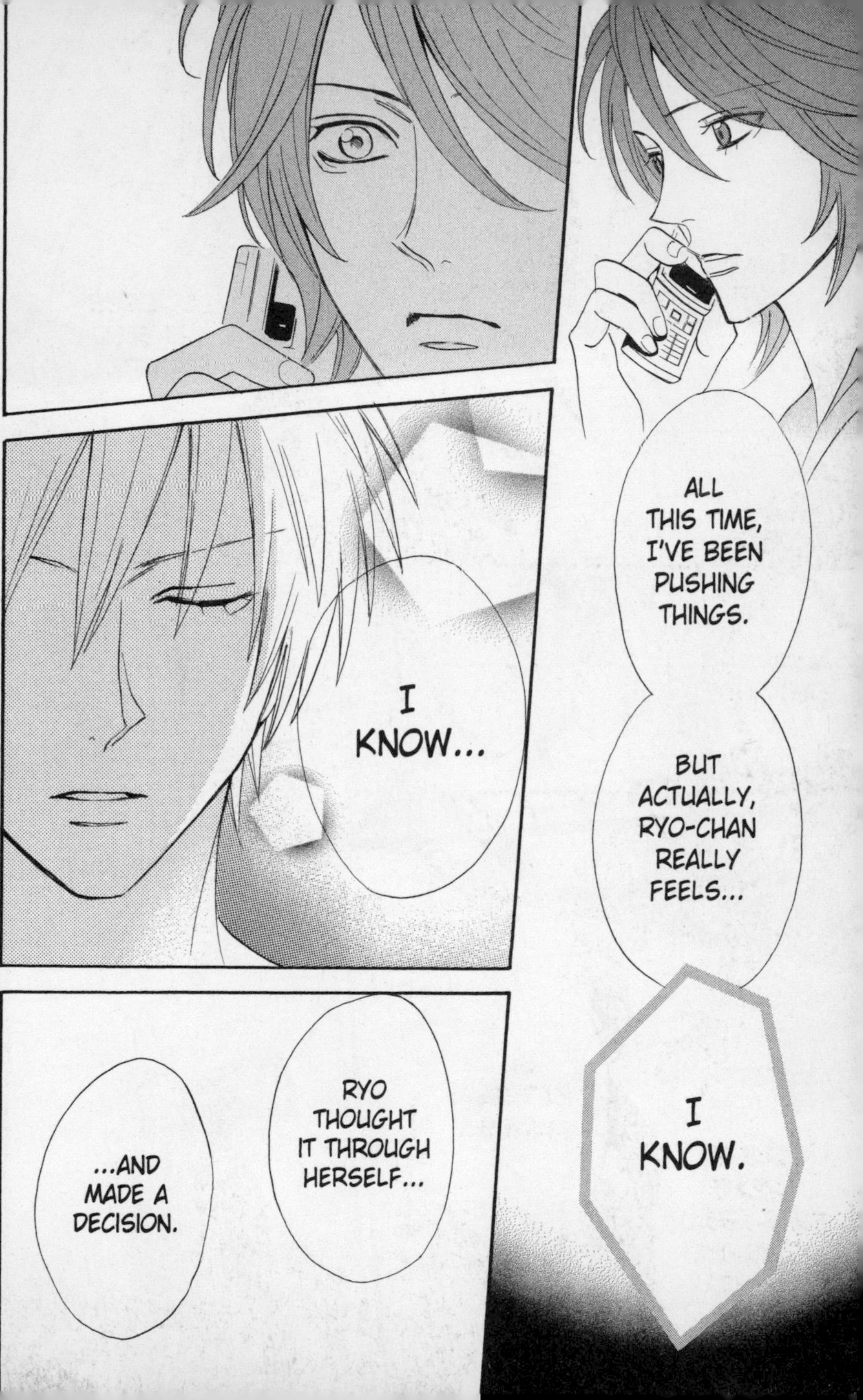
ALL THIS TIME, I'VE BEEN PUSHING THINGS.
BUT ACTUALLY, RYO-CHAN REALLY FEELS...
I KNOW.
I KNOW...
RYO THOUGHT IT THROUGH HERSELF...
...AND MADE A DECISION.

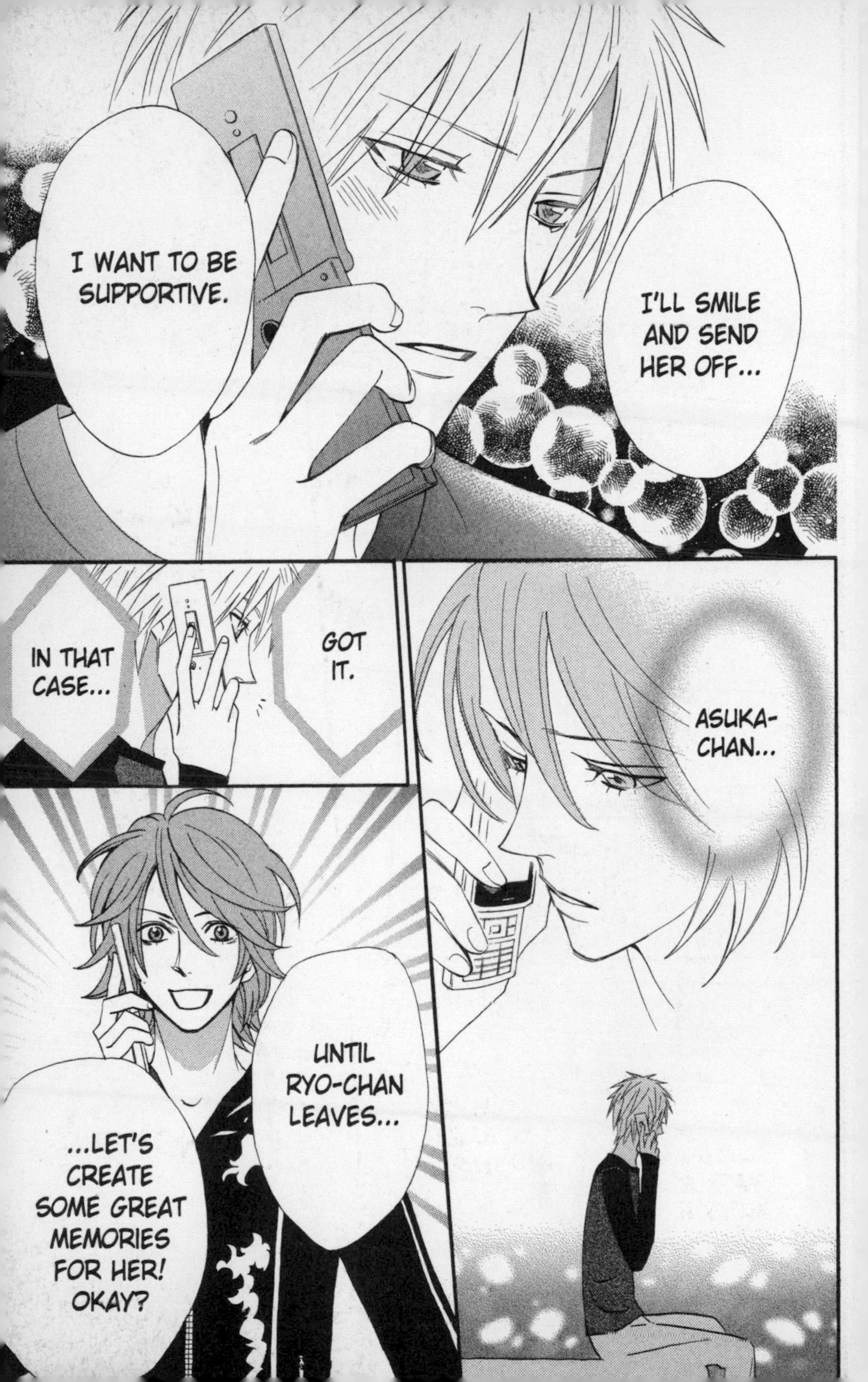
I'LL SMILE AND SEND HER OFF...
I WANT TO BE SUPPORTIVE.
ASUKA-CHAN...
GOT IT.
IN THAT CASE...
UNTIL RYO-CHAN LEAVES...
...LET'S CREATE SOME GREAT MEMORIES FOR HER! OKAY?

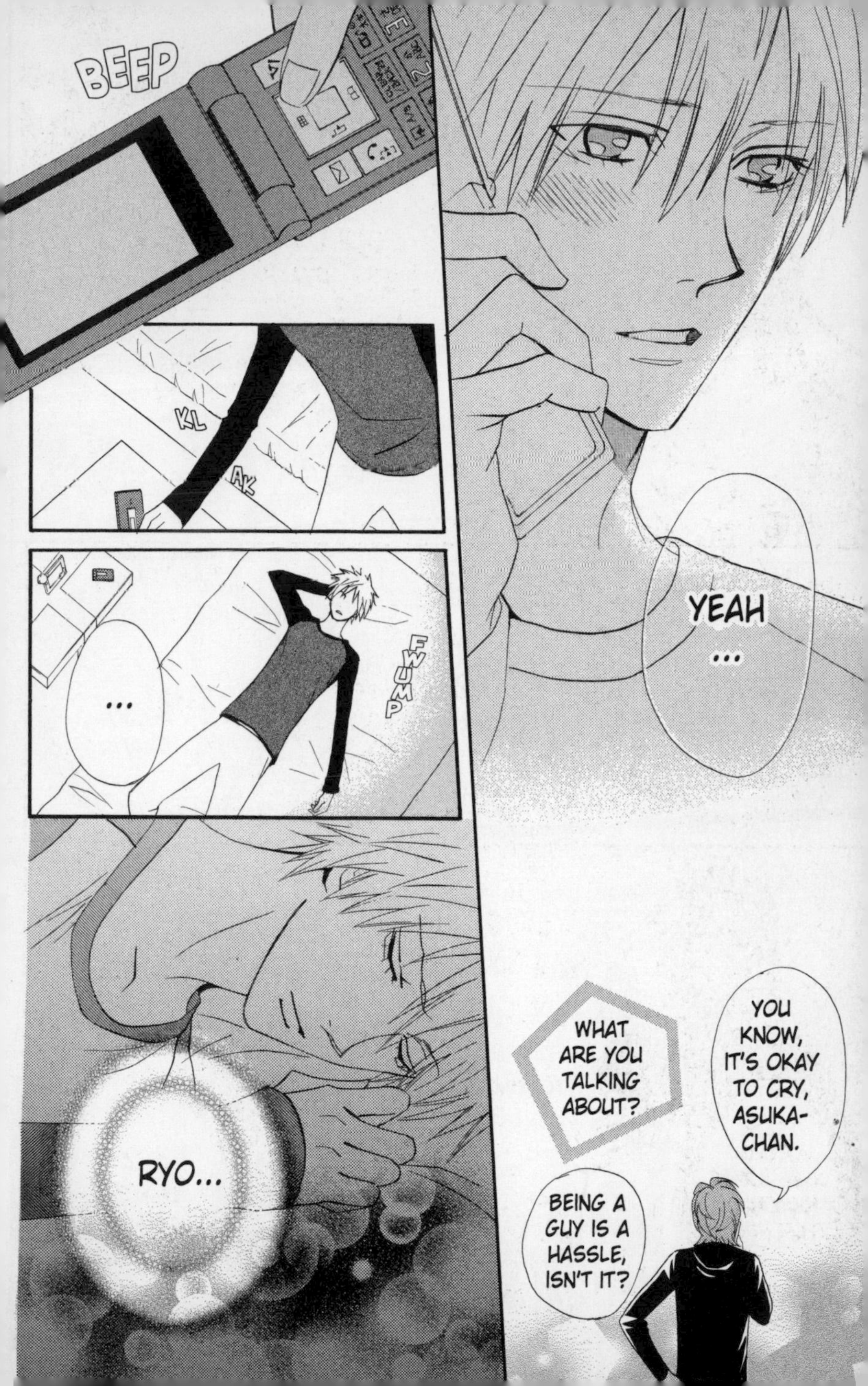
YEAH ...
YOU KNOW, IT'S OKAY TO CRY, ASUKA-CHAN.
WHAT ARE YOU TALKING ABOUT?
BEING A GUY IS A HASSLE, ISN'T IT?
BEEP
KL
AK
FWUMP
...
RYO...

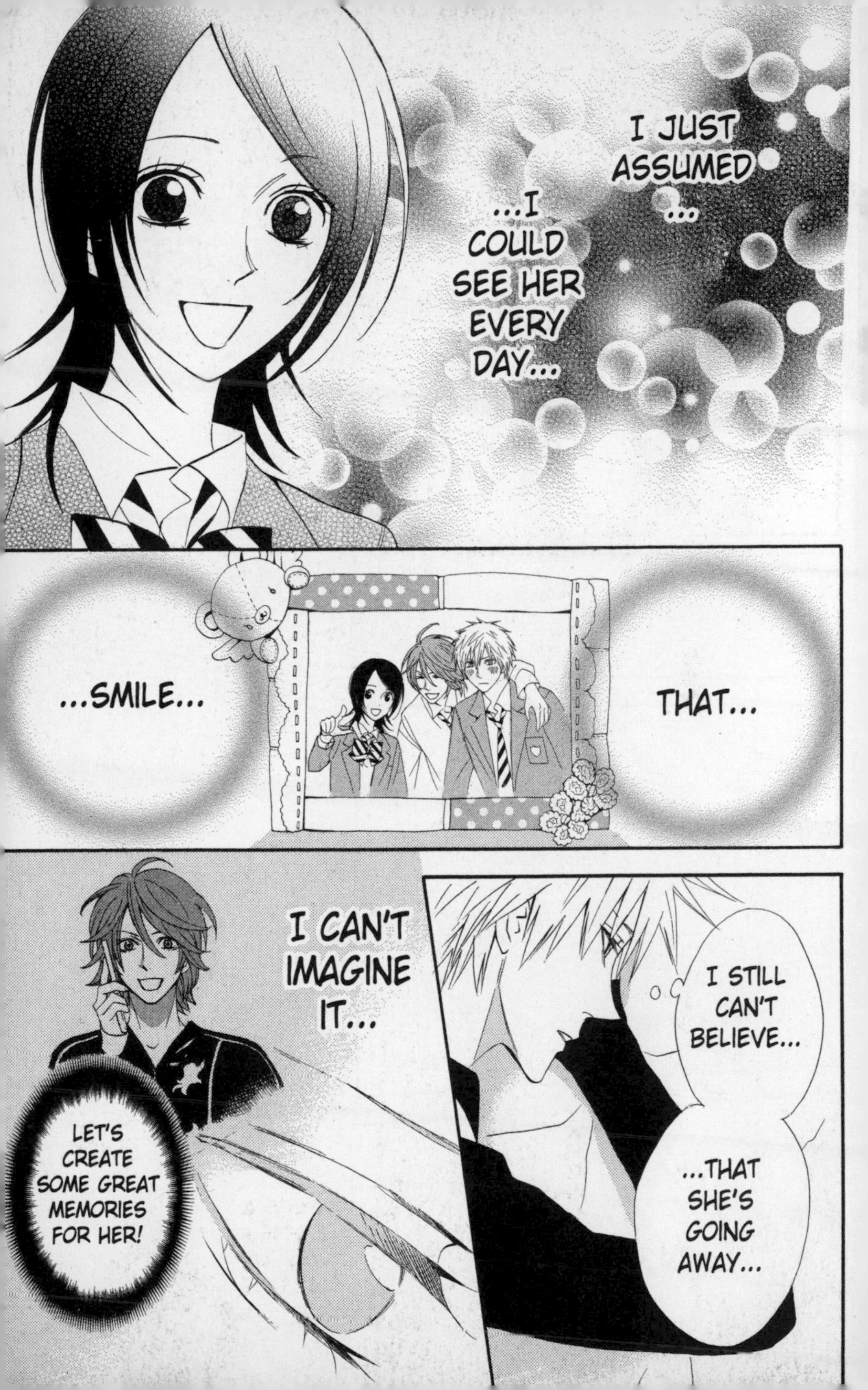
I JUST ASSUMED...
...I COULD SEE HER EVERY DAY...
THAT...
...SMILE...
I STILL CAN'T BELIEVE...
...THAT SHE'S GOING AWAY...
I CAN'T IMAGINE IT...
LET'S CREATE SOME GREAT MEMORIES FOR HER!

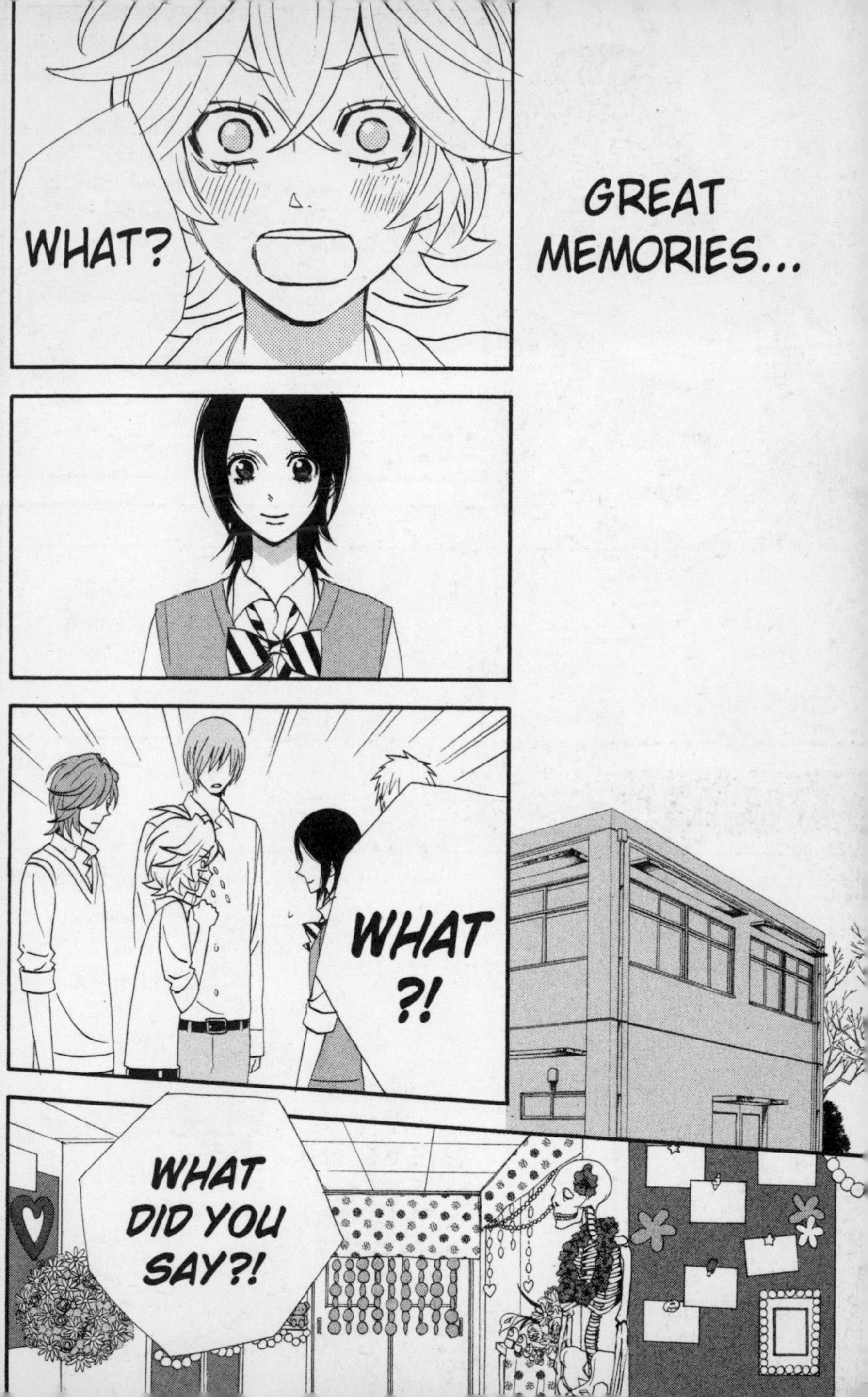
GREAT MEMORIES...
WHAT?
WHAT ?!
WHAT DID YOU SAY?!

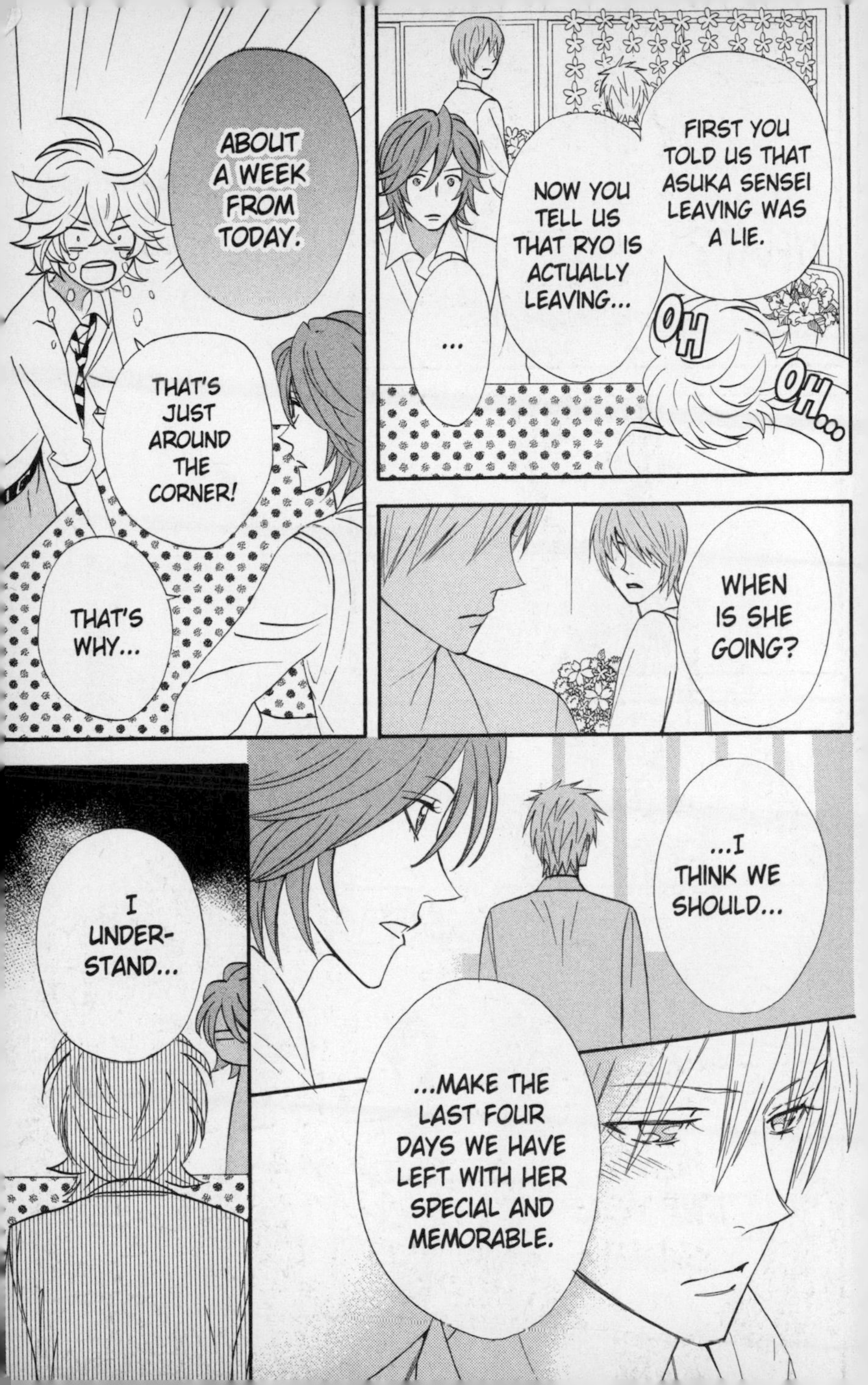
FIRST YOU TOLD US THAT ASUKA SENSEI LEAVING WAS A LIE.
NOW YOU TELL US THAT RYO IS ACTUALLY LEAVING...
...
OH
OH...
WHEN IS SHE GOING?
ABOUT A WEEK FROM TODAY.
THAT'S JUST AROUND THE CORNER!
THAT'S WHY...
...I THINK WE SHOULD...
...MAKE THE LAST FOUR DAYS WE HAVE LEFT WITH HER SPECIAL AND MEMORABLE.
I UNDER-STAND...

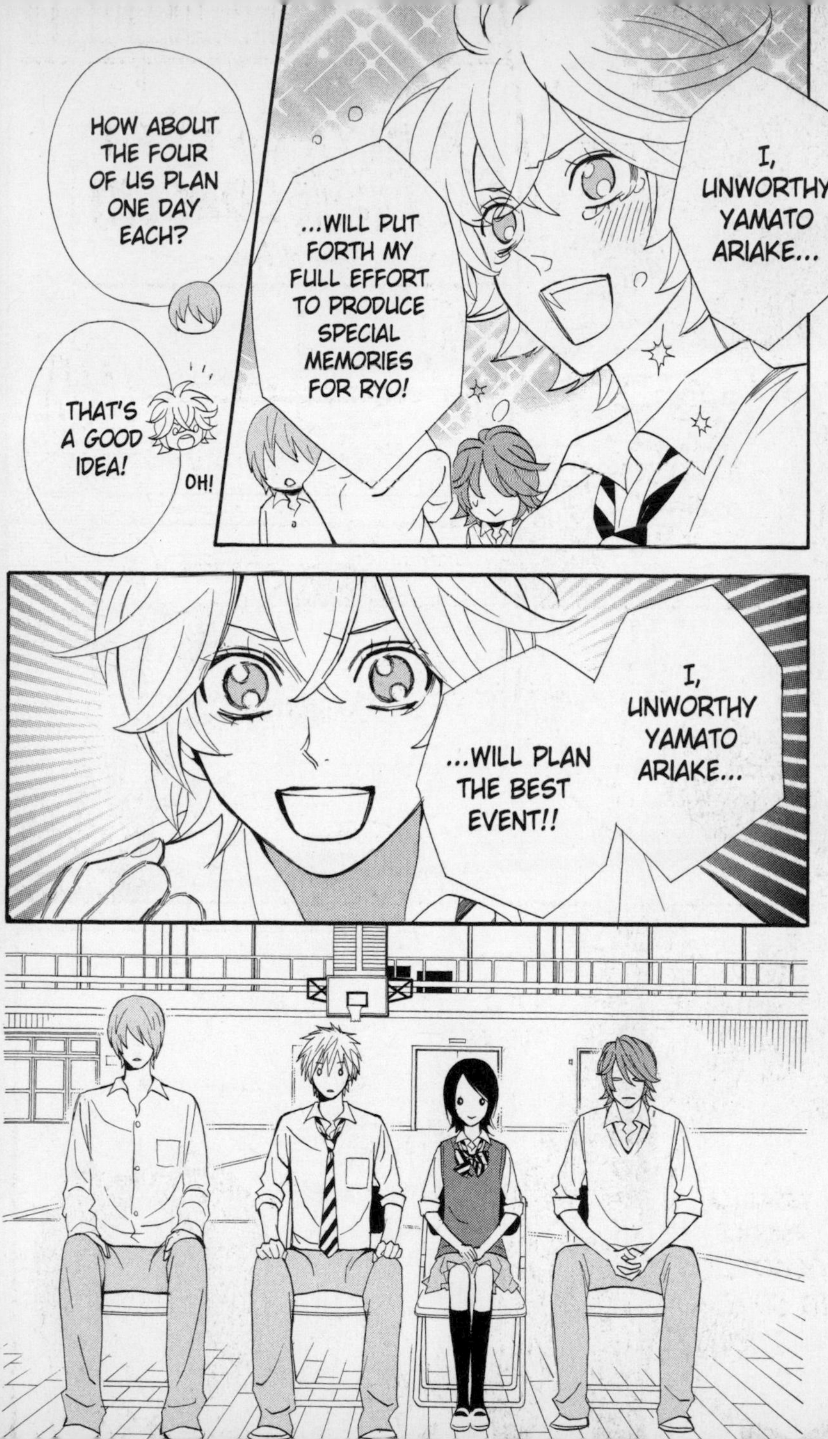
I, UNWORTHY YAMATO ARIAKE...
...WILL PUT FORTH MY FULL EFFORT TO PRODUCE SPECIAL MEMORIES FOR RYO!
HOW ABOUT THE FOUR OF US PLAN ONE DAY EACH?
OH!
THAT'S A GOOD IDEA!
I, UNWORTHY YAMATO ARIAKE...
...WILL PLAN THE BEST EVENT!!

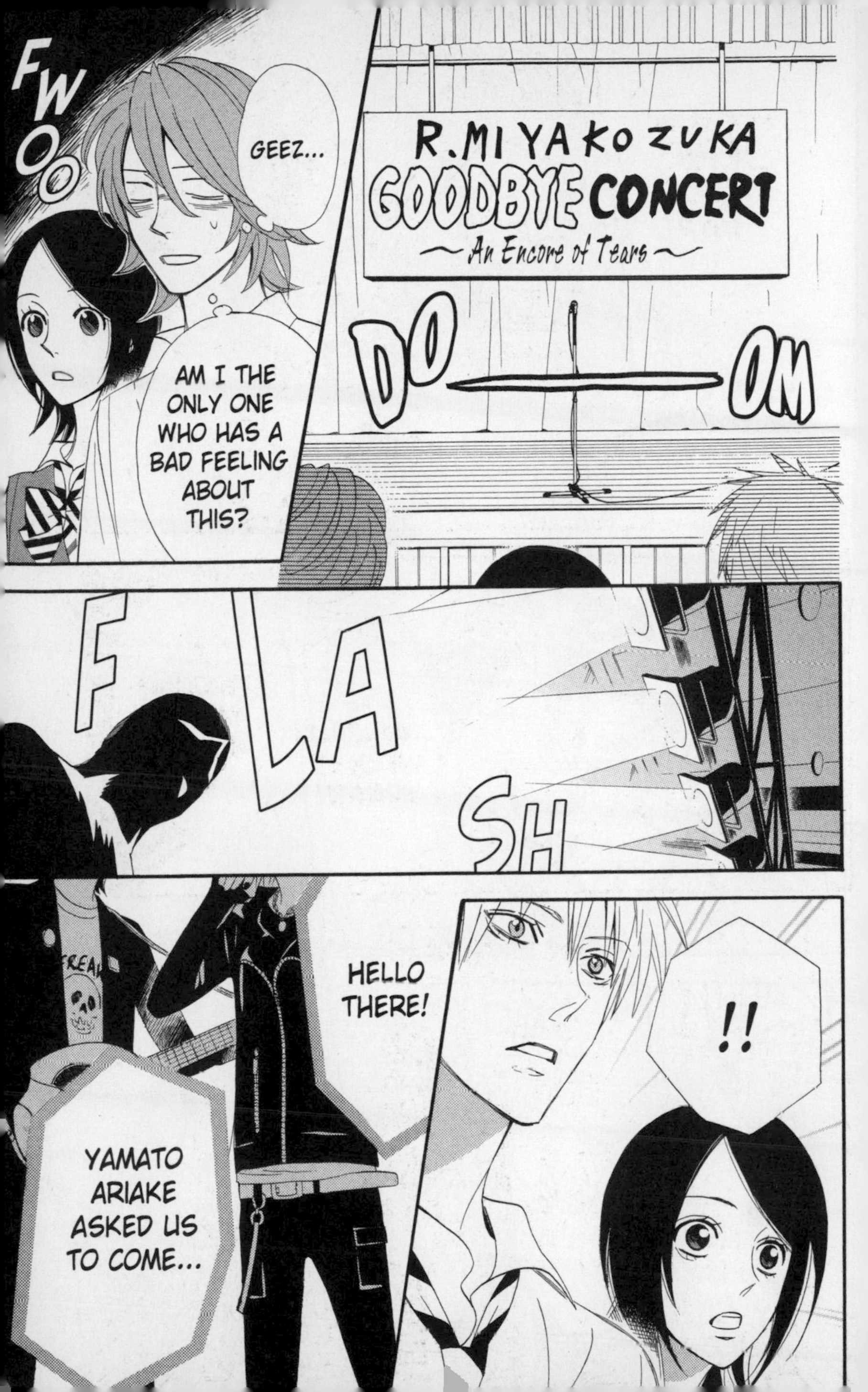
R. MIYAKOZUKA
GOODBYE CONCERT
~An Encore of Tears~
DOOM
GEEZ...
AM I THE ONLY ONE WHO HAS A BAD FEELING ABOUT THIS?
FWOOO
FLASH
!!
HELLO THERE!
YAMATO ARIAKE ASKED US TO COME...

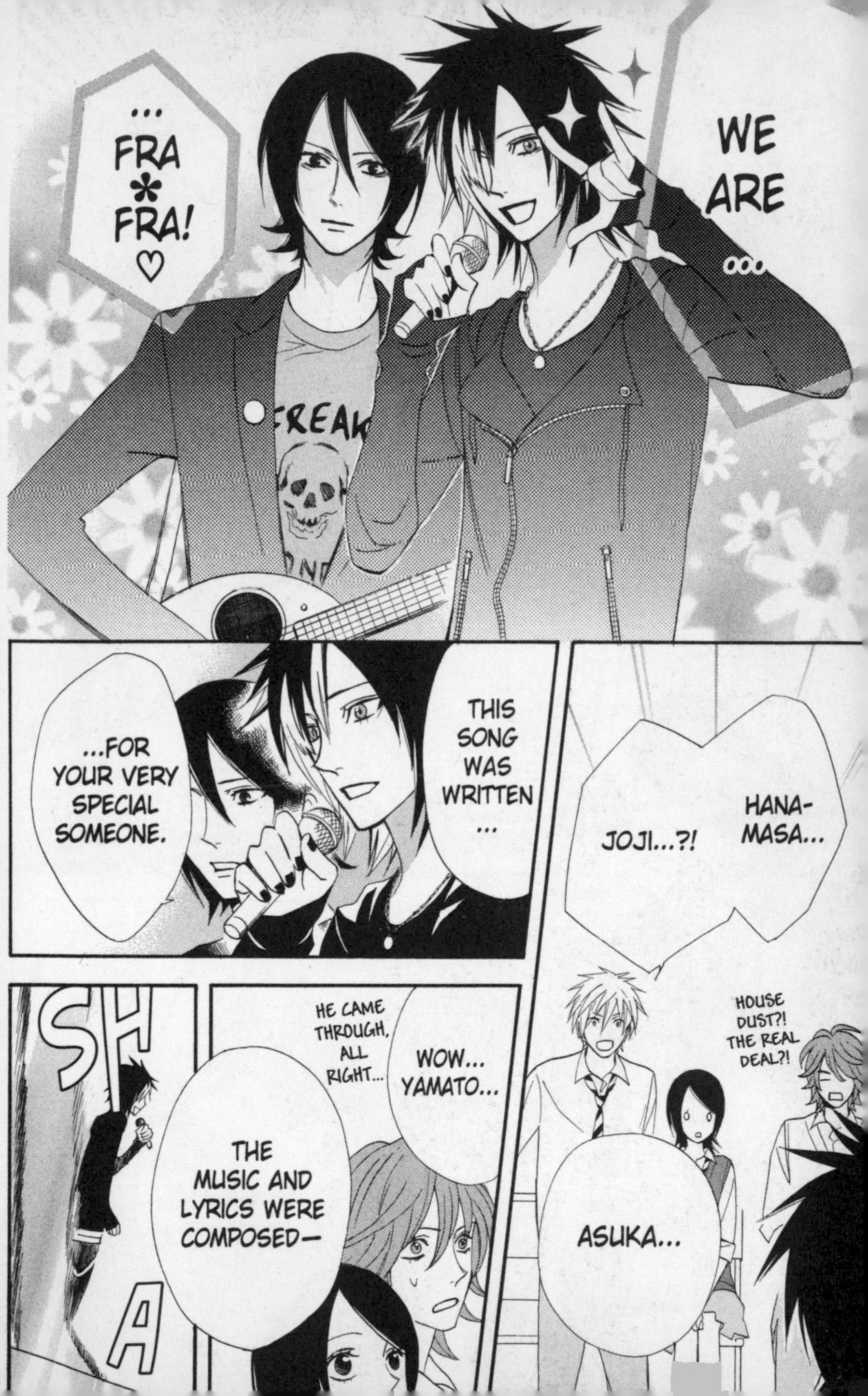
WE ARE ...
... FRA * FRA! ♡
HANA-MASA...
JOJI...?!
HOUSE DUST?! THE REAL DEAL?!
ASUKA...
THIS SONG WAS WRITTEN ...
...FOR YOUR VERY SPECIAL SOMEONE.
WOW... YAMATO...
HE CAME THROUGH, ALL RIGHT...
THE MUSIC AND LYRICS WERE COMPOSED—
SH
A

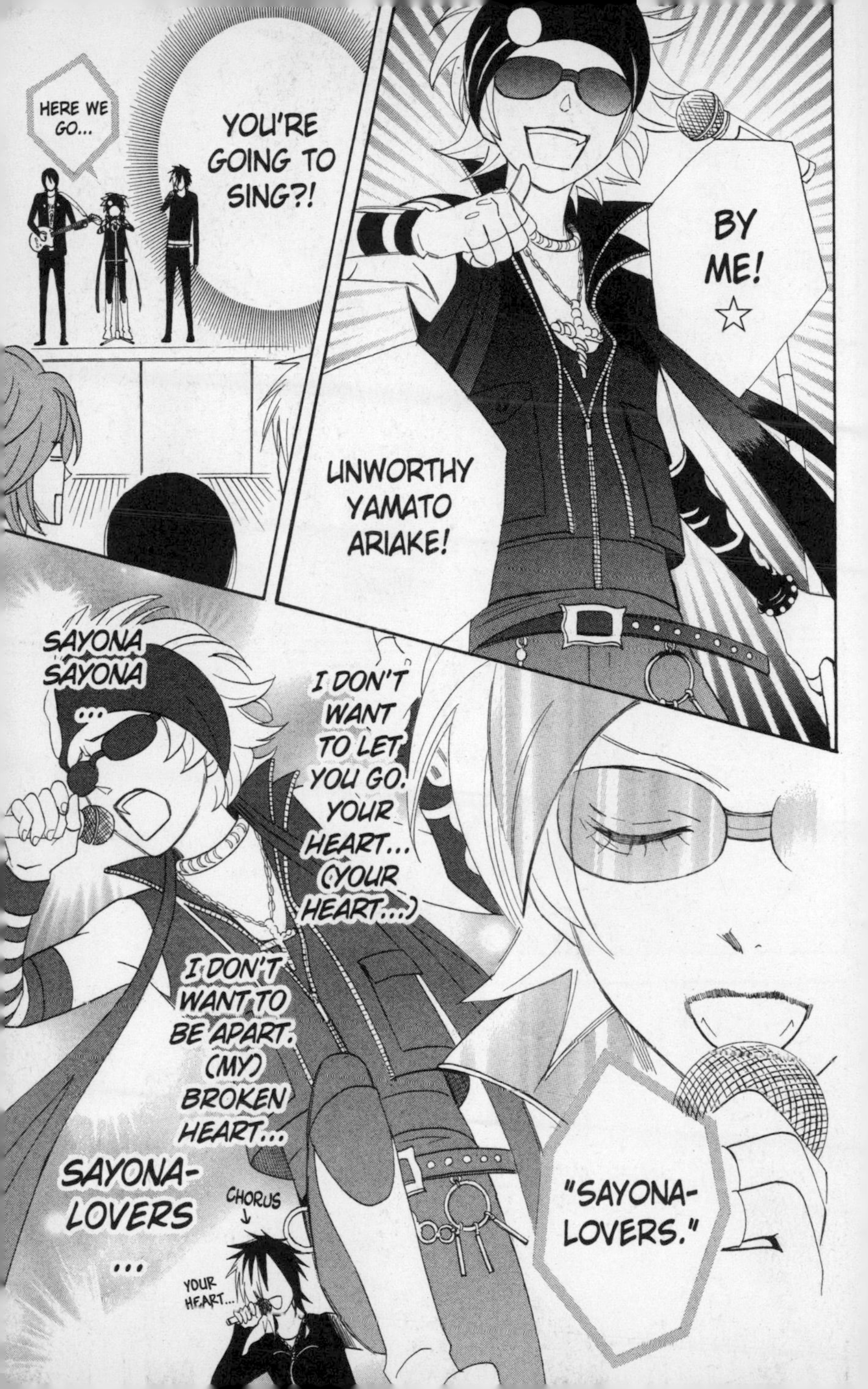
BY ME! ☆
UNWORTHY YAMATO ARIAKE!
HERE WE GO...
YOU'RE GOING TO SING?!
"SAYONA-LOVERS."
I DON'T WANT TO LET YOU GO. YOUR HEART... (YOUR HEART...)
SAYONA SAYONA ...
I DON'T WANT TO BE APART. (MY) BROKEN HEART...
SAYONA-LOVERS ...
CHORUS
YOUR HEART...

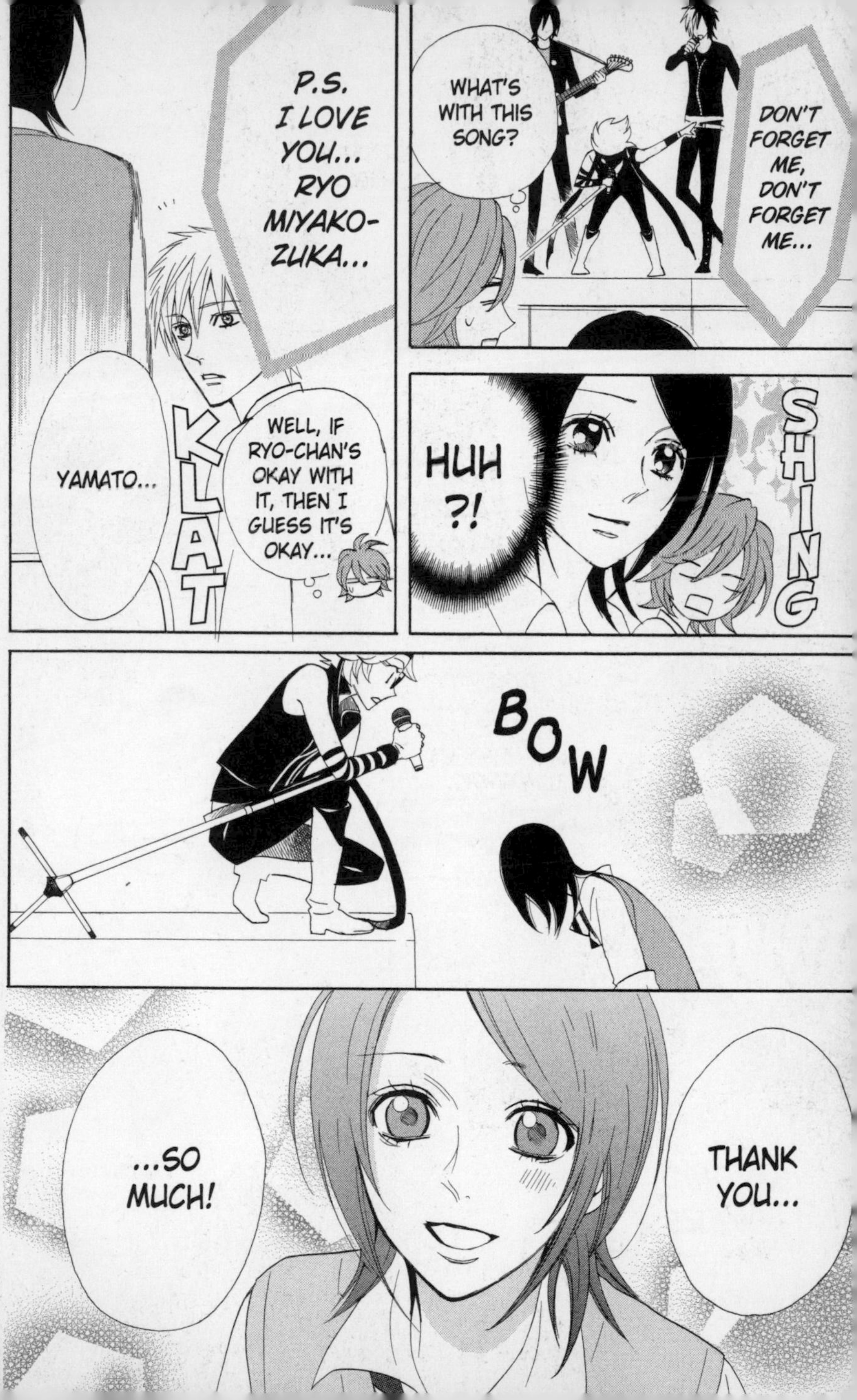
DON'T FORGET ME, DON'T FORGET ME...
WHAT'S WITH THIS SONG?
SHING
HUH ?!
P.S. I LOVE YOU... RYO MIYAKO-ZUKA...
WELL, IF RYO-CHAN'S OKAY WITH IT, THEN I GUESS IT'S OKAY...
KLAT
YAMATO...
BOW
THANK YOU...
...SO MUCH!

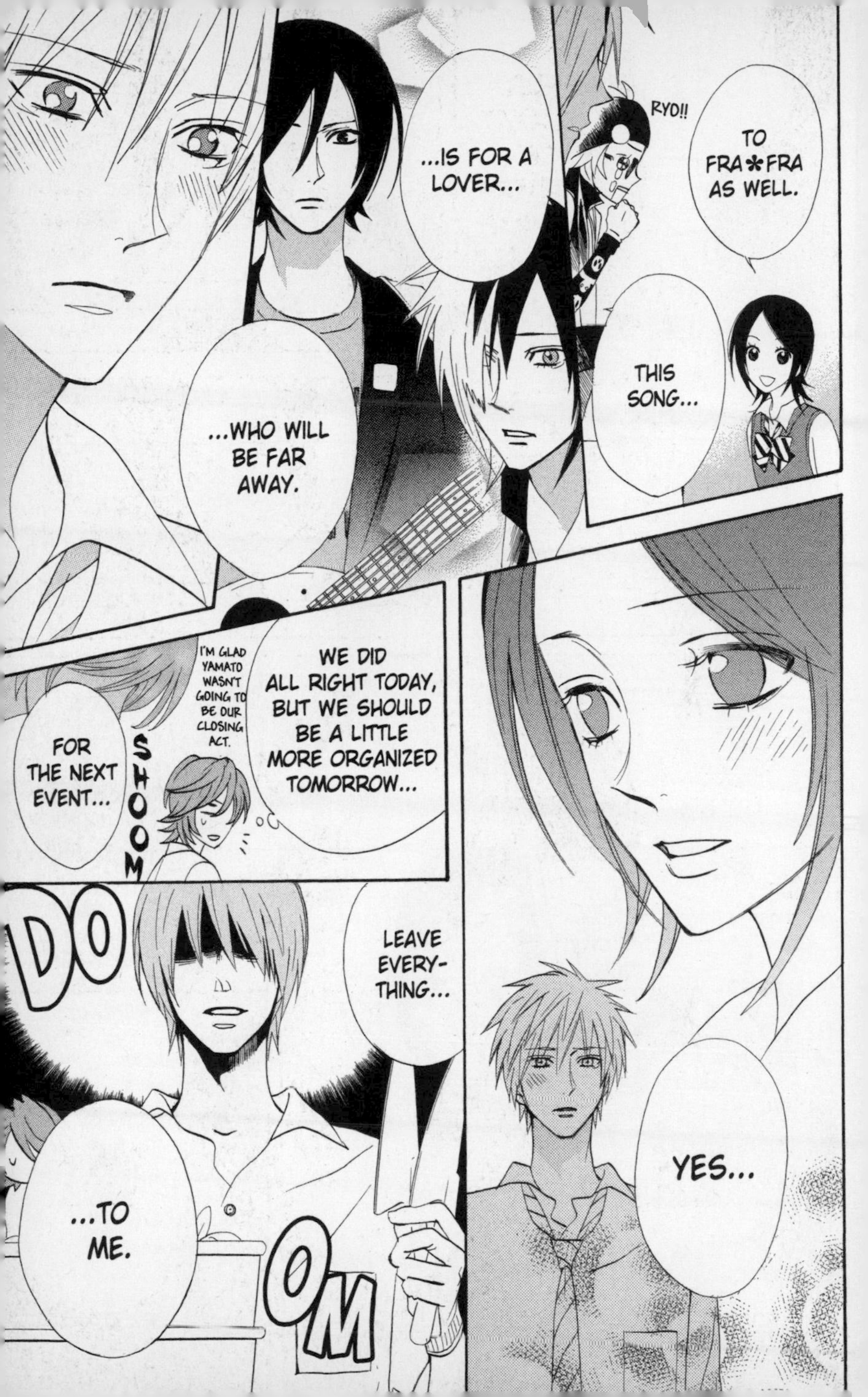
TO FRA✻FRA AS WELL.
RYO!!
THIS SONG...
...IS FOR A LOVER...
...WHO WILL BE FAR AWAY.
YES...
WE DID ALL RIGHT TODAY, BUT WE SHOULD BE A LITTLE MORE ORGANIZED TOMORROW...
I'M GLAD YAMATO WASN'T GOING TO BE OUR CLOSING ACT.
SHOOM
FOR THE NEXT EVENT...
LEAVE EVERY-THING...
DO
OM
...TO ME.

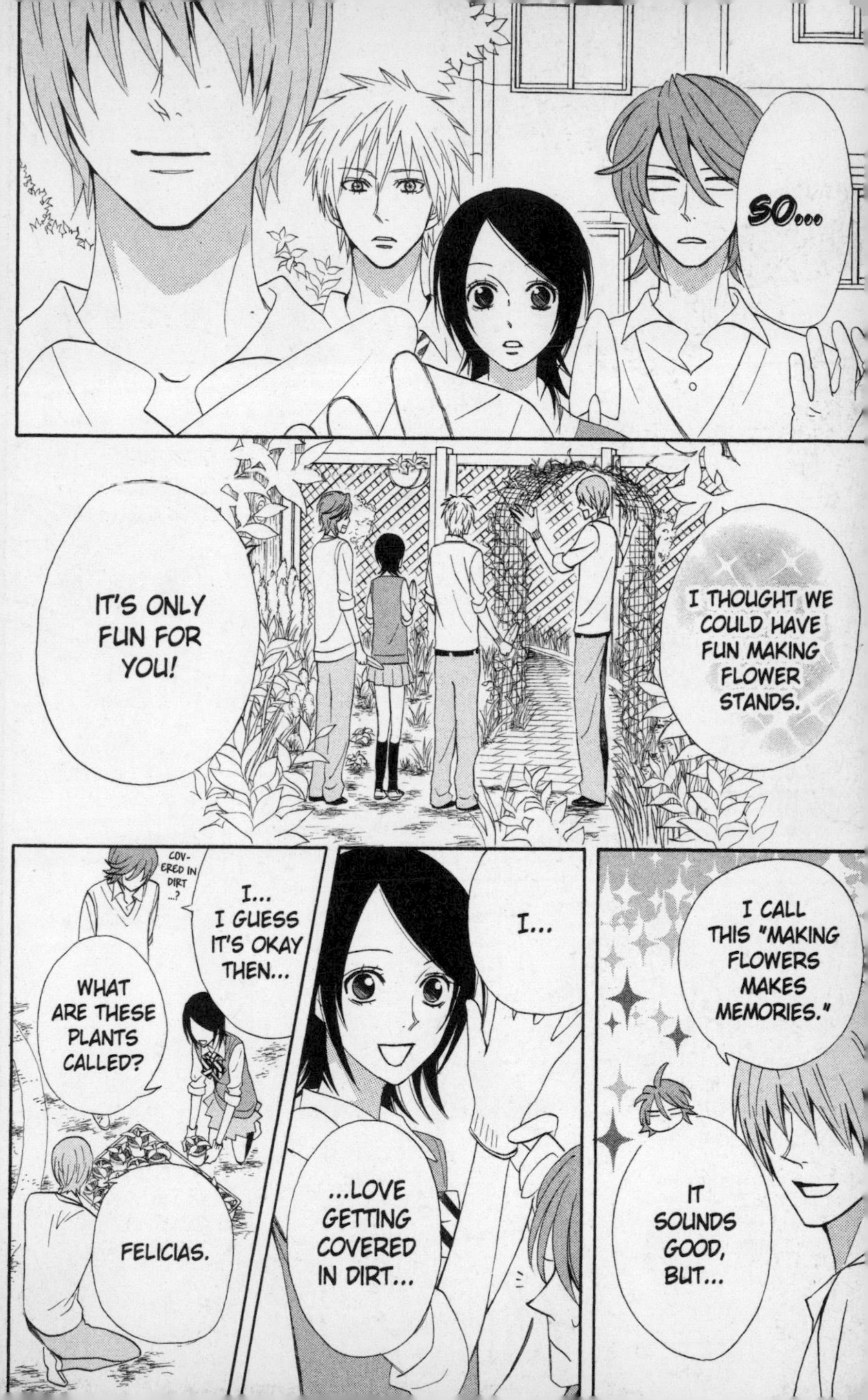
SO...
I THOUGHT WE COULD HAVE FUN MAKING FLOWER STANDS.
IT'S ONLY FUN FOR YOU!
I CALL THIS "MAKING FLOWERS MAKES MEMORIES."
IT SOUNDS GOOD, BUT...
I...
...LOVE GETTING COVERED IN DIRT...
COVERED IN DIRT ...?
I... I GUESS IT'S OKAY THEN...
WHAT ARE THESE PLANTS CALLED?
FELICIAS.

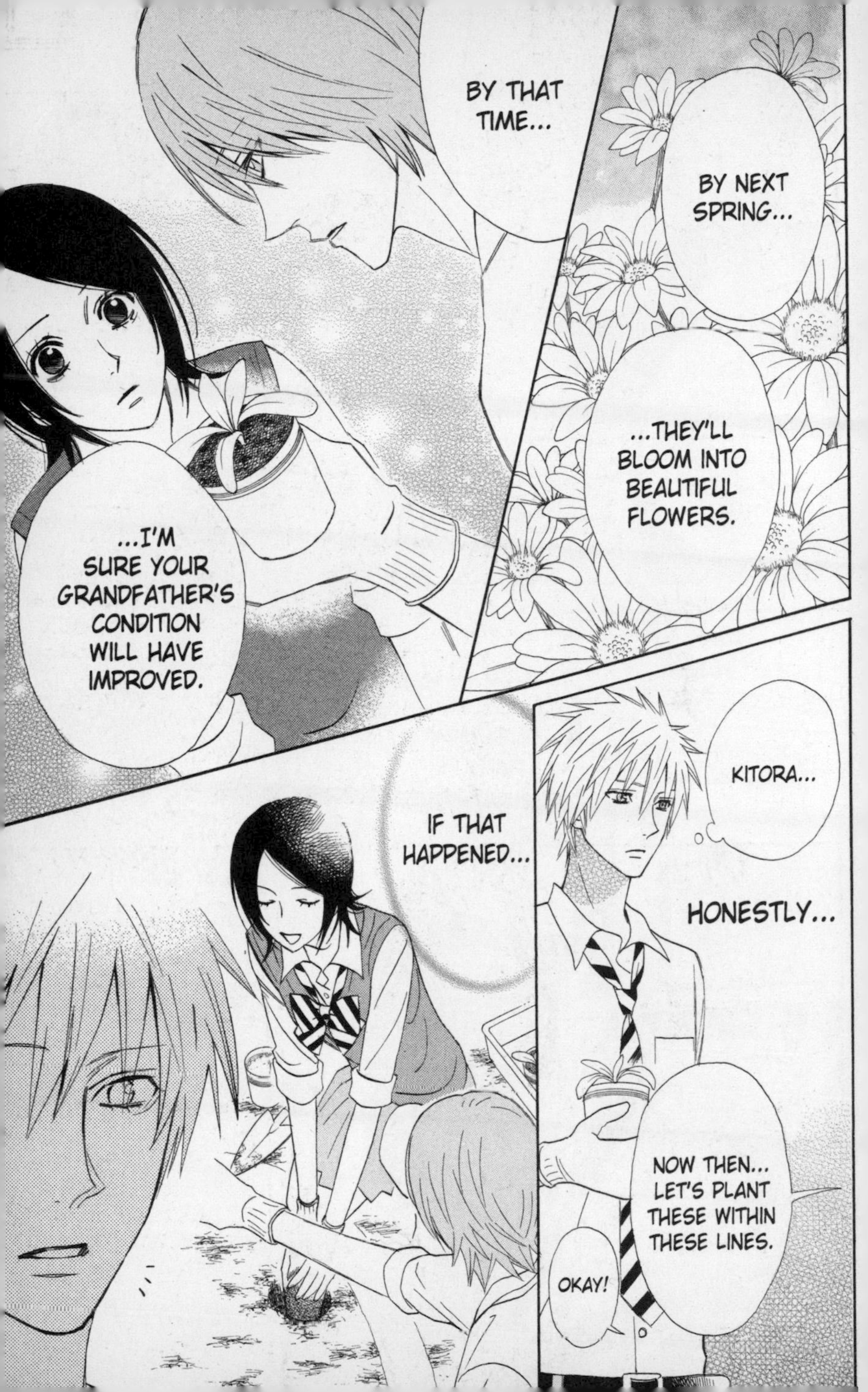
BY NEXT SPRING...
...THEY'LL BLOOM INTO BEAUTIFUL FLOWERS.
BY THAT TIME...
...I'M SURE YOUR GRANDFATHER'S CONDITION WILL HAVE IMPROVED.
KITORA...
HONESTLY...
NOW THEN... LET'S PLANT THESE WITHIN THESE LINES.
OKAY!
IF THAT HAPPENED...

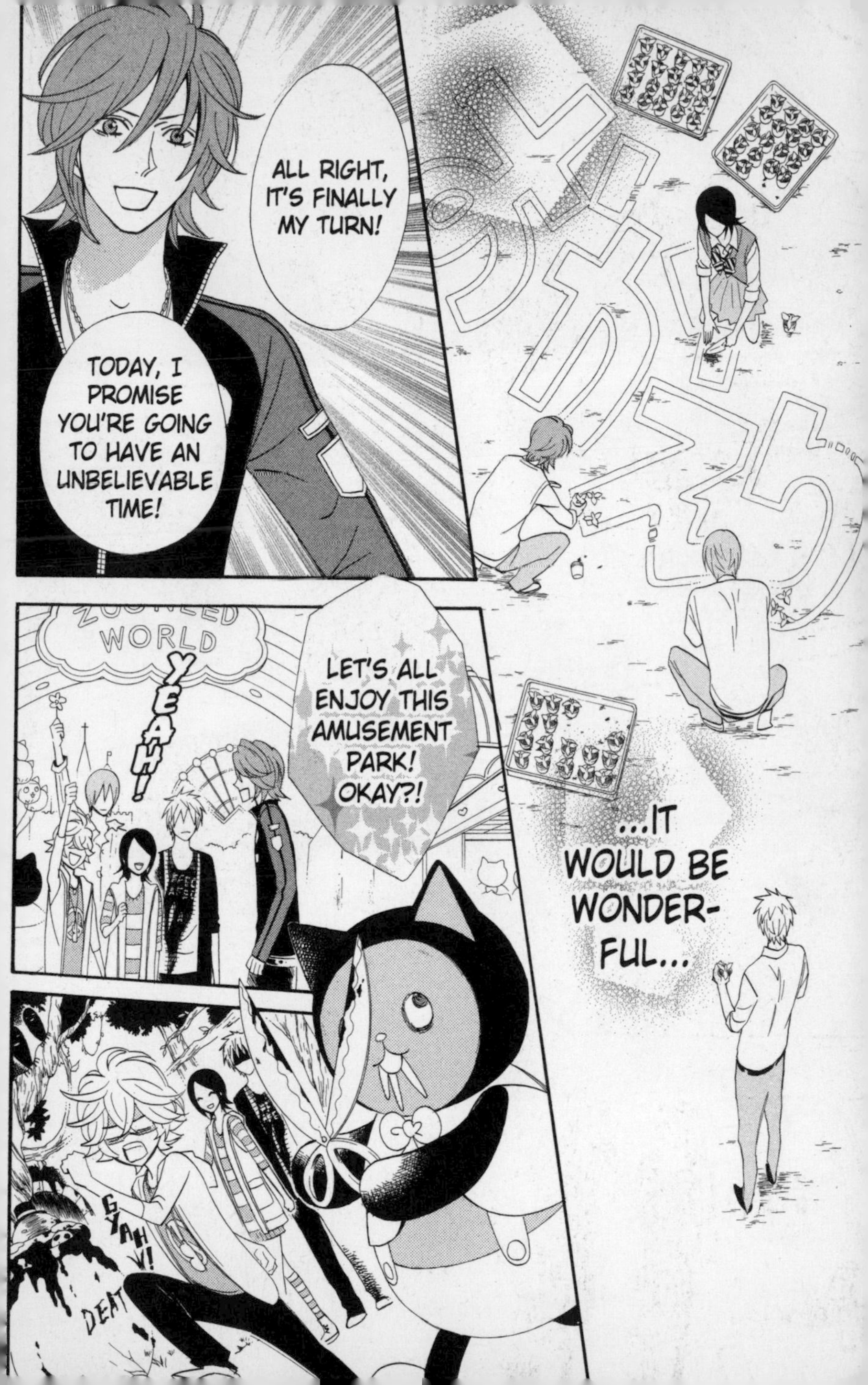
...IT WOULD BE WONDER-FUL...
ALL RIGHT, IT'S FINALLY MY TURN!
TODAY, I PROMISE YOU'RE GOING TO HAVE AN UNBELIEVABLE TIME!
LET'S ALL ENJOY THIS AMUSEMENT PARK! OKAY?!
WORLD
YEAH!
GYAHH!

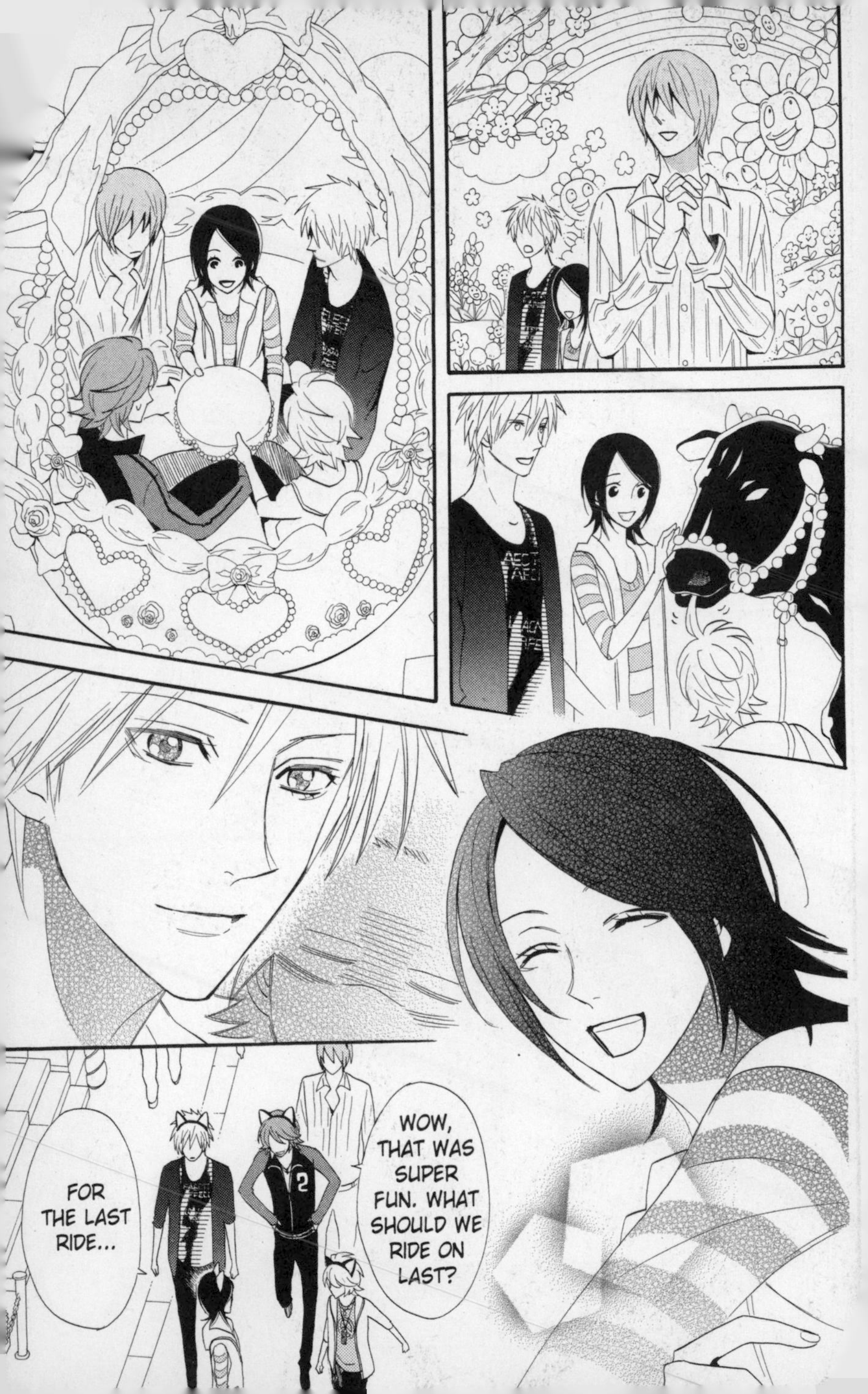
WOW, THAT WAS SUPER FUN. WHAT SHOULD WE RIDE ON LAST?
FOR THE LAST RIDE...

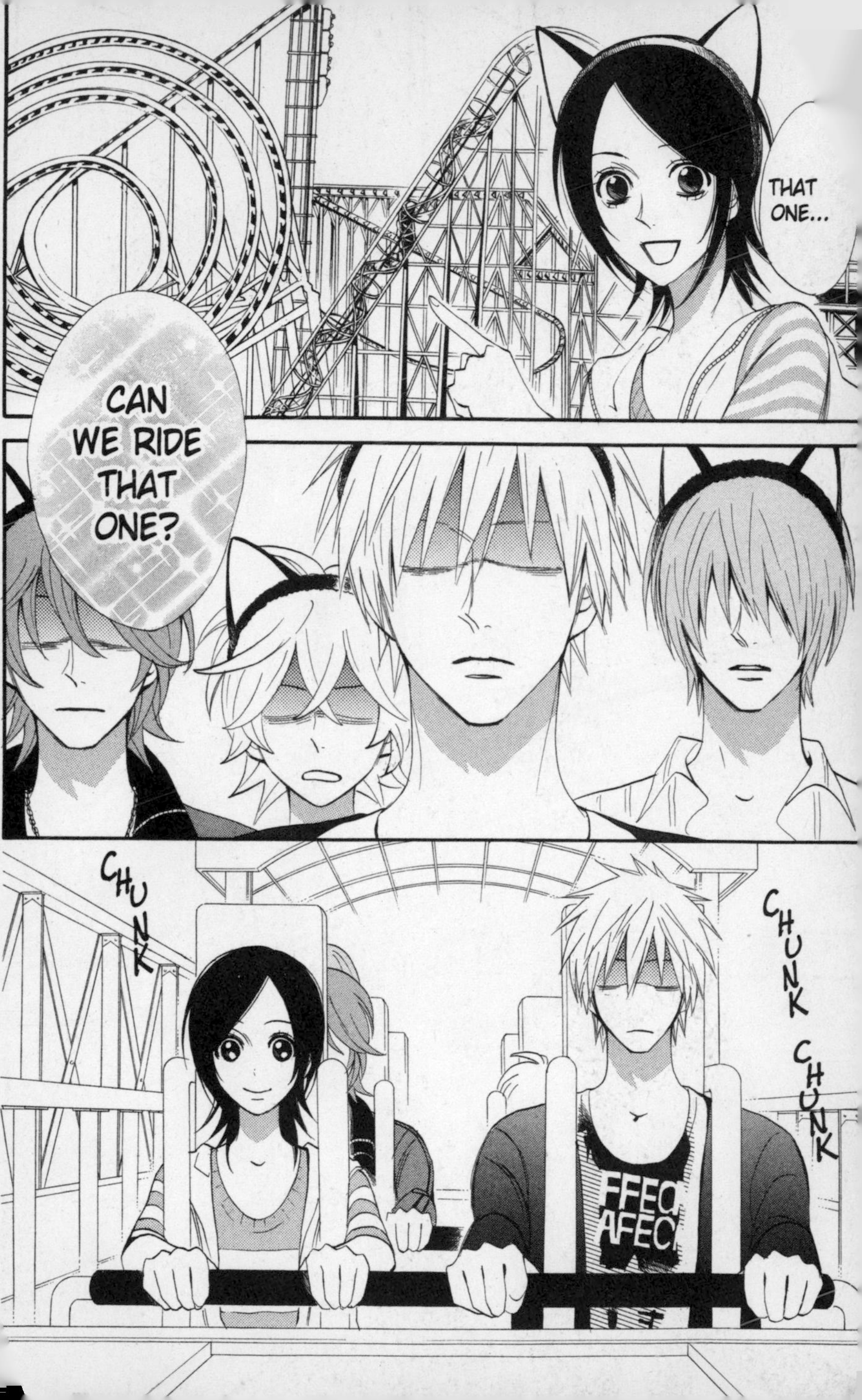
THAT ONE...
CAN WE RIDE THAT ONE?
CHUNK
CHUNK
CHUNK

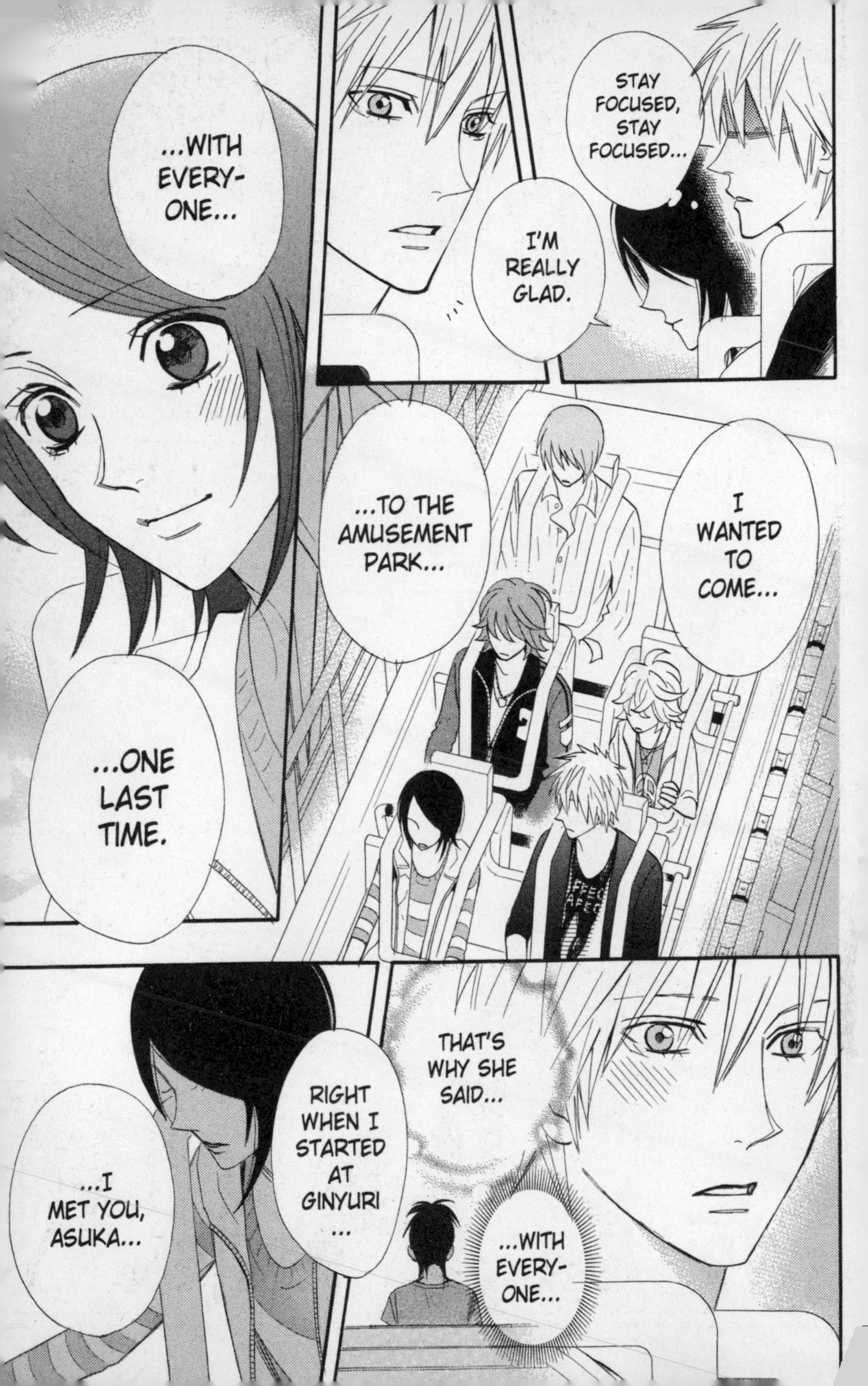
STAY FOCUSED, STAY FOCUSED...
I'M REALLY GLAD.
I WANTED TO COME...
...TO THE AMUSEMENT PARK...
...WITH EVERY-ONE...
...ONE LAST TIME.
THAT'S WHY SHE SAID...
...WITH EVERY-ONE...
RIGHT WHEN I STARTED AT GINYURI ...
...I MET YOU, ASUKA...

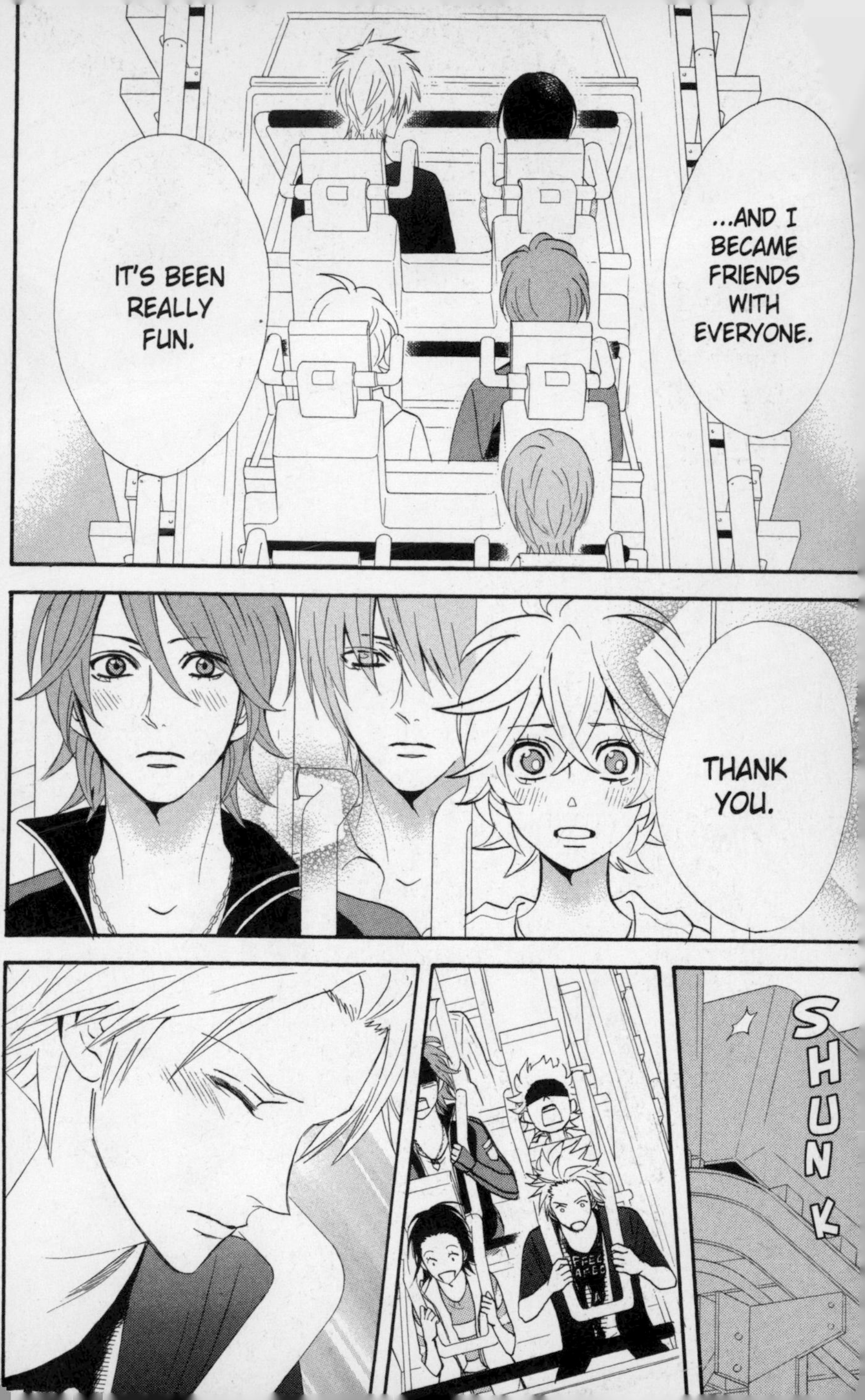
...AND I BECAME FRIENDS WITH EVERYONE.
IT'S BEEN REALLY FUN.
THANK YOU.
SHUNK

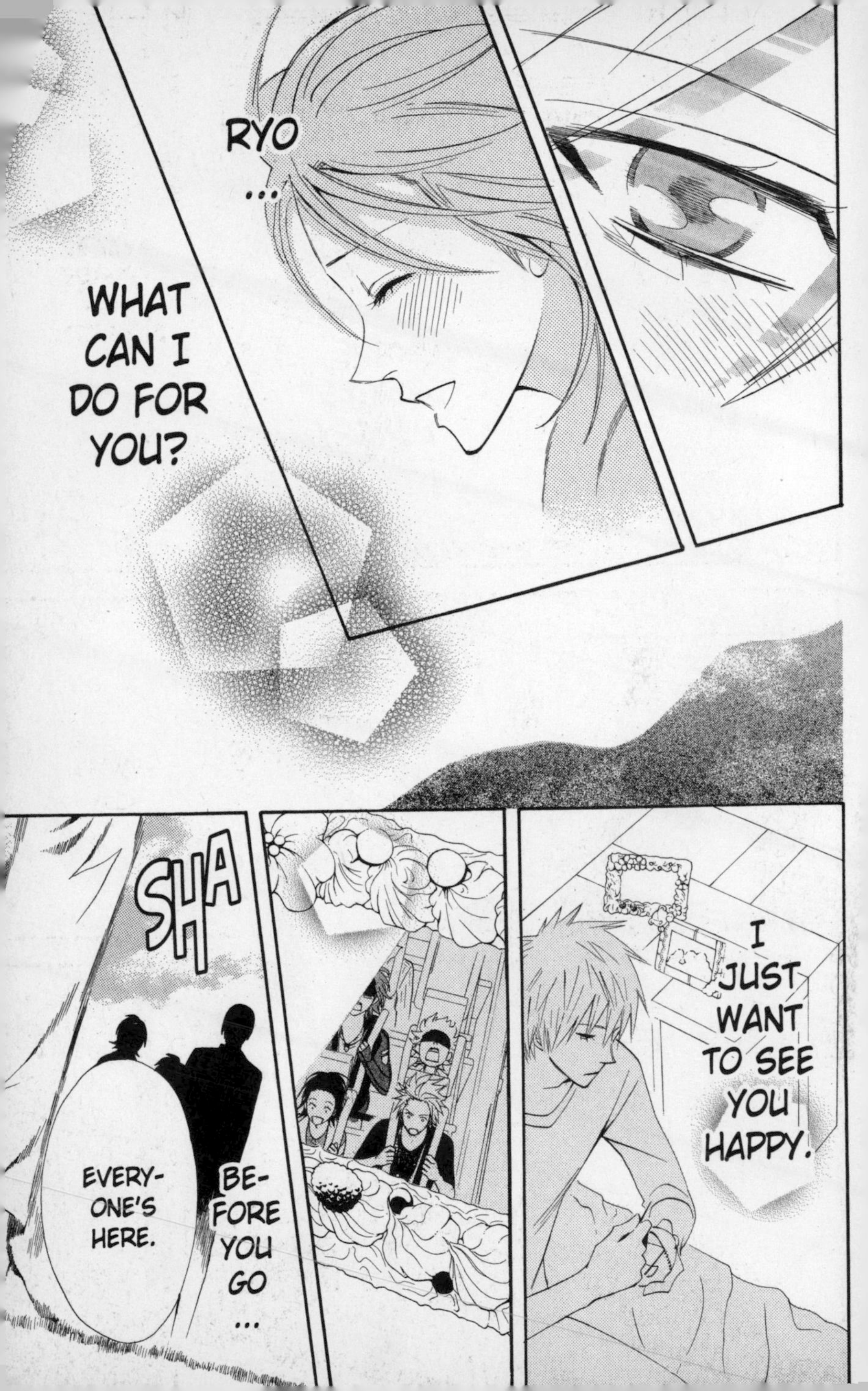
RYO ...
WHAT CAN I DO FOR YOU?
I JUST WANT TO SEE YOU HAPPY.
BEFORE YOU GO ...
SHA
EVERYONE'S HERE.

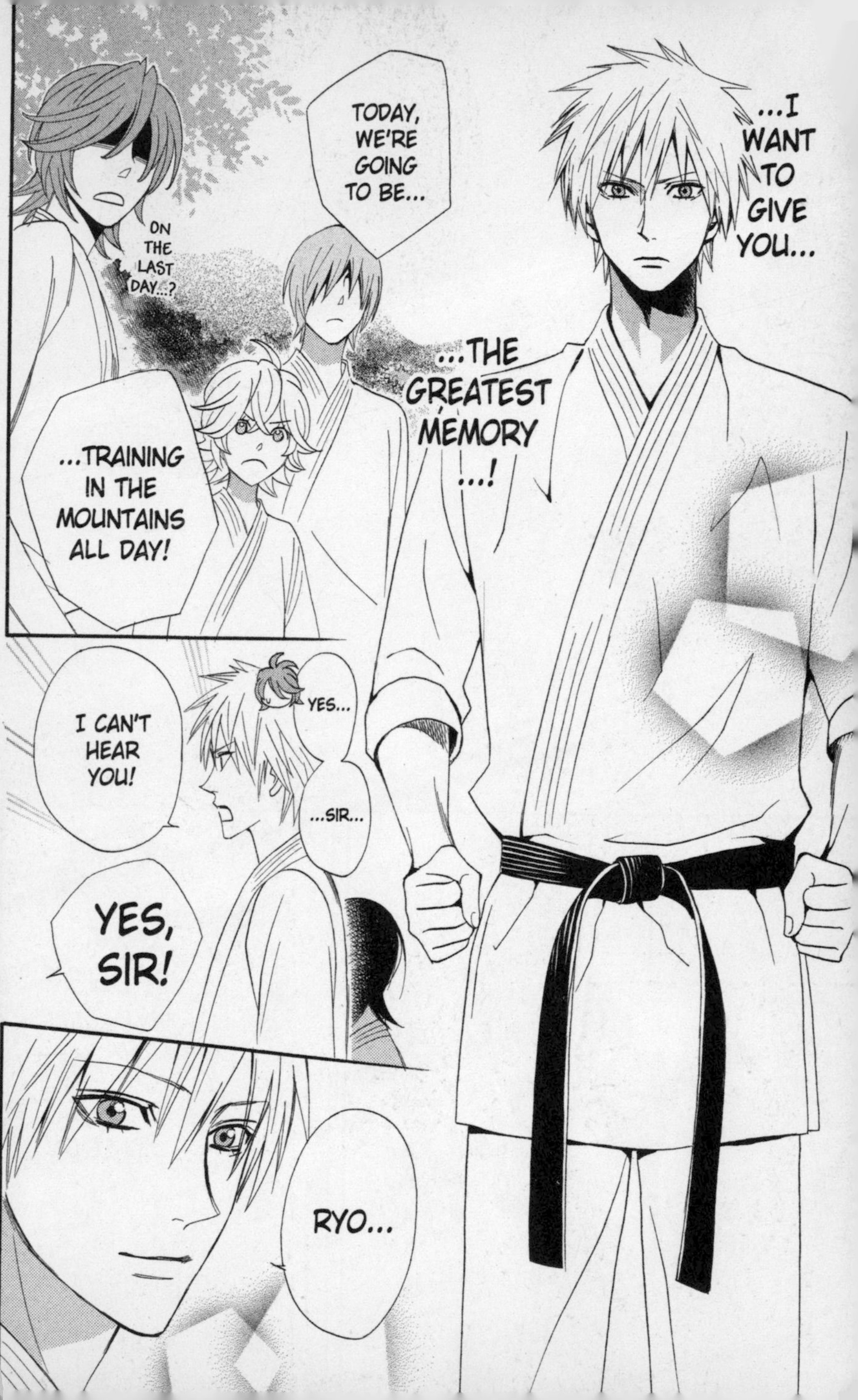
...I WANT TO GIVE YOU...
...THE GREATEST MEMORY ...!
TODAY, WE'RE GOING TO BE...
ON THE LAST DAY...?
...TRAINING IN THE MOUNTAINS ALL DAY!
YES...
...SIR...
I CAN'T HEAR YOU!
YES, SIR!
RYO...

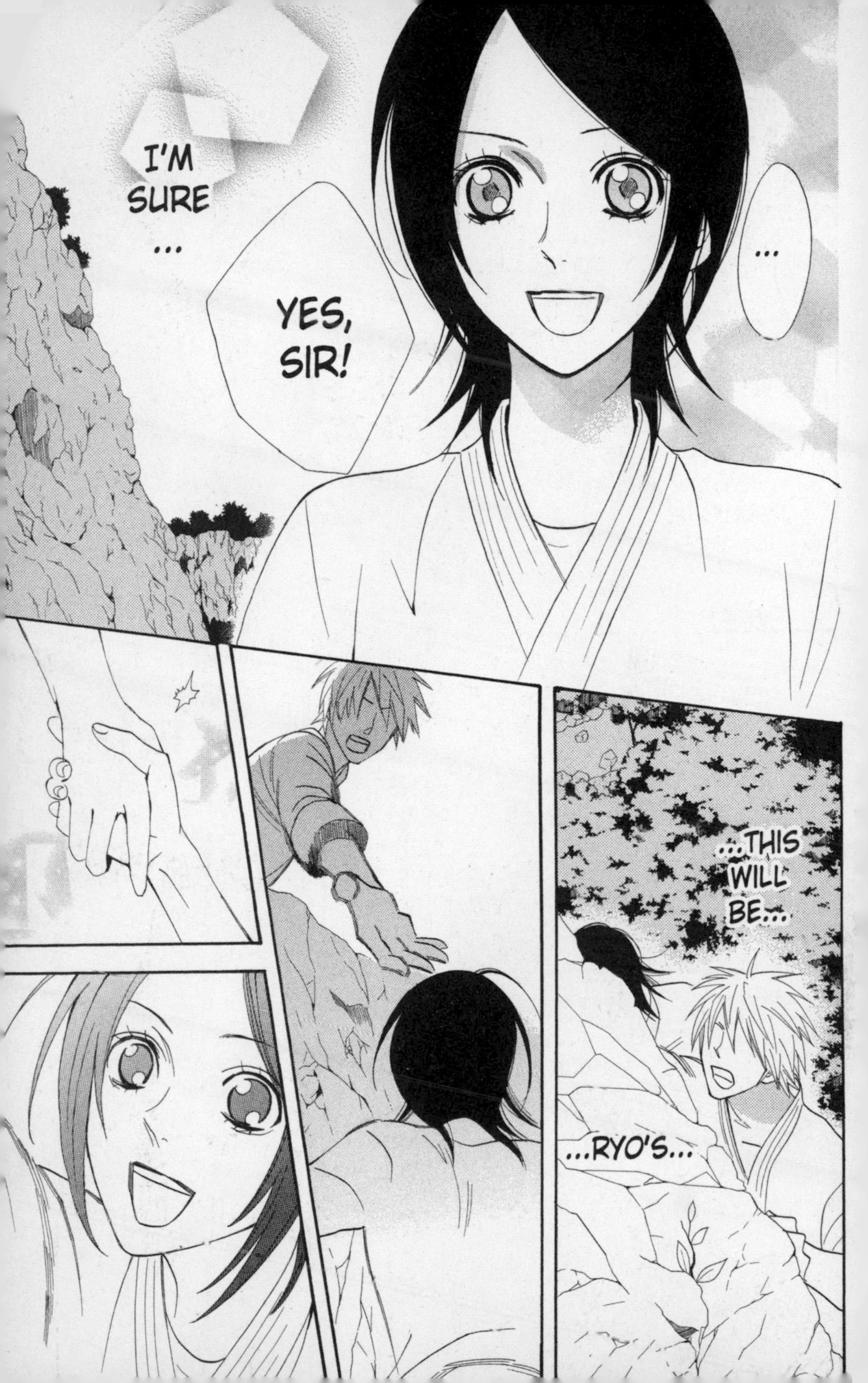
...
YES, SIR!
I'M SURE ...
...THIS WILL BE...
...RYO'S...

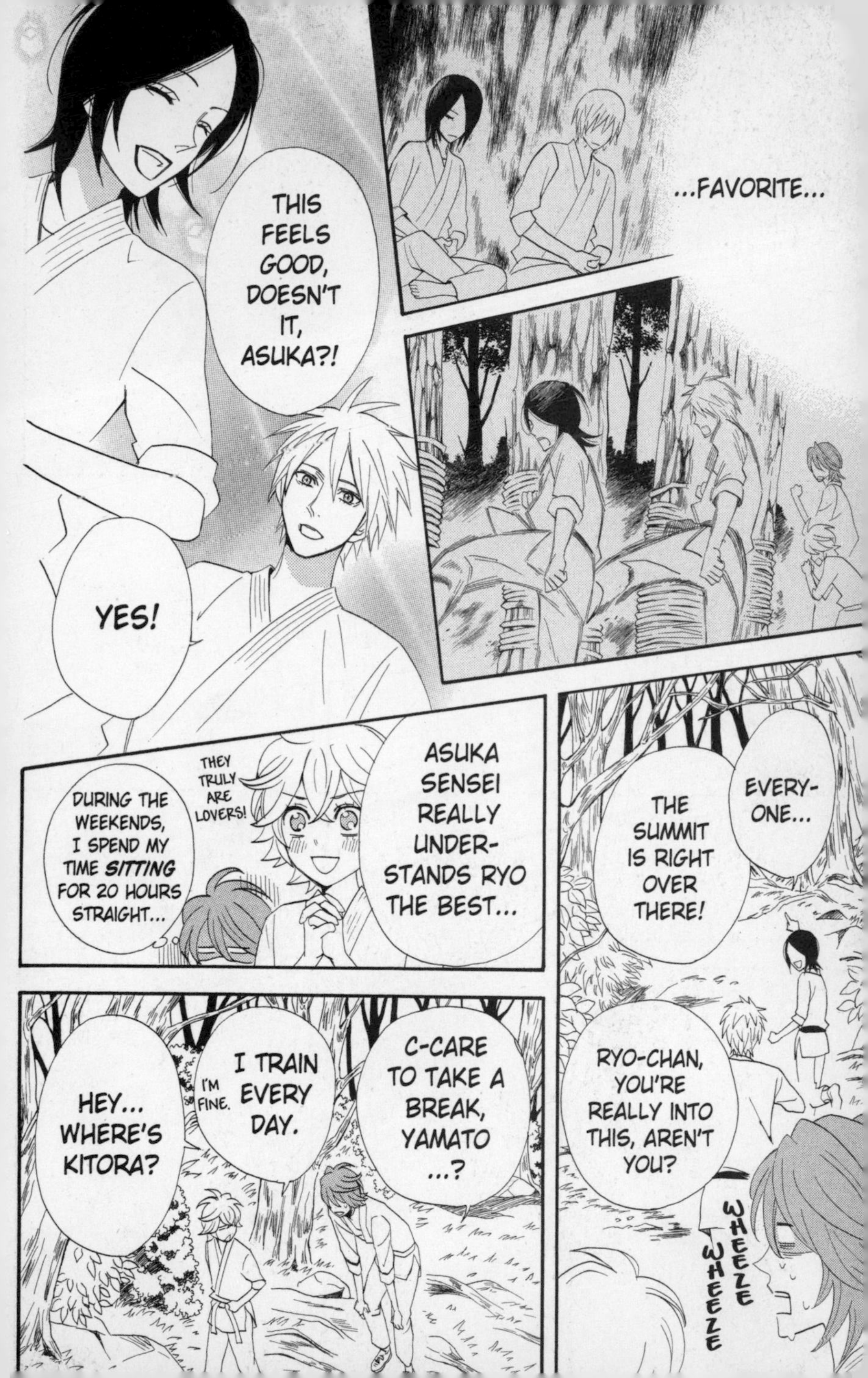
...FAVORITE...
THIS FEELS GOOD, DOESN'T IT, ASUKA?!
YES!
EVERY-ONE...
THE SUMMIT IS RIGHT OVER THERE!
RYO-CHAN, YOU'RE REALLY INTO THIS, AREN'T YOU?
WHEEZE WHEEZE
ASUKA SENSEI REALLY UNDER-STANDS RYO THE BEST...
THEY TRULY ARE LOVERS!
DURING THE WEEKENDS, I SPEND MY TIME SITTING FOR 20 HOURS STRAIGHT...
C-CARE TO TAKE A BREAK, YAMATO ...?
I TRAIN EVERY DAY.
I'M FINE.
HEY... WHERE'S KITORA?

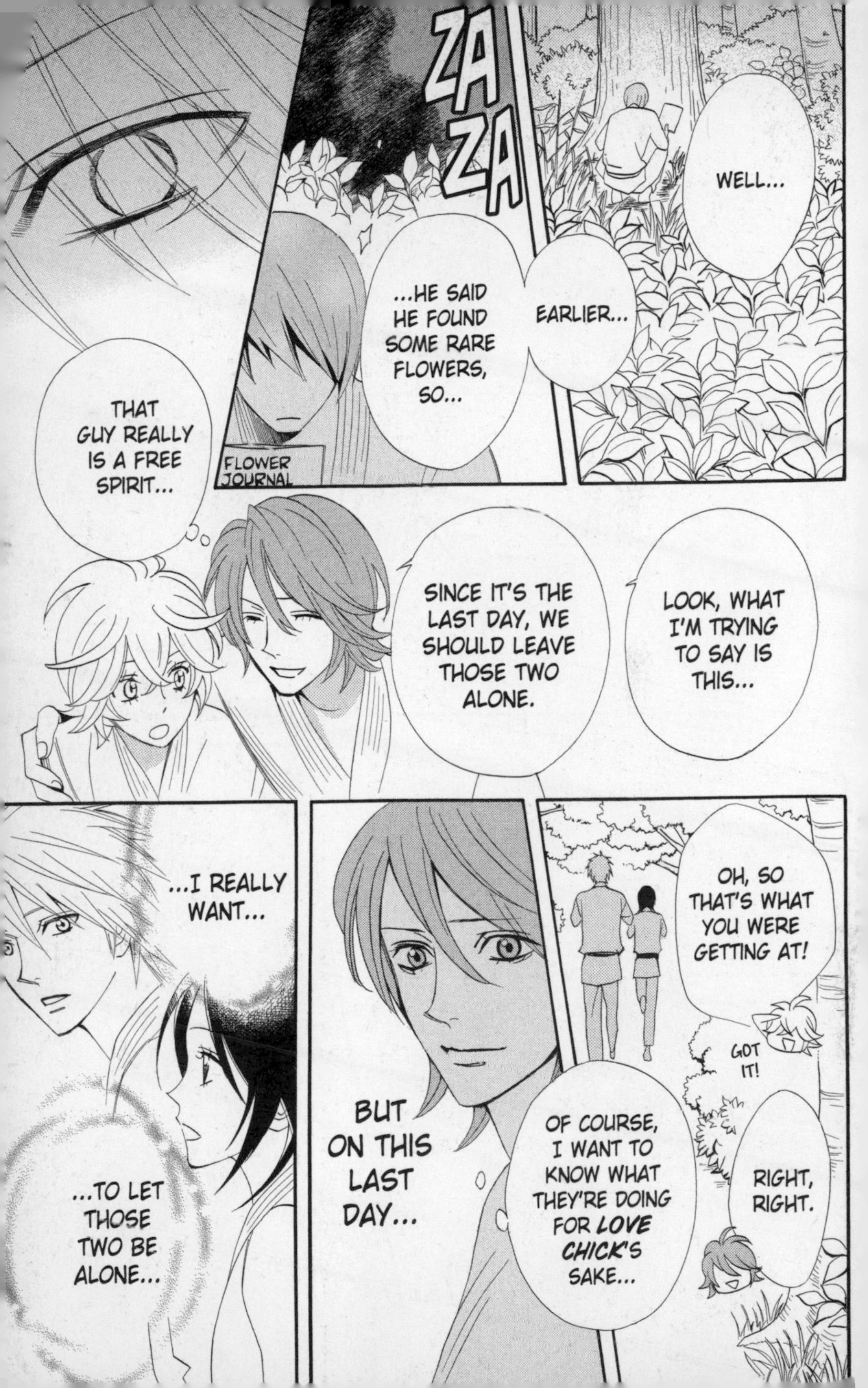
WELL...
EARLIER...
ZA ZA
...HE SAID HE FOUND SOME RARE FLOWERS, SO...
FLOWER JOURNAL
THAT GUY REALLY IS A FREE SPIRIT...
LOOK, WHAT I'M TRYING TO SAY IS THIS...
SINCE IT'S THE LAST DAY, WE SHOULD LEAVE THOSE TWO ALONE.
OH, SO THAT'S WHAT YOU WERE GETTING AT!
GOT IT!
RIGHT, RIGHT.
OF COURSE, I WANT TO KNOW WHAT THEY'RE DOING FOR *LOVE CHICK*'S SAKE...
BUT ON THIS LAST DAY...
...I REALLY WANT...
...TO LET THOSE TWO BE ALONE...

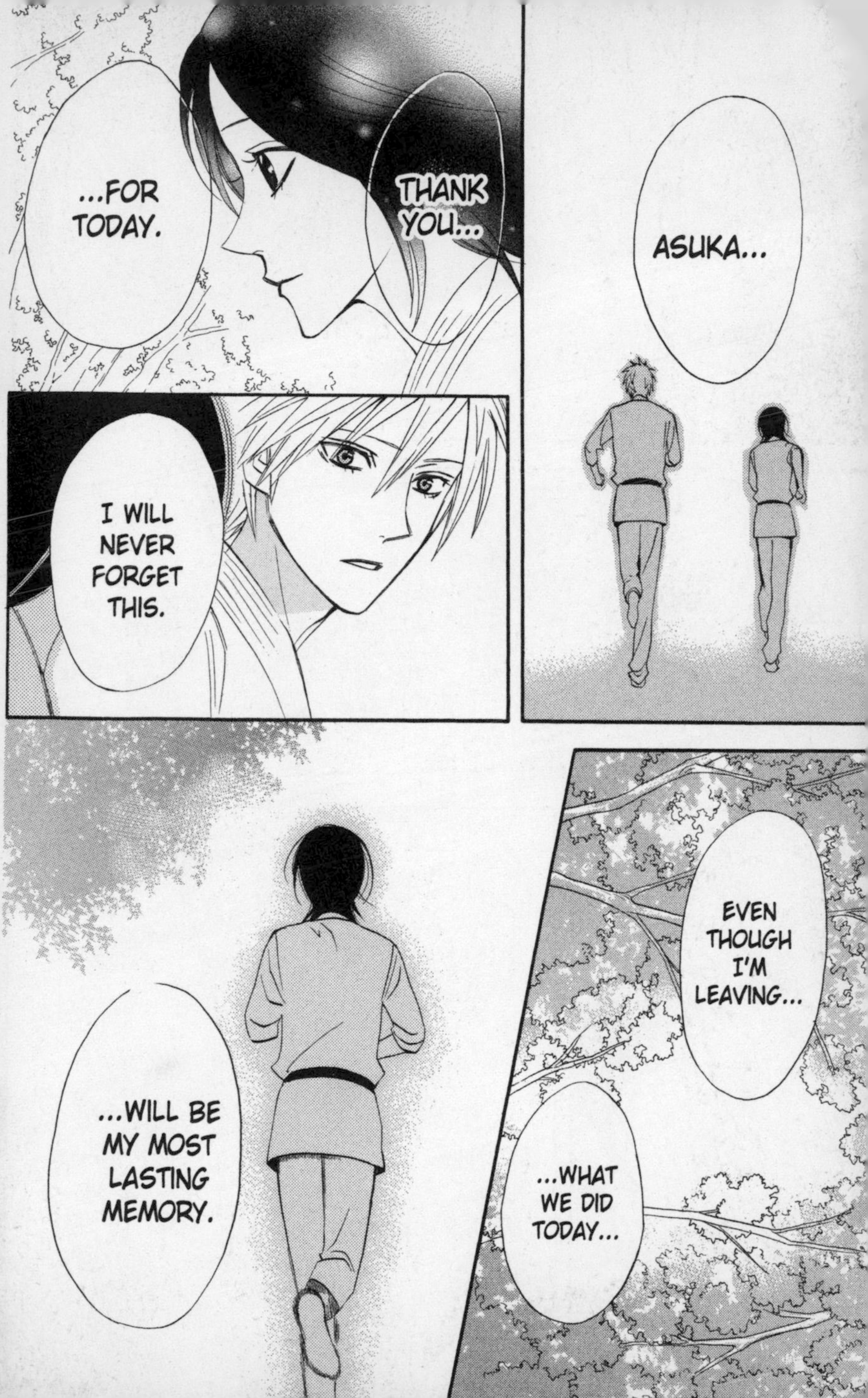
ASUKA...
THANK YOU...
...FOR TODAY.
I WILL NEVER FORGET THIS.
EVEN THOUGH I'M LEAVING...
...WHAT WE DID TODAY...
...WILL BE MY MOST LASTING MEMORY.

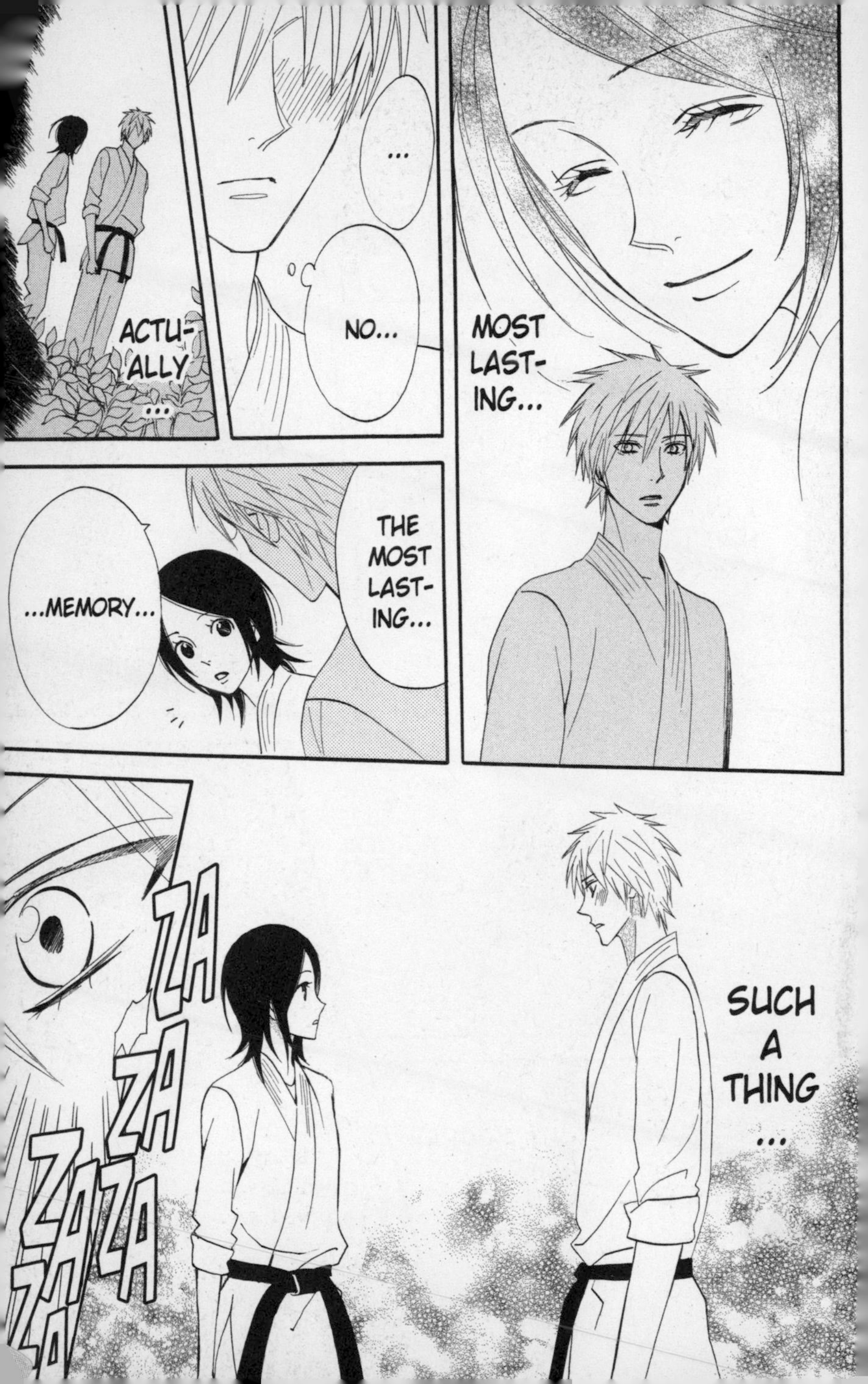
MOST LAST-ING...
...
NO...
ACTU-ALLY ...
THE MOST LAST-ING...
...MEMORY...
SUCH A THING ...
ZA
ZA
ZA
ZA
ZA

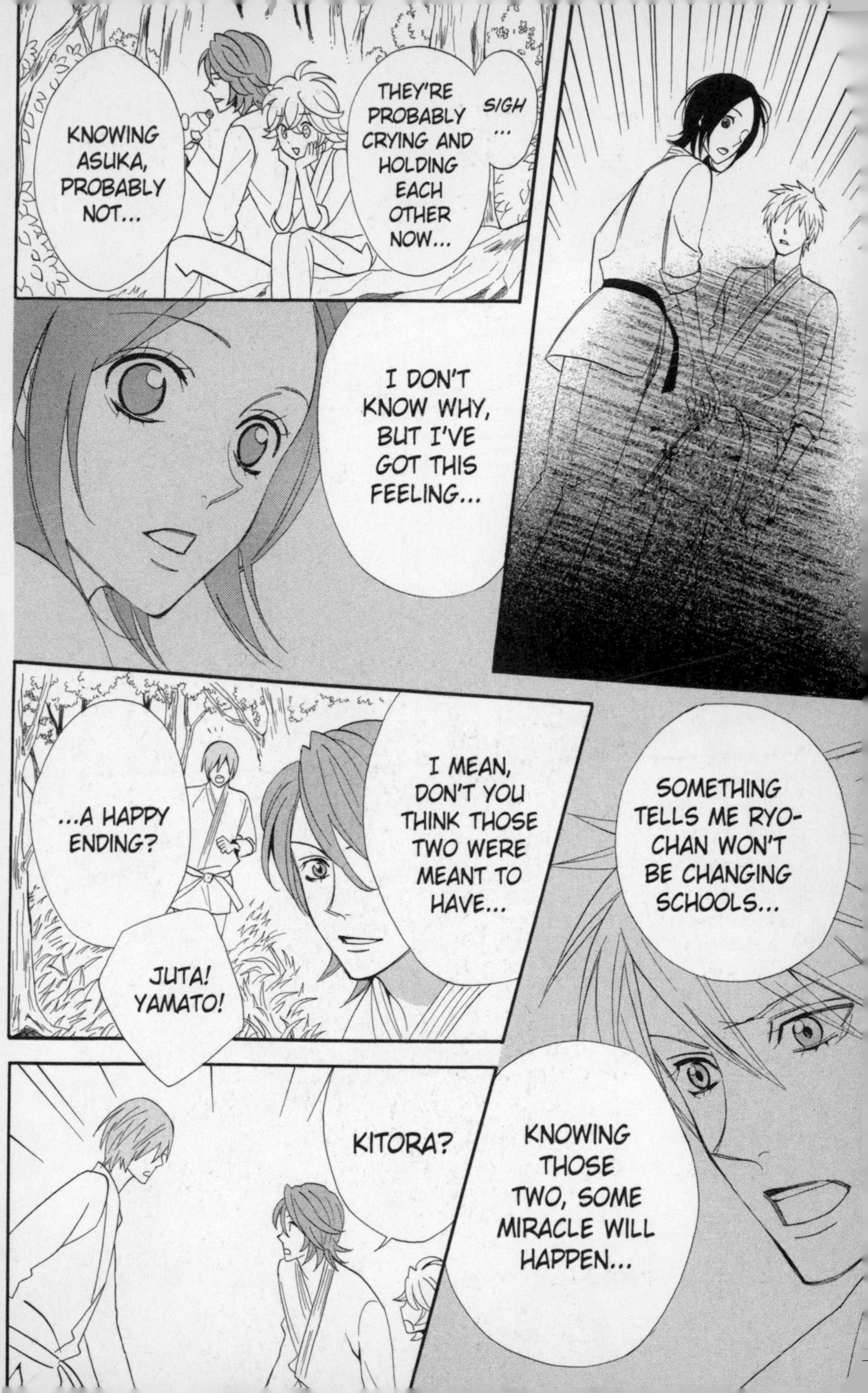
THEY'RE PROBABLY CRYING AND HOLDING EACH OTHER NOW...
SIGH...
KNOWING ASUKA, PROBABLY NOT...
I DON'T KNOW WHY, BUT I'VE GOT THIS FEELING...
SOMETHING TELLS ME RYO-CHAN WON'T BE CHANGING SCHOOLS...
KNOWING THOSE TWO, SOME MIRACLE WILL HAPPEN...
I MEAN, DON'T YOU THINK THOSE TWO WERE MEANT TO HAVE...
...A HAPPY ENDING?
JUTA! YAMATO!
KITORA?

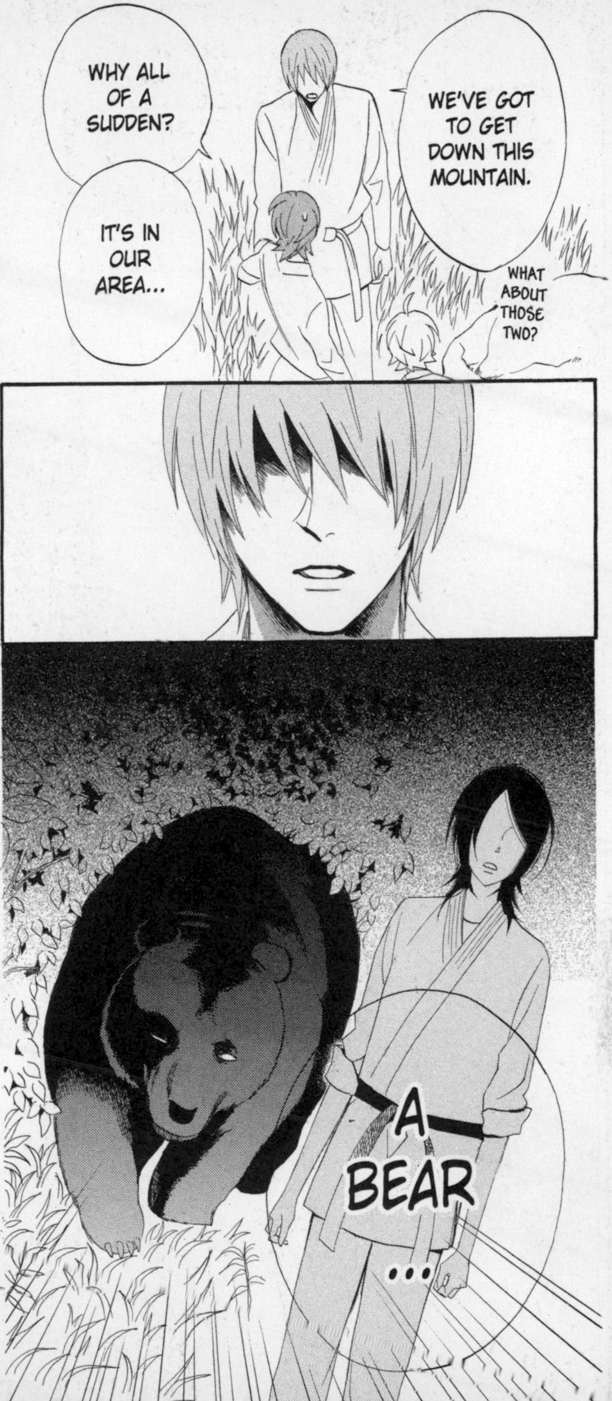
WE'VE GOT TO GET DOWN THIS MOUNTAIN.
WHY ALL OF A SUDDEN?
IT'S IN OUR AREA...
WHAT ABOUT THOSE TWO?
A BEAR...

This is volume 8.
I'm Aya Kanno.

I received a request from a reader, so for some of these note sections, I'd like to write the profiles for the main characters.

First, our main character:

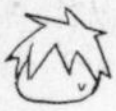

Asuka Masamune

Ginyuri Academy High School
Second-year, Class A
Born September 6
Virgo, Blood Type A
Height: 180 cm
Hobbies: Cooking and needlework
Favorite books include *Bushido*, *Rongo* (*Analects of Confucius*) and *Love Chick*.

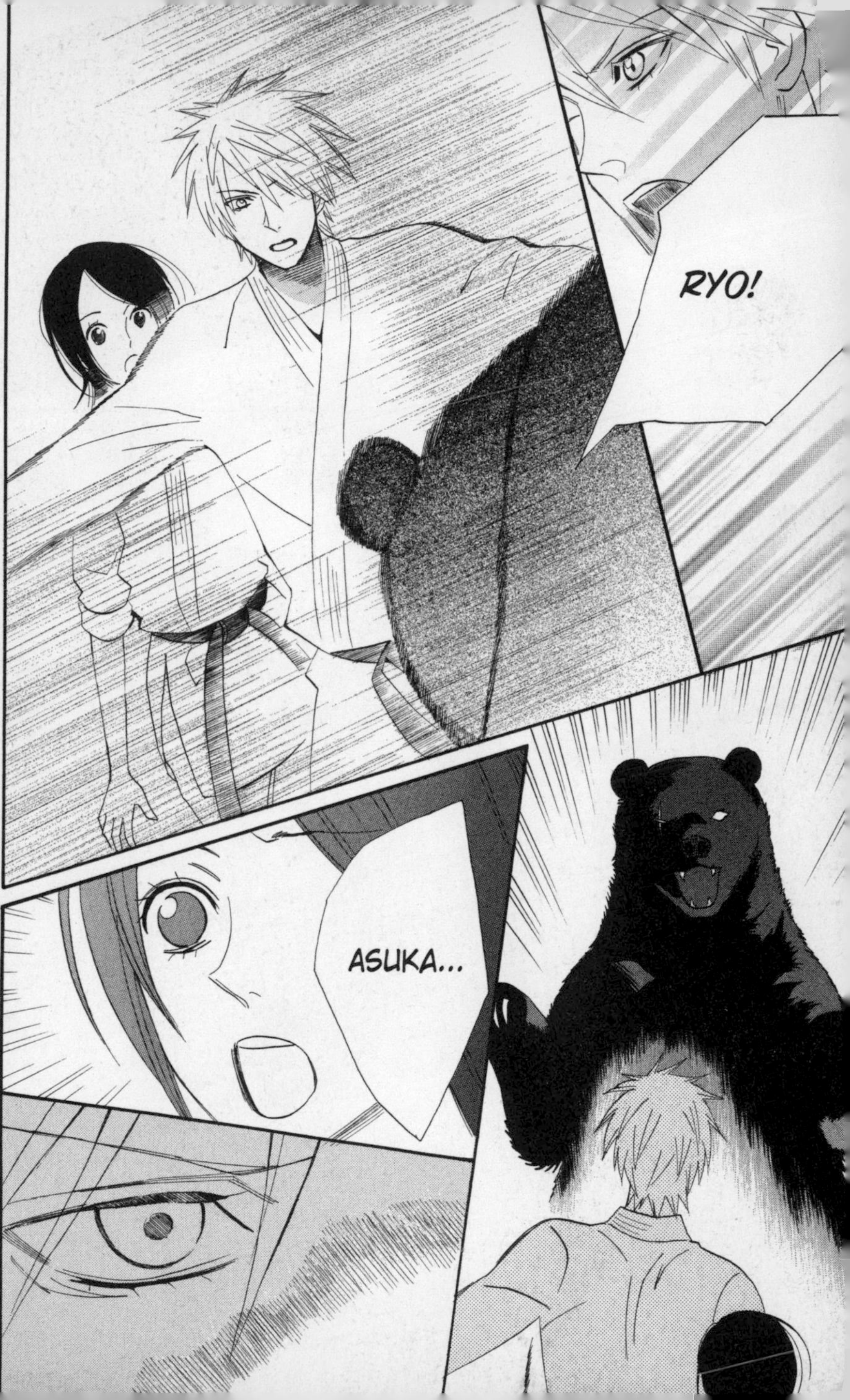
RYO!
ASUKA...

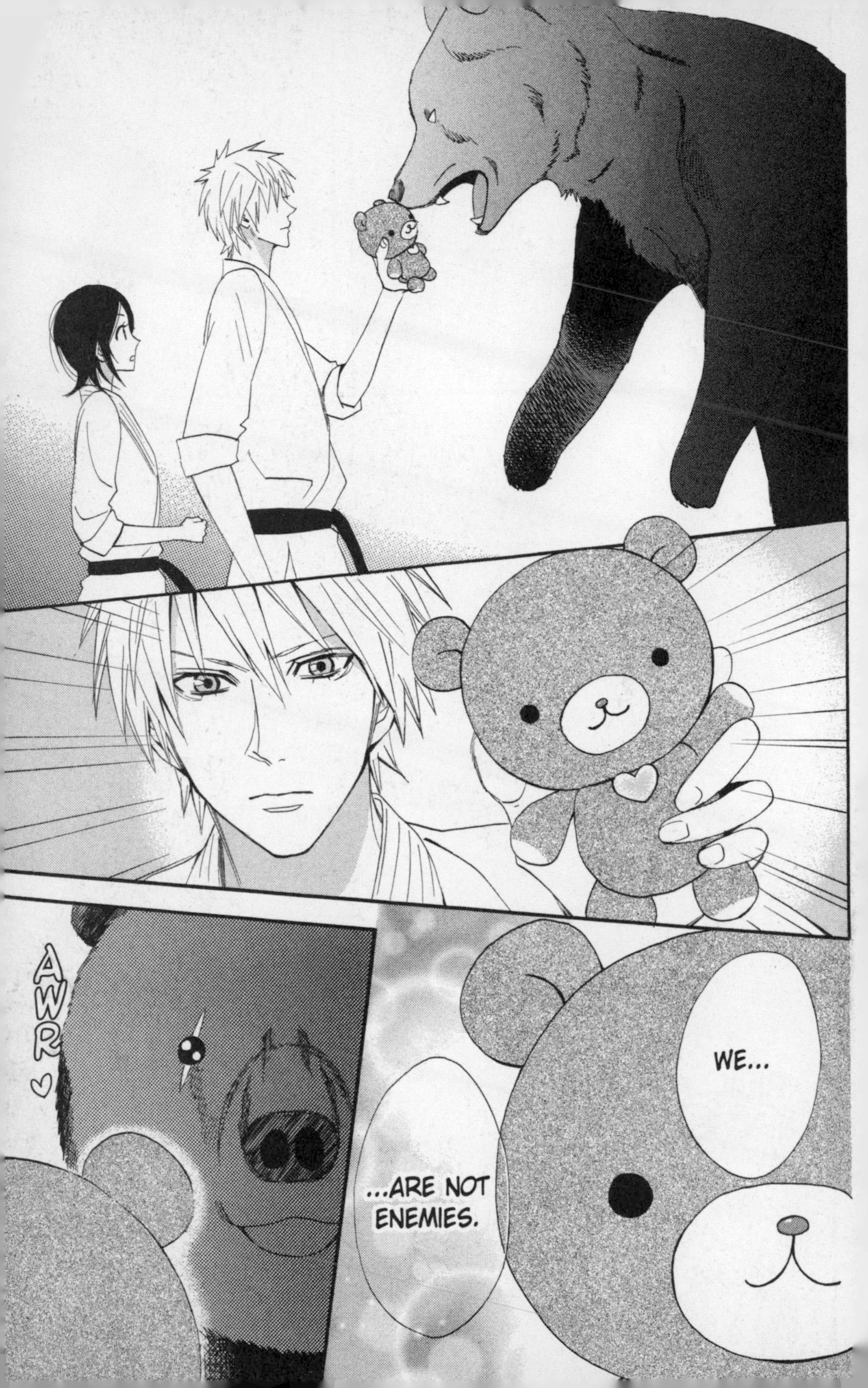
AWR ♡
WE...
...ARE NOT ENEMIES.

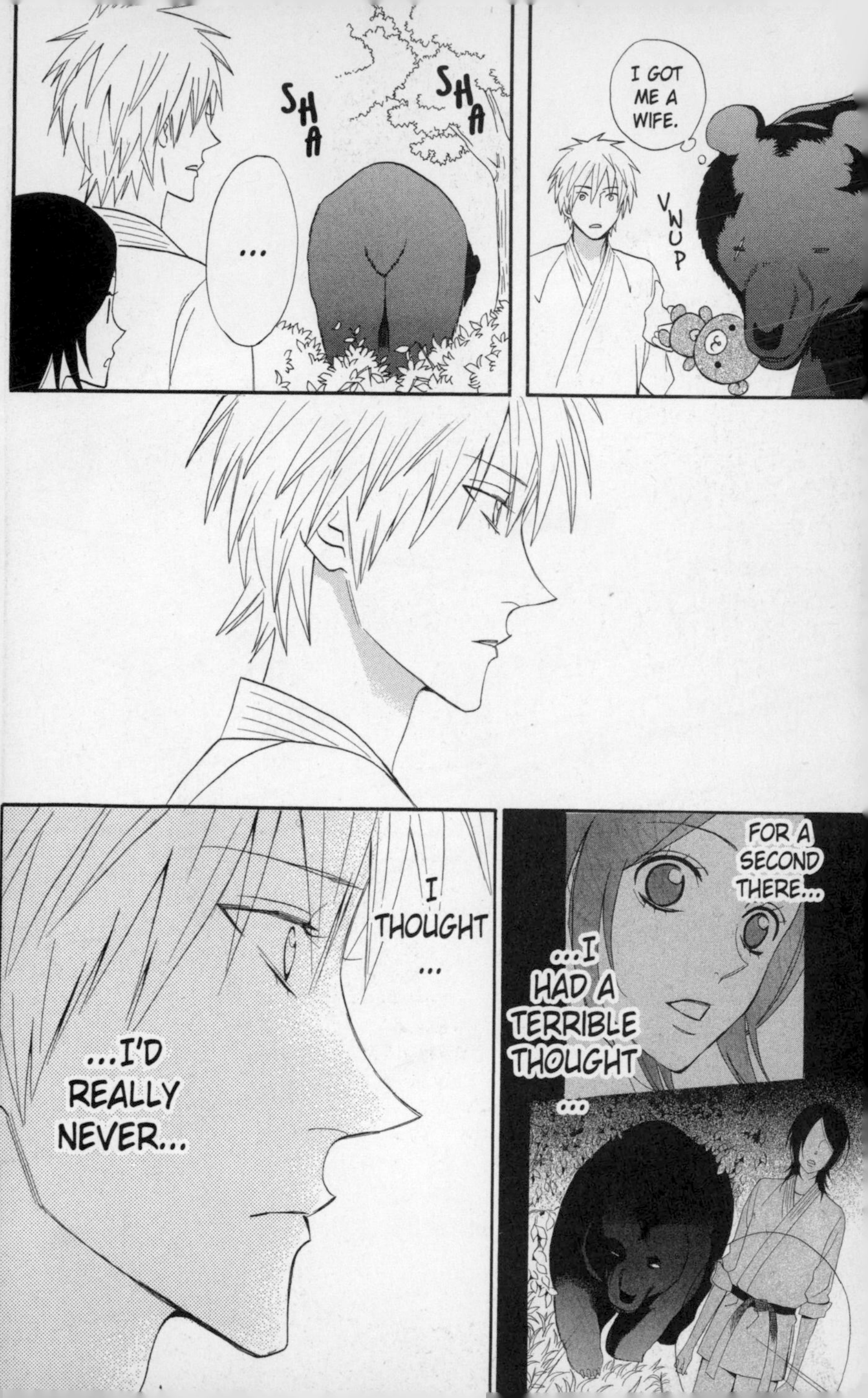
I GOT ME A WIFE.
VWUP
SHA
SHA
...
FOR A SECOND THERE...
...I HAD A TERRIBLE THOUGHT...
I THOUGHT...
...I'D REALLY NEVER...

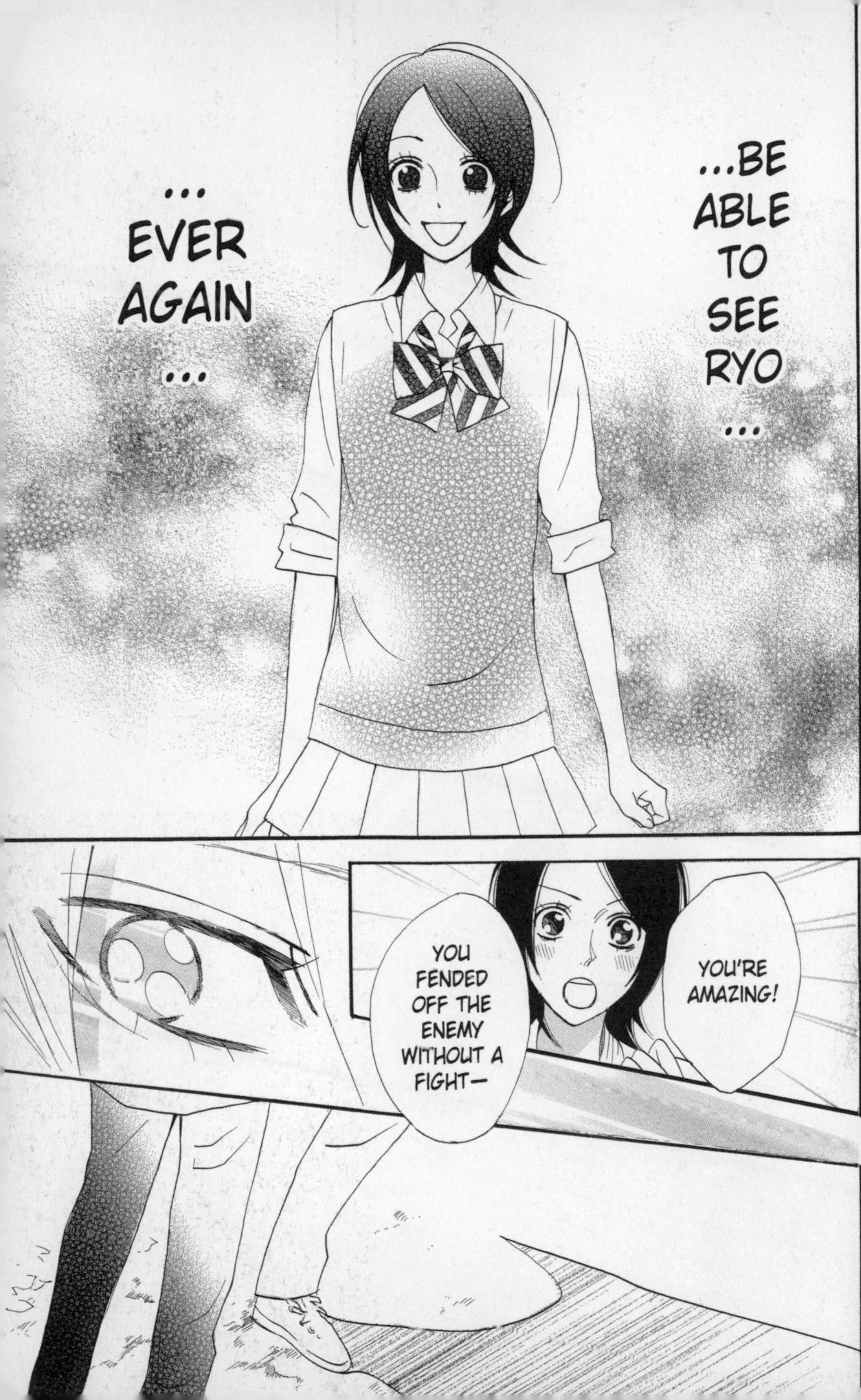
...BE ABLE TO SEE RYO ...
... EVER AGAIN ...
YOU'RE AMAZING!
YOU FENDED OFF THE ENEMY WITHOUT A FIGHT—

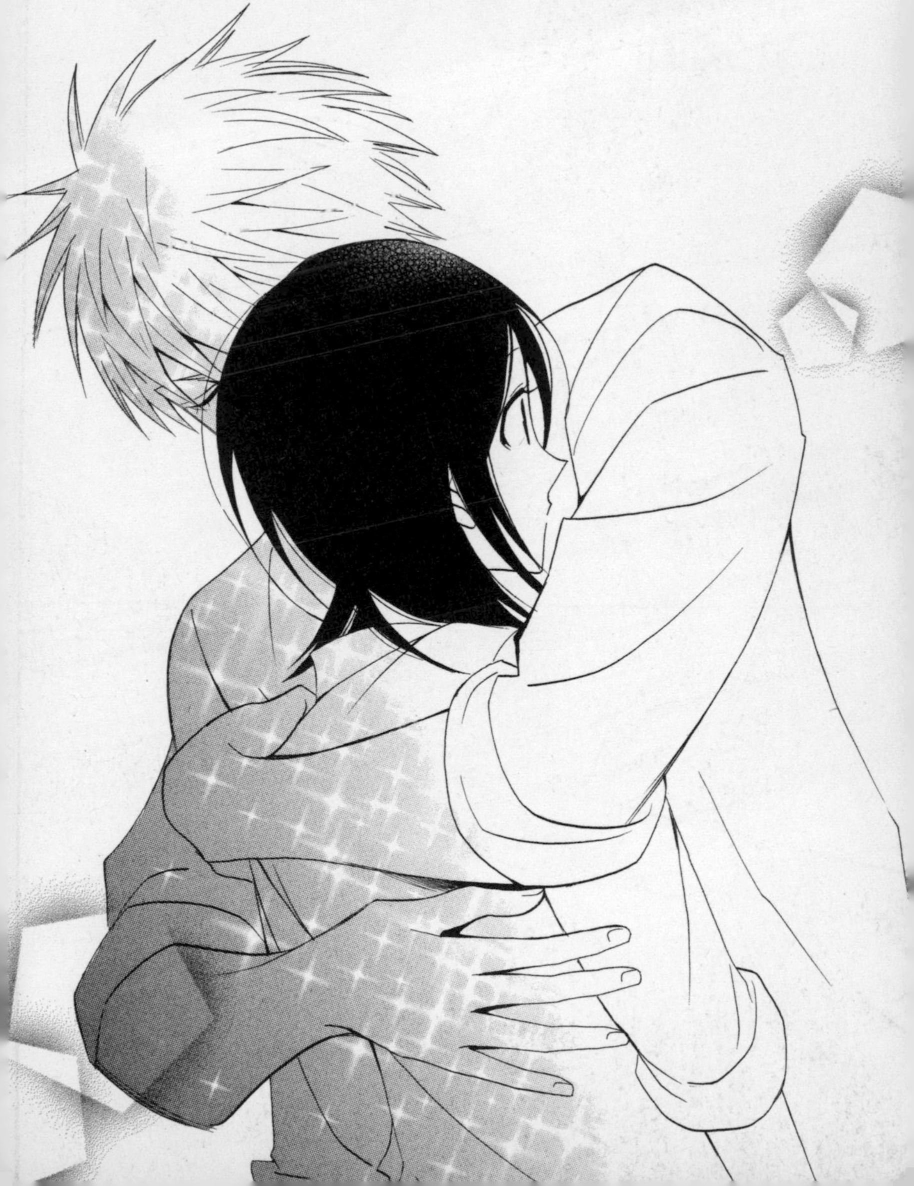

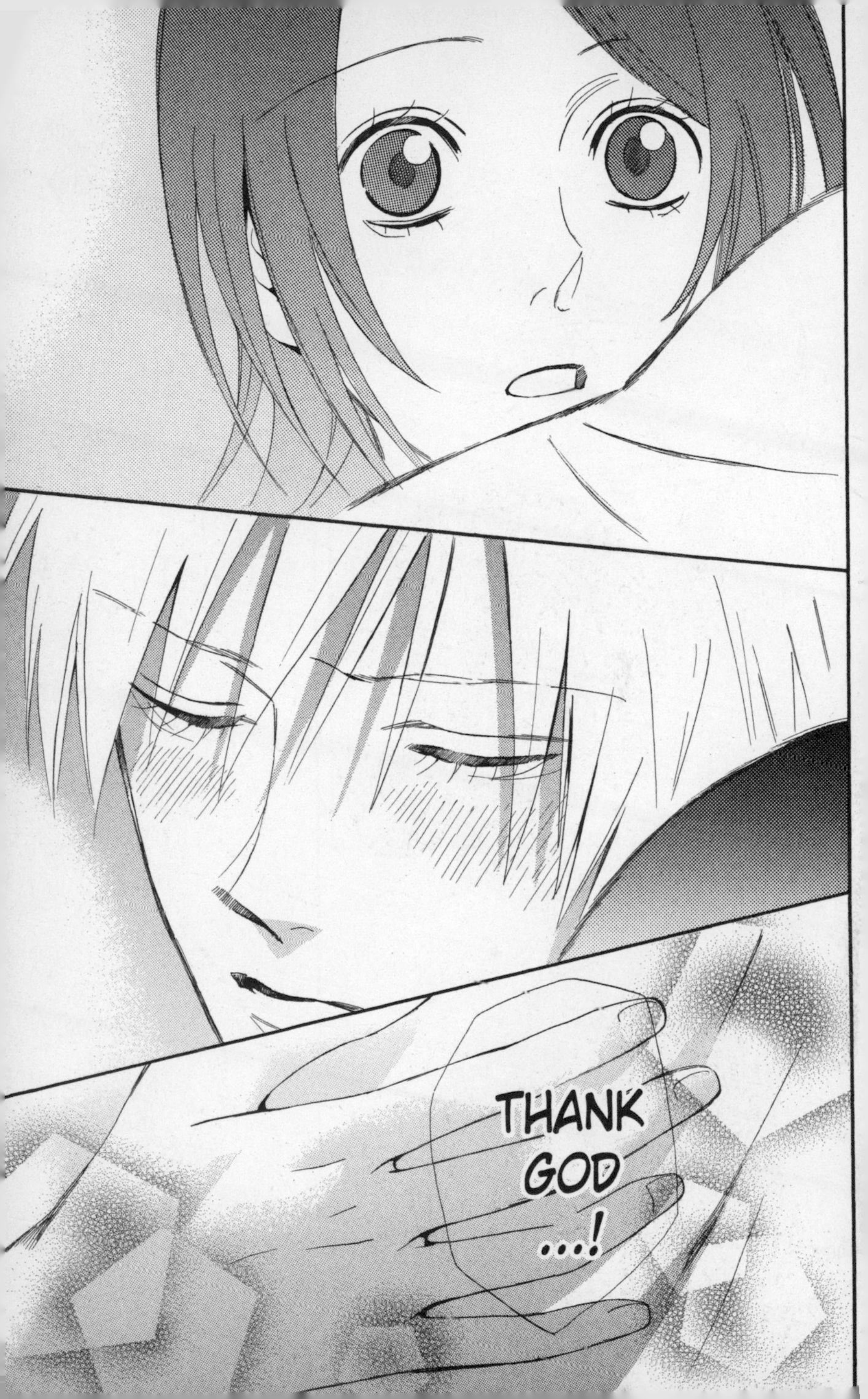
THANK GOD ...!

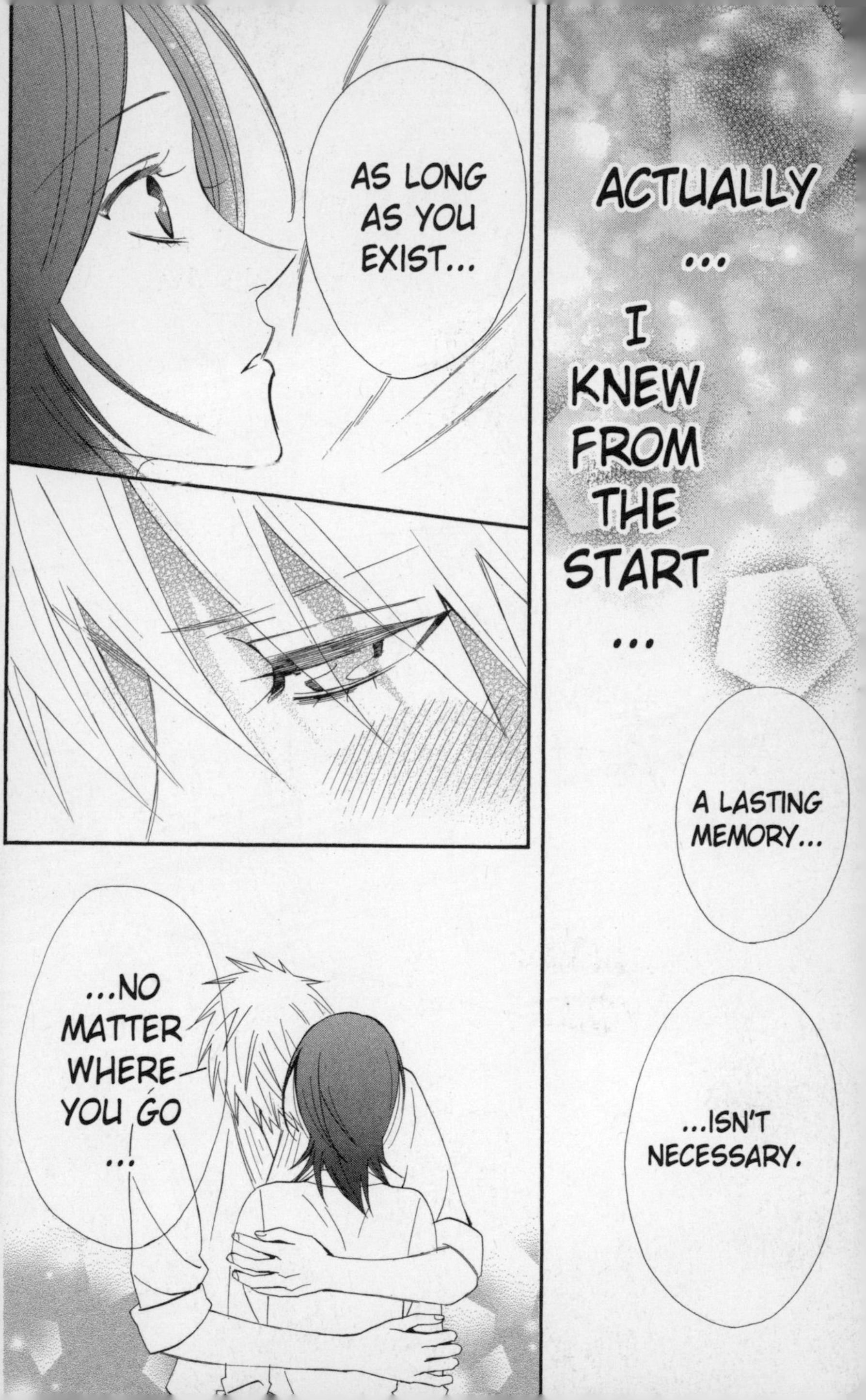
ACTUALLY ... I KNEW FROM THE START ...
A LASTING MEMORY...
...ISN'T NECESSARY.
AS LONG AS YOU EXIST...
...NO MATTER WHERE YOU GO ...

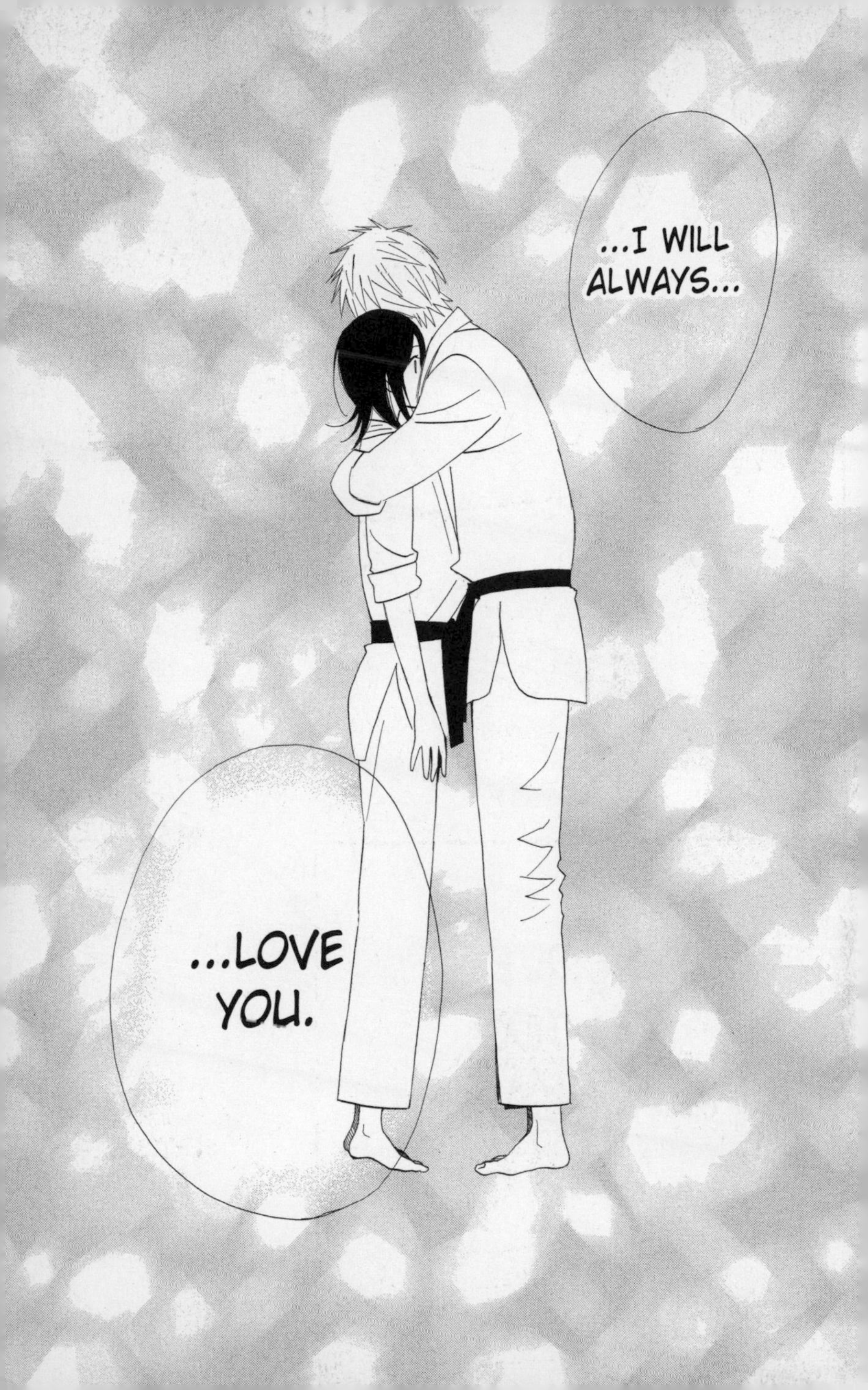
...I WILL ALWAYS...
...LOVE YOU.

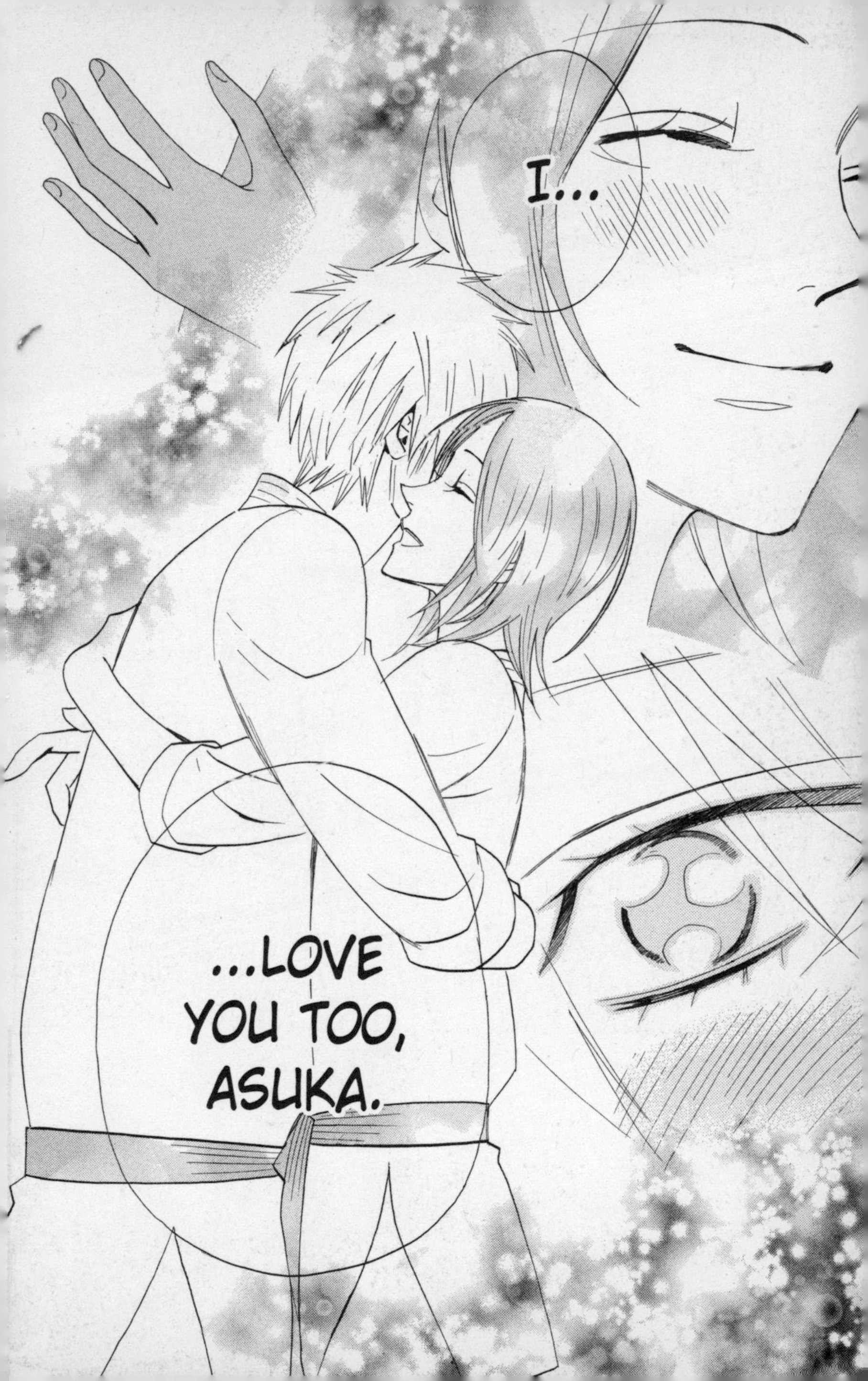
I...
...LOVE YOU TOO, ASUKA.

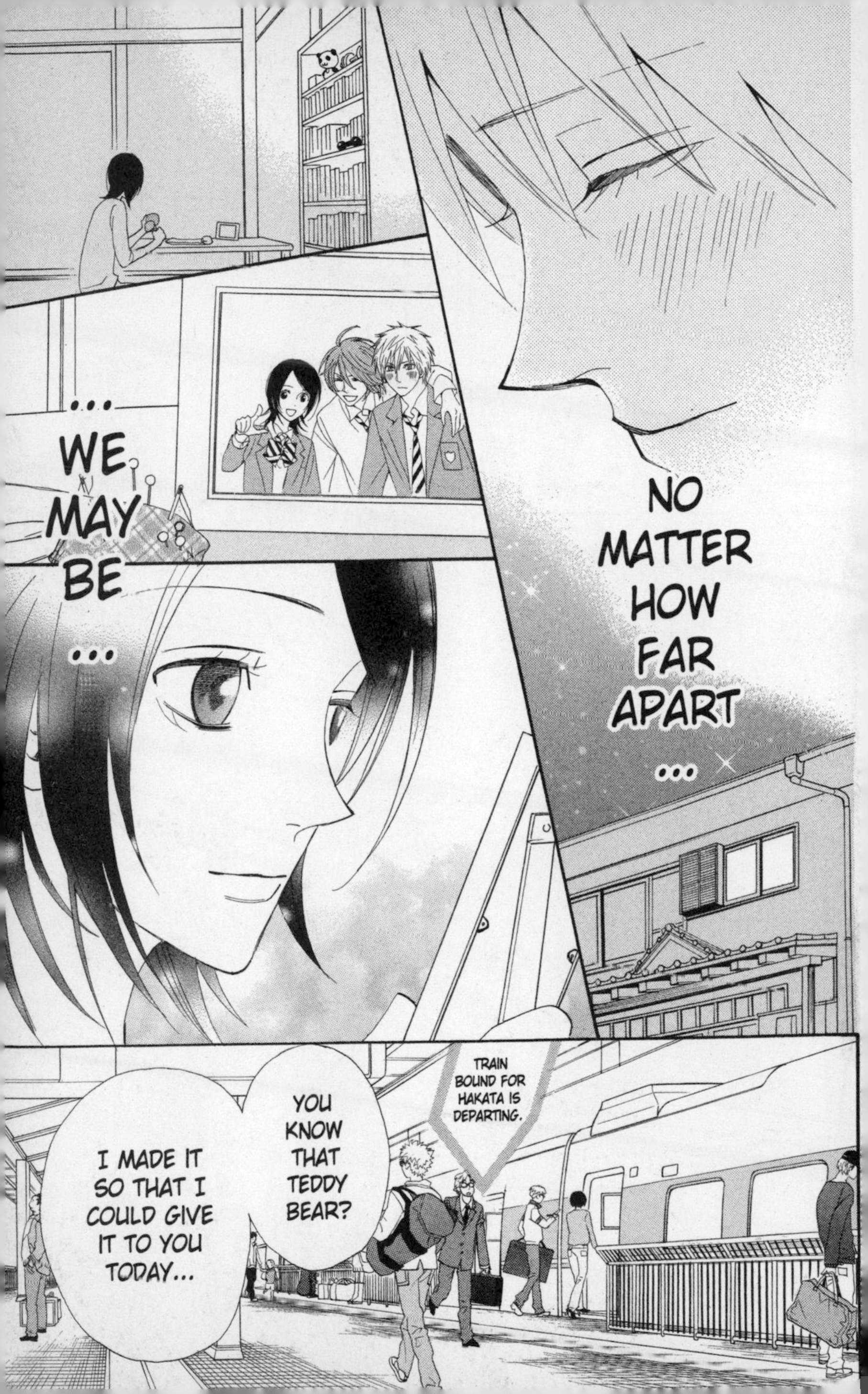
NO MATTER HOW FAR APART ...
... WE MAY BE ...
TRAIN BOUND FOR HAKATA IS DEPARTING.
YOU KNOW THAT TEDDY BEAR?
I MADE IT SO THAT I COULD GIVE IT TO YOU TODAY...

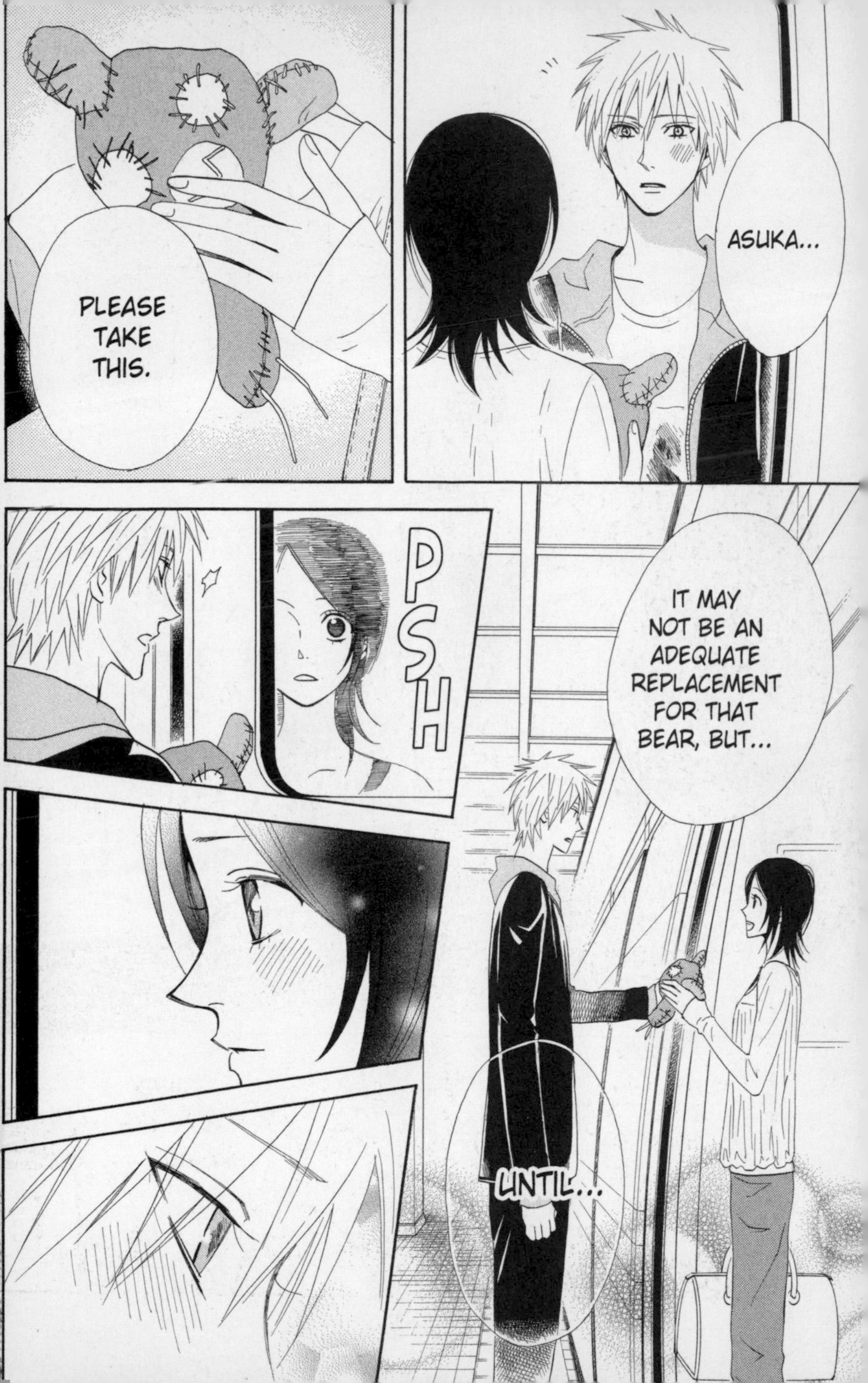
ASUKA...
PLEASE TAKE THIS.
IT MAY NOT BE AN ADEQUATE REPLACEMENT FOR THAT BEAR, BUT...
UNTIL...
PSH

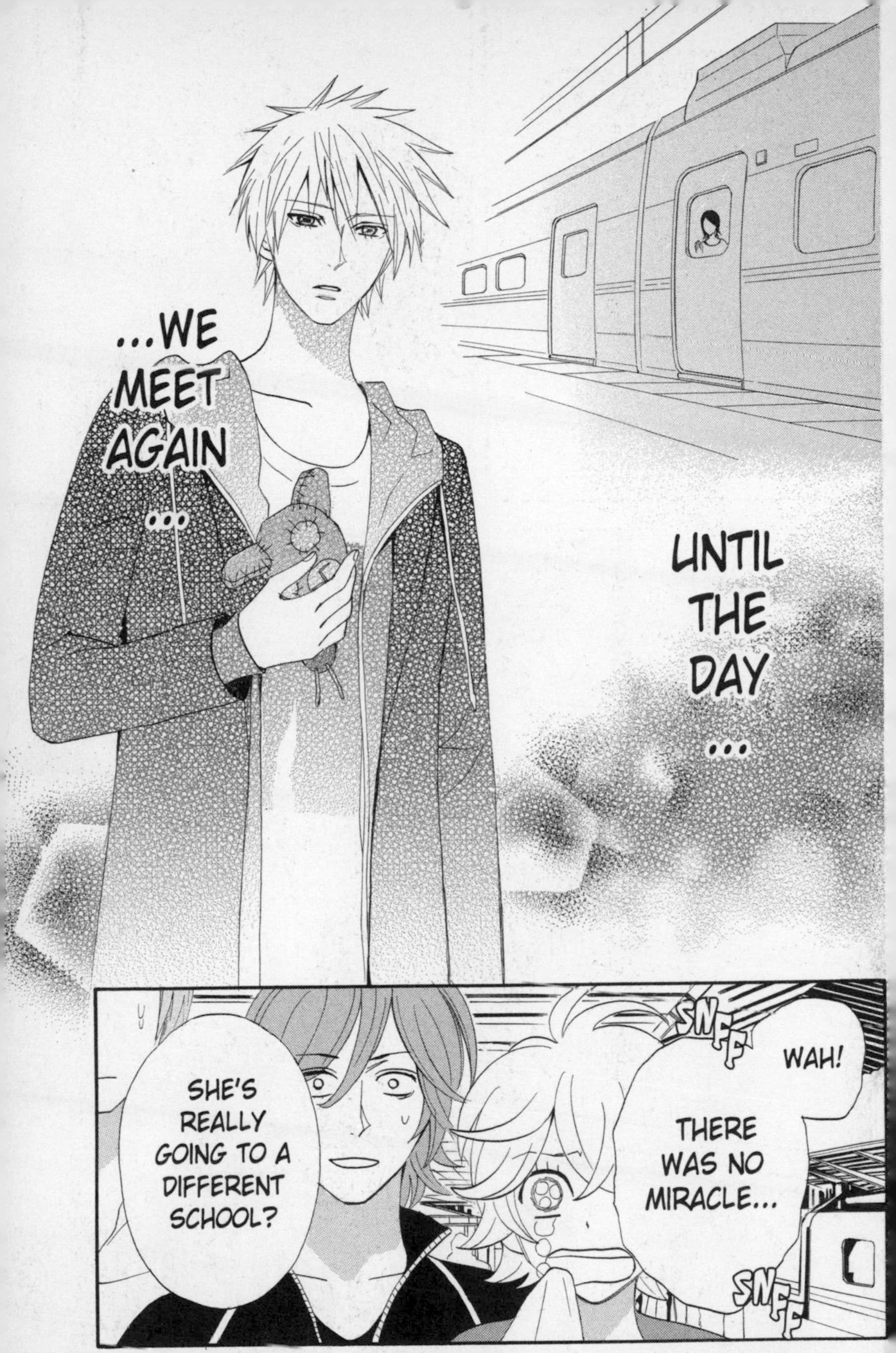
UNTIL THE DAY ...
...WE MEET AGAIN ...
SNFF
WAH!
THERE WAS NO MIRACLE...
SNFF
SHE'S REALLY GOING TO A DIFFERENT SCHOOL?

OTOMEN

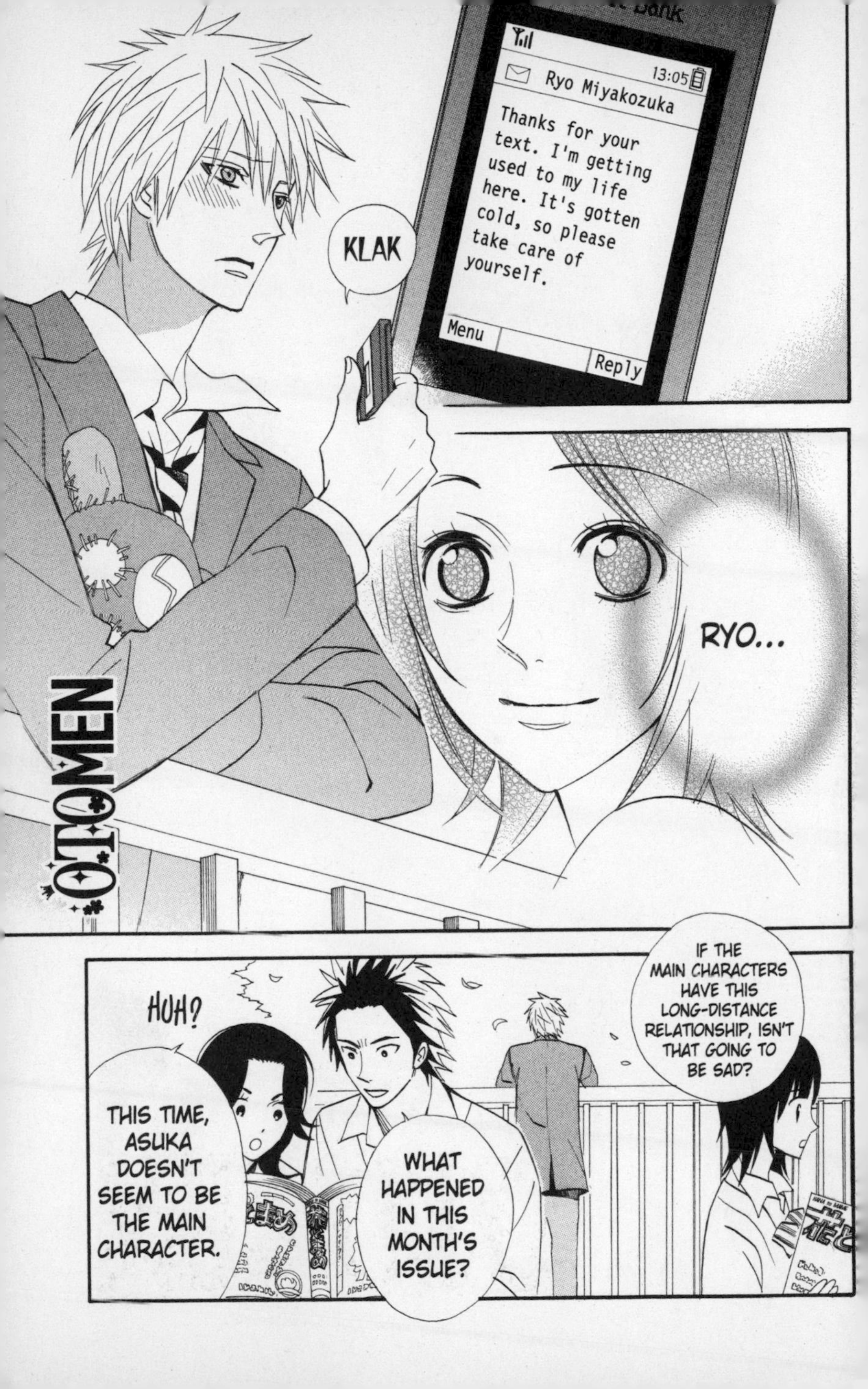
13:05
Ryo Miyakozuka
Thanks for your text. I'm getting used to my life here. It's gotten cold, so please take care of yourself.
Menu
Reply
KLAK
RYO...
OTOMEN
IF THE MAIN CHARACTERS HAVE THIS LONG-DISTANCE RELATIONSHIP, ISN'T THAT GOING TO BE SAD?
HUH?
WHAT HAPPENED IN THIS MONTH'S ISSUE?
THIS TIME, ASUKA DOESN'T SEEM TO BE THE MAIN CHARACTER.

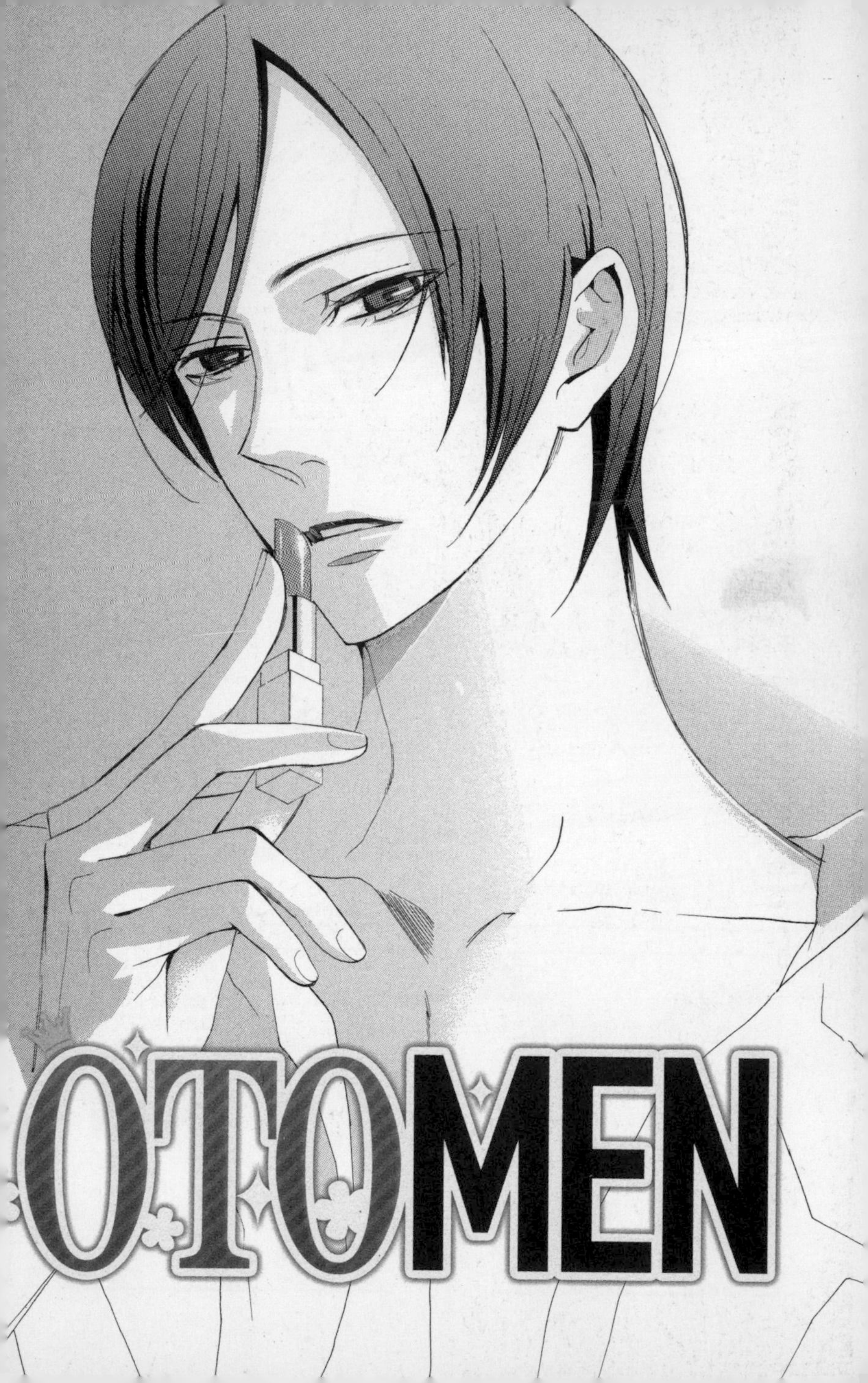
OTOMEN

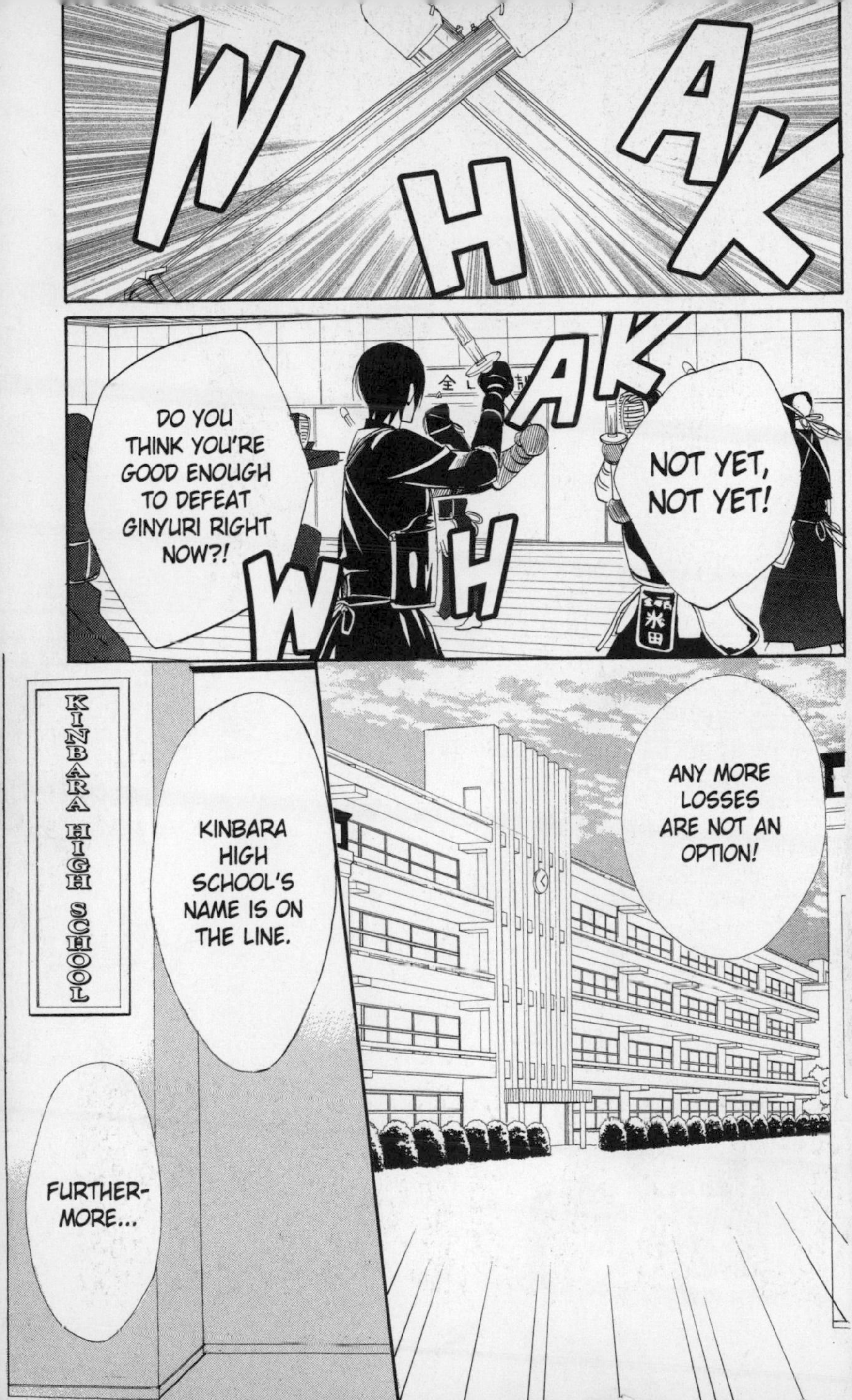
WHAK
WHAK
NOT YET, NOT YET!
DO YOU THINK YOU'RE GOOD ENOUGH TO DEFEAT GINYURI RIGHT NOW?!
KINBARA HIGH SCHOOL
ANY MORE LOSSES ARE NOT AN OPTION!
KINBARA HIGH SCHOOL'S NAME IS ON THE LINE.
FURTHER-MORE...

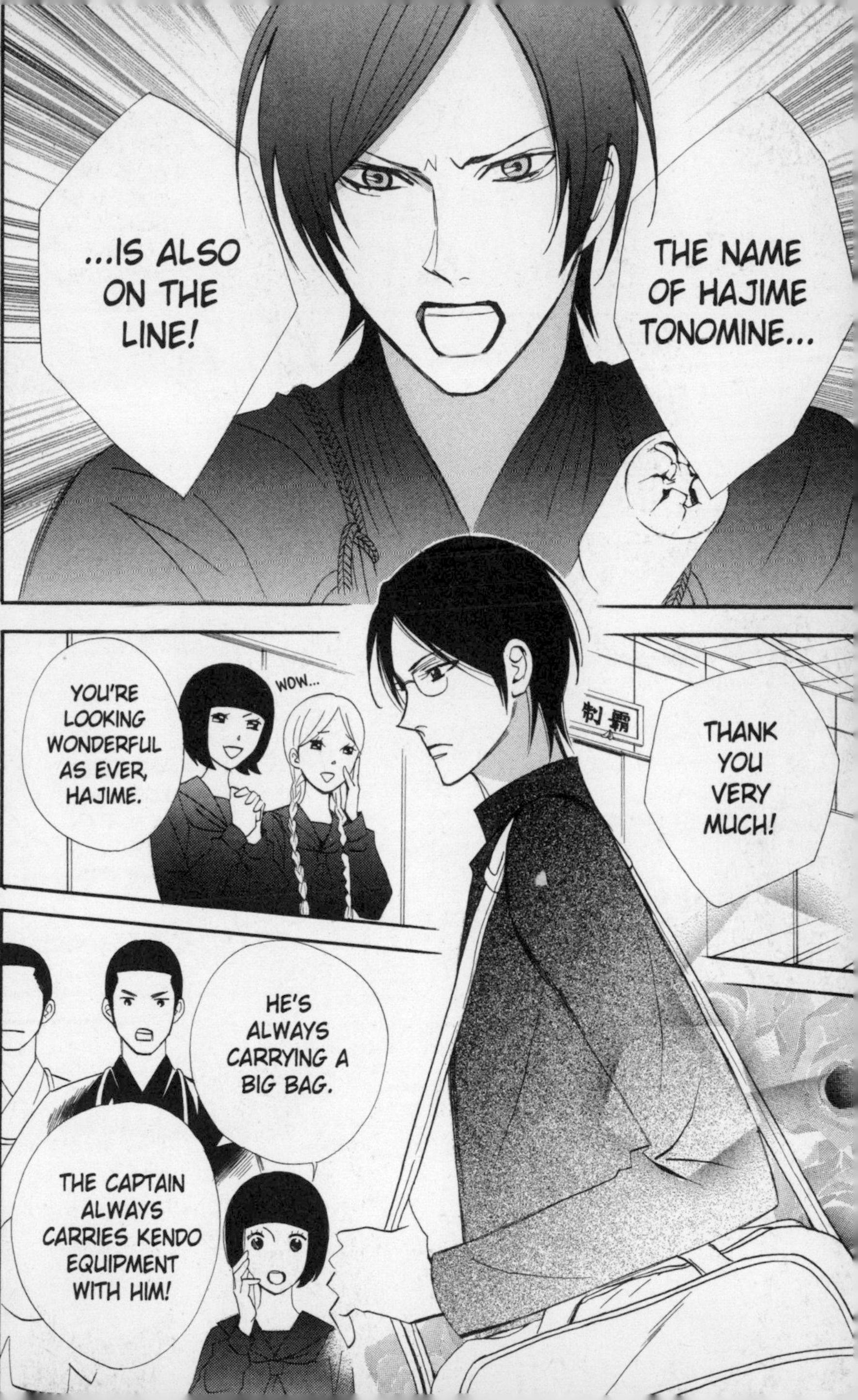
THE NAME OF HAJIME TONOMINE...
...IS ALSO ON THE LINE!
THANK YOU VERY MUCH!
WOW...
YOU'RE LOOKING WONDERFUL AS EVER, HAJIME.
制覇
HE'S ALWAYS CARRYING A BIG BAG.
THE CAPTAIN ALWAYS CARRIES KENDO EQUIPMENT WITH HIM!

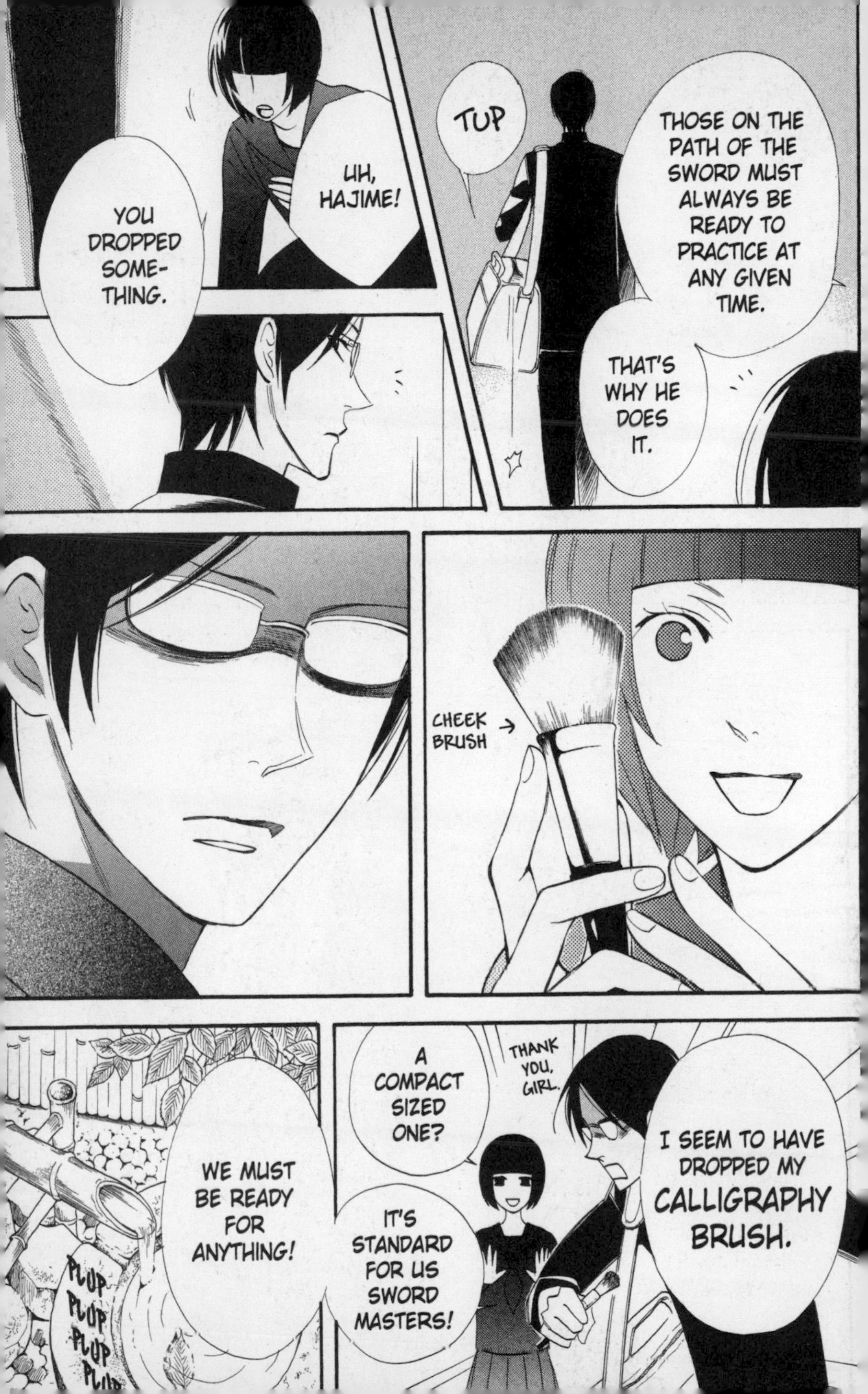
THOSE ON THE PATH OF THE SWORD MUST ALWAYS BE READY TO PRACTICE AT ANY GIVEN TIME.
TUP
THAT'S WHY HE DOES IT.
UH, HAJIME!
YOU DROPPED SOME-THING.
CHEEK BRUSH
I SEEM TO HAVE DROPPED MY CALLIGRAPHY BRUSH.
THANK YOU, GIRL.
A COMPACT SIZED ONE?
IT'S STANDARD FOR US SWORD MASTERS!
WE MUST BE READY FOR ANYTHING!
PLUP PLUP PLUP PLUP

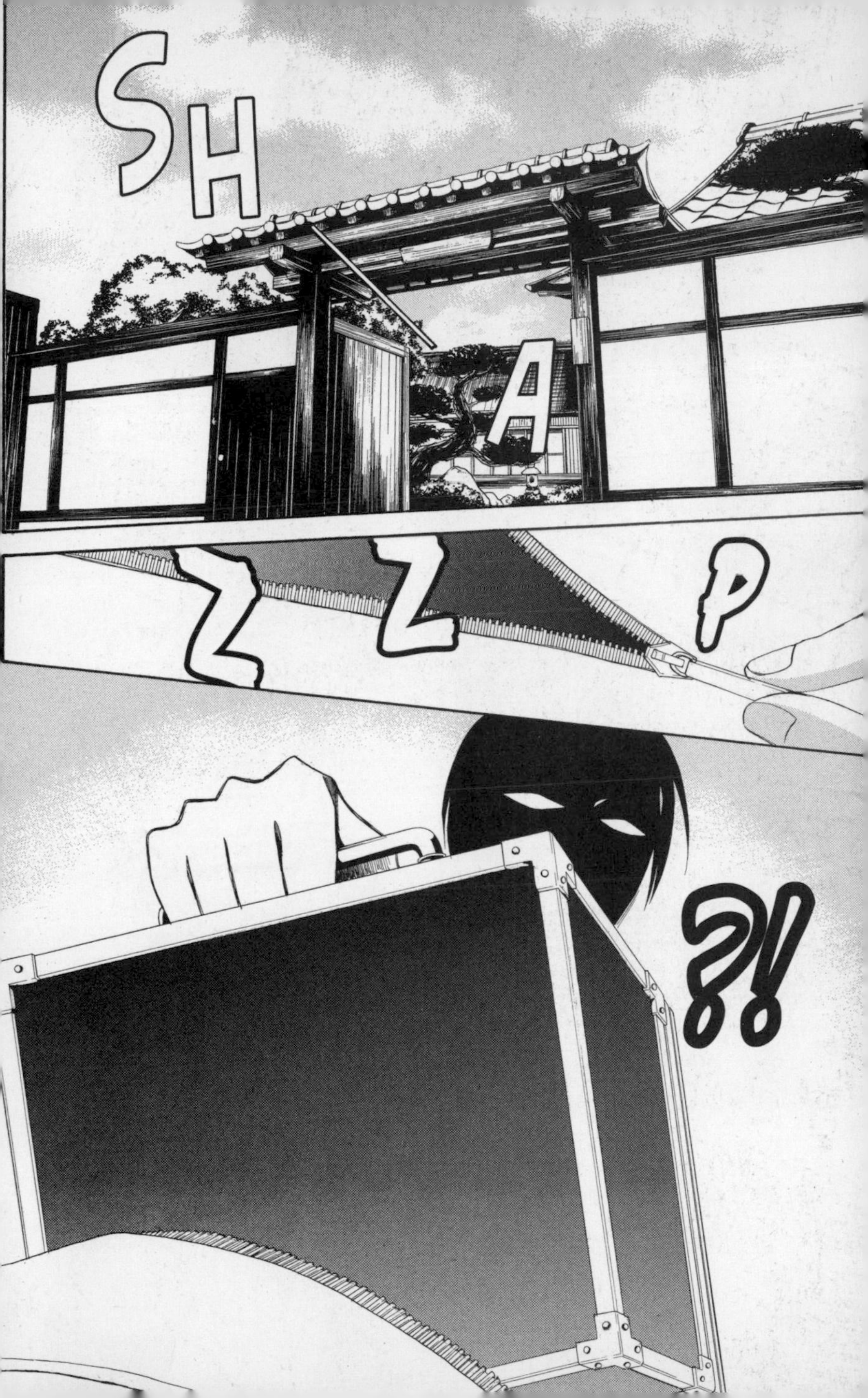
SHA
ZZP
?!

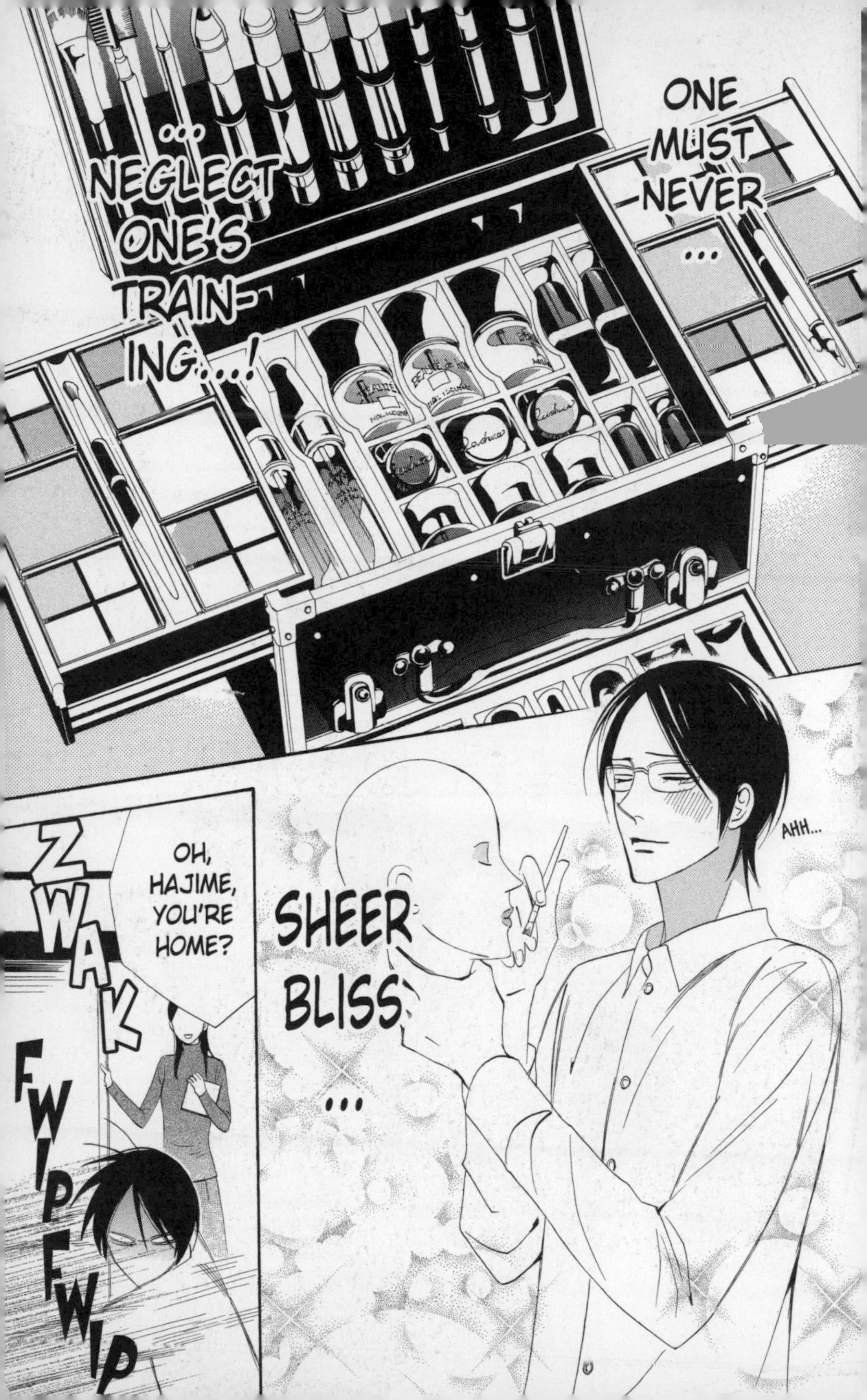
ONE MUST NEVER ...
... NEGLECT ONE'S TRAIN-ING...!
AHH...
SHEER BLISS
...
ZWAK
OH, HAJIME, YOU'RE HOME?
FWIP FWIP

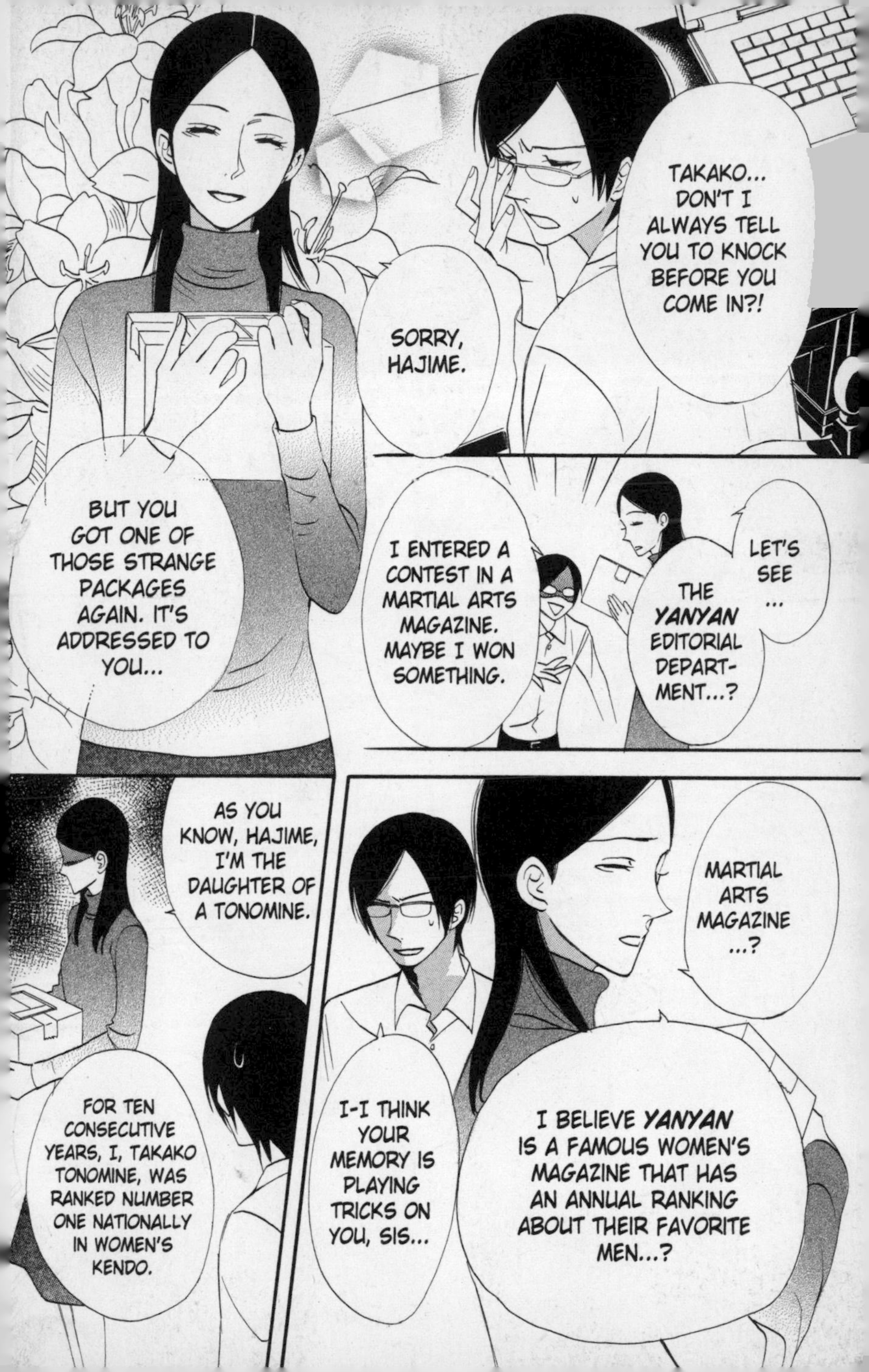
TAKAKO... DON'T I ALWAYS TELL YOU TO KNOCK BEFORE YOU COME IN?!
SORRY, HAJIME.
BUT YOU GOT ONE OF THOSE STRANGE PACKAGES AGAIN. IT'S ADDRESSED TO YOU...
LET'S SEE ...
THE *YANYAN* EDITORIAL DEPART-MENT...?
I ENTERED A CONTEST IN A MARTIAL ARTS MAGAZINE. MAYBE I WON SOMETHING.
MARTIAL ARTS MAGAZINE ...?
I BELIEVE *YANYAN* IS A FAMOUS WOMEN'S MAGAZINE THAT HAS AN ANNUAL RANKING ABOUT THEIR FAVORITE MEN...?
I-I THINK YOUR MEMORY IS PLAYING TRICKS ON YOU, SIS...
AS YOU KNOW, HAJIME, I'M THE DAUGHTER OF A TONOMINE.
FOR TEN CONSECUTIVE YEARS, I, TAKAKO TONOMINE, WAS RANKED NUMBER ONE NATIONALLY IN WOMEN'S KENDO.

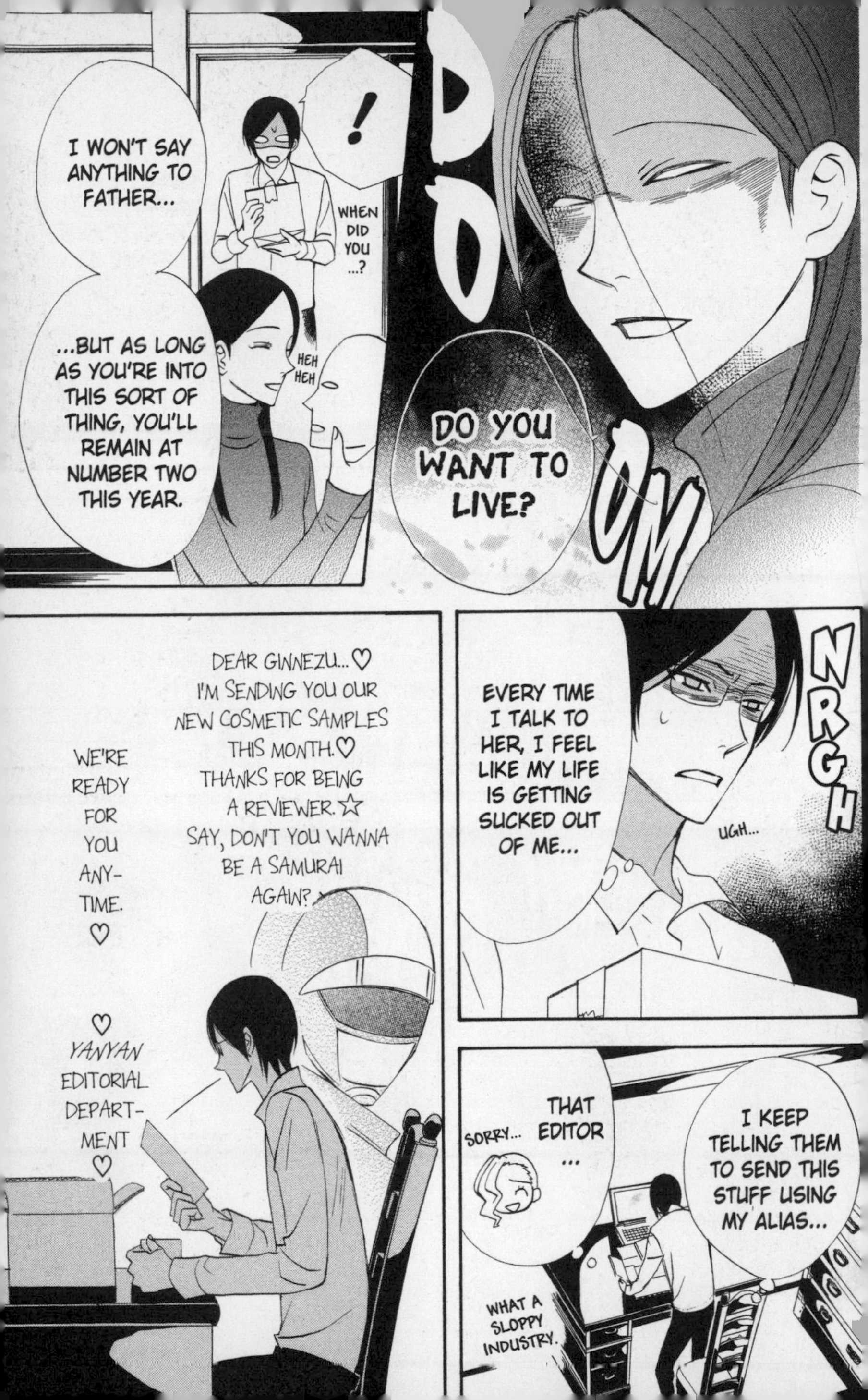
DOOM
DO YOU WANT TO LIVE?
!
WHEN DID YOU ...?
I WON'T SAY ANYTHING TO FATHER...
...BUT AS LONG AS YOU'RE INTO THIS SORT OF THING, YOU'LL REMAIN AT NUMBER TWO THIS YEAR.
HEH HEH
NRGH
EVERY TIME I TALK TO HER, I FEEL LIKE MY LIFE IS GETTING SUCKED OUT OF ME...
UGH...
I KEEP TELLING THEM TO SEND THIS STUFF USING MY ALIAS...
THAT EDITOR ...
SORRY...
WHAT A SLOPPY INDUSTRY.
DEAR GINNEZU...♡ I'M SENDING YOU OUR NEW COSMETIC SAMPLES THIS MONTH.♡ THANKS FOR BEING A REVIEWER.☆ SAY, DON'T YOU WANNA BE A SAMURAI AGAIN?
WE'RE READY FOR YOU ANY-TIME. ♡
♡ YANYAN EDITORIAL DEPART-MENT ♡

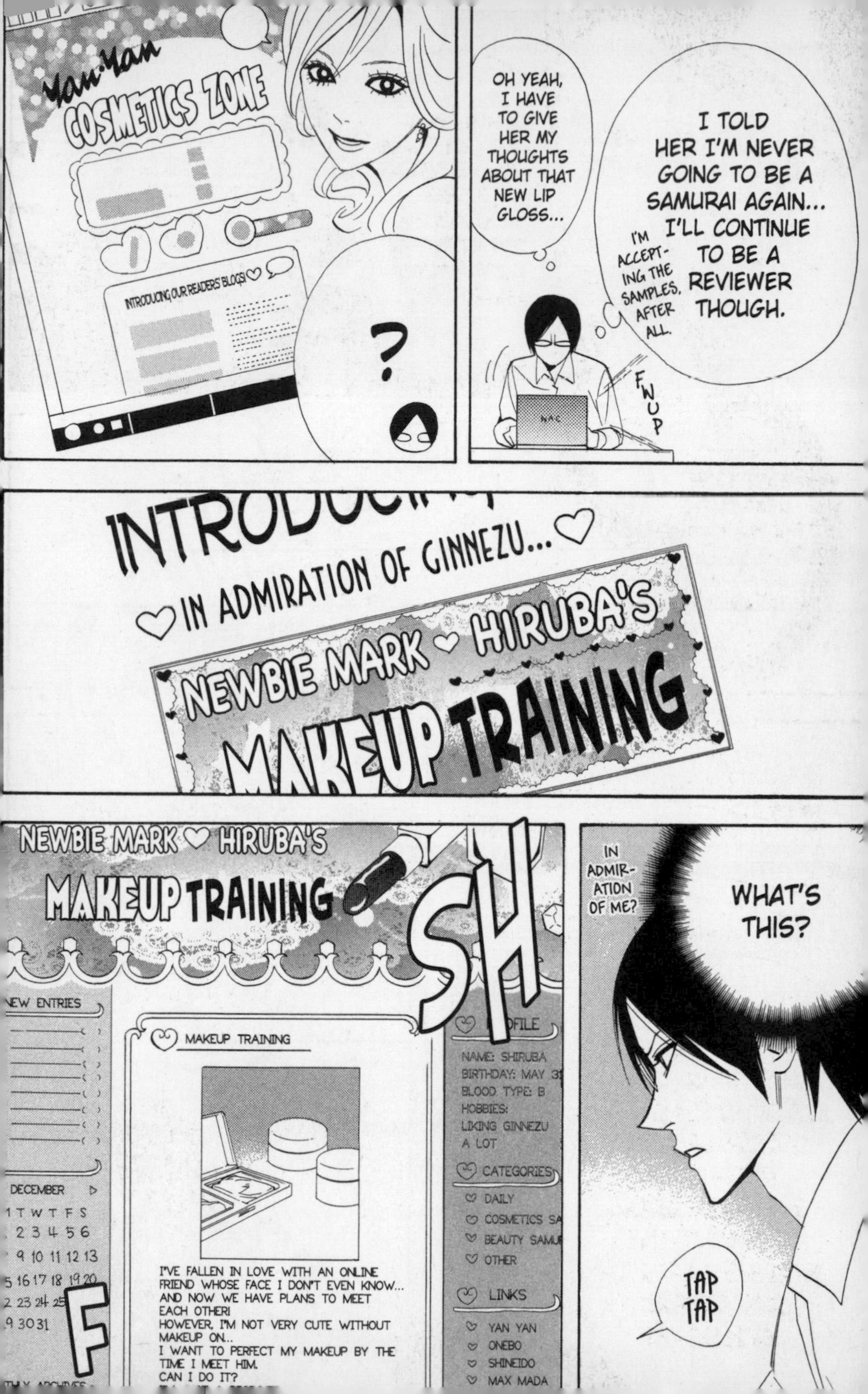
I TOLD HER I'M NEVER GOING TO BE A SAMURAI AGAIN... I'LL CONTINUE TO BE A REVIEWER THOUGH.
I'M ACCEPTING THE SAMPLES, AFTER ALL.
OH YEAH, I HAVE TO GIVE HER MY THOUGHTS ABOUT THAT NEW LIP GLOSS...
FWUP
?
Yan·Yan
COSMETICS ZONE
INTRODUCING OUR READERS' BLOGS!
INTRODUCING
IN ADMIRATION OF GINNEZU...
NEWBIE MARK HIRUBA'S
MAKEUP TRAINING
WHAT'S THIS?
IN ADMIRATION OF ME?
TAP TAP
NEWBIE MARK HIRUBA'S
MAKEUP TRAINING
SH
F
NEW ENTRIES
MAKEUP TRAINING
I'VE FALLEN IN LOVE WITH AN ONLINE FRIEND WHOSE FACE I DON'T EVEN KNOW... AND NOW WE HAVE PLANS TO MEET EACH OTHER!
HOWEVER, I'M NOT VERY CUTE WITHOUT MAKEUP ON...
I WANT TO PERFECT MY MAKEUP BY THE TIME I MEET HIM.
CAN I DO IT?
NAME: SHIRUBA
BIRTHDAY: MAY 31
BLOOD TYPE: B
HOBBIES:
LIKING GINNEZU A LOT
CATEGORIES
DAILY
OTHER
LINKS
YAN YAN
ONEBO
SHINEIDO
MAX MADA
DECEMBER

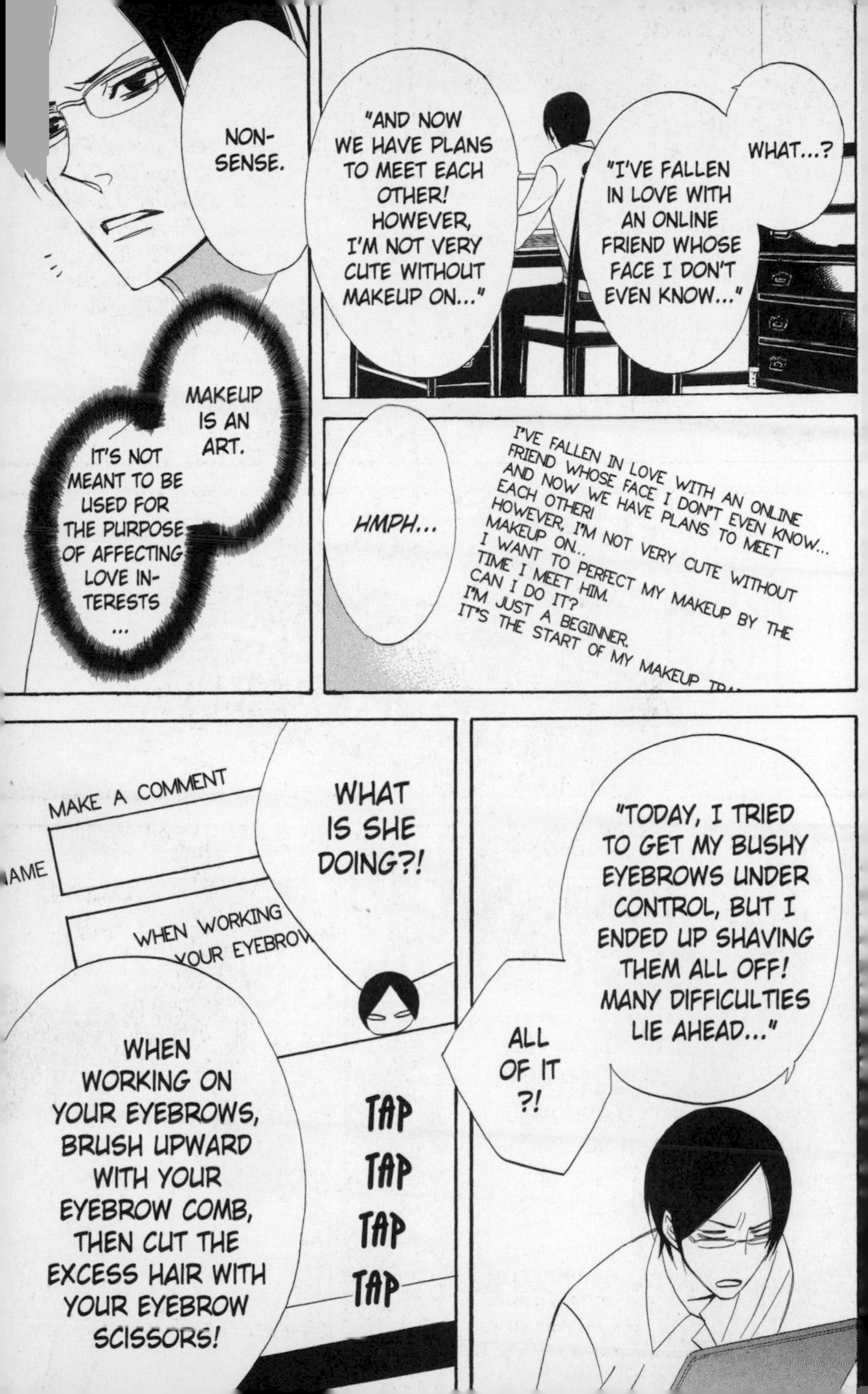
WHAT...?
"I'VE FALLEN IN LOVE WITH AN ONLINE FRIEND WHOSE FACE I DON'T EVEN KNOW..."
"AND NOW WE HAVE PLANS TO MEET EACH OTHER! HOWEVER, I'M NOT VERY CUTE WITHOUT MAKEUP ON..."
I'VE FALLEN IN LOVE WITH AN ONLINE FRIEND WHOSE FACE I DON'T EVEN KNOW...
AND NOW WE HAVE PLANS TO MEET EACH OTHER!
HOWEVER, I'M NOT VERY CUTE WITHOUT MAKEUP ON...
I WANT TO PERFECT MY MAKEUP BY THE TIME I MEET HIM.
CAN I DO IT?
I'M JUST A BEGINNER.
IT'S THE START OF MY MAKEUP
HMPH...
NON-SENSE.
MAKEUP IS AN ART.
IT'S NOT MEANT TO BE USED FOR THE PURPOSE OF AFFECTING LOVE INTERESTS...
"TODAY, I TRIED TO GET MY BUSHY EYEBROWS UNDER CONTROL, BUT I ENDED UP SHAVING THEM ALL OFF! MANY DIFFICULTIES LIE AHEAD..."
ALL OF IT?!
WHAT IS SHE DOING?!
MAKE A COMMENT
WHEN WORKING
WHEN WORKING ON YOUR EYEBROWS, BRUSH UPWARD WITH YOUR EYEBROW COMB, THEN CUT THE EXCESS HAIR WITH YOUR EYEBROW SCISSORS!
TAP TAP TAP TAP

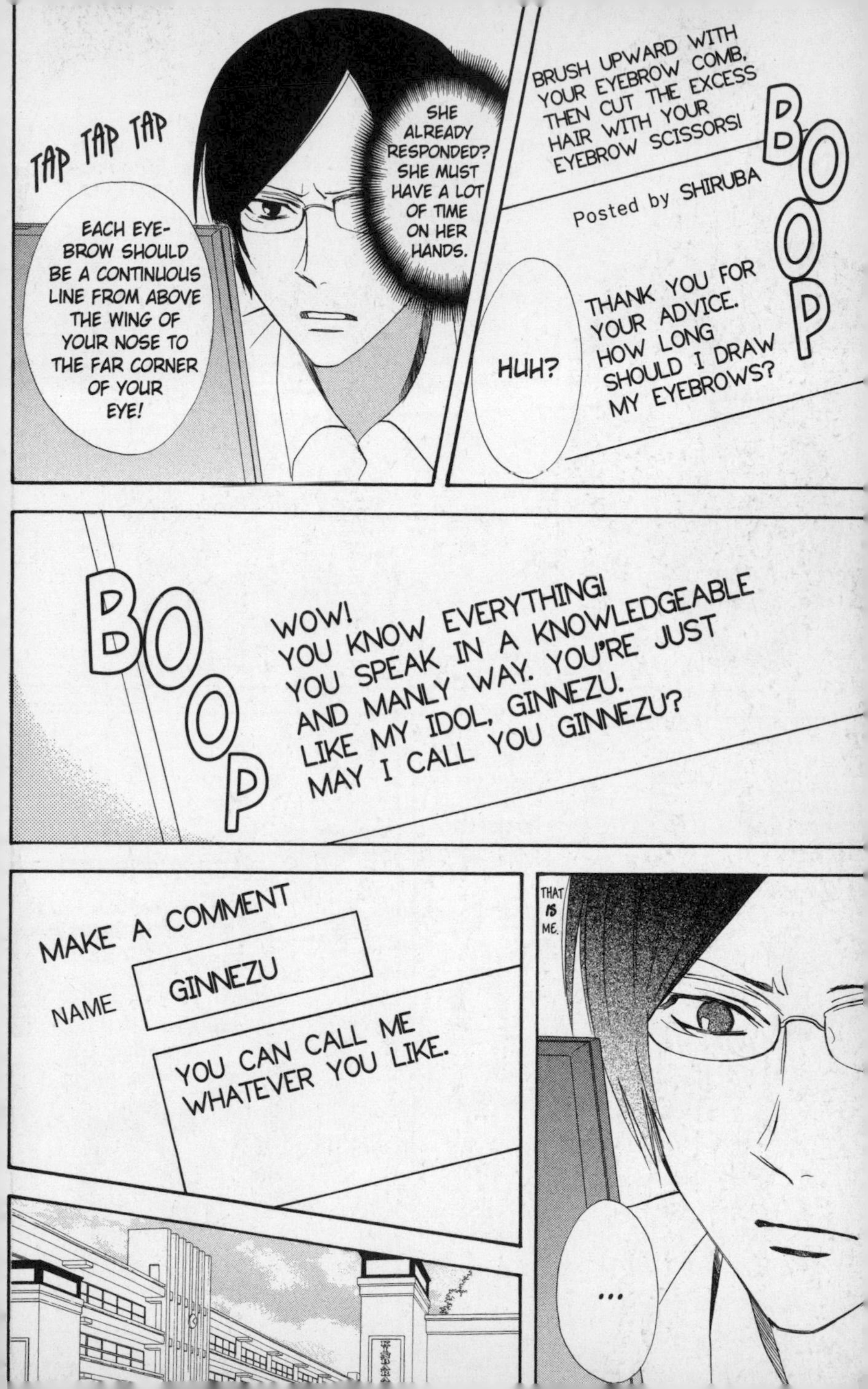
BRUSH UPWARD WITH YOUR EYEBROW COMB, THEN CUT THE EXCESS HAIR WITH YOUR EYEBROW SCISSORS!
Posted by SHIRUBA
BOOP
THANK YOU FOR YOUR ADVICE. HOW LONG SHOULD I DRAW MY EYEBROWS?
HUH?
SHE ALREADY RESPONDED? SHE MUST HAVE A LOT OF TIME ON HER HANDS.
TAP TAP TAP
EACH EYE-BROW SHOULD BE A CONTINUOUS LINE FROM ABOVE THE WING OF YOUR NOSE TO THE FAR CORNER OF YOUR EYE!
BOOP
WOW! YOU KNOW EVERYTHING! YOU SPEAK IN A KNOWLEDGEABLE AND MANLY WAY. YOU'RE JUST LIKE MY IDOL, GINNEZU. MAY I CALL YOU GINNEZU?
THAT IS ME.
...
MAKE A COMMENT
NAME
GINNEZU
YOU CAN CALL ME WHATEVER YOU LIKE.

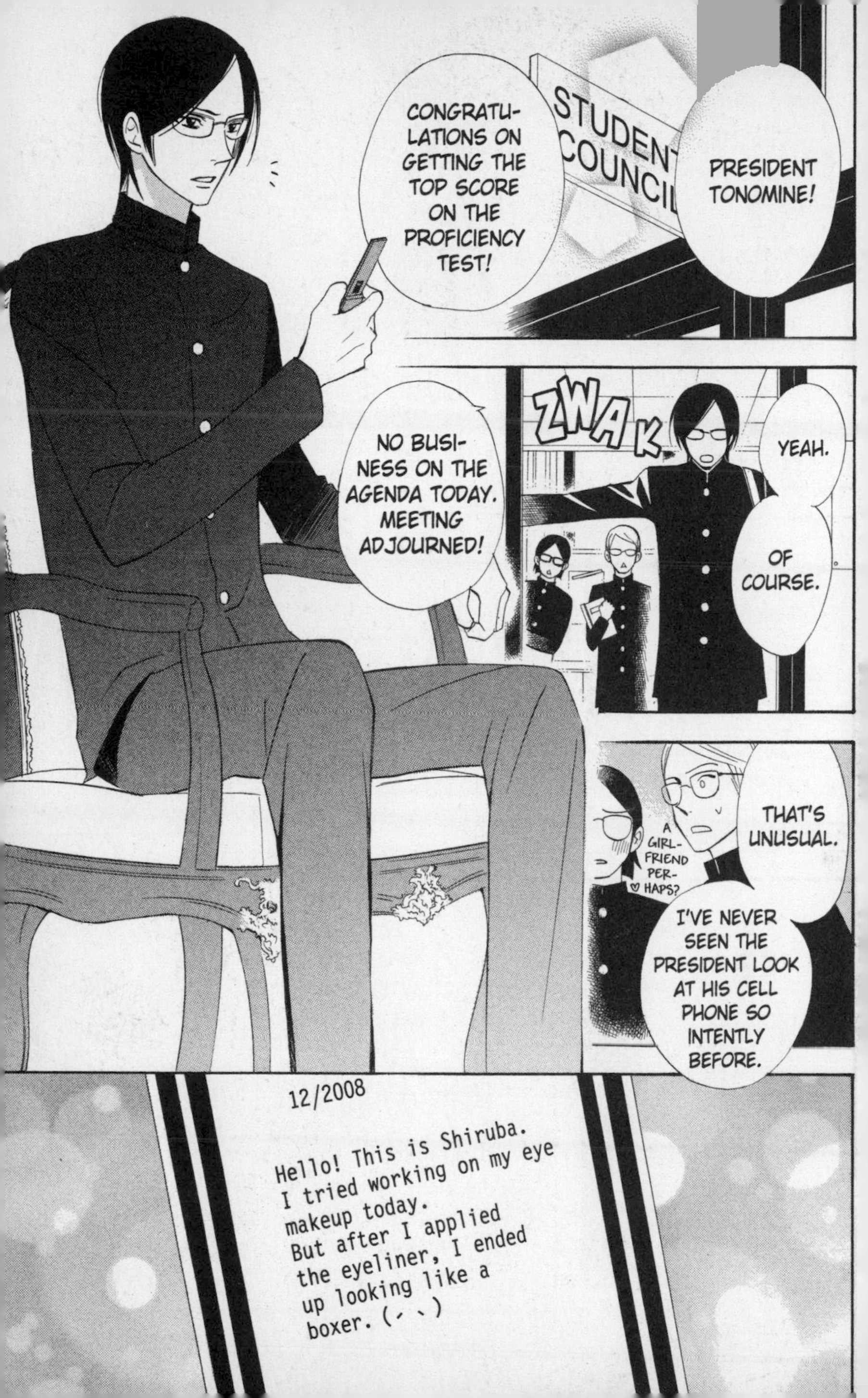
STUDENT COUNCIL
PRESIDENT TONOMINE!
CONGRATULATIONS ON GETTING THE TOP SCORE ON THE PROFICIENCY TEST!
NO BUSINESS ON THE AGENDA TODAY. MEETING ADJOURNED!
ZWAK
YEAH.
OF COURSE.
THAT'S UNUSUAL.
I'VE NEVER SEEN THE PRESIDENT LOOK AT HIS CELL PHONE SO INTENTLY BEFORE.
A GIRLFRIEND PERHAPS? ♡
12/2008
Hello! This is Shiruba.
I tried working on my eye makeup today.
But after I applied the eyeliner, I ended up looking like a boxer. (╭ ╮)

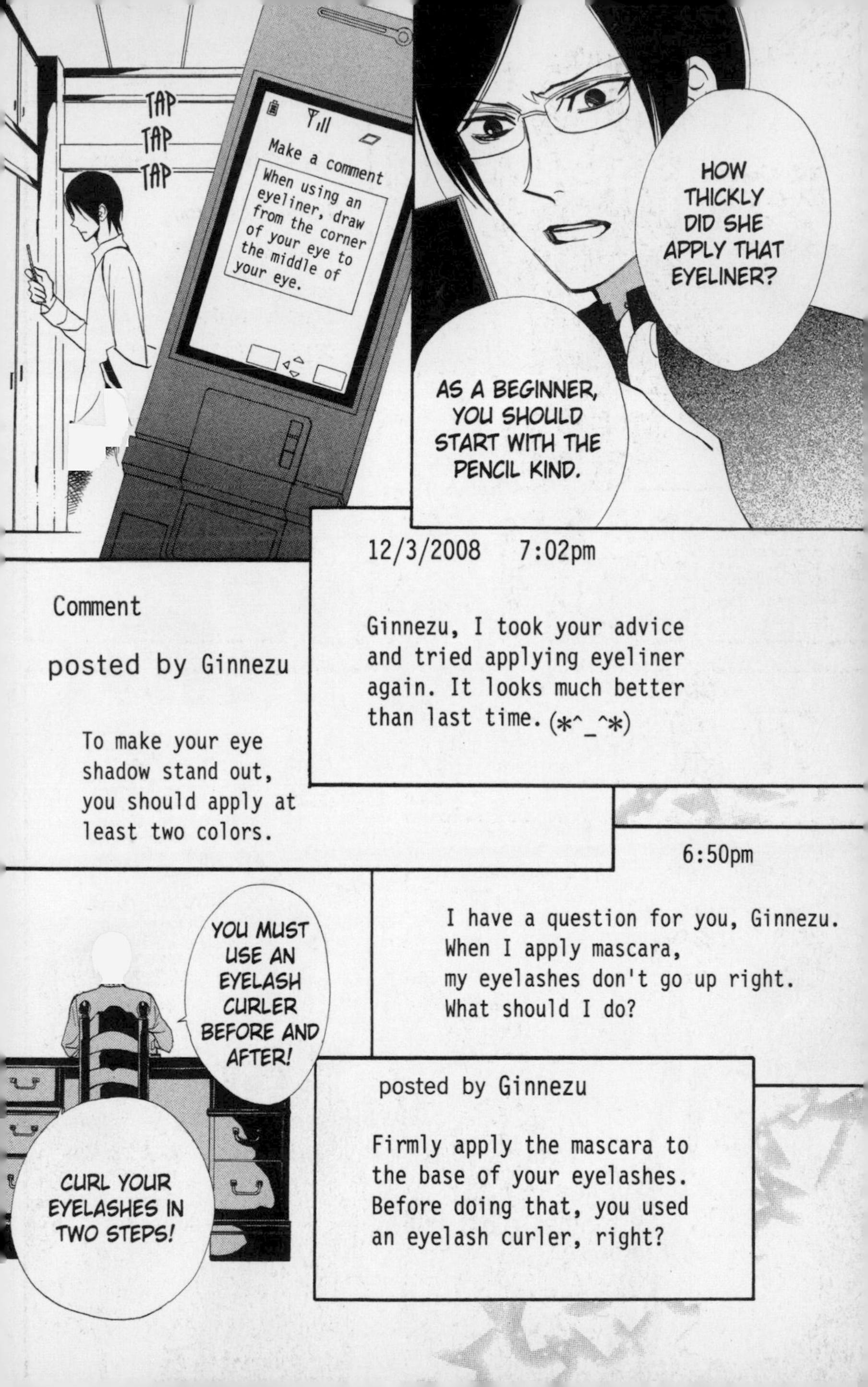
HOW THICKLY DID SHE APPLY THAT EYELINER?
AS A BEGINNER, YOU SHOULD START WITH THE PENCIL KIND.
TAP
TAP
TAP
Make a comment
When using an eyeliner, draw from the corner of your eye to the middle of your eye.
12/3/2008 7:02pm
Ginnezu, I took your advice and tried applying eyeliner again. It looks much better than last time. (*^_^*)
Comment
posted by Ginnezu
To make your eye shadow stand out, you should apply at least two colors.
6:50pm
I have a question for you, Ginnezu. When I apply mascara, my eyelashes don't go up right. What should I do?
posted by Ginnezu
Firmly apply the mascara to the base of your eyelashes. Before doing that, you used an eyelash curler, right?
YOU MUST USE AN EYELASH CURLER BEFORE AND AFTER!
CURL YOUR EYELASHES IN TWO STEPS!

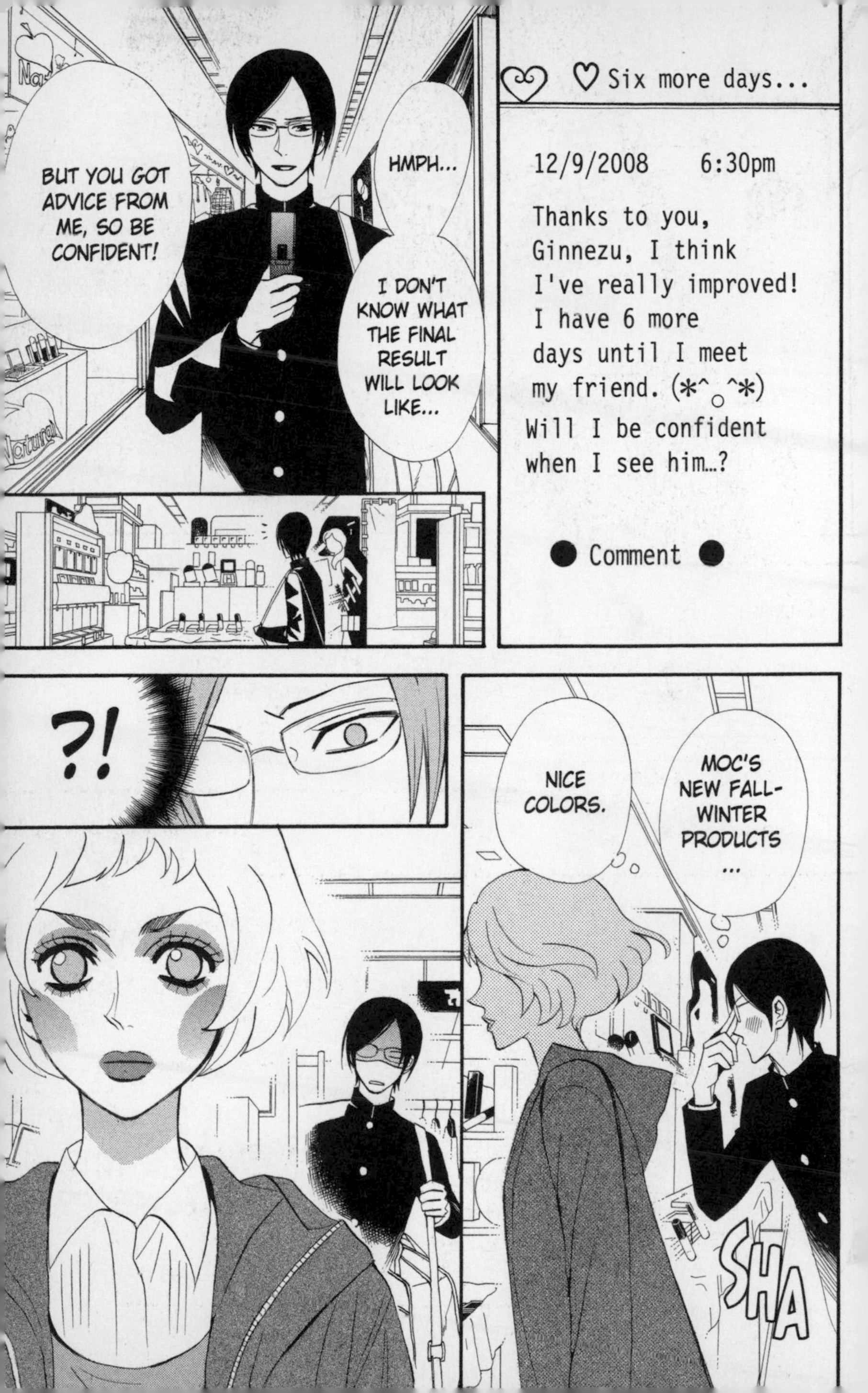
♡ Six more days...
12/9/2008 6:30pm
Thanks to you, Ginnezu, I think I've really improved! I have 6 more days until I meet my friend. (*^o^*) Will I be confident when I see him...?
● Comment ●
HMPH...
I DON'T KNOW WHAT THE FINAL RESULT WILL LOOK LIKE...
BUT YOU GOT ADVICE FROM ME, SO BE CONFIDENT!
MOC'S NEW FALL-WINTER PRODUCTS ...
NICE COLORS.
SHA
?!

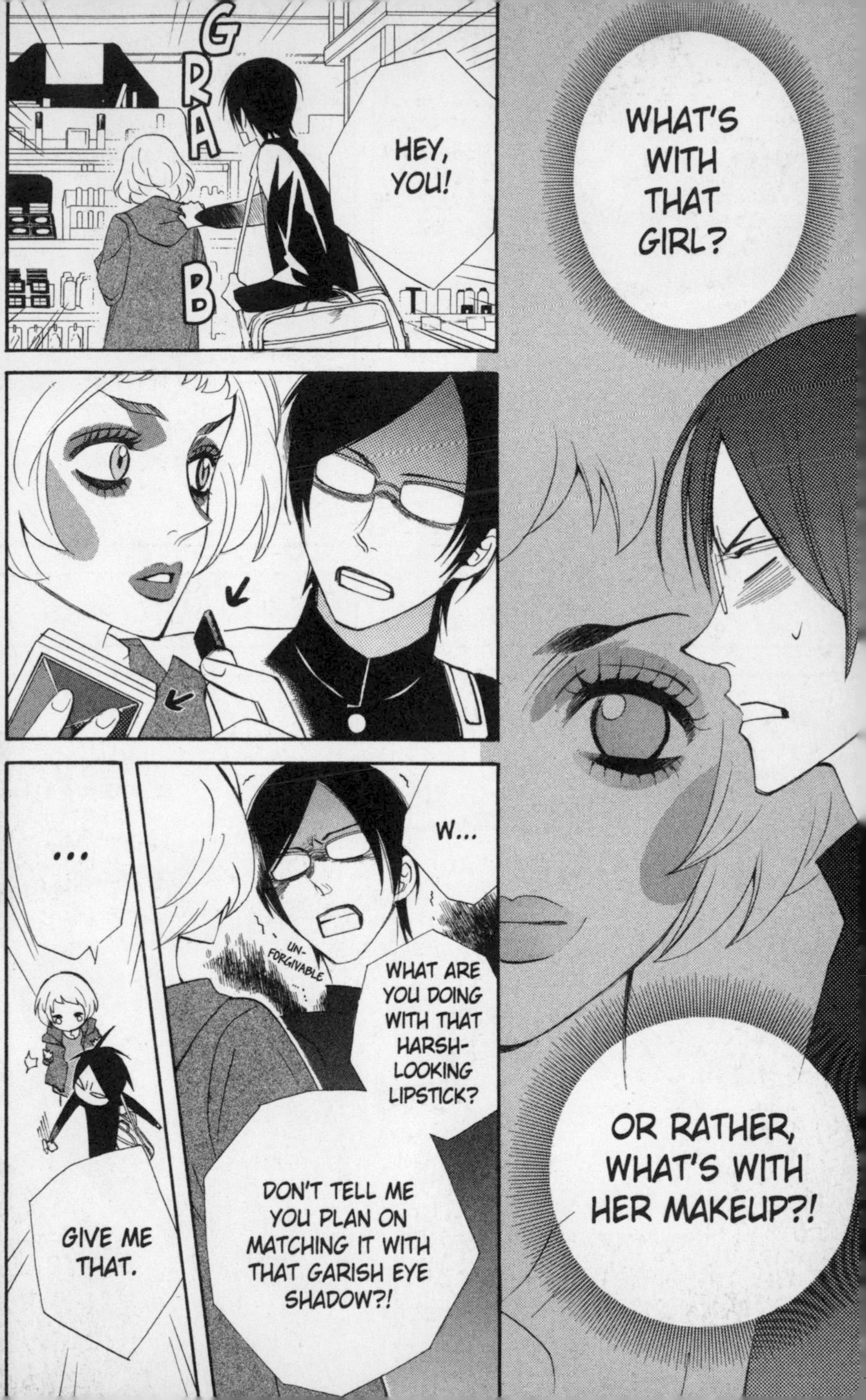
WHAT'S WITH THAT GIRL?
OR RATHER, WHAT'S WITH HER MAKEUP?!
GRAB
HEY, YOU!
W...
UN-FORGIVABLE
WHAT ARE YOU DOING WITH THAT HARSH-LOOKING LIPSTICK?
DON'T TELL ME YOU PLAN ON MATCHING IT WITH THAT GARISH EYE SHADOW?!
...
GIVE ME THAT.

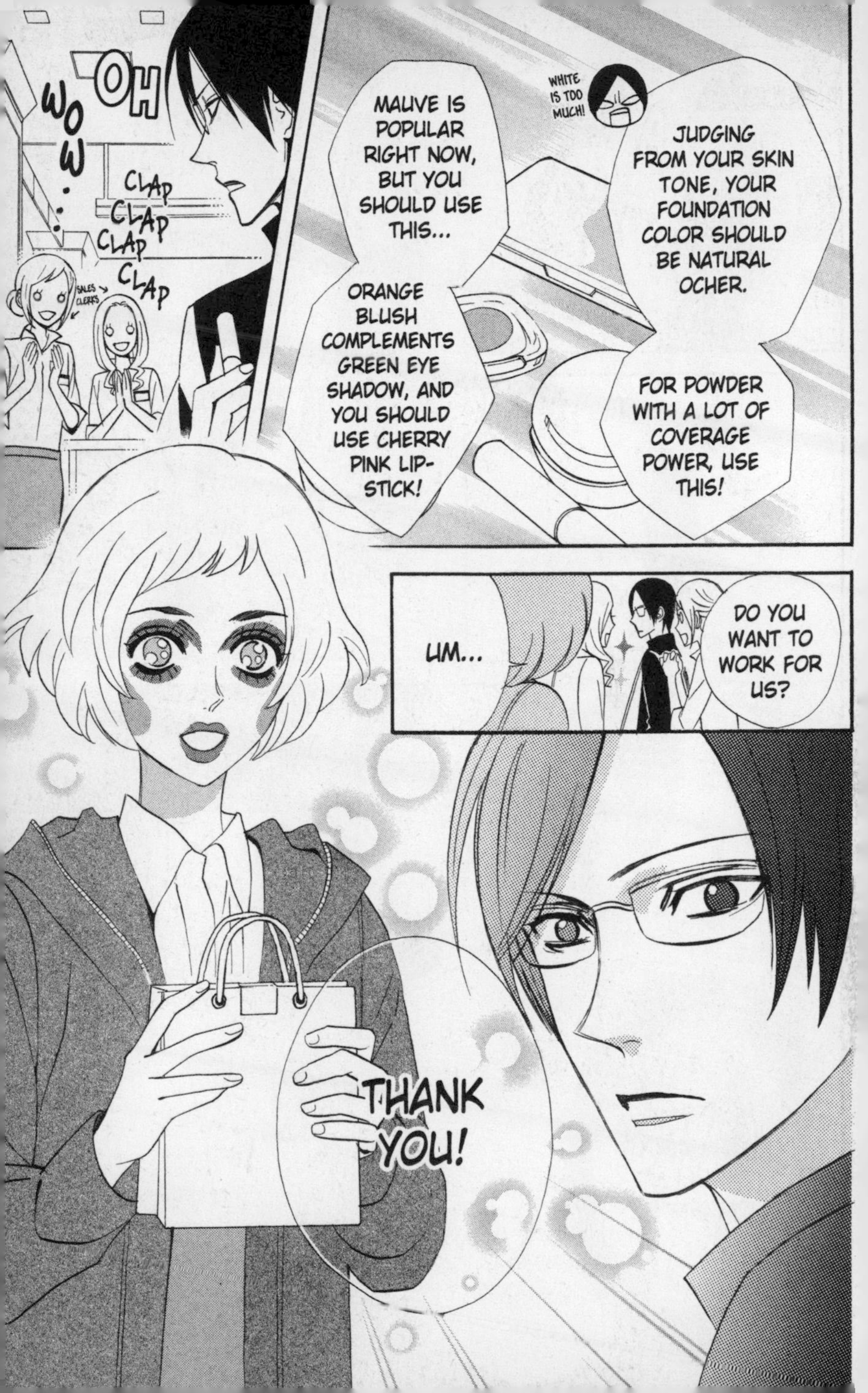
WHITE IS TOO MUCH!
JUDGING FROM YOUR SKIN TONE, YOUR FOUNDATION COLOR SHOULD BE NATURAL OCHER.
MAUVE IS POPULAR RIGHT NOW, BUT YOU SHOULD USE THIS...
FOR POWDER WITH A LOT OF COVERAGE POWER, USE THIS!
ORANGE BLUSH COMPLEMENTS GREEN EYE SHADOW, AND YOU SHOULD USE CHERRY PINK LIP-STICK!
OH
WOW...
CLAP CLAP CLAP CLAP
SALES CLERKS
DO YOU WANT TO WORK FOR US?
UM...
THANK YOU!

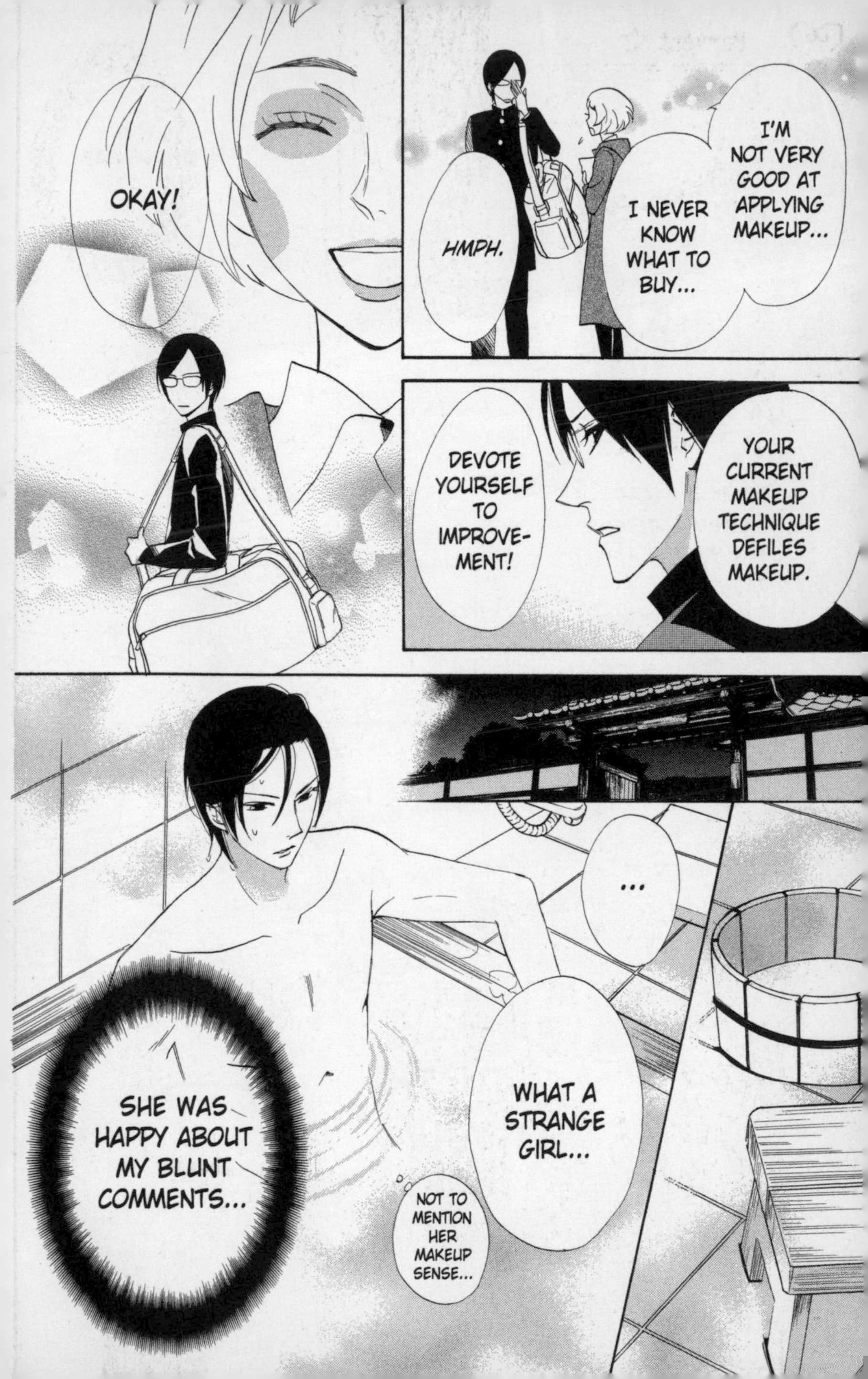
I'M NOT VERY GOOD AT APPLYING MAKEUP...
I NEVER KNOW WHAT TO BUY...
HMPH.
YOUR CURRENT MAKEUP TECHNIQUE DEFILES MAKEUP.
DEVOTE YOURSELF TO IMPROVEMENT!
OKAY!
...
WHAT A STRANGE GIRL...
SHE WAS HAPPY ABOUT MY BLUNT COMMENTS...
NOT TO MENTION HER MAKEUP SENSE...

Harvest ☆

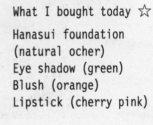

What I bought today ☆

Hanasui foundation
(natural ocher)
Eye shadow (green)
Blush (orange)
Lipstick (cherry pink)

IT'S AS
IF...

...

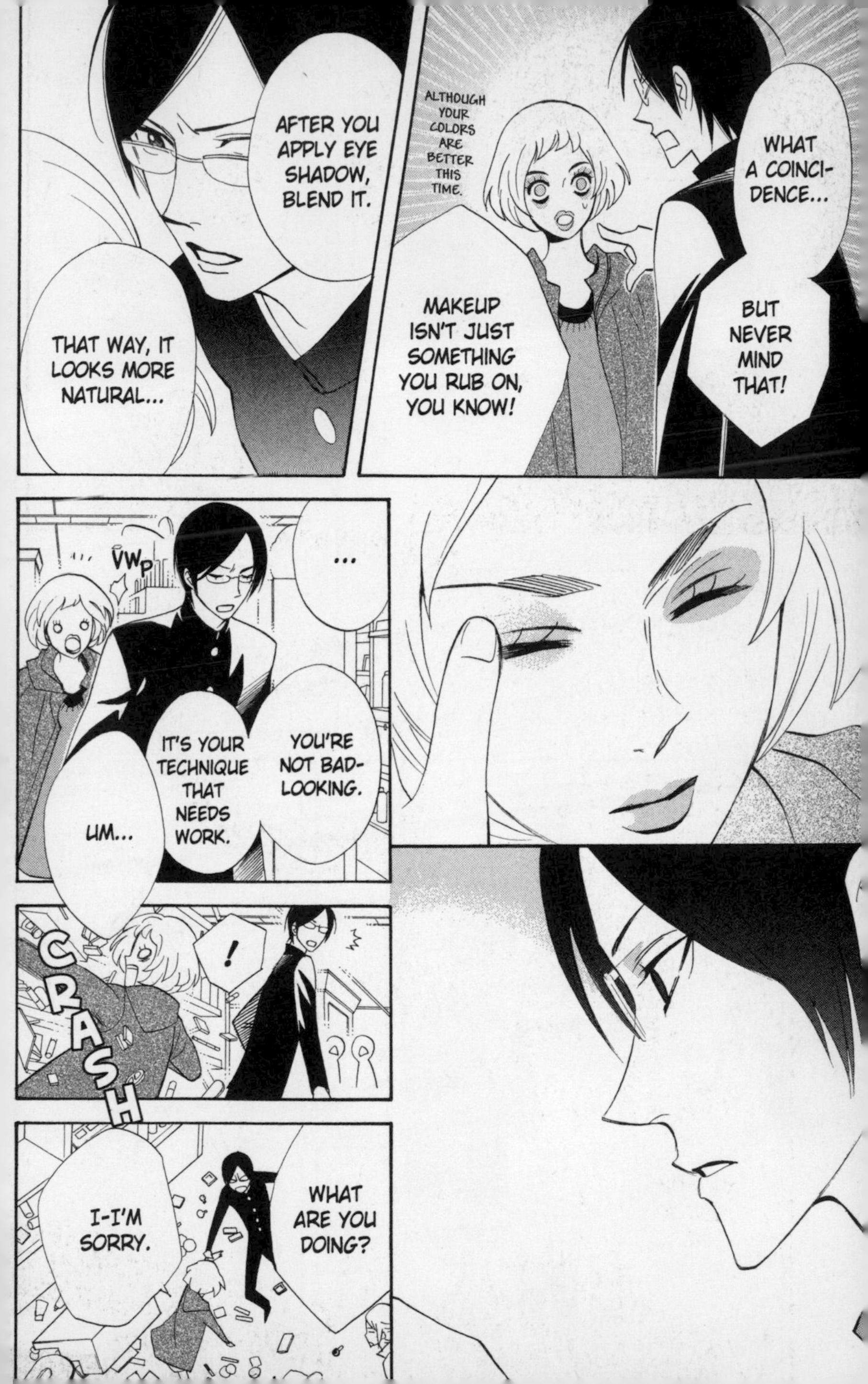
WHAT A COINCIDENCE...
BUT NEVER MIND THAT!
ALTHOUGH YOUR COLORS ARE BETTER THIS TIME.
MAKEUP ISN'T JUST SOMETHING YOU RUB ON, YOU KNOW!
AFTER YOU APPLY EYE SHADOW, BLEND IT.
THAT WAY, IT LOOKS MORE NATURAL...
...
YOU'RE NOT BAD-LOOKING.
IT'S YOUR TECHNIQUE THAT NEEDS WORK.
VWP
UM...
!
CRASH
WHAT ARE YOU DOING?
I-I'M SORRY.

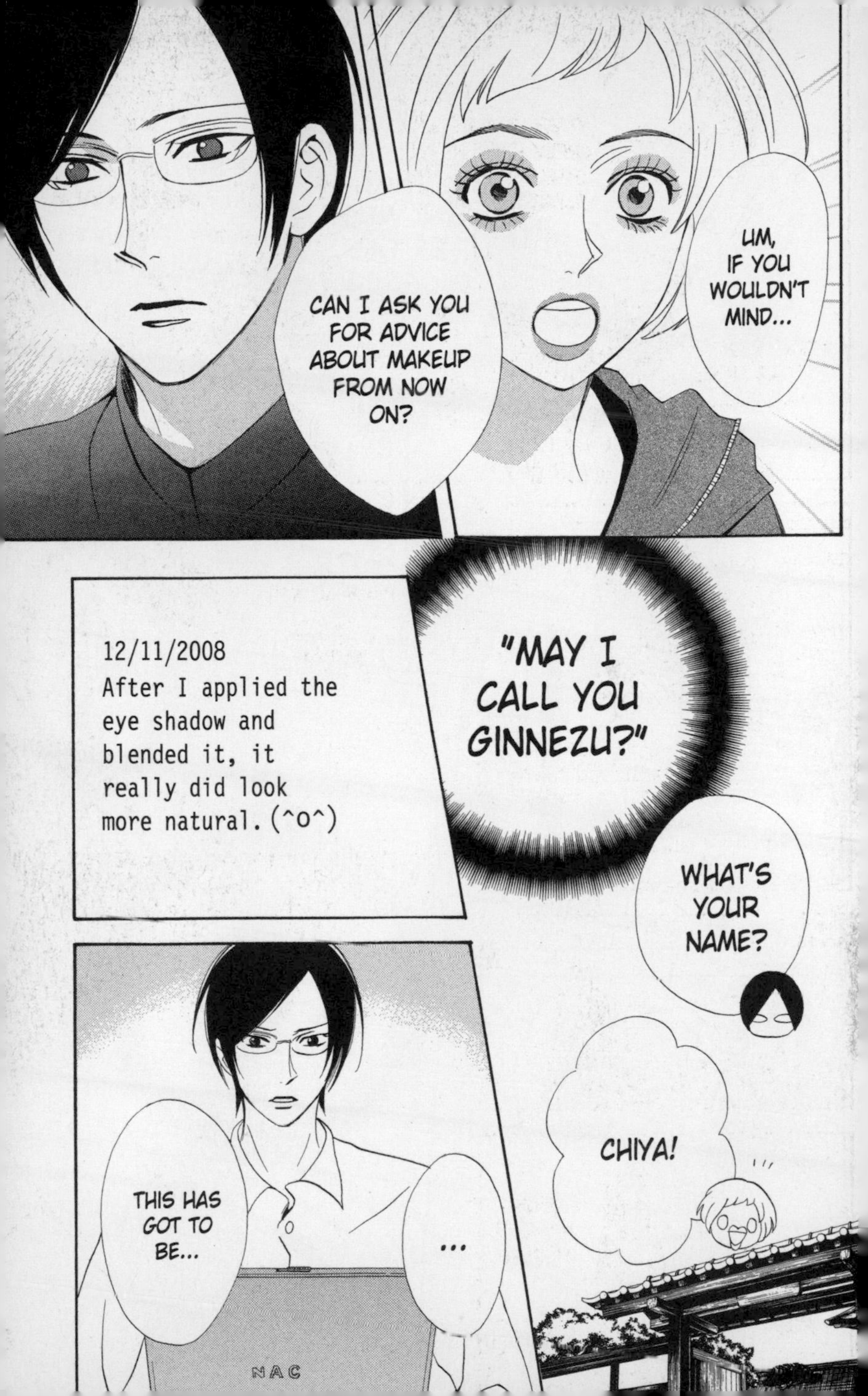
UM, IF YOU WOULDN'T MIND...
CAN I ASK YOU FOR ADVICE ABOUT MAKEUP FROM NOW ON?
"MAY I CALL YOU GINNEZU?"
WHAT'S YOUR NAME?
CHIYA!
12/11/2008
After I applied the eye shadow and blended it, it really did look more natural. (^o^)
...
THIS HAS GOT TO BE...
NAC

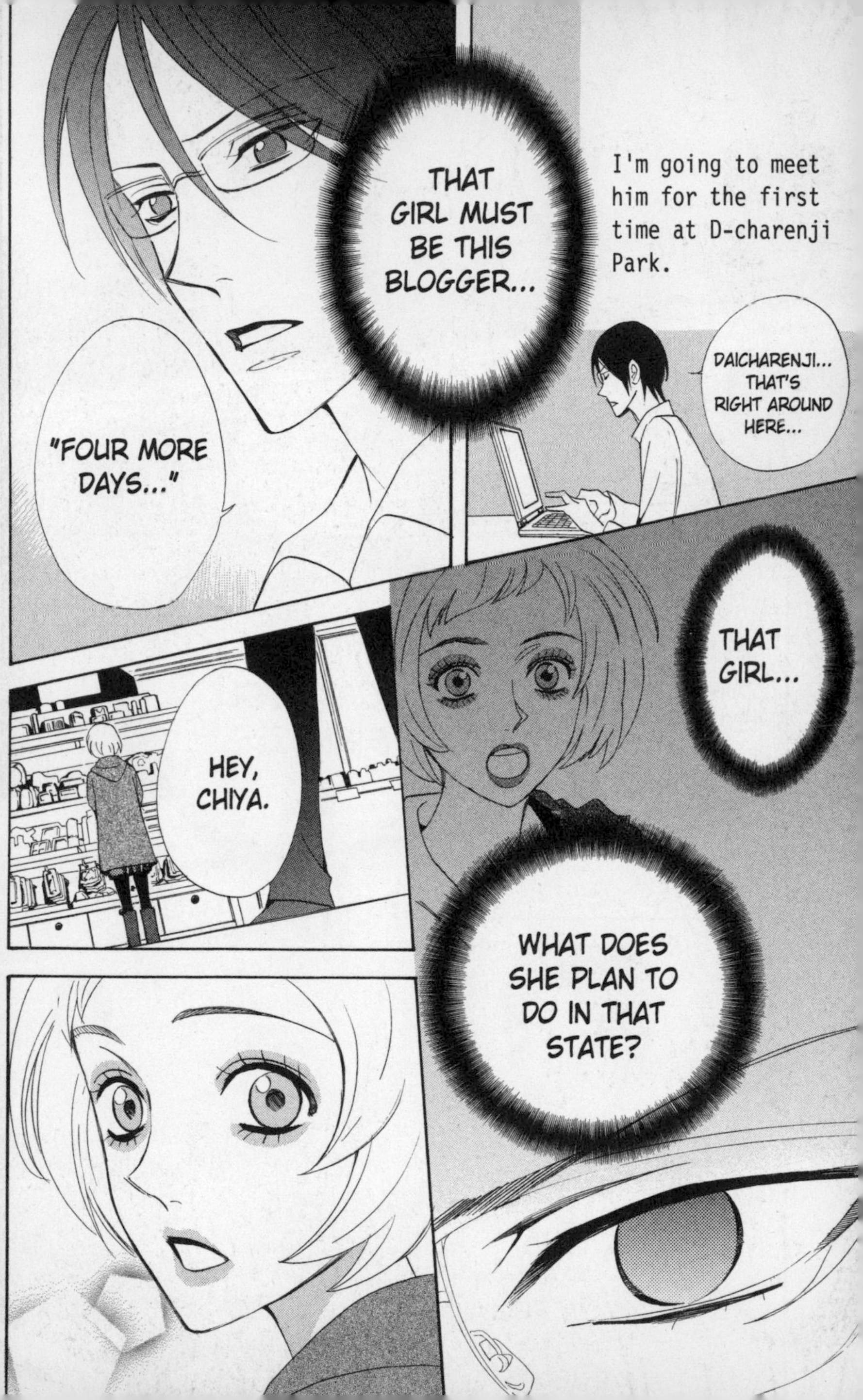
I'm going to meet him for the first time at D-charenji Park.
DAICHARENJI... THAT'S RIGHT AROUND HERE...
THAT GIRL MUST BE THIS BLOGGER...
"FOUR MORE DAYS..."
THAT GIRL...
HEY, CHIYA.
WHAT DOES SHE PLAN TO DO IN THAT STATE?

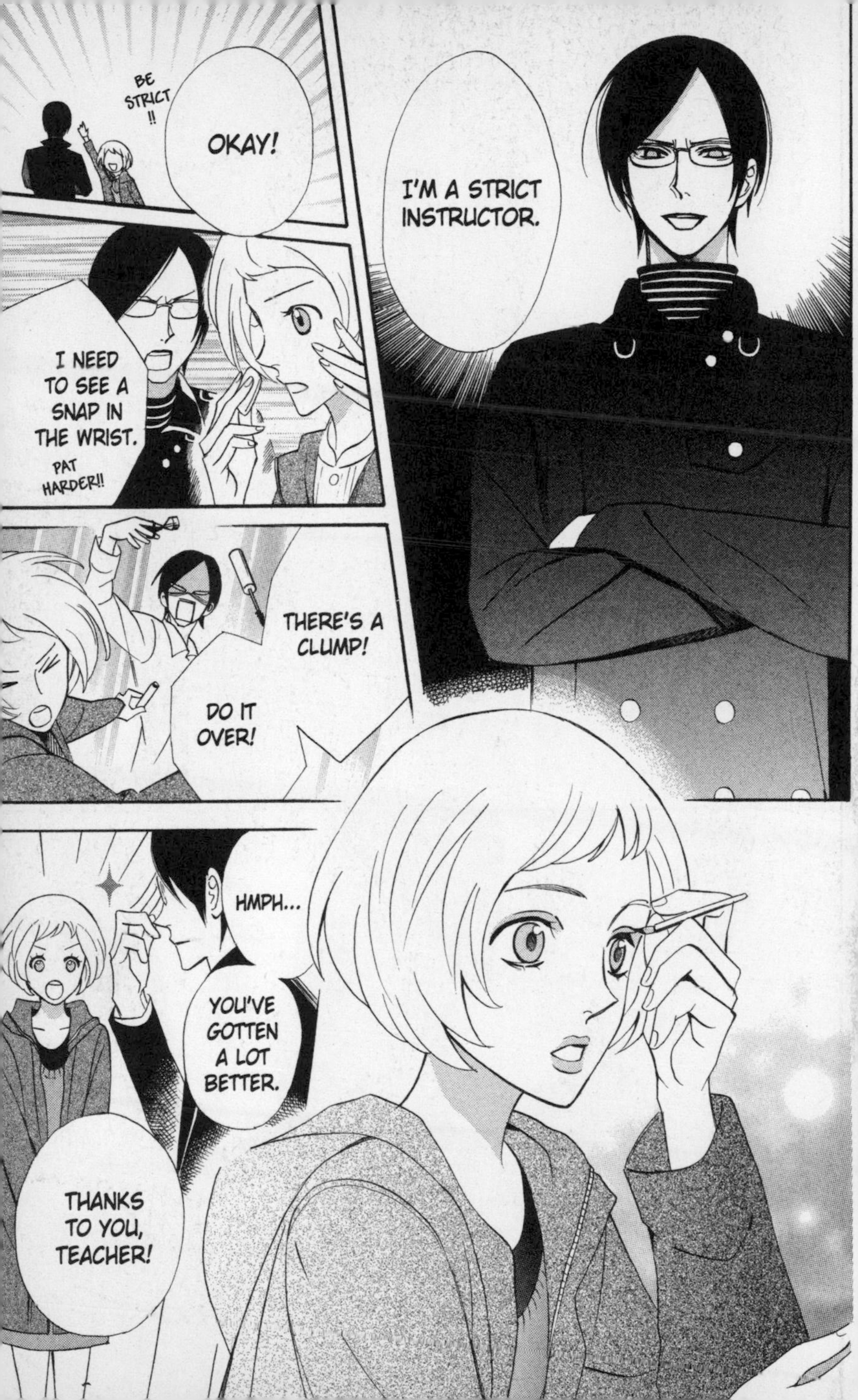
I'M A STRICT INSTRUCTOR.
OKAY!
BE STRICT!!
I NEED TO SEE A SNAP IN THE WRIST.
PAT HARDER!!
THERE'S A CLUMP!
DO IT OVER!
HMPH...
YOU'VE GOTTEN A LOT BETTER.
THANKS TO YOU, TEACHER!

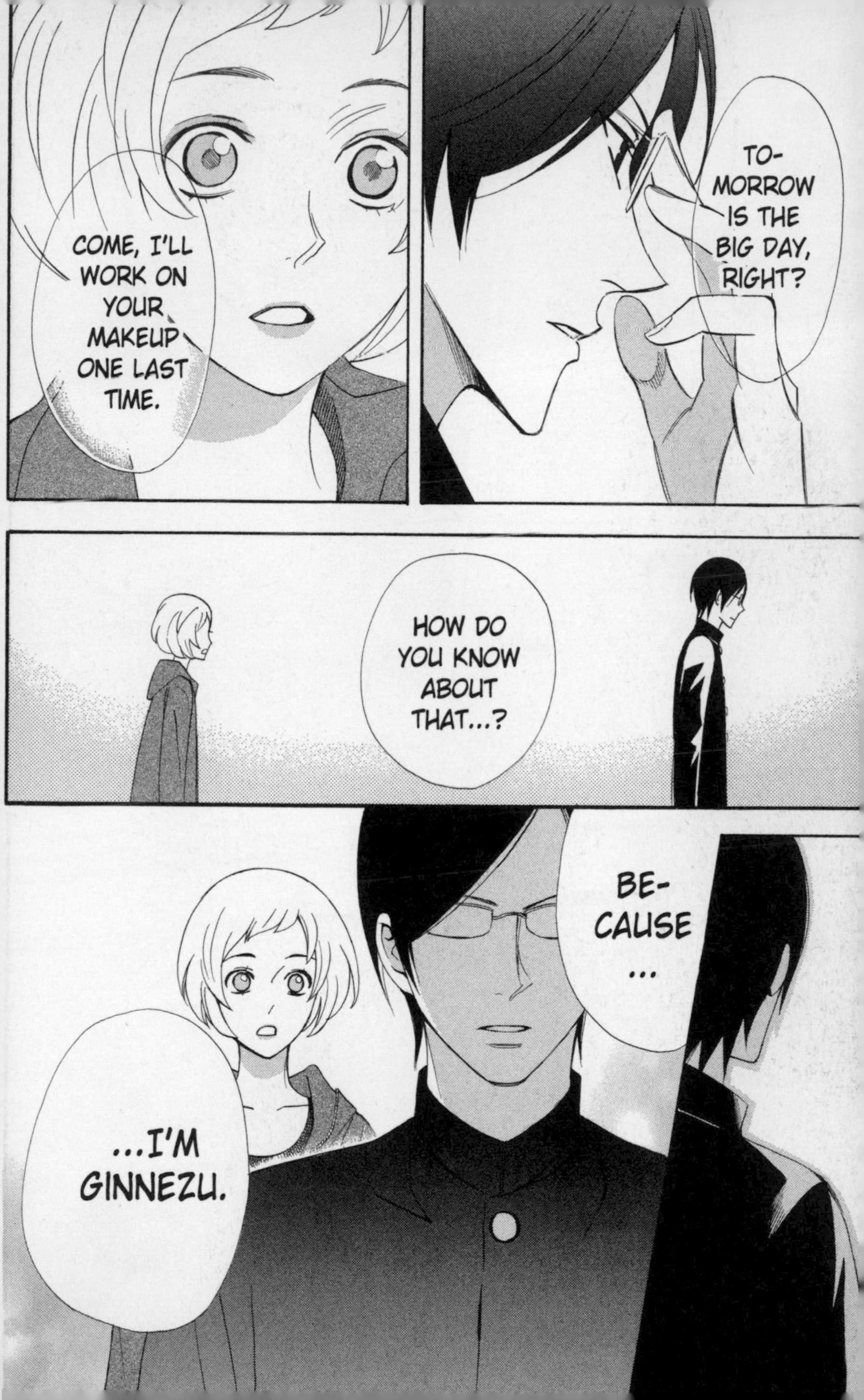
TO-MORROW IS THE BIG DAY, RIGHT?
COME, I'LL WORK ON YOUR MAKEUP ONE LAST TIME.
HOW DO YOU KNOW ABOUT THAT...?
BE-CAUSE ...
...I'M GINNEZU.

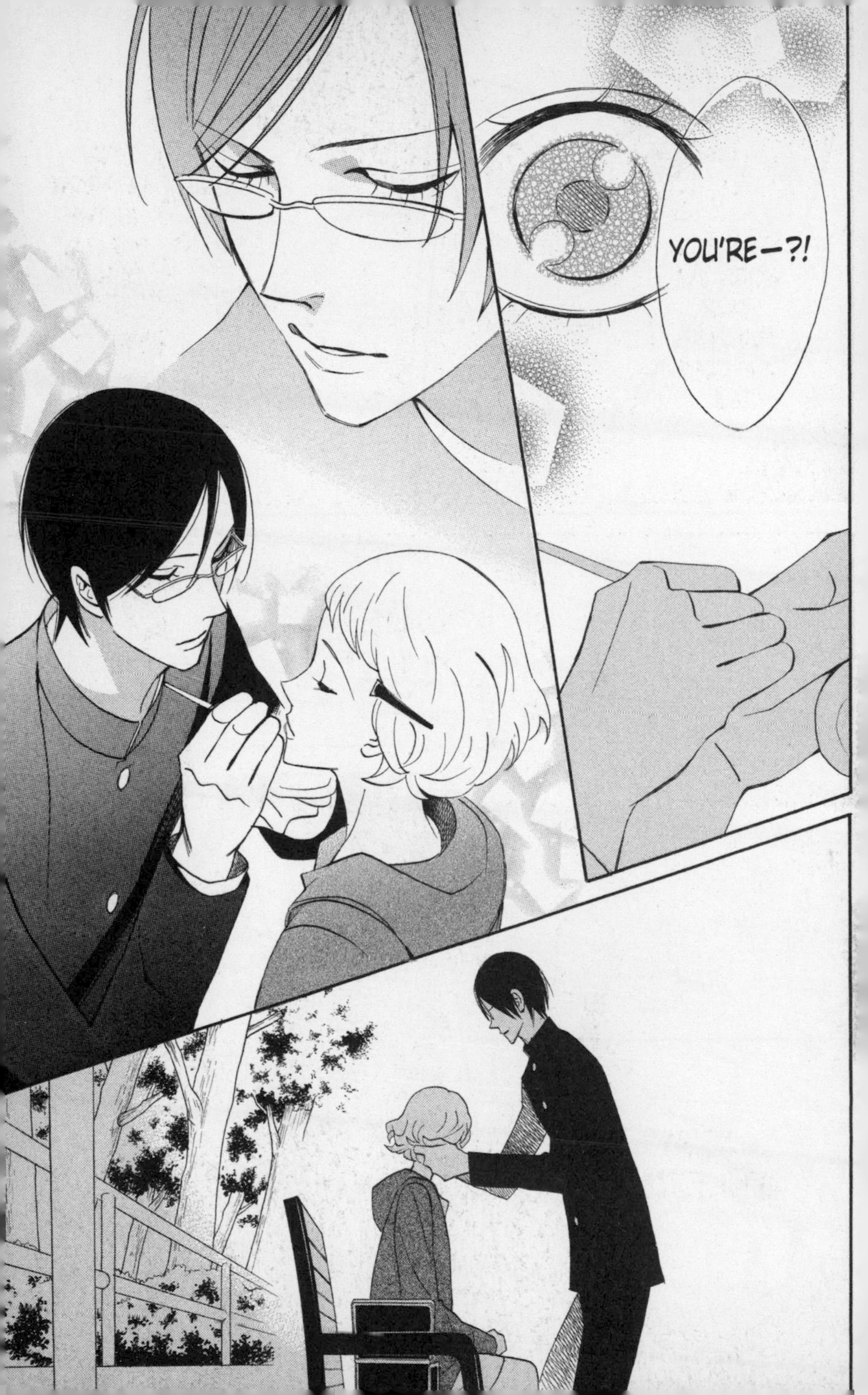
YOU'RE—?!

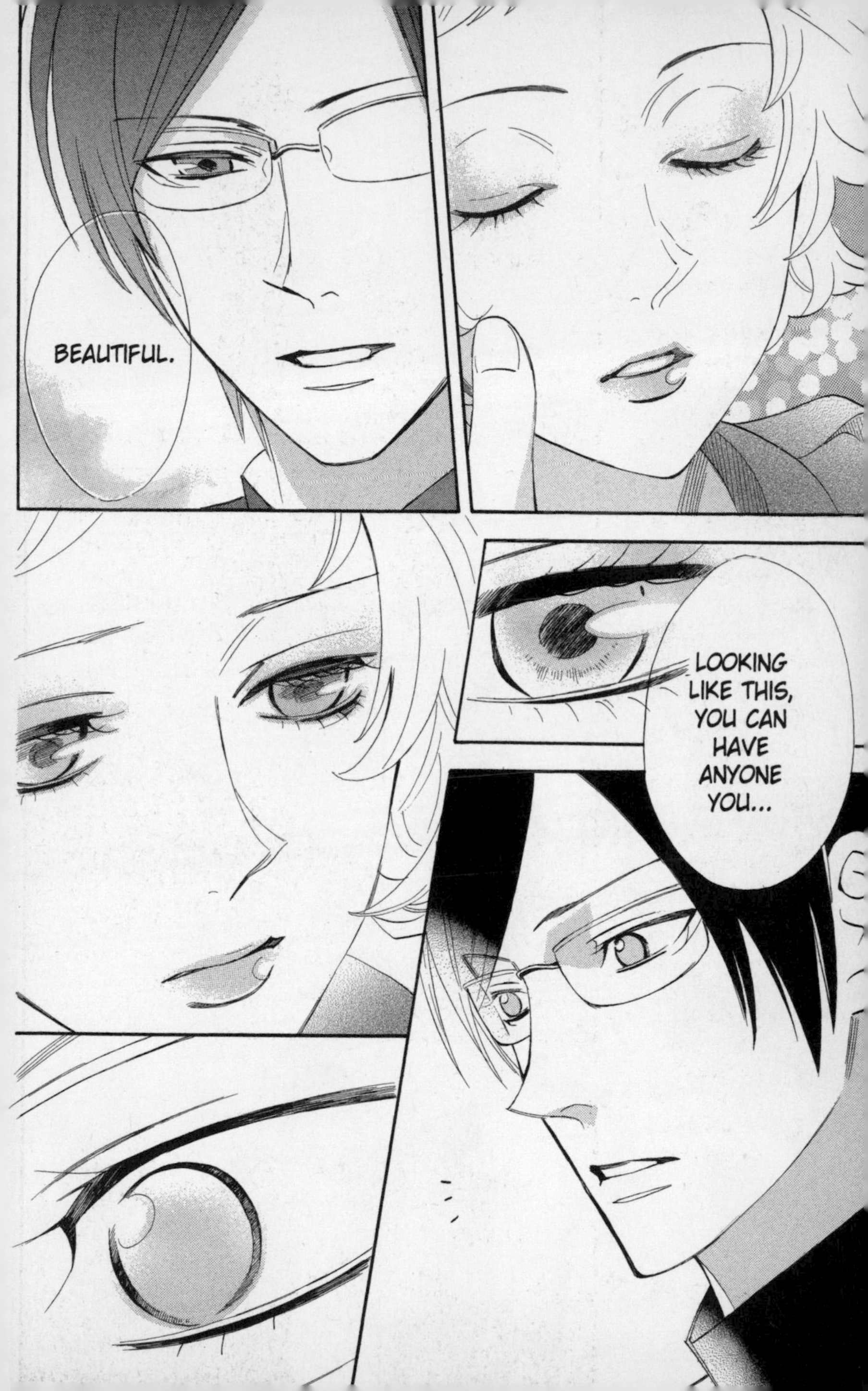
BEAUTIFUL.
LOOKING LIKE THIS, YOU CAN HAVE ANYONE YOU...

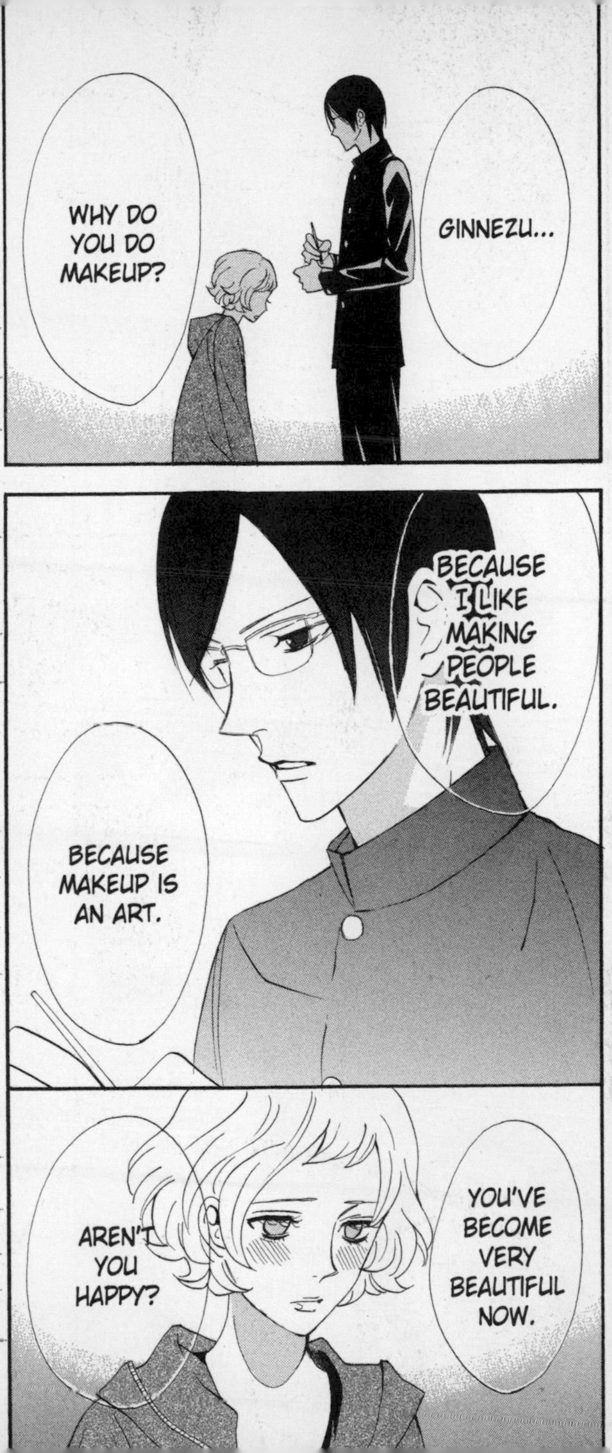
GINNEZU...
WHY DO YOU DO MAKEUP?
BECAUSE I LIKE MAKING PEOPLE BEAUTIFUL.
BECAUSE MAKEUP IS AN ART.
YOU'VE BECOME VERY BEAUTIFUL NOW.
AREN'T YOU HAPPY?

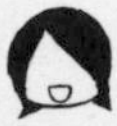

Ryo Miyakozuka

Ginyuri Academy
High School
Second-year, Class C
Born May 5
Taurus, Blood Type O
Height: 160 cm
Hobby: Training
People she admires:
Her father and
Mas Oyama

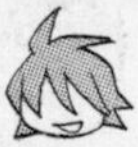

Juta Tachibana

Ginyuri Academy
High School
Second-year,
Class A
Born March 9
Pisces,
Blood Type A
Height: 178 cm
Hobby: Women
His Dream: To
become a popular
shojo manga artist
like Mira Jonouchi

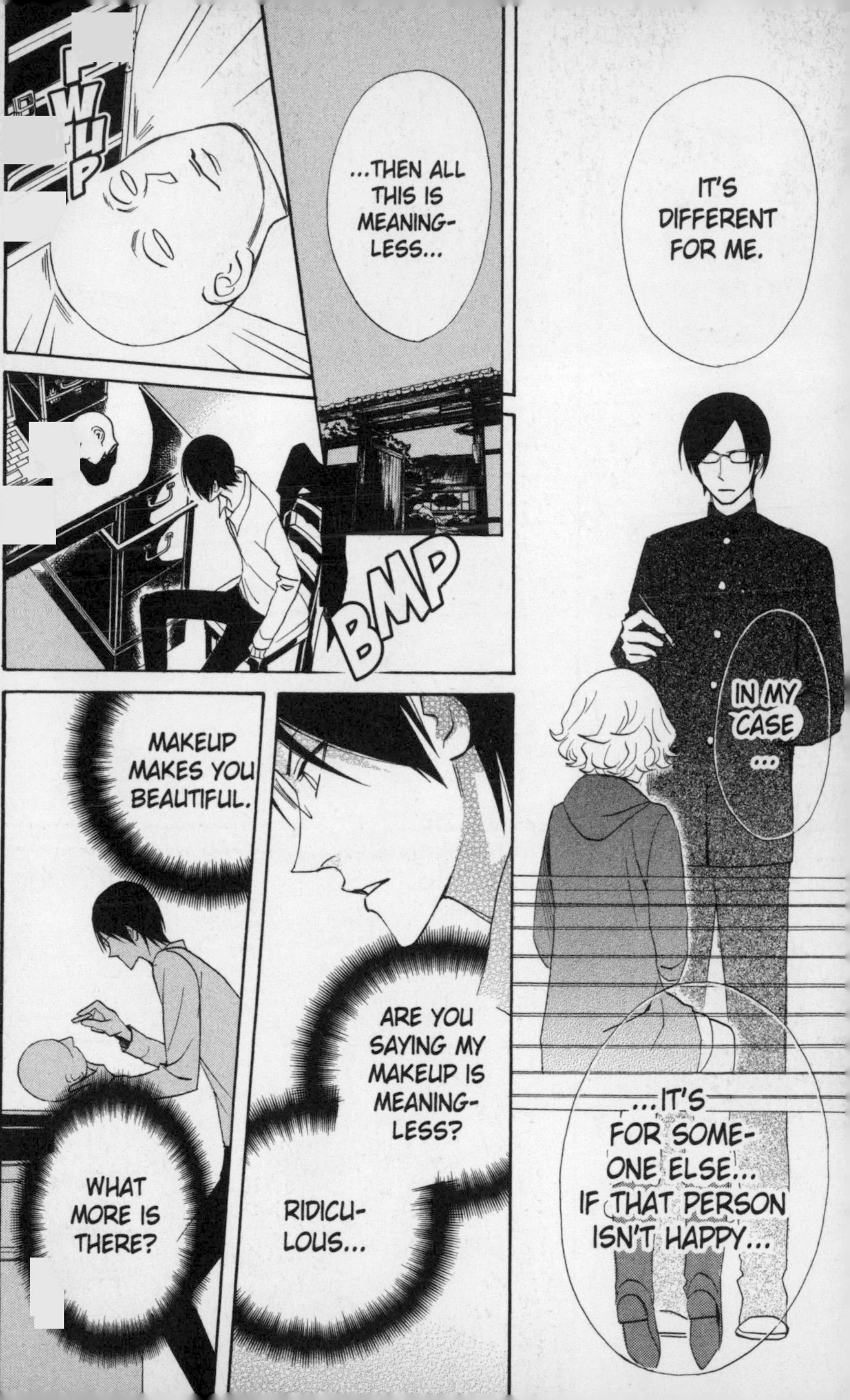
IT'S DIFFERENT FOR ME.
IN MY CASE...
...IT'S FOR SOME-ONE ELSE... IF THAT PERSON ISN'T HAPPY...
...THEN ALL THIS IS MEANING-LESS...
FWUP
BMP
ARE YOU SAYING MY MAKEUP IS MEANING-LESS?
RIDICU-LOUS...
MAKEUP MAKES YOU BEAUTIFUL.
WHAT MORE IS THERE?

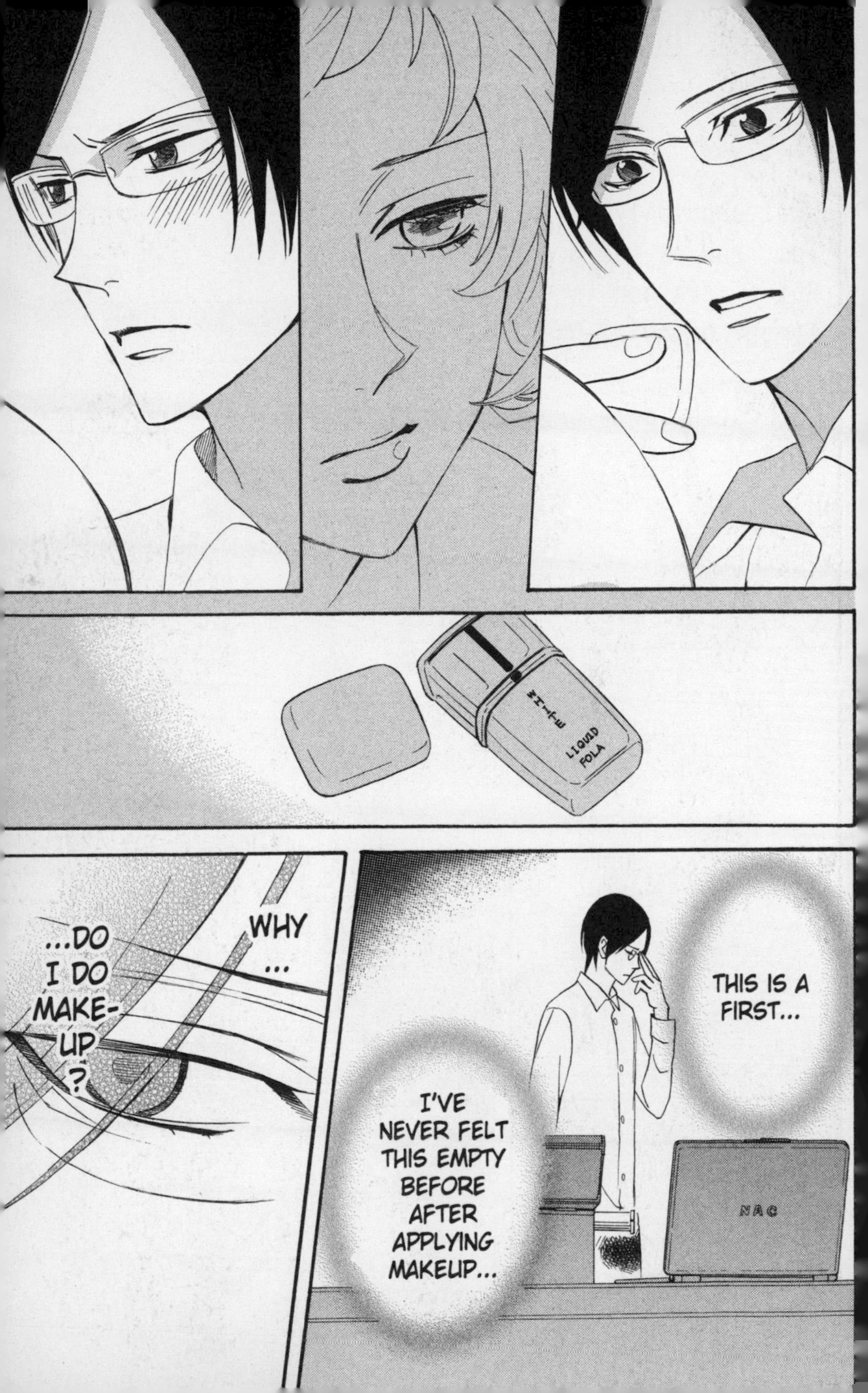
LIQUID
FOLA
THIS IS A FIRST...
I'VE NEVER FELT THIS EMPTY BEFORE AFTER APPLYING MAKEUP...
NAC
WHY ...
...DO I DO MAKE-UP ?

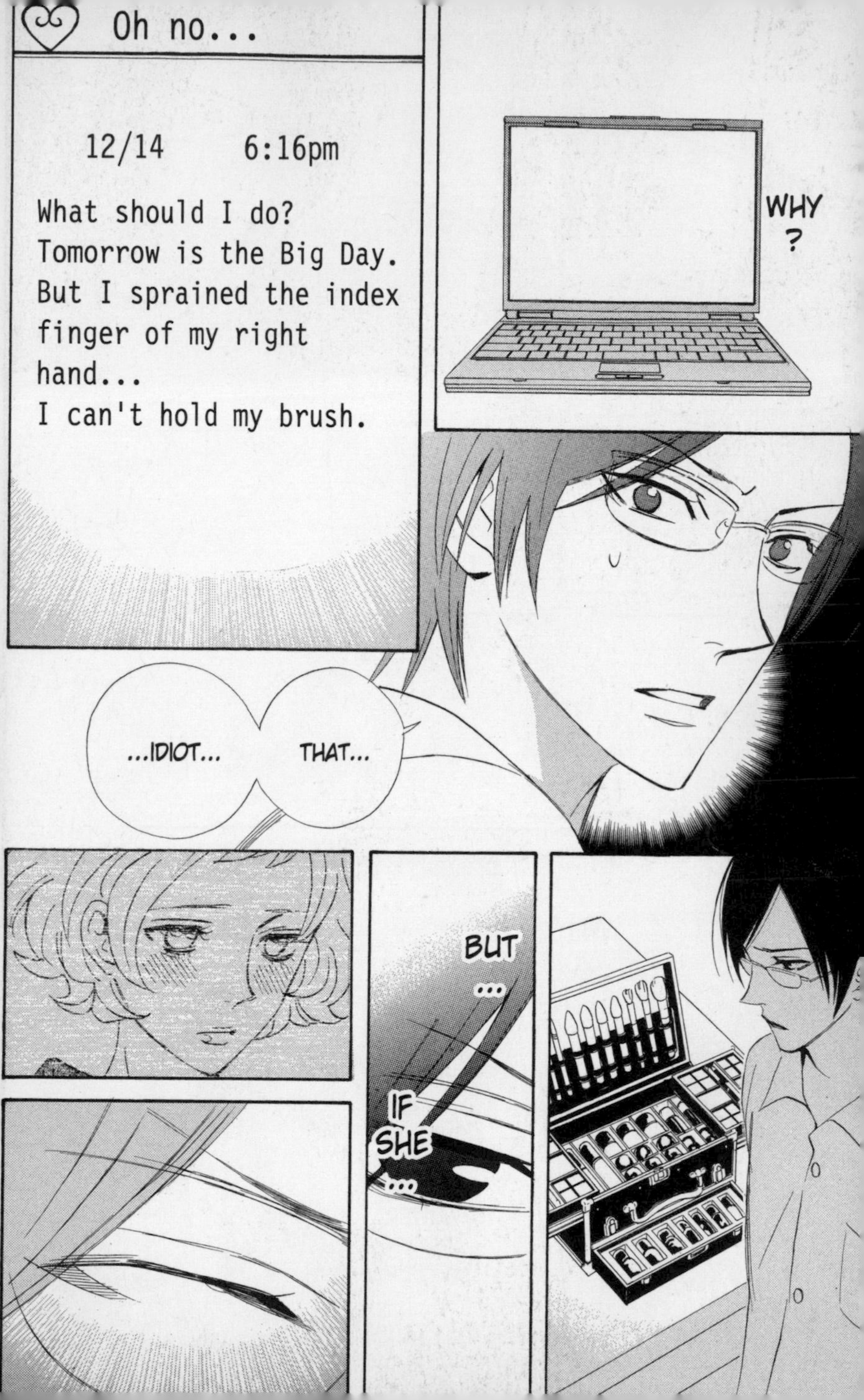
WHY ?
Oh no...
12/14 6:16pm
What should I do?
Tomorrow is the Big Day.
But I sprained the index finger of my right hand...
I can't hold my brush.
THAT...
...IDIOT...
BUT ...
IF SHE ...

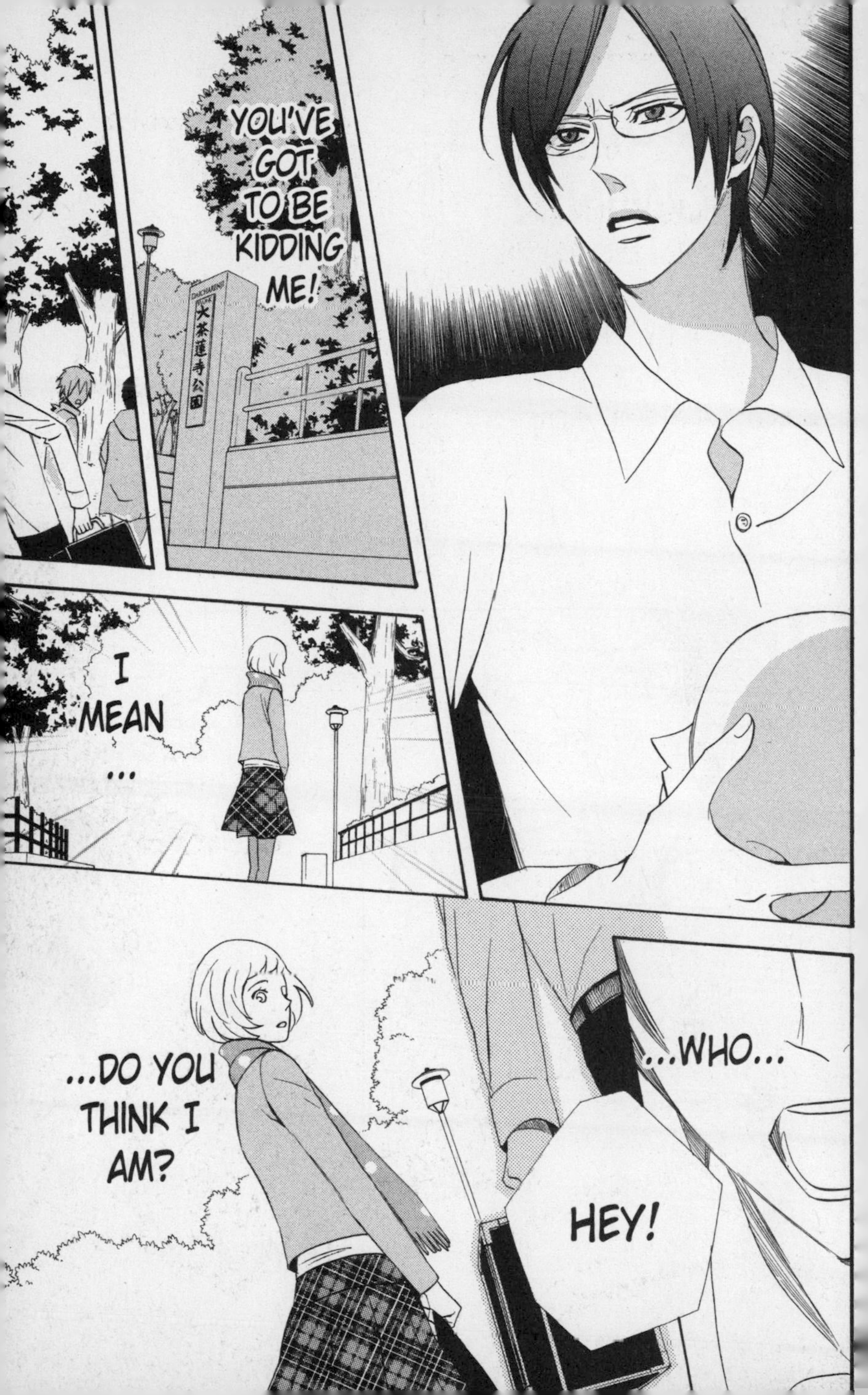
YOU'VE GOT TO BE KIDDING ME!
大茶蓮寺公園
I MEAN...
...WHO...
HEY!
...DO YOU THINK I AM?

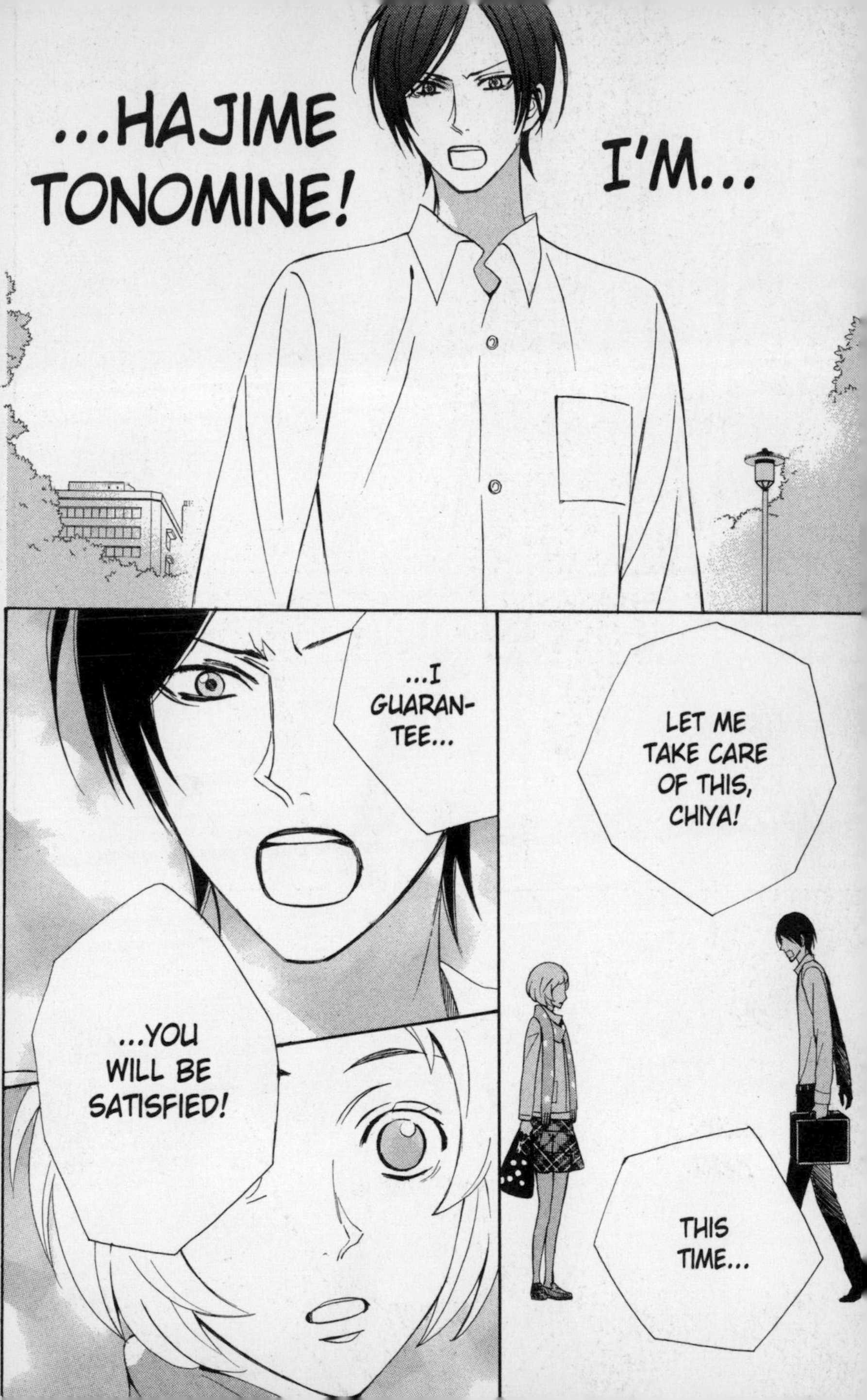
I'M...
...HAJIME TONOMINE!
LET ME TAKE CARE OF THIS, CHIYA!
THIS TIME...
...I GUARAN-TEE...
...YOU WILL BE SATISFIED!

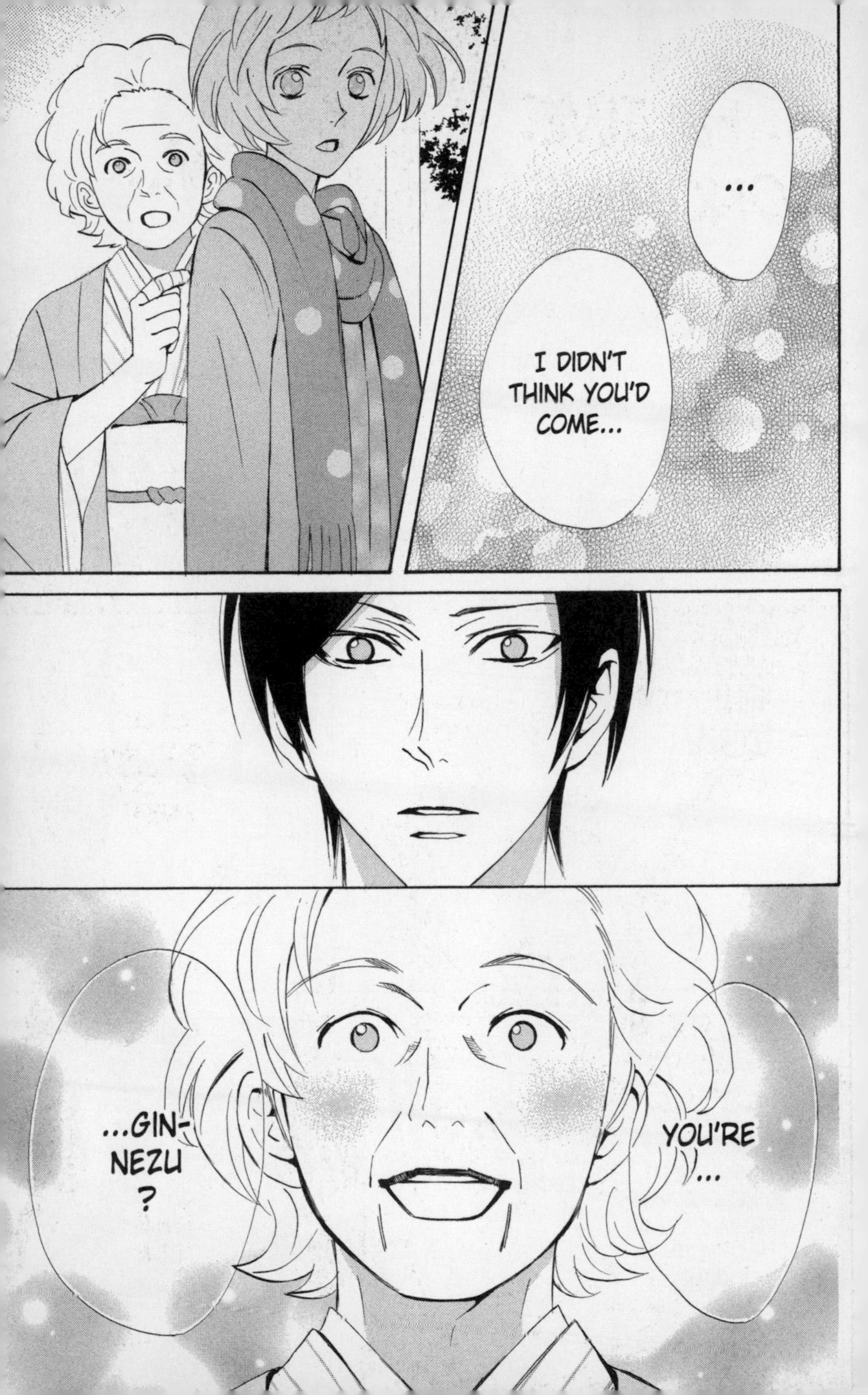
...
I DIDN'T THINK YOU'D COME...
YOU'RE ...
...GIN-NEZU ?

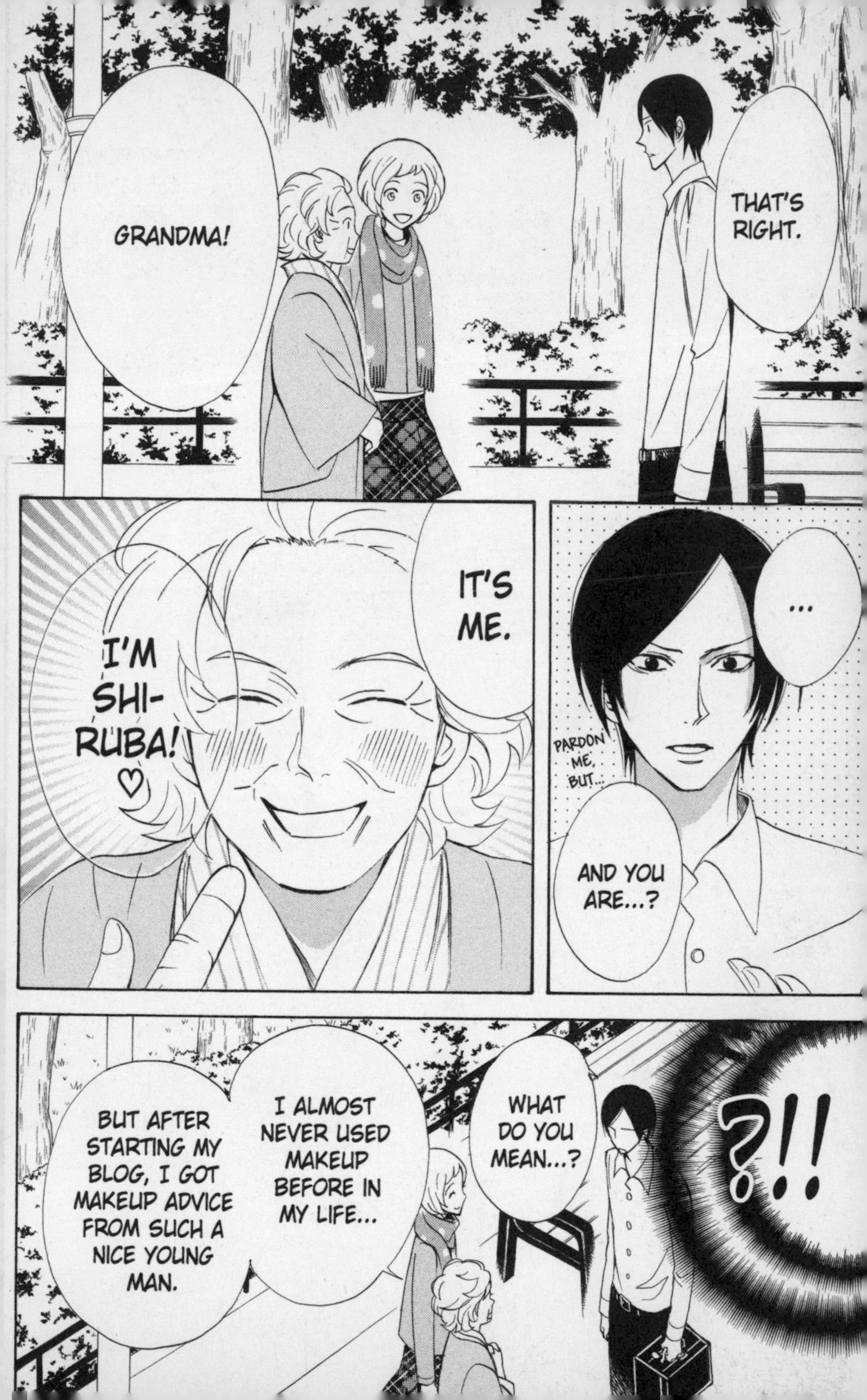
THAT'S RIGHT.
GRANDMA!
...
PARDON ME, BUT...
AND YOU ARE...?
IT'S ME.
I'M SHI-RUBA! ♡
?!!
WHAT DO YOU MEAN...?
I ALMOST NEVER USED MAKEUP BEFORE IN MY LIFE...
BUT AFTER STARTING MY BLOG, I GOT MAKEUP ADVICE FROM SUCH A NICE YOUNG MAN.

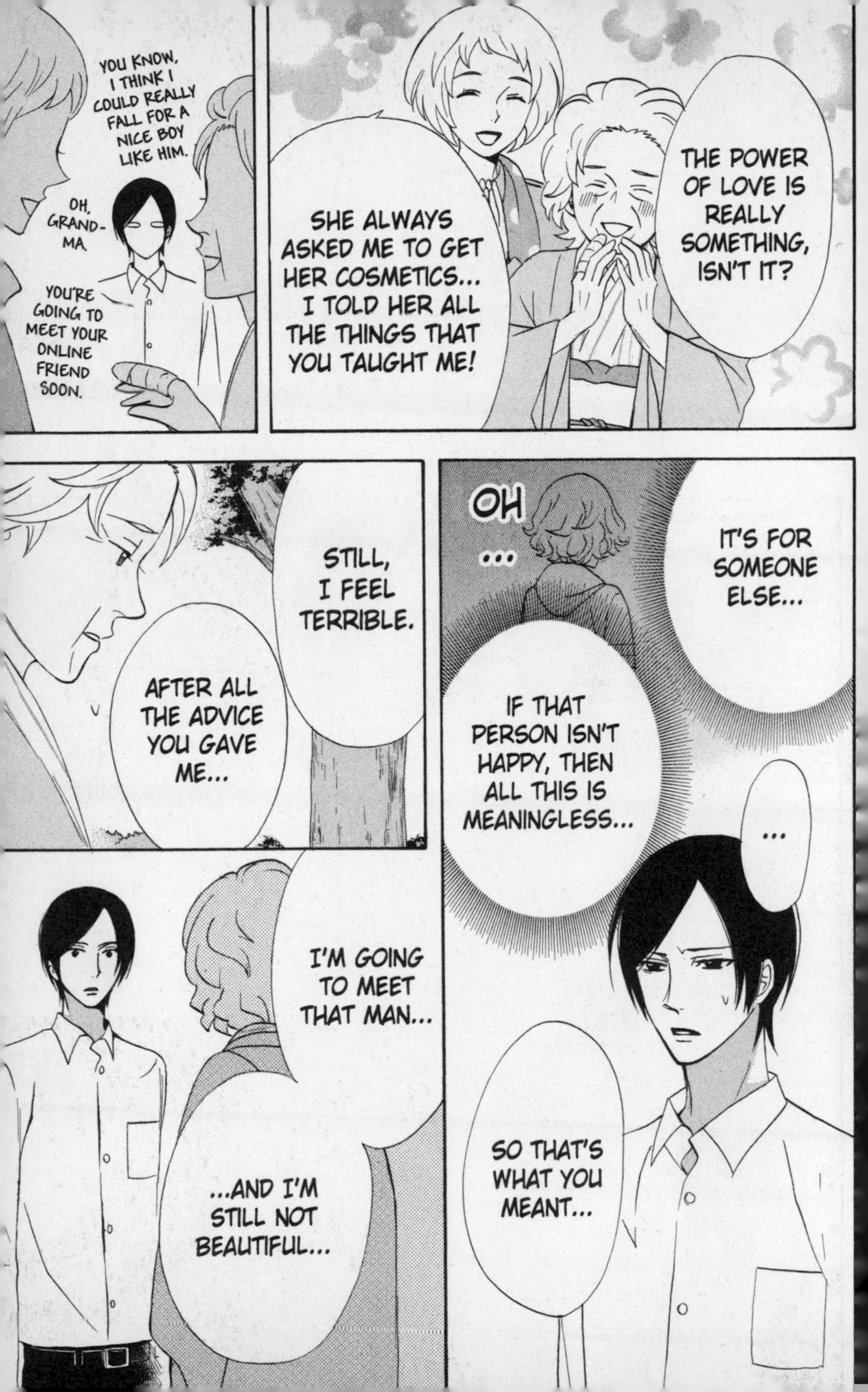
THE POWER OF LOVE IS REALLY SOMETHING, ISN'T IT?
SHE ALWAYS ASKED ME TO GET HER COSMETICS... I TOLD HER ALL THE THINGS THAT YOU TAUGHT ME!
YOU KNOW, I THINK I COULD REALLY FALL FOR A NICE BOY LIKE HIM.
OH, GRAND-MA.
YOU'RE GOING TO MEET YOUR ONLINE FRIEND SOON.
IT'S FOR SOMEONE ELSE...
OH...
IF THAT PERSON ISN'T HAPPY, THEN ALL THIS IS MEANINGLESS...
...
SO THAT'S WHAT YOU MEANT...
STILL, I FEEL TERRIBLE.
AFTER ALL THE ADVICE YOU GAVE ME...
I'M GOING TO MEET THAT MAN...
...AND I'M STILL NOT BEAUTIFUL...

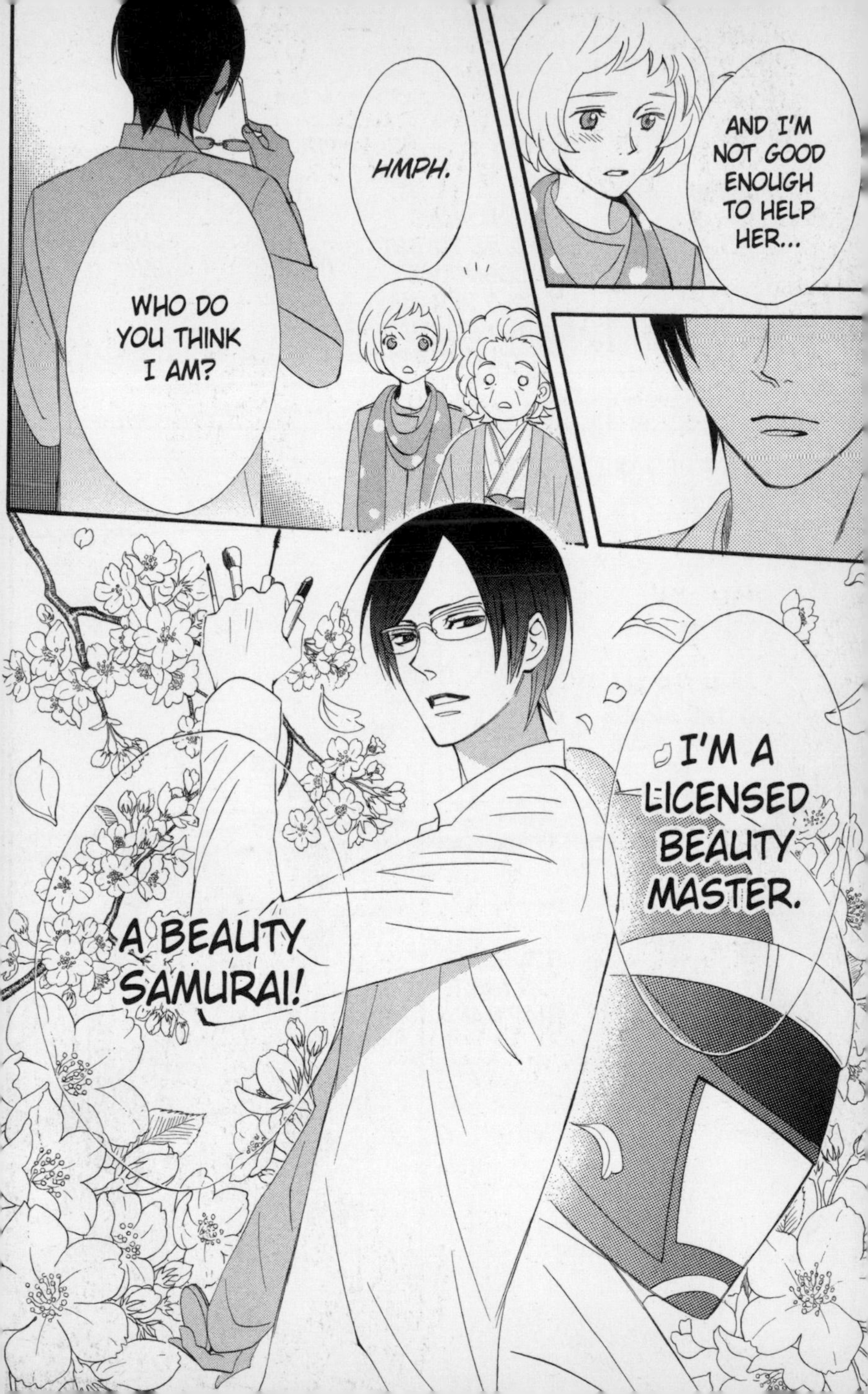
AND I'M NOT GOOD ENOUGH TO HELP HER...
HMPH.
WHO DO YOU THINK I AM?
I'M A LICENSED BEAUTY MASTER.
A BEAUTY SAMURAI!

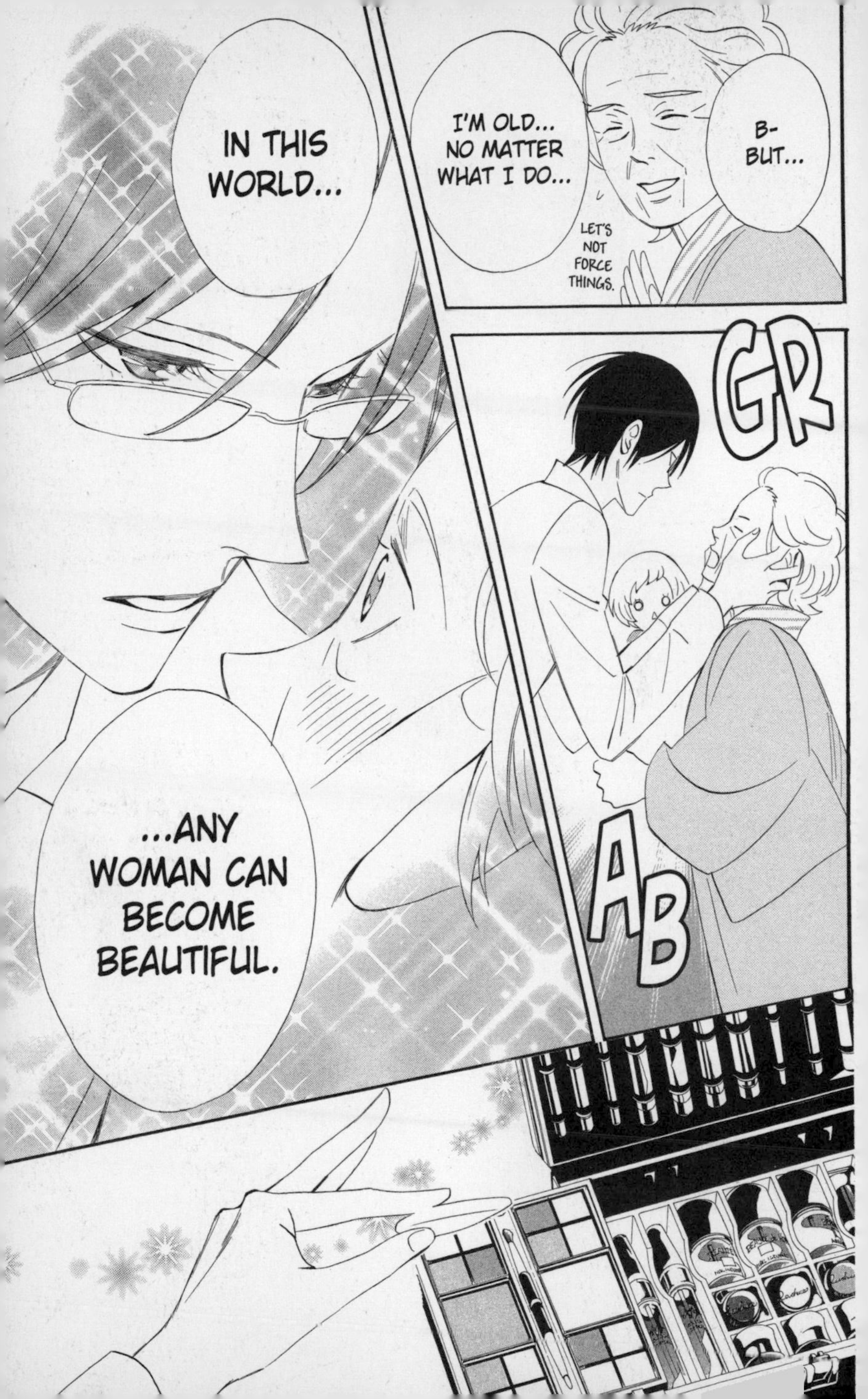
B-BUT...
I'M OLD... NO MATTER WHAT I DO...
LET'S NOT FORCE THINGS.
GRAB
IN THIS WORLD...
...ANY WOMAN CAN BECOME BEAUTIFUL.

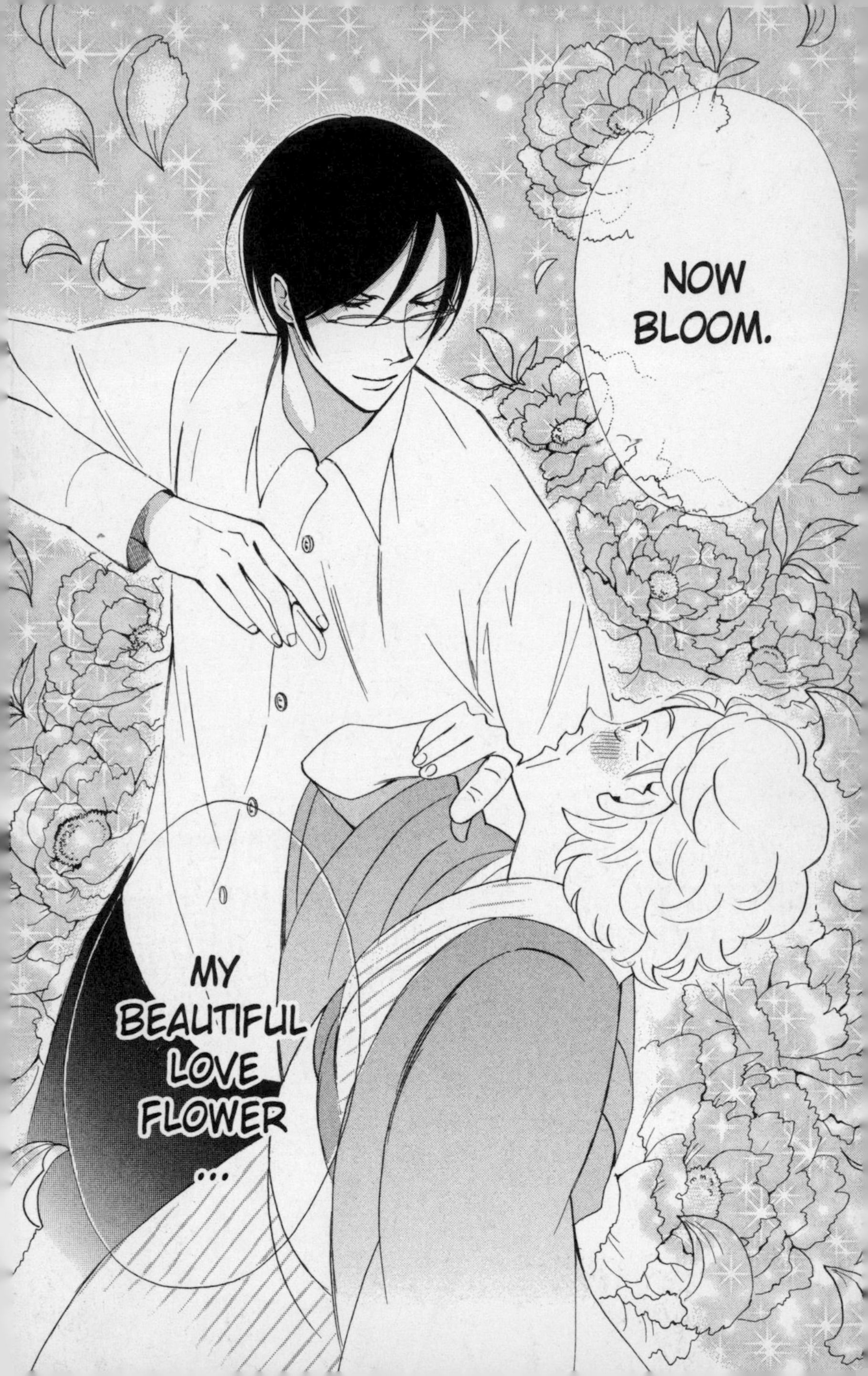
NOW BLOOM.
MY BEAUTIFUL LOVE FLOWER...

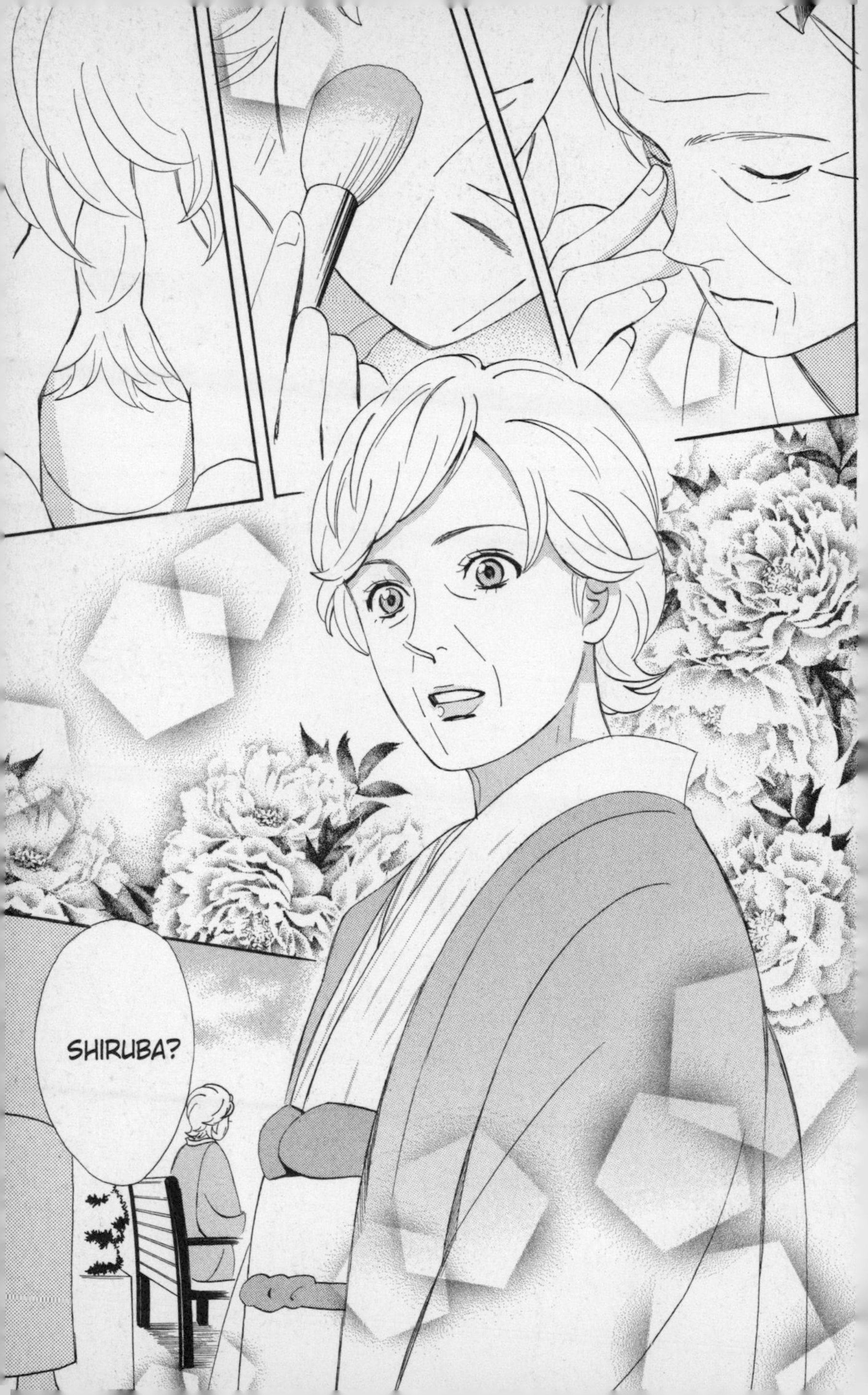
SHIRUBA?

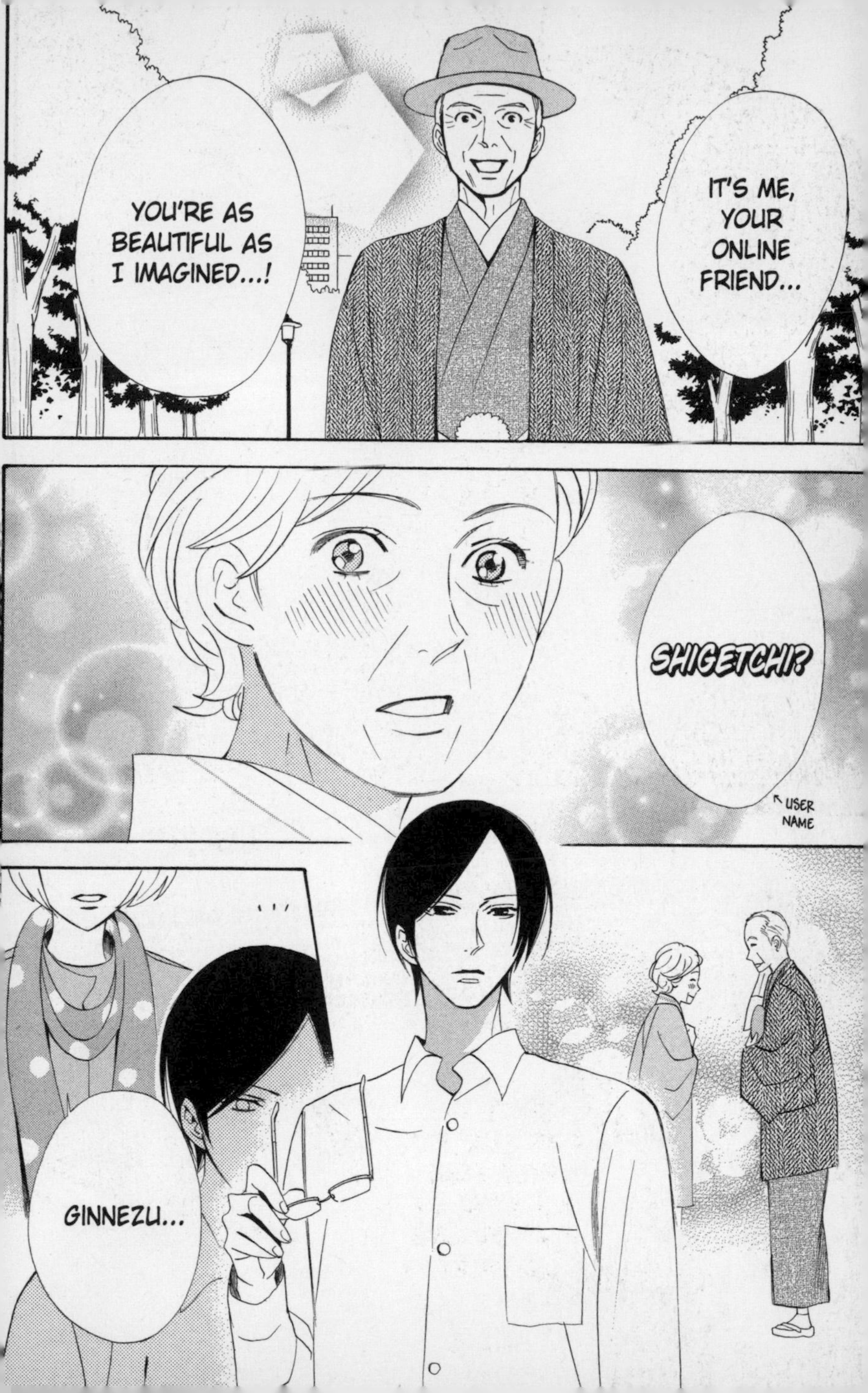
IT'S ME, YOUR ONLINE FRIEND...
YOU'RE AS BEAUTIFUL AS I IMAGINED...!
SHIGETCHI?
USER NAME
...
GINNEZU...

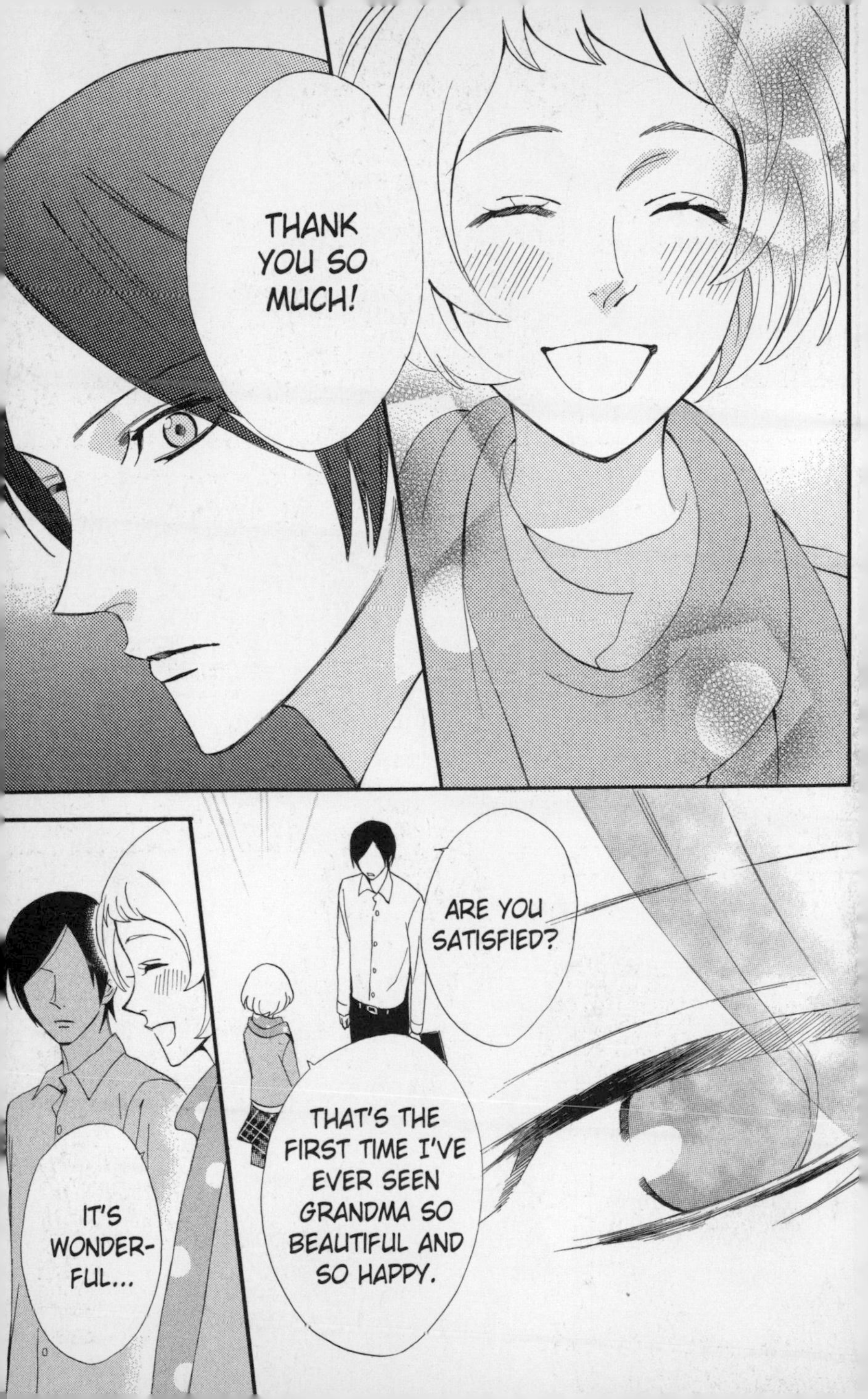
THANK YOU SO MUCH!
ARE YOU SATISFIED?
THAT'S THE FIRST TIME I'VE EVER SEEN GRANDMA SO BEAUTIFUL AND SO HAPPY.
IT'S WONDER-FUL...

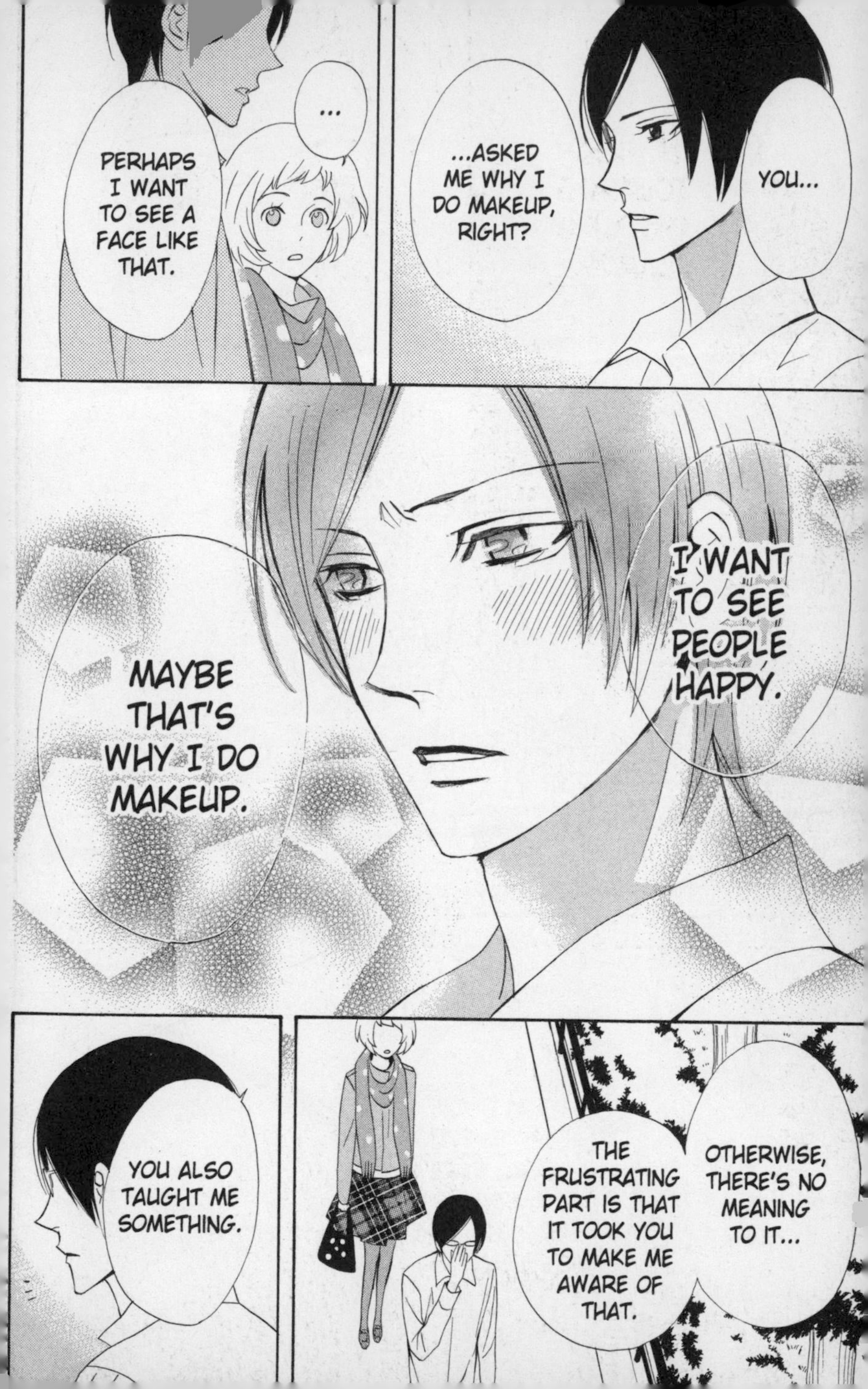
YOU...
...ASKED ME WHY I DO MAKEUP, RIGHT?
...
PERHAPS I WANT TO SEE A FACE LIKE THAT.
I WANT TO SEE PEOPLE HAPPY.
MAYBE THAT'S WHY I DO MAKEUP.
OTHERWISE, THERE'S NO MEANING TO IT...
THE FRUSTRATING PART IS THAT IT TOOK YOU TO MAKE ME AWARE OF THAT.
YOU ALSO TAUGHT ME SOMETHING.

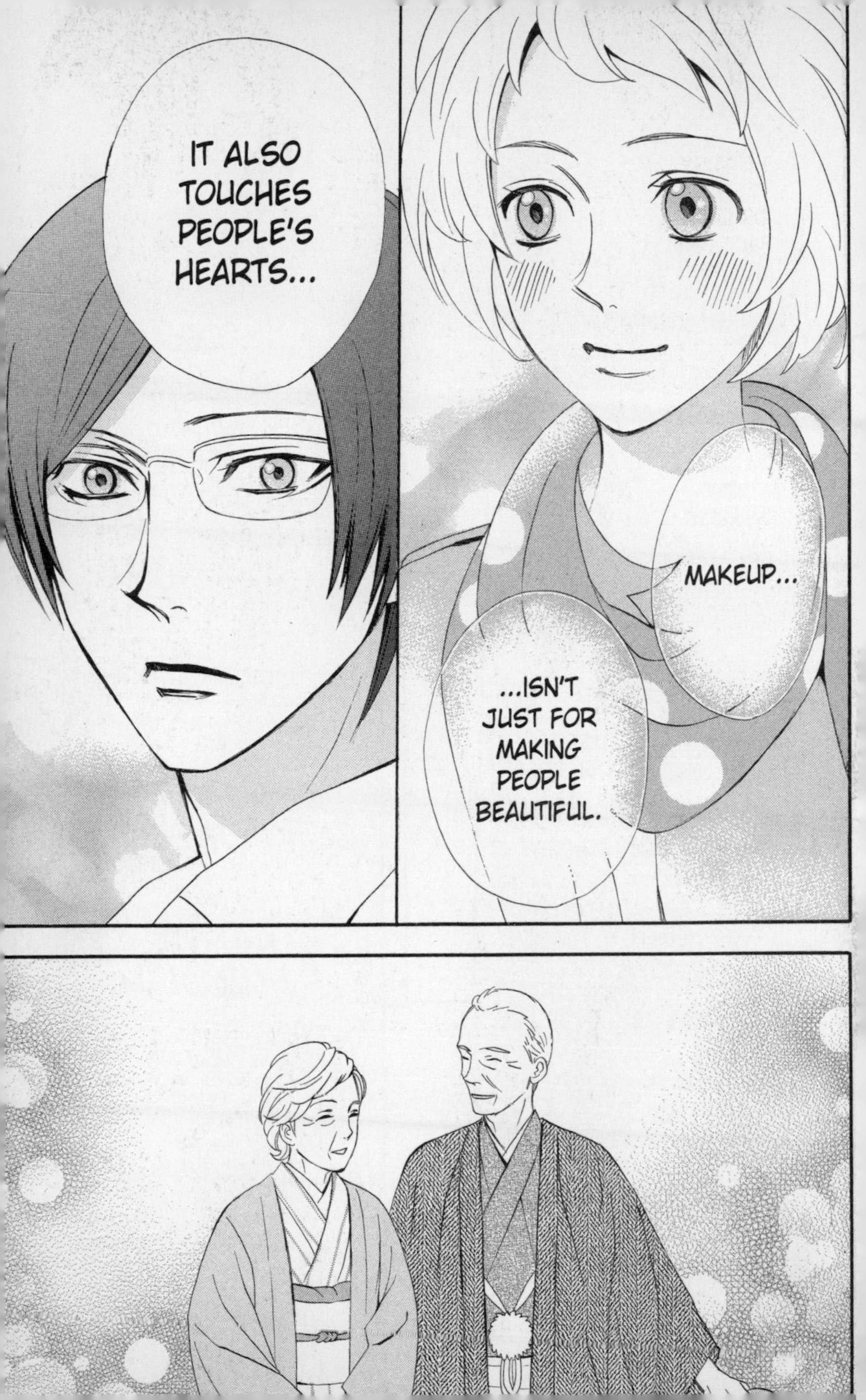
MAKEUP...
...ISN'T JUST FOR MAKING PEOPLE BEAUTIFUL.
IT ALSO TOUCHES PEOPLE'S HEARTS...

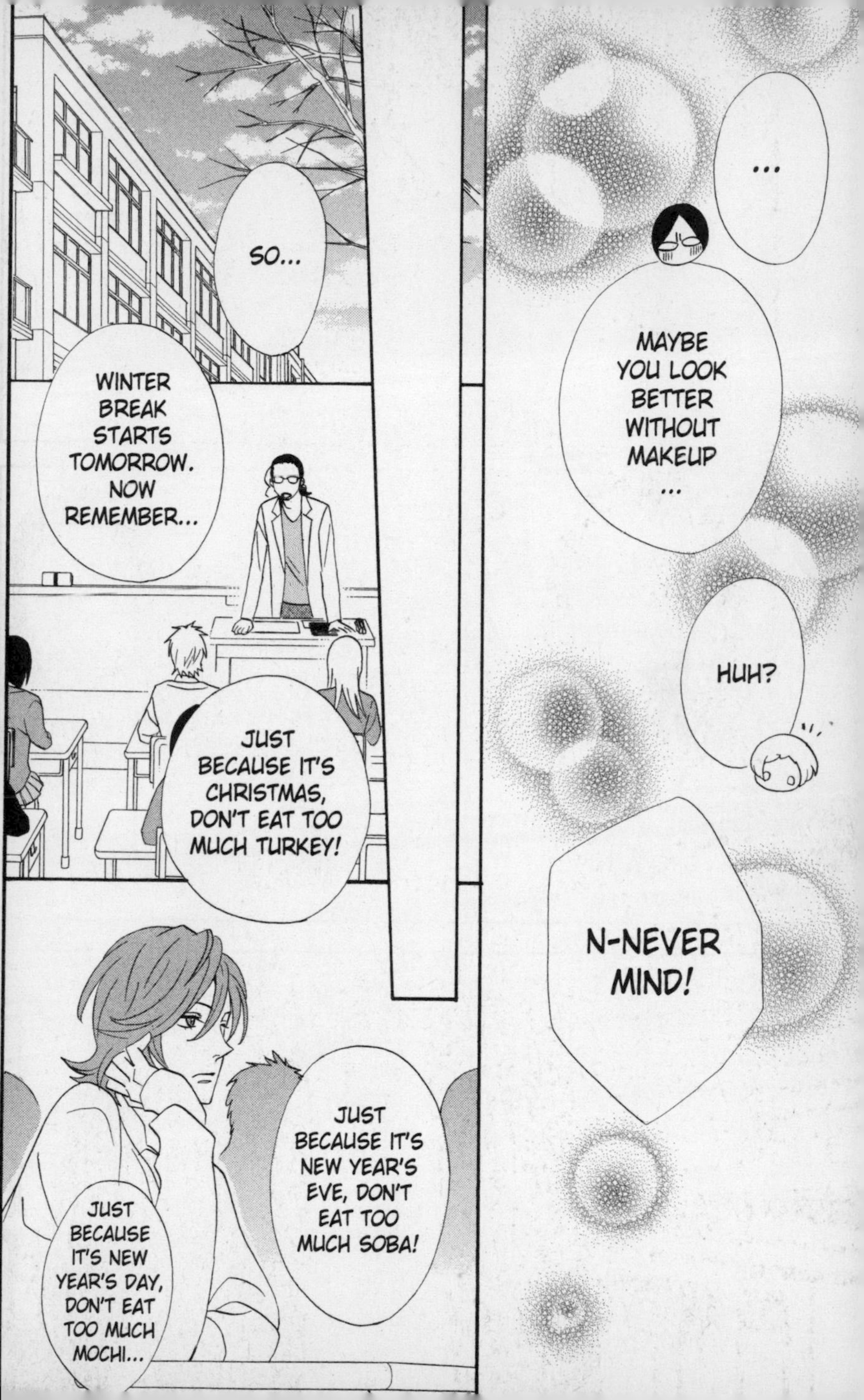
...
MAYBE YOU LOOK BETTER WITHOUT MAKEUP ...
HUH?
N-NEVER MIND!
SO...
WINTER BREAK STARTS TOMORROW. NOW REMEMBER...
JUST BECAUSE IT'S CHRISTMAS, DON'T EAT TOO MUCH TURKEY!
JUST BECAUSE IT'S NEW YEAR'S EVE, DON'T EAT TOO MUCH SOBA!
JUST BECAUSE IT'S NEW YEAR'S DAY, DON'T EAT TOO MUCH MOCHI...

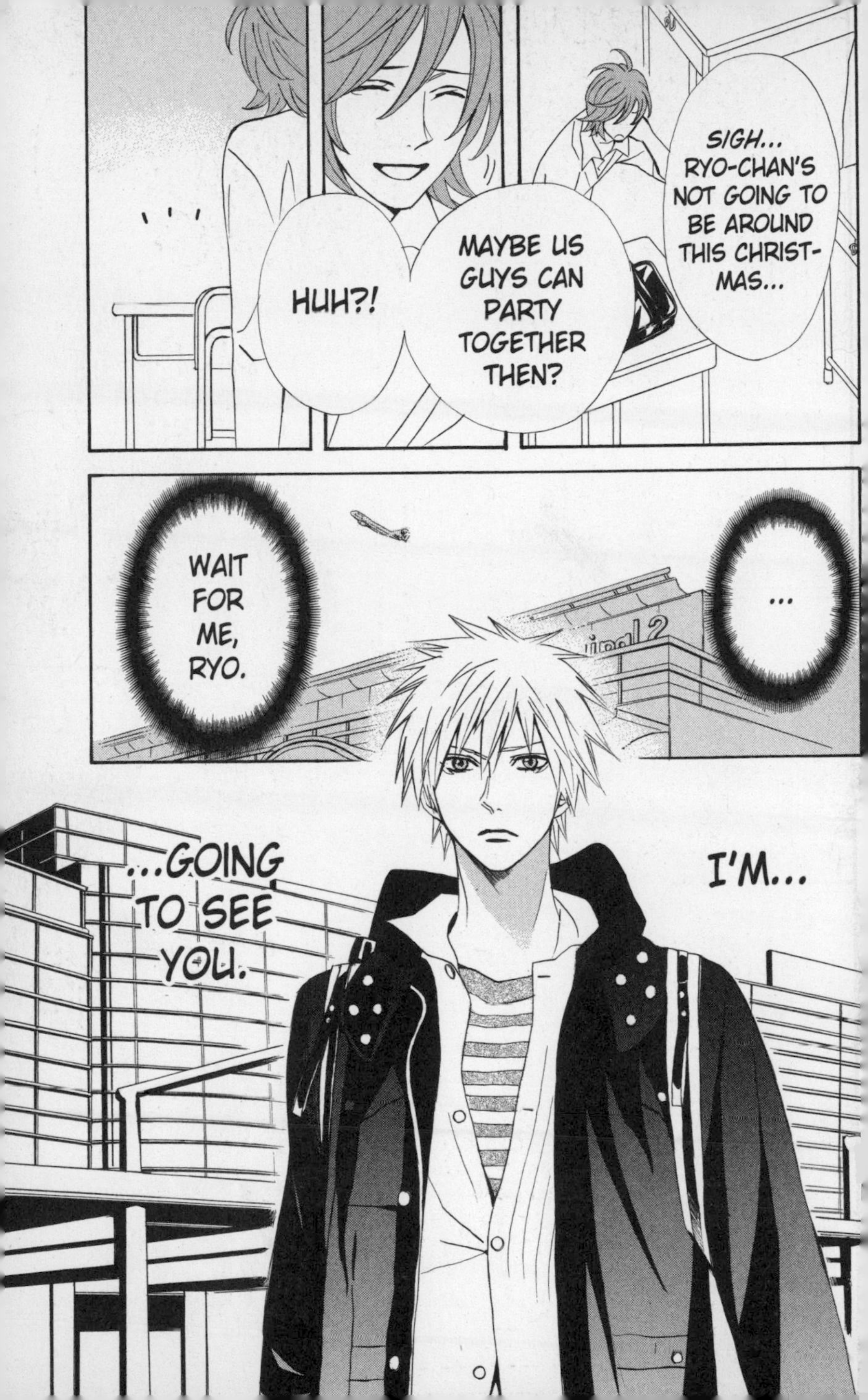
SIGH... RYO-CHAN'S NOT GOING TO BE AROUND THIS CHRIST-MAS...
MAYBE US GUYS CAN PARTY TOGETHER THEN?
HUH?!
...
WAIT FOR ME, RYO.
I'M...
...GOING TO SEE YOU.

OTOMEN

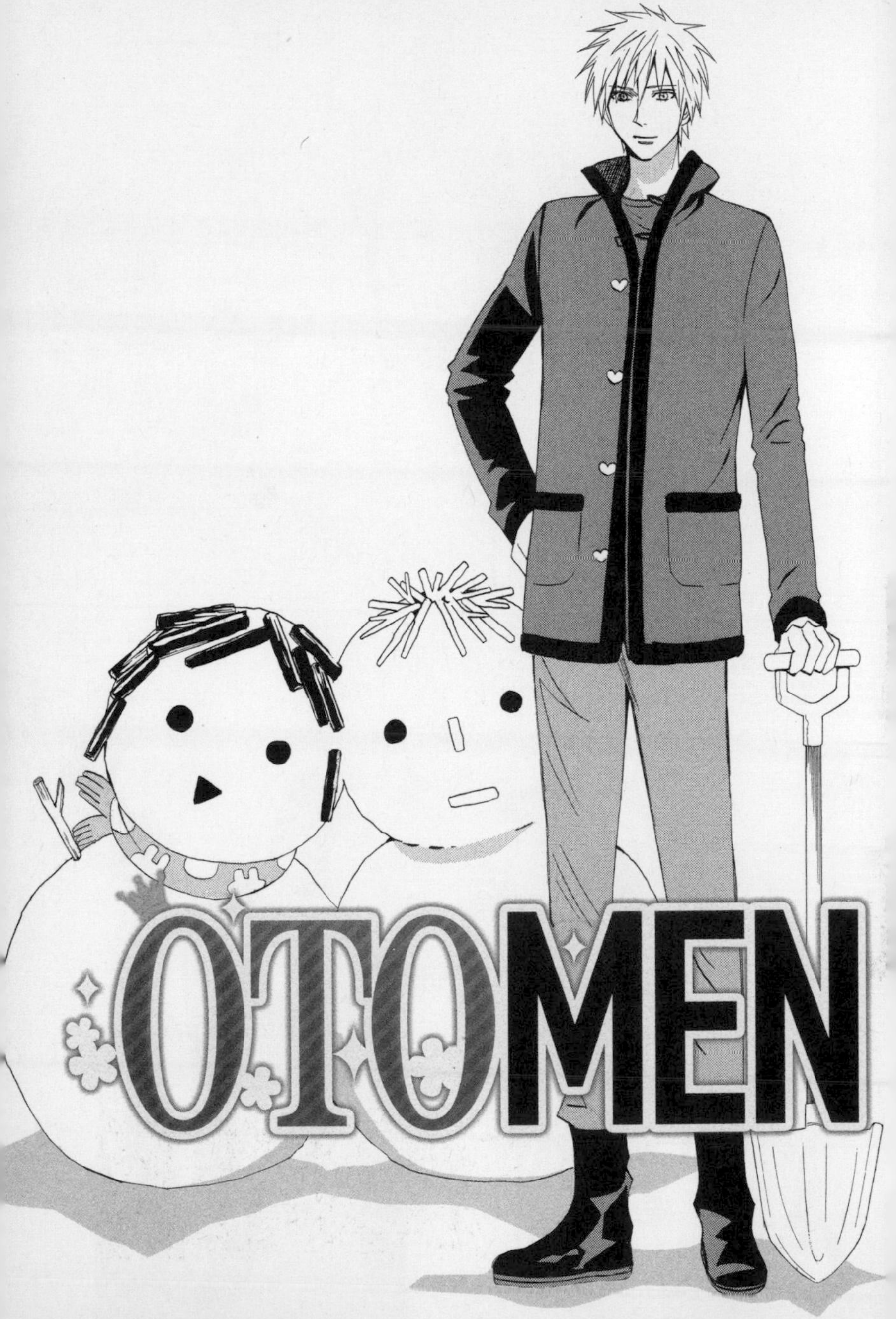
OTOMEN

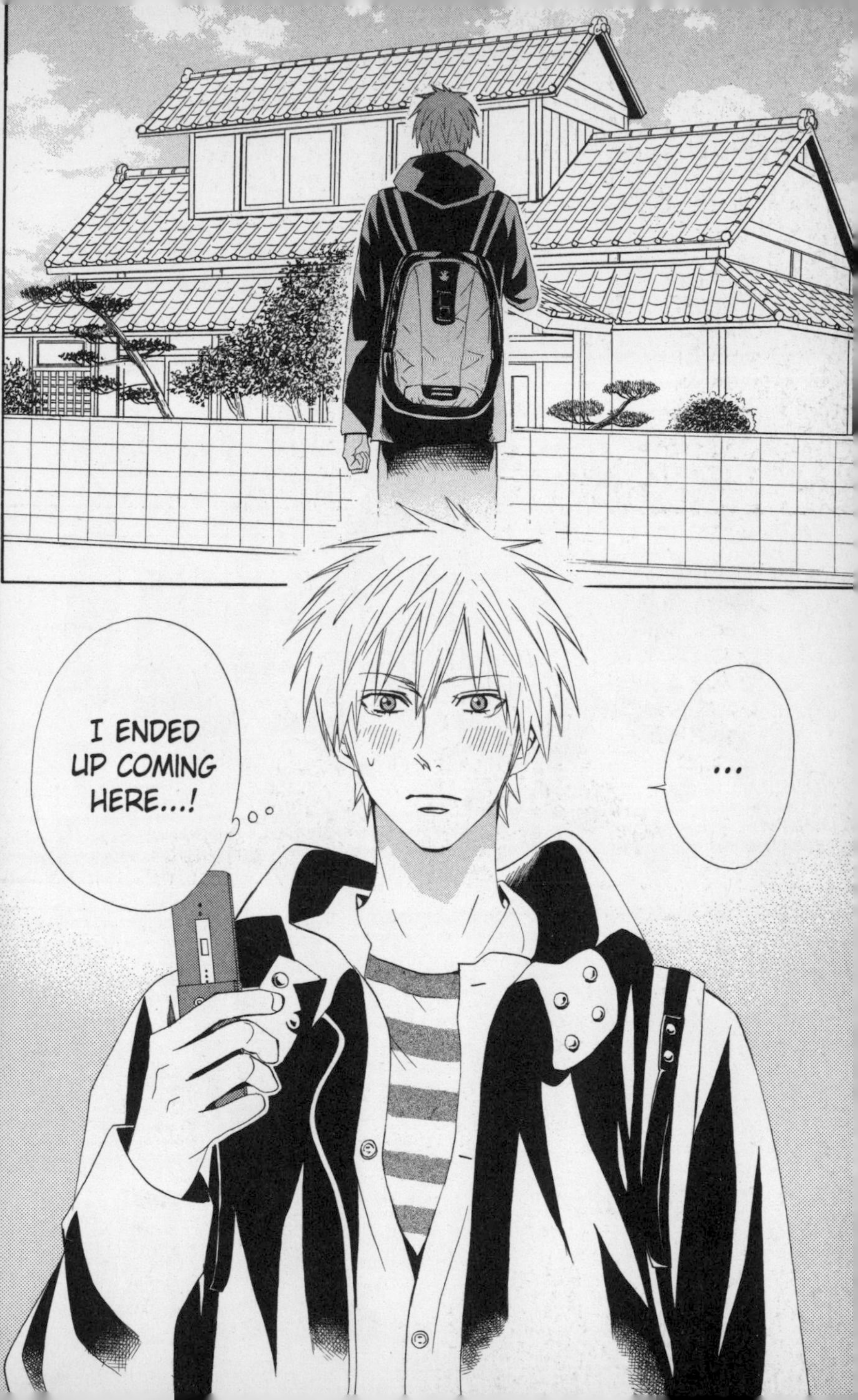
...
I ENDED UP COMING HERE...!

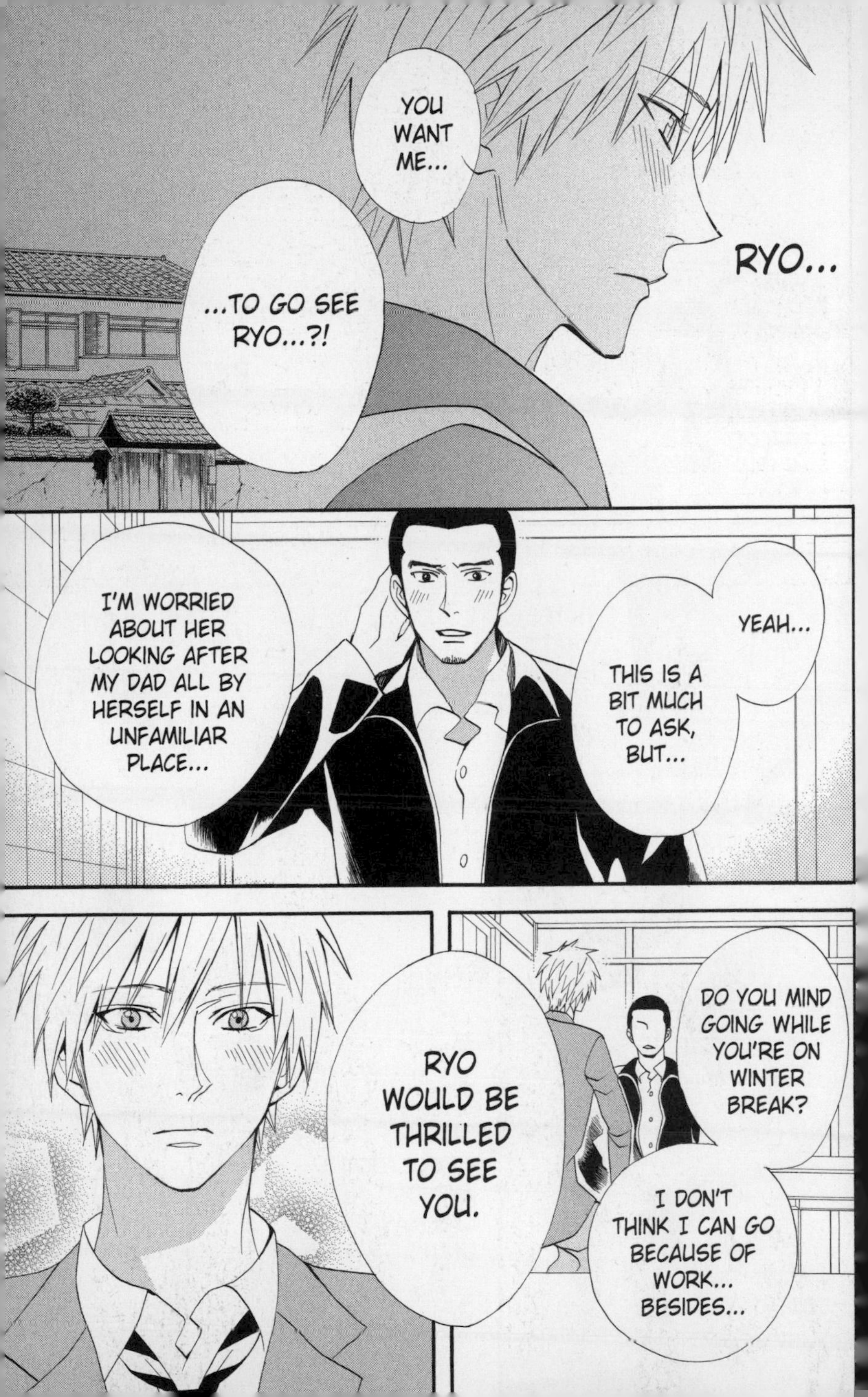
YOU WANT ME...
...TO GO SEE RYO...?!
RYO...
YEAH...
THIS IS A BIT MUCH TO ASK, BUT...
I'M WORRIED ABOUT HER LOOKING AFTER MY DAD ALL BY HERSELF IN AN UNFAMILIAR PLACE...
DO YOU MIND GOING WHILE YOU'RE ON WINTER BREAK?
I DON'T THINK I CAN GO BECAUSE OF WORK... BESIDES...
RYO WOULD BE THRILLED TO SEE YOU.

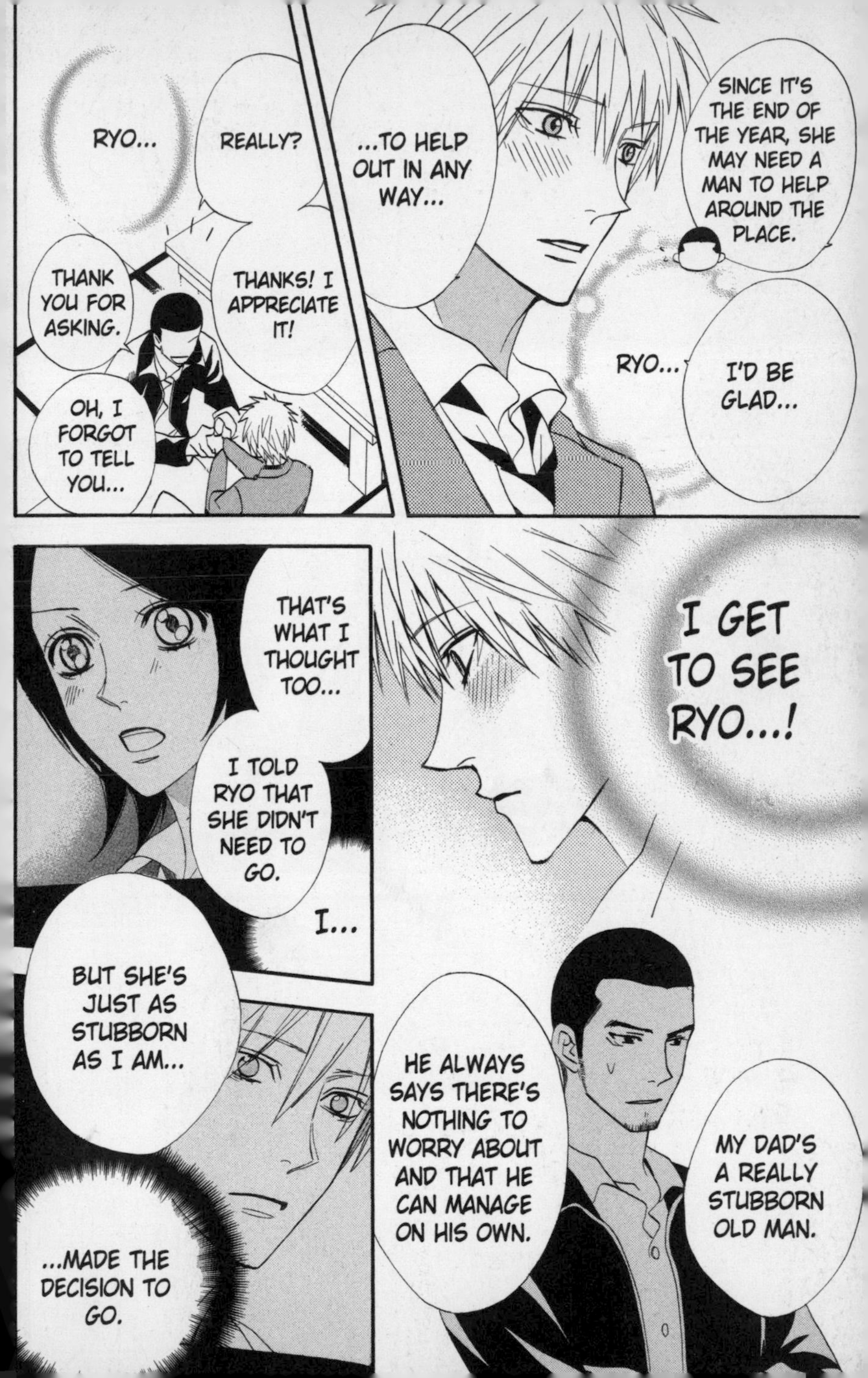
SINCE IT'S THE END OF THE YEAR, SHE MAY NEED A MAN TO HELP AROUND THE PLACE.
RYO...
I'D BE GLAD...
...TO HELP OUT IN ANY WAY...
REALLY?
RYO...
THANKS! I APPRECIATE IT!
THANK YOU FOR ASKING.
OH, I FORGOT TO TELL YOU...
I GET TO SEE RYO...!
THAT'S WHAT I THOUGHT TOO...
I TOLD RYO THAT SHE DIDN'T NEED TO GO.
MY DAD'S A REALLY STUBBORN OLD MAN.
HE ALWAYS SAYS THERE'S NOTHING TO WORRY ABOUT AND THAT HE CAN MANAGE ON HIS OWN.
BUT SHE'S JUST AS STUBBORN AS I AM...
I...
...MADE THE DECISION TO GO.

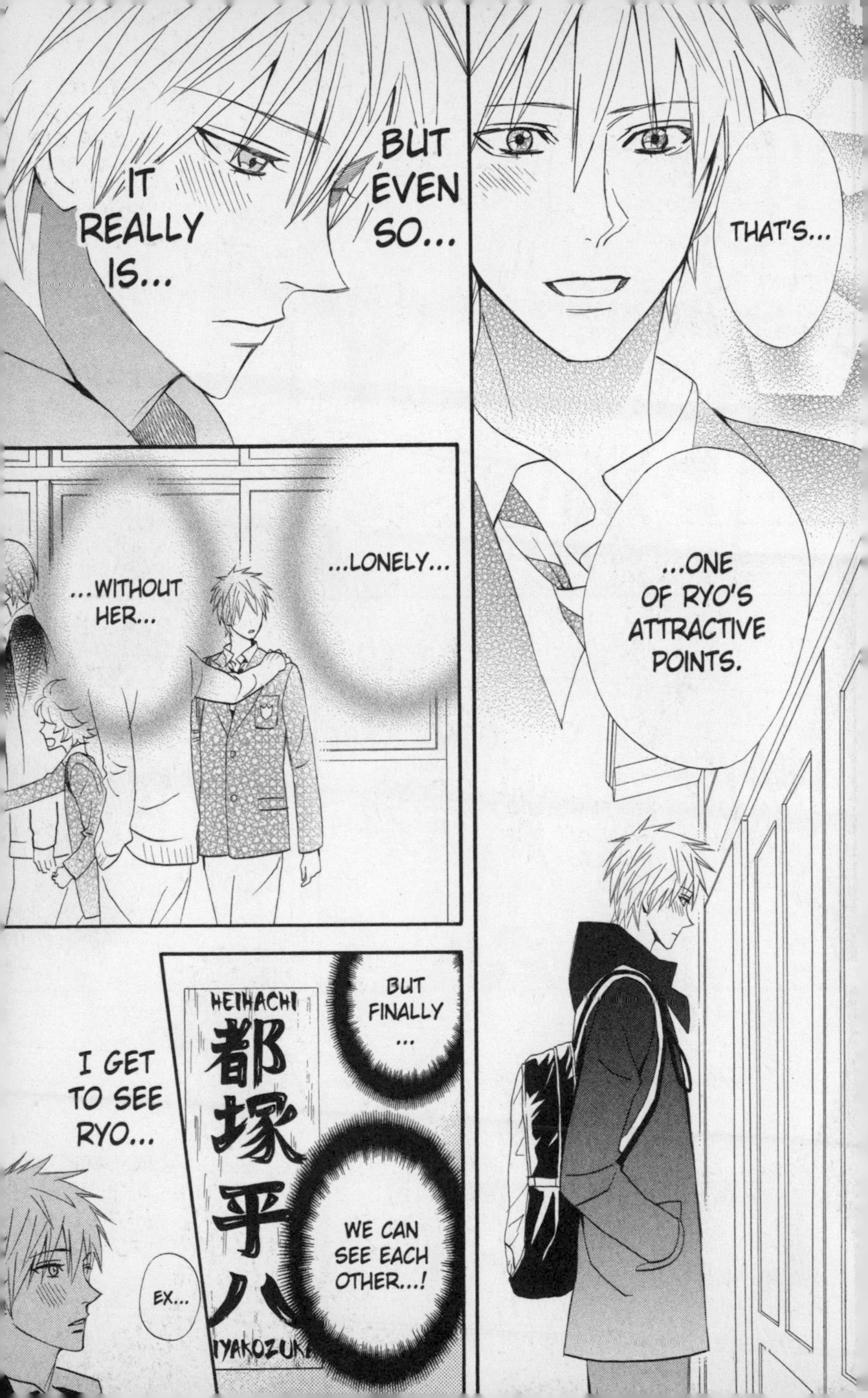
THAT'S...
...ONE OF RYO'S ATTRACTIVE POINTS.
BUT EVEN SO...
IT REALLY IS...
...LONELY...
...WITHOUT HER...
BUT FINALLY...
WE CAN SEE EACH OTHER...!
I GET TO SEE RYO...
HEIHACHI
都塚平八
EX...

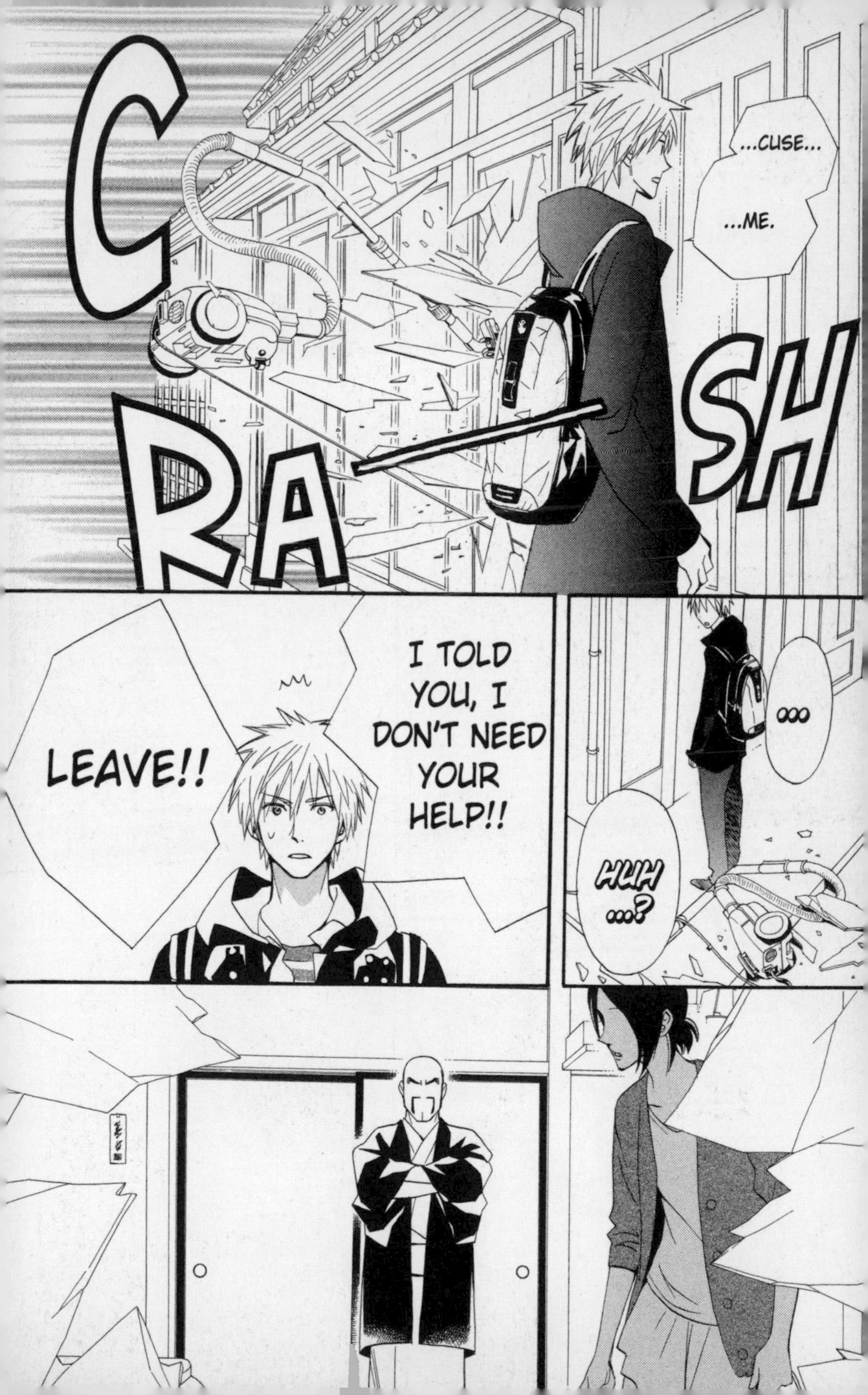
...CUSE...
...ME.
CRASH
...
HUH ...?
I TOLD YOU, I DON'T NEED YOUR HELP!!
LEAVE!!

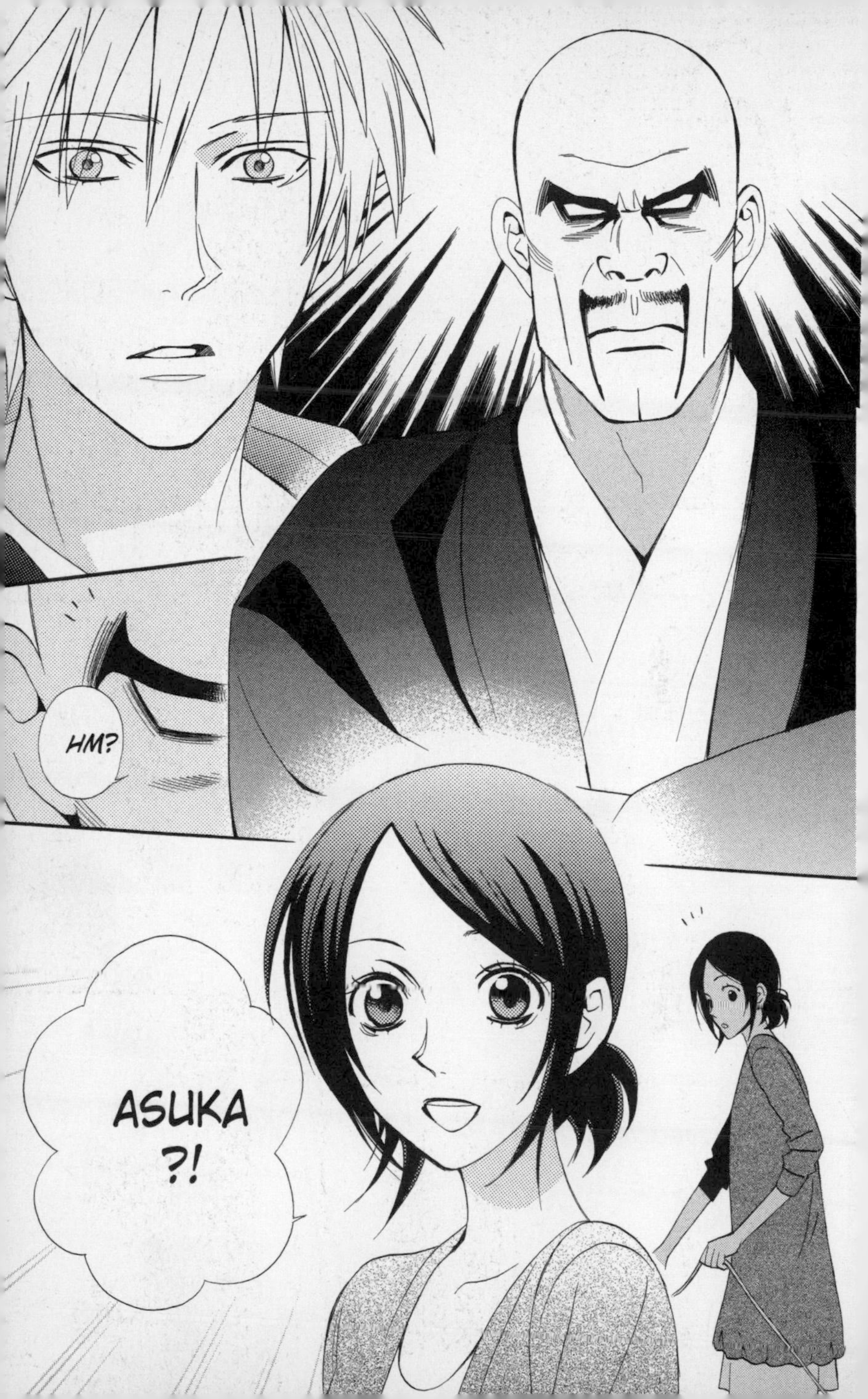
HM?
ASUKA ?!

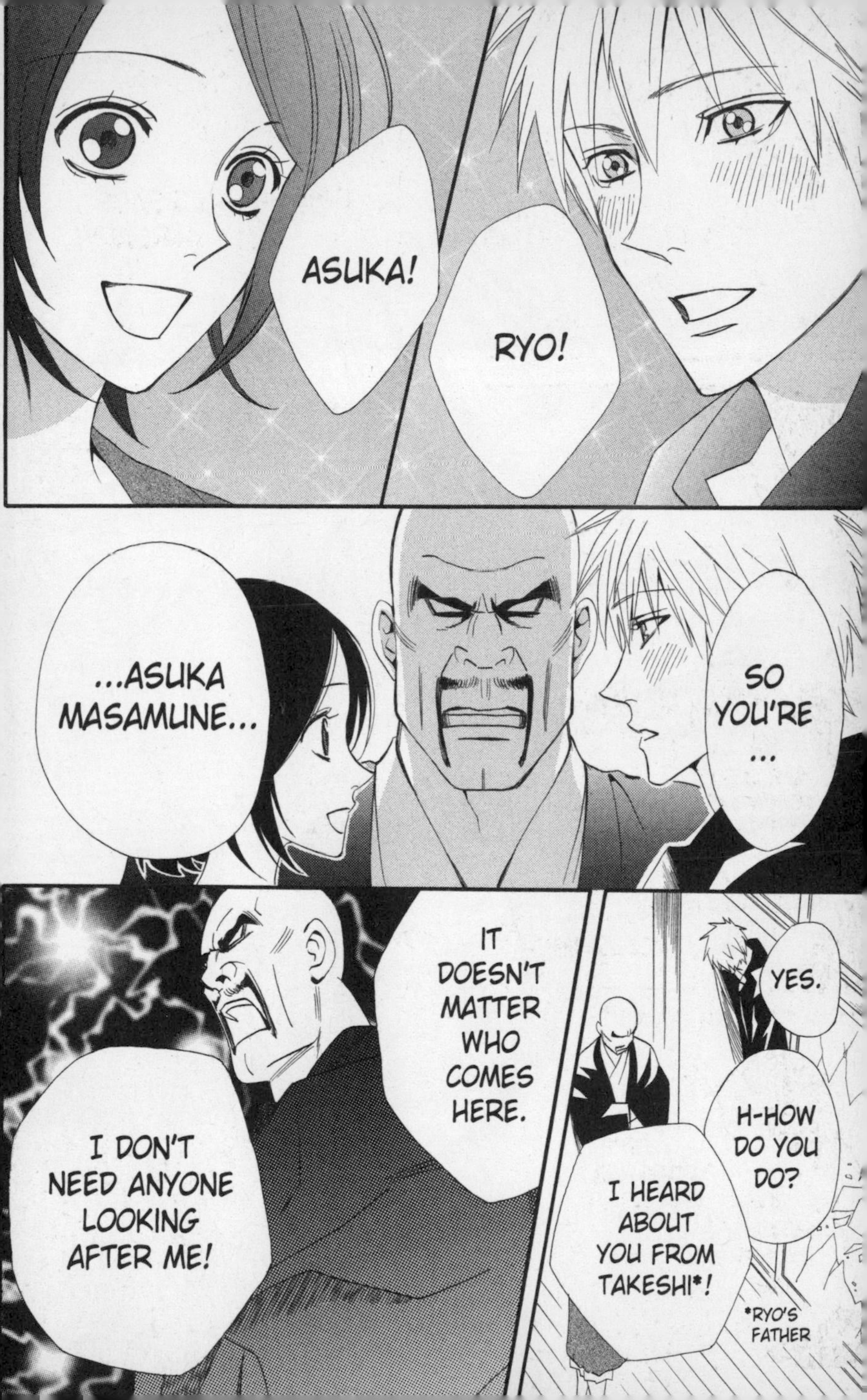
RYO!
ASUKA!
SO YOU'RE ...
...ASUKA MASAMUNE...
YES.
H-HOW DO YOU DO?
I HEARD ABOUT YOU FROM TAKESHI*!
*RYO'S FATHER
IT DOESN'T MATTER WHO COMES HERE.
I DON'T NEED ANYONE LOOKING AFTER ME!

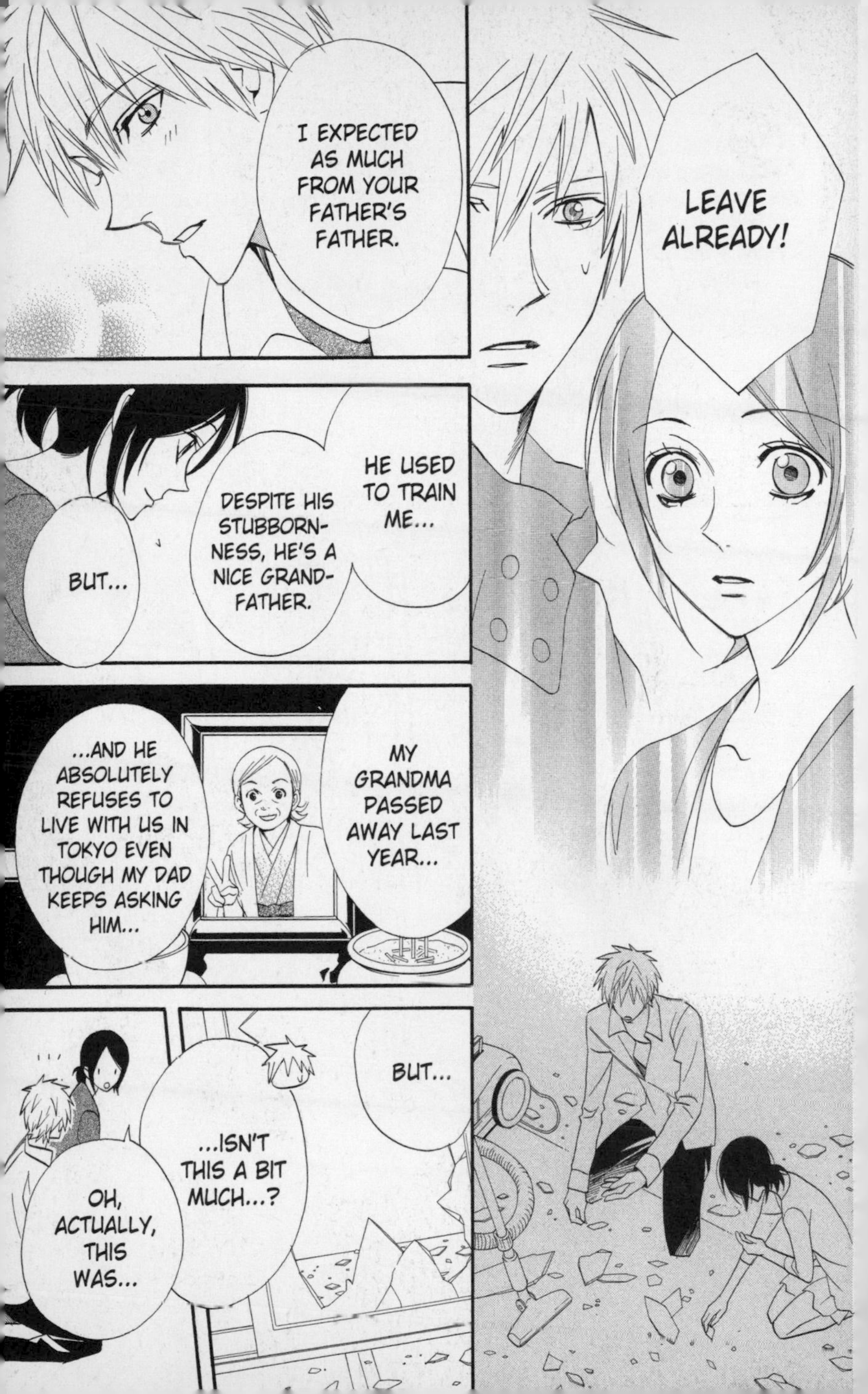
LEAVE ALREADY!
I EXPECTED AS MUCH FROM YOUR FATHER'S FATHER.
HE USED TO TRAIN ME...
DESPITE HIS STUBBORNNESS, HE'S A NICE GRANDFATHER.
BUT...
MY GRANDMA PASSED AWAY LAST YEAR...
...AND HE ABSOLUTELY REFUSES TO LIVE WITH US IN TOKYO EVEN THOUGH MY DAD KEEPS ASKING HIM...
BUT...
...ISN'T THIS A BIT MUCH...?
OH, ACTUALLY, THIS WAS...

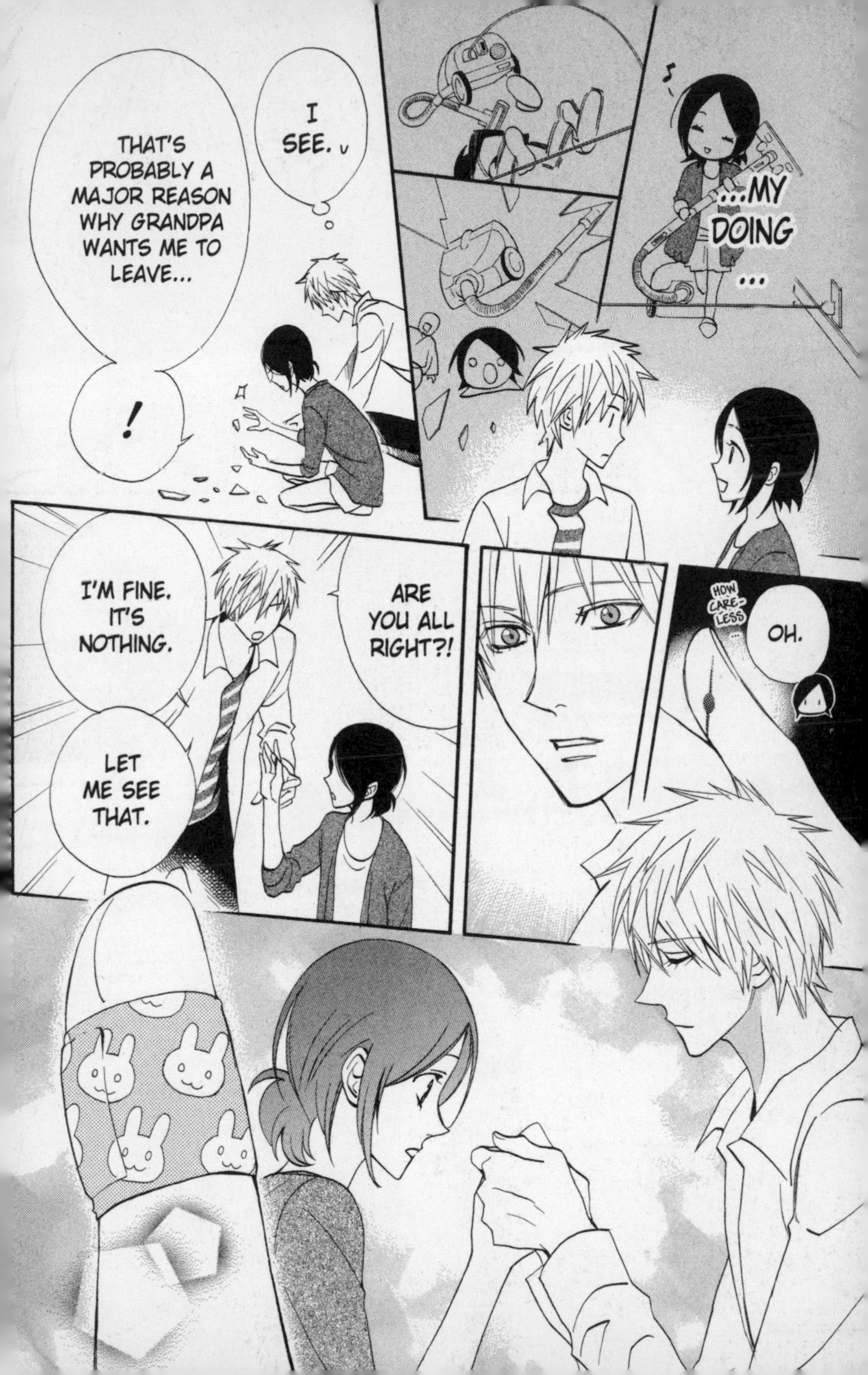
...MY DOING ...
I SEE.
THAT'S PROBABLY A MAJOR REASON WHY GRANDPA WANTS ME TO LEAVE...
!
OH.
HOW CARE-LESS...
ARE YOU ALL RIGHT?!
I'M FINE. IT'S NOTHING.
LET ME SEE THAT.

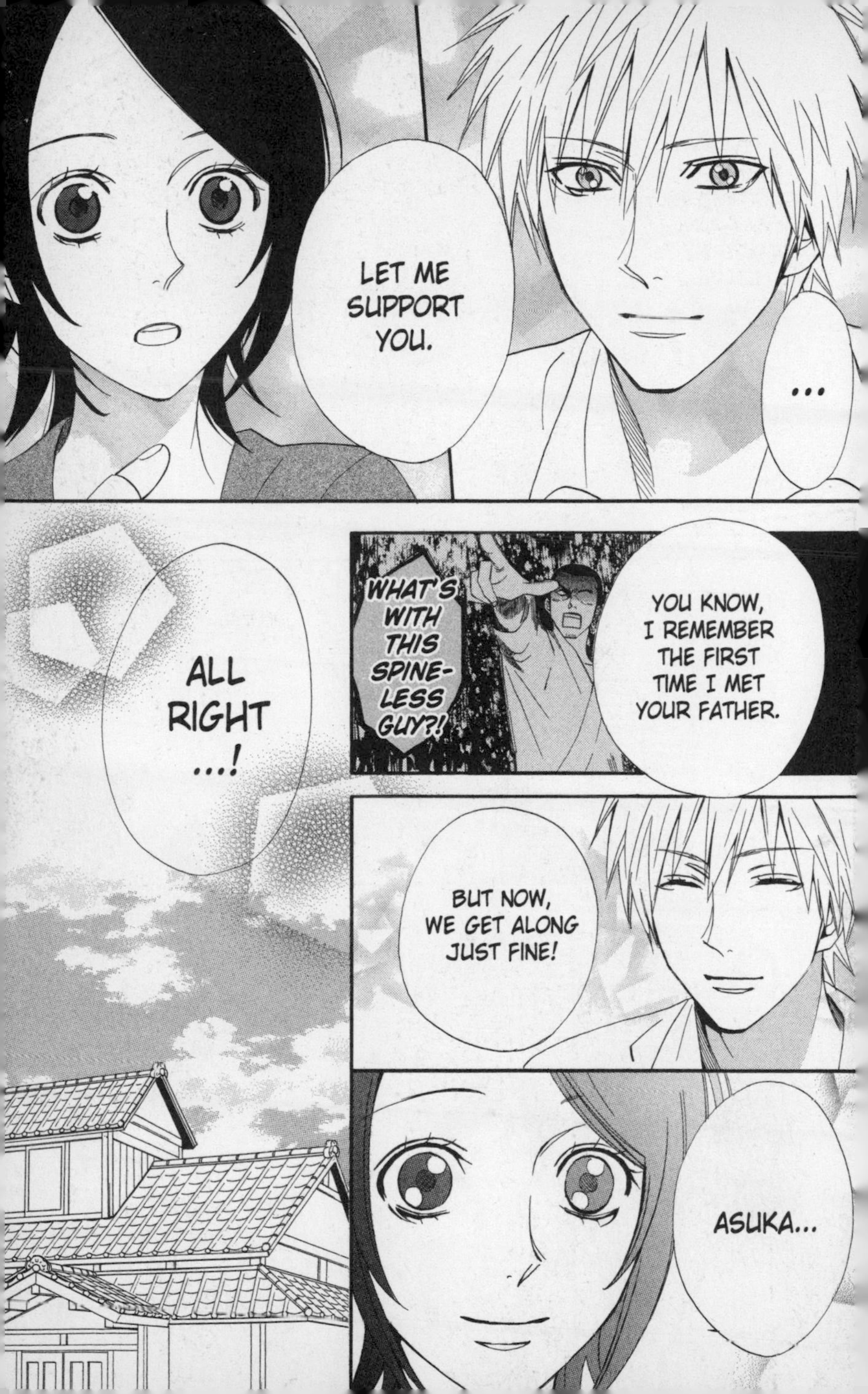
...
LET ME SUPPORT YOU.
YOU KNOW, I REMEMBER THE FIRST TIME I MET YOUR FATHER.
WHAT'S WITH THIS SPINE-LESS GUY?!
BUT NOW, WE GET ALONG JUST FINE!
ASUKA...
ALL RIGHT ...!

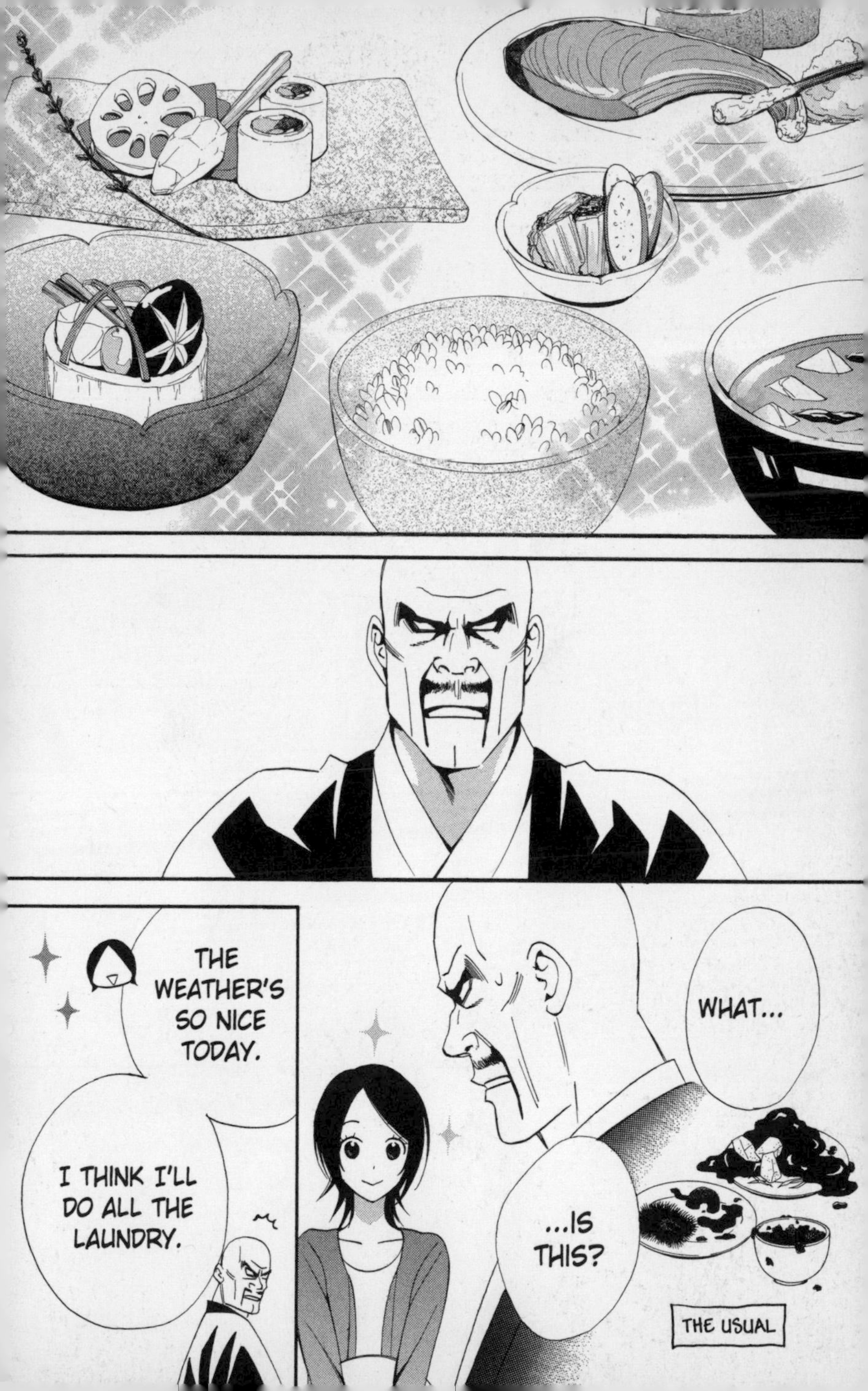
WHAT...
...IS THIS?
THE USUAL
THE WEATHER'S SO NICE TODAY.
I THINK I'LL DO ALL THE LAUNDRY.

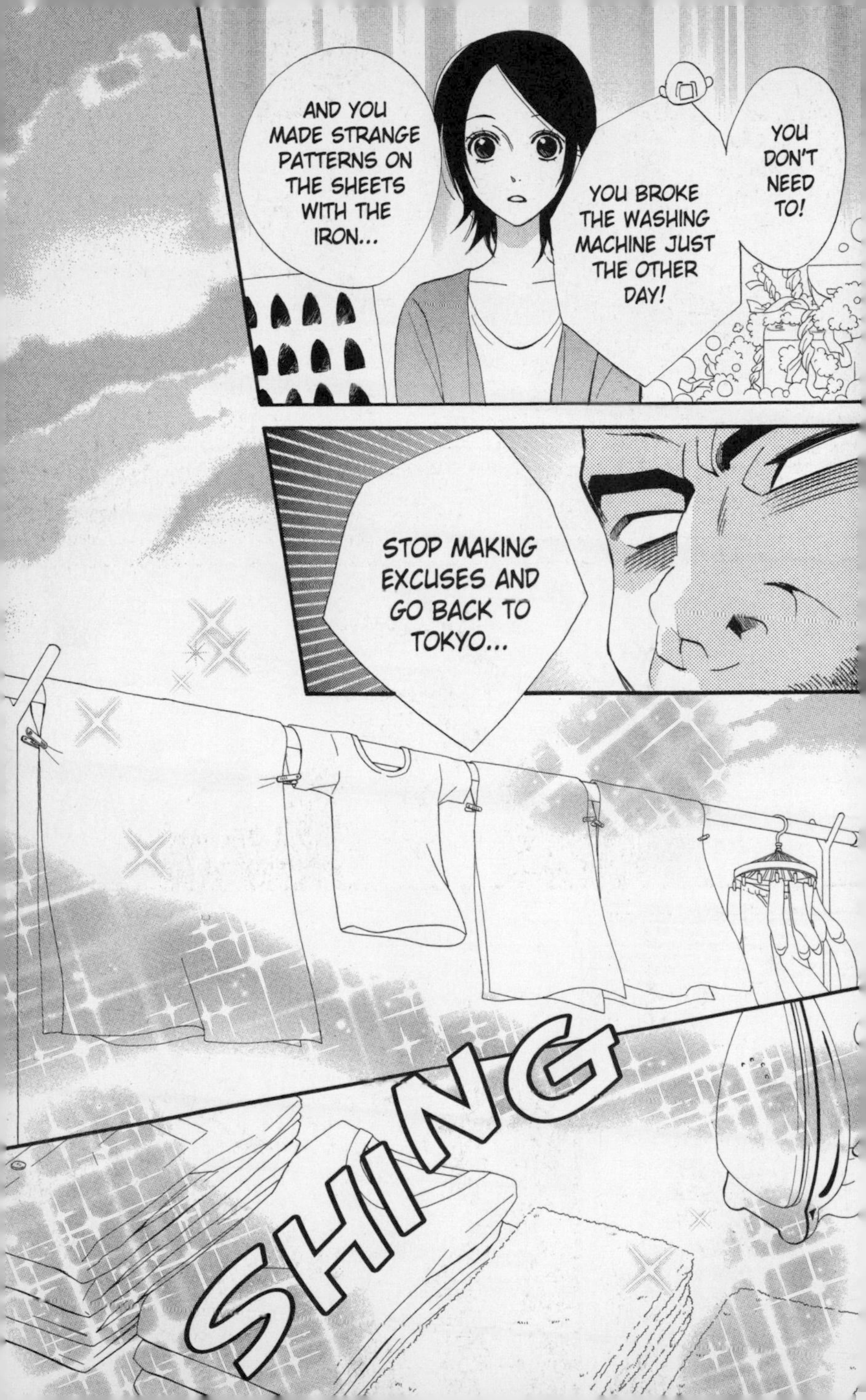
YOU DON'T NEED TO!
YOU BROKE THE WASHING MACHINE JUST THE OTHER DAY!
AND YOU MADE STRANGE PATTERNS ON THE SHEETS WITH THE IRON...
STOP MAKING EXCUSES AND GO BACK TO TOKYO...
SHING

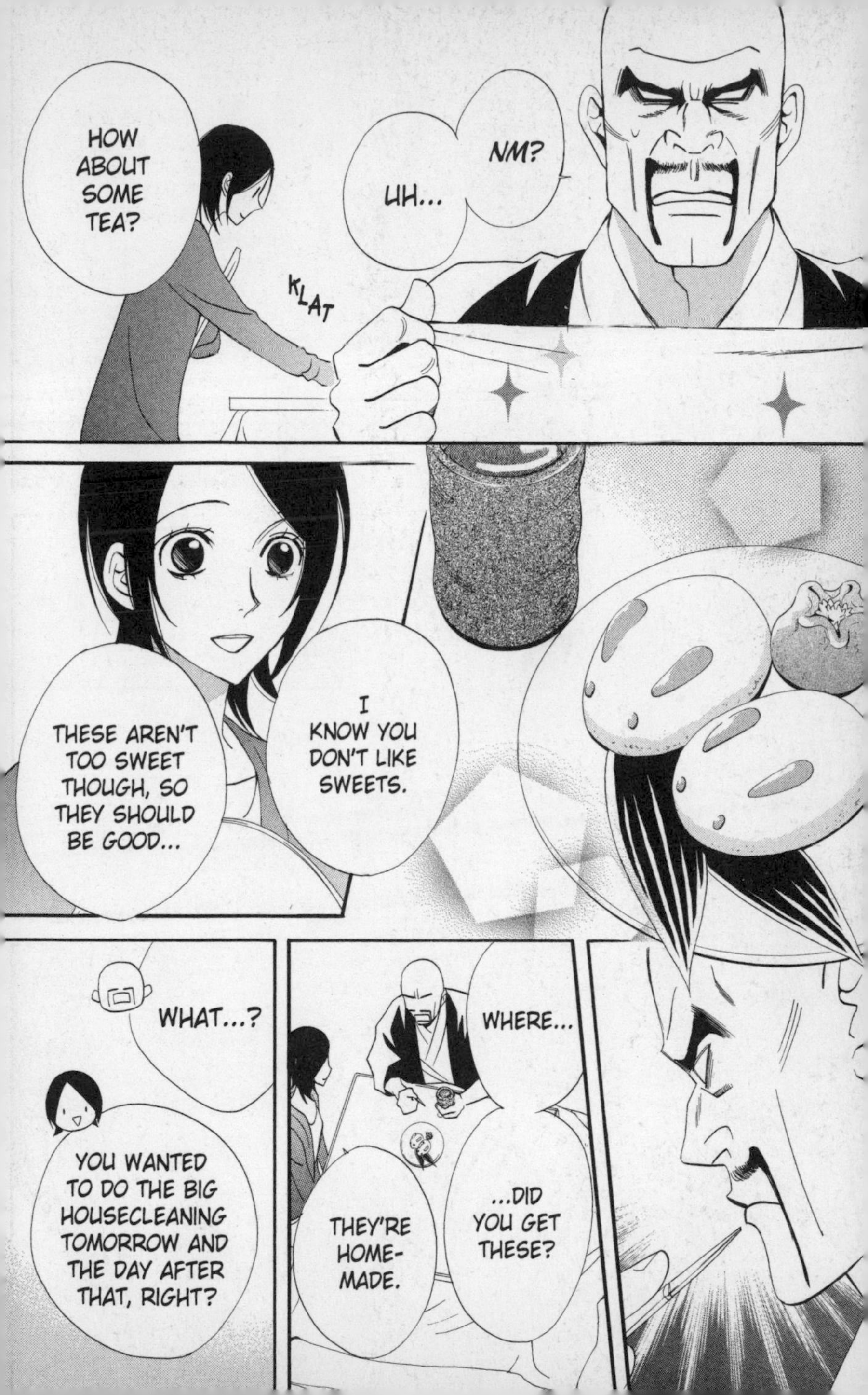
NM?
UH...
HOW ABOUT SOME TEA?
KLAT
I KNOW YOU DON'T LIKE SWEETS.
THESE AREN'T TOO SWEET THOUGH, SO THEY SHOULD BE GOOD...
WHERE...
...DID YOU GET THESE?
THEY'RE HOME-MADE.
WHAT...?
YOU WANTED TO DO THE BIG HOUSECLEANING TOMORROW AND THE DAY AFTER THAT, RIGHT?

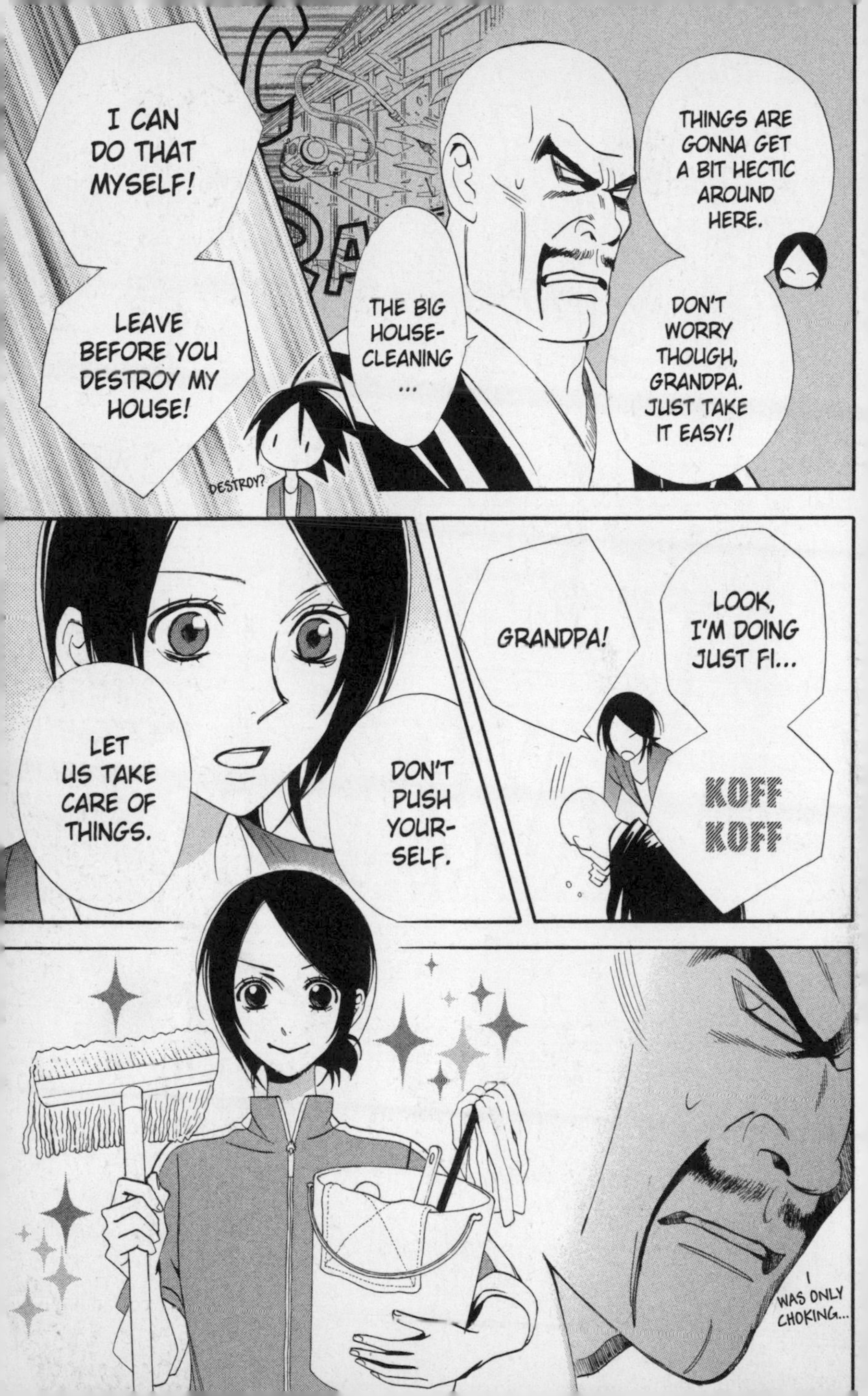
THINGS ARE GONNA GET A BIT HECTIC AROUND HERE.
DON'T WORRY THOUGH, GRANDPA. JUST TAKE IT EASY!
THE BIG HOUSE-CLEANING...
I CAN DO THAT MYSELF!
LEAVE BEFORE YOU DESTROY MY HOUSE!
DESTROY?
LOOK, I'M DOING JUST FI...
GRANDPA!
KOFF KOFF
DON'T PUSH YOURSELF.
LET US TAKE CARE OF THINGS.
I WAS ONLY CHOKING...

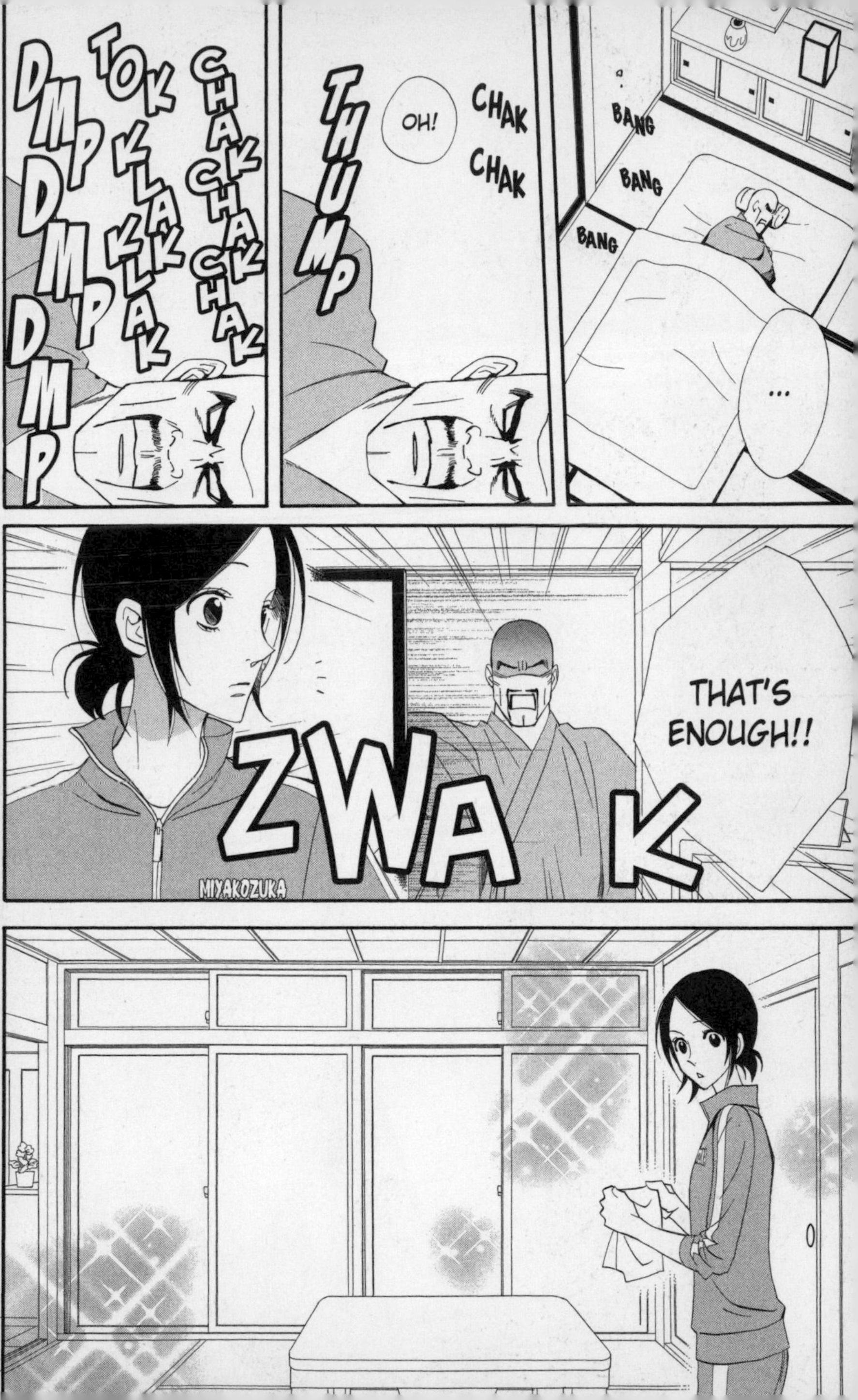
BANG
BANG
BANG
...
CHAK
CHAK
OH!
THUMP
CHAKCHAKCHAK
TOK
KLAKLAKLAK
DMPDMPDMP
THAT'S ENOUGH!!
ZWAK
MIYAKOZUKA

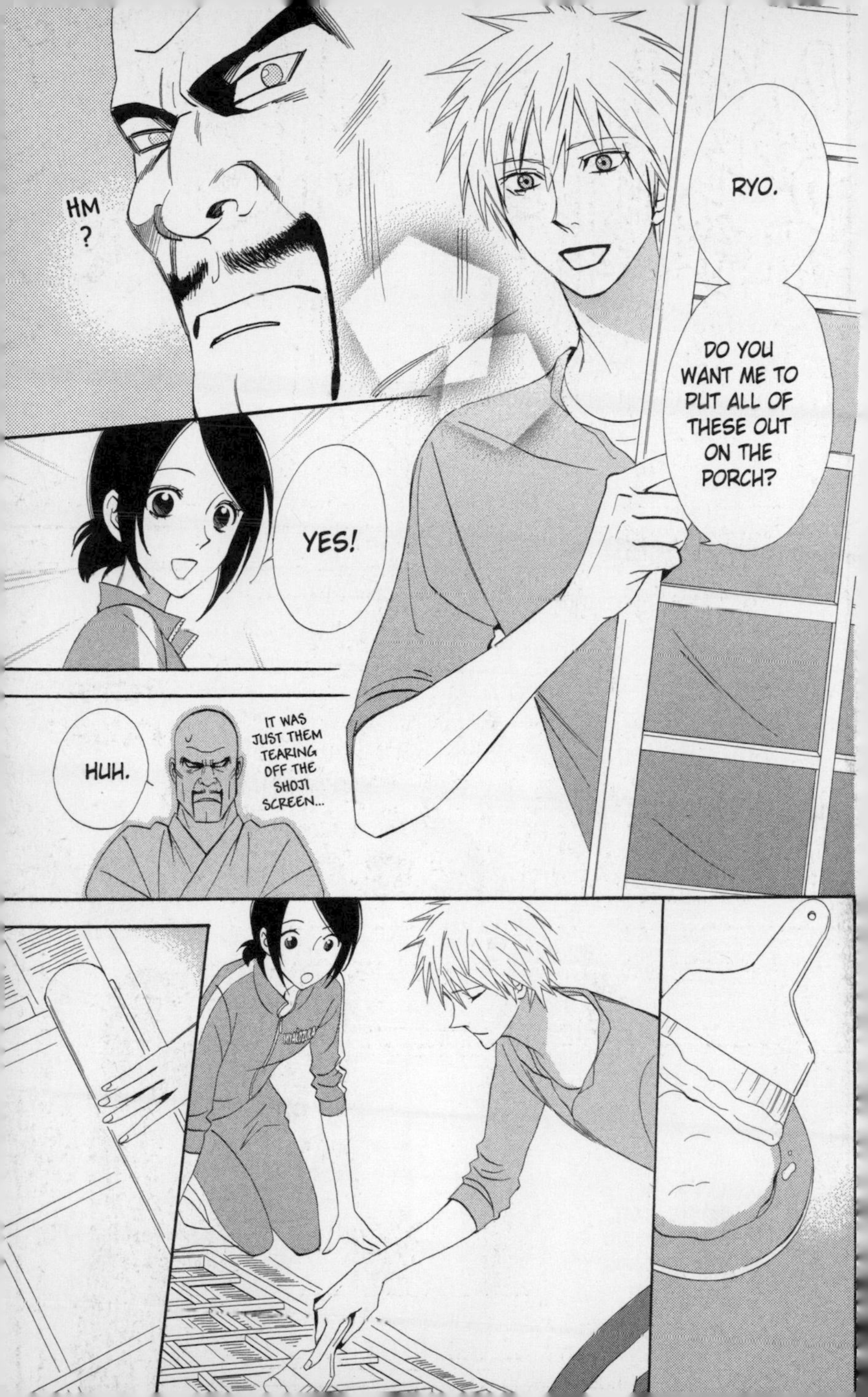
RYO.
DO YOU WANT ME TO PUT ALL OF THESE OUT ON THE PORCH?
HM?
YES!
HUH.
IT WAS JUST THEM TEARING OFF THE SHOJI SCREEN...

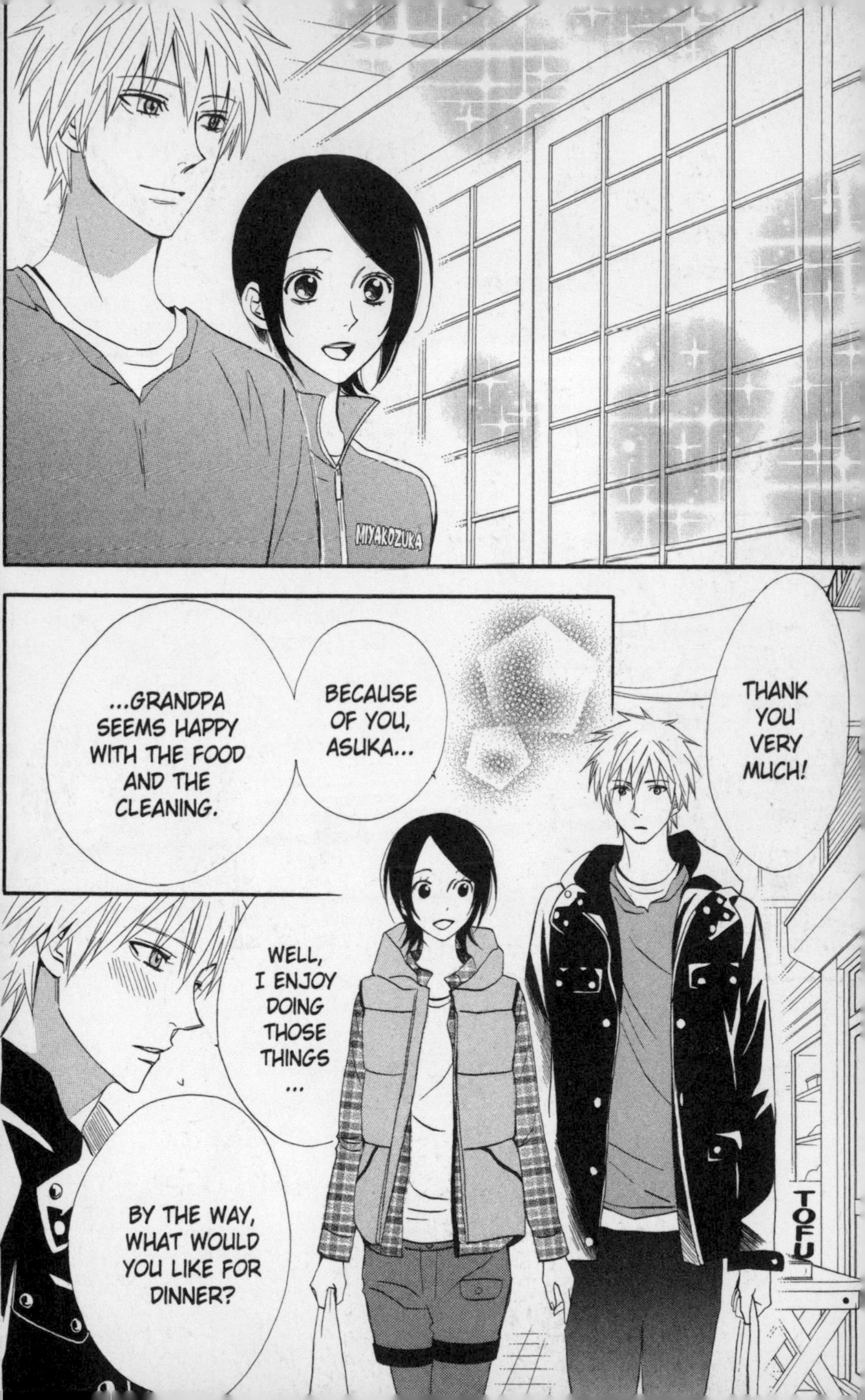
MIYAKOZUKA
THANK YOU VERY MUCH!
BECAUSE OF YOU, ASUKA...
...GRANDPA SEEMS HAPPY WITH THE FOOD AND THE CLEANING.
TOFU
WELL, I ENJOY DOING THOSE THINGS ...
BY THE WAY, WHAT WOULD YOU LIKE FOR DINNER?

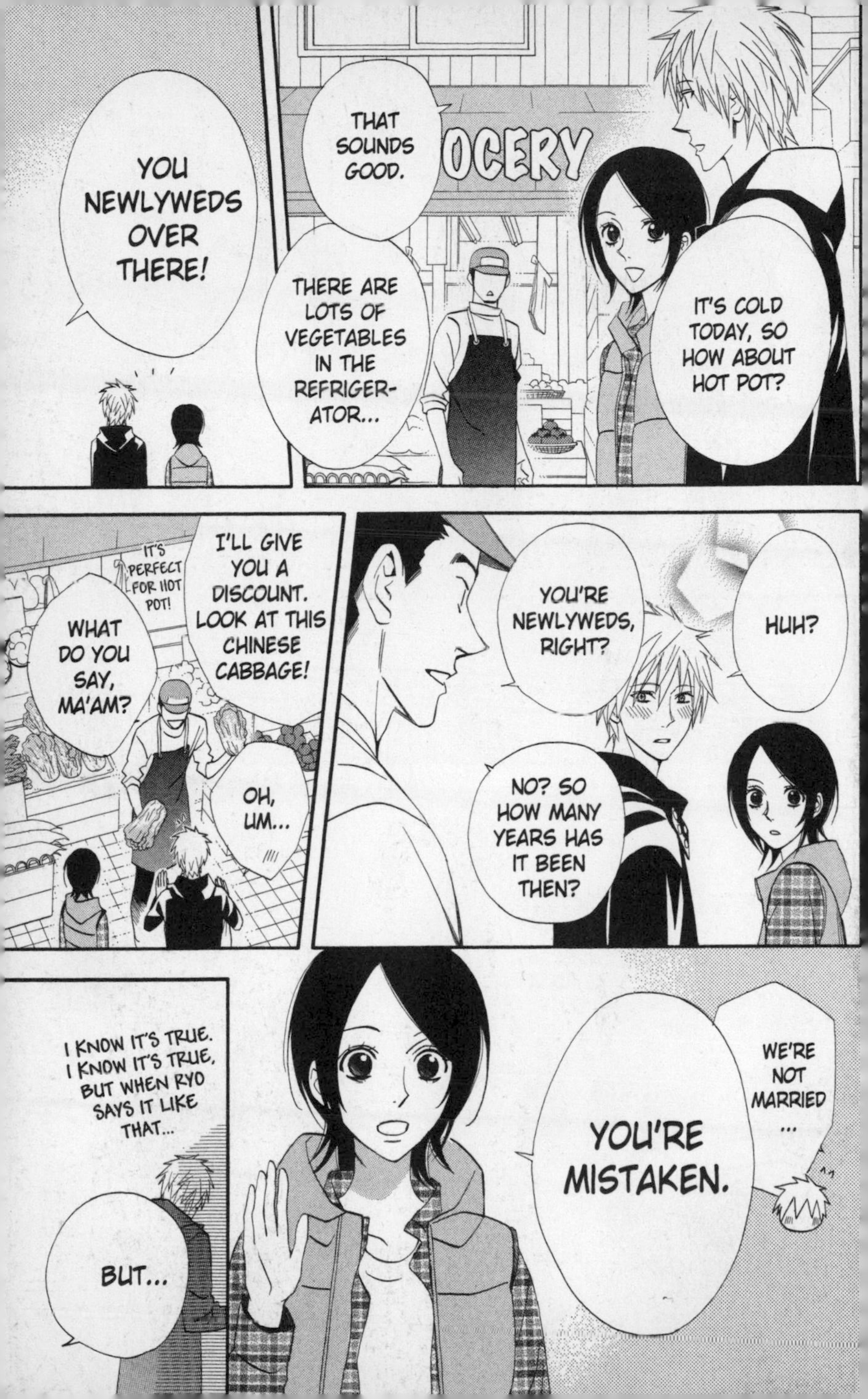
IT'S COLD TODAY, SO HOW ABOUT HOT POT?
OCERY
THAT SOUNDS GOOD.
THERE ARE LOTS OF VEGETABLES IN THE REFRIGERATOR...
YOU NEWLYWEDS OVER THERE!
HUH?
YOU'RE NEWLYWEDS, RIGHT?
NO? SO HOW MANY YEARS HAS IT BEEN THEN?
I'LL GIVE YOU A DISCOUNT. LOOK AT THIS CHINESE CABBAGE!
IT'S PERFECT FOR HOT POT!
WHAT DO YOU SAY, MA'AM?
OH, UM...
WE'RE NOT MARRIED...
YOU'RE MISTAKEN.
I KNOW IT'S TRUE. I KNOW IT'S TRUE, BUT WHEN RYO SAYS IT LIKE THAT...
BUT...

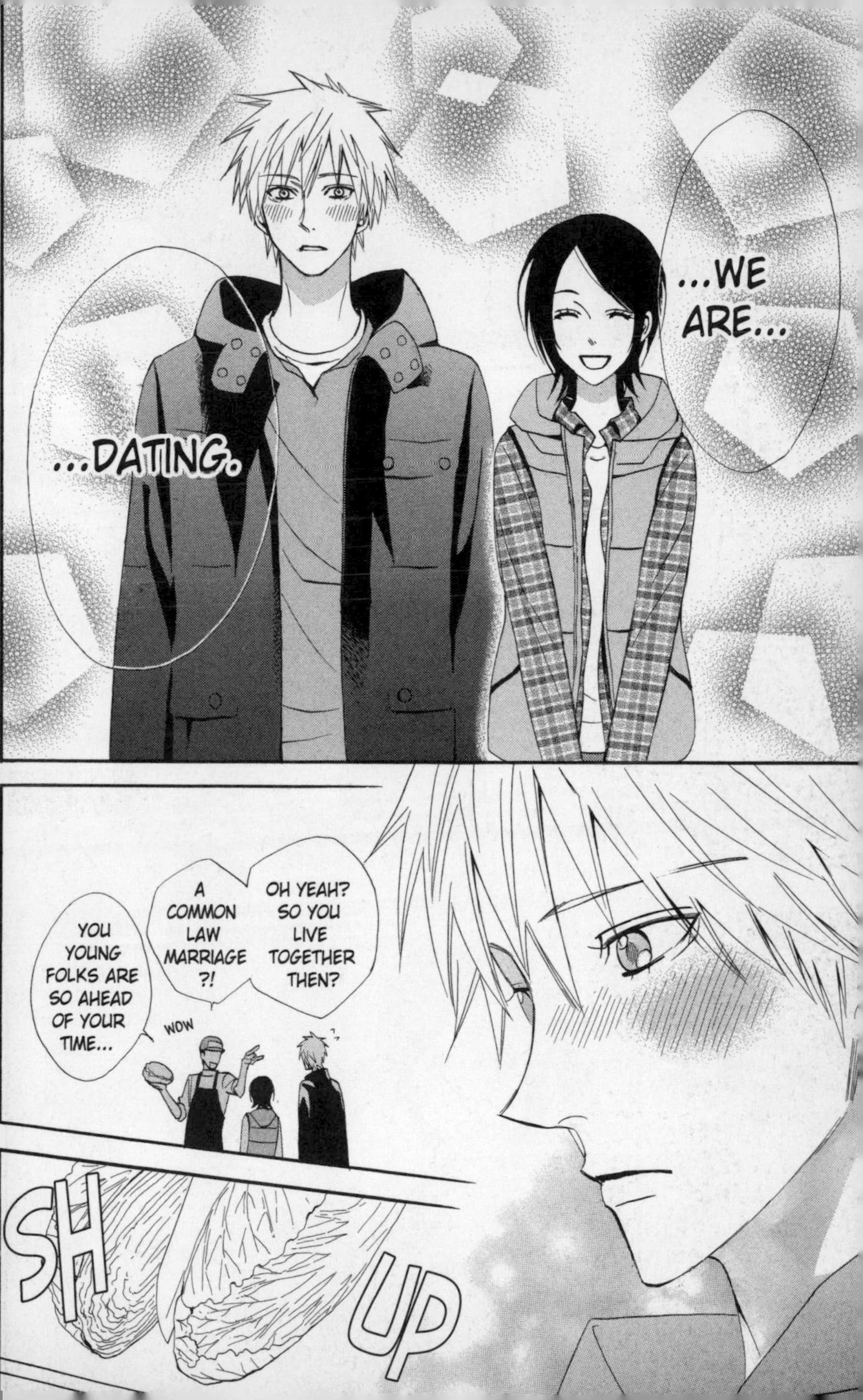
...WE ARE...
...DATING.
OH YEAH? SO YOU LIVE TOGETHER THEN?
A COMMON LAW MARRIAGE ?!
YOU YOUNG FOLKS ARE SO AHEAD OF YOUR TIME...
WOW
SH UP

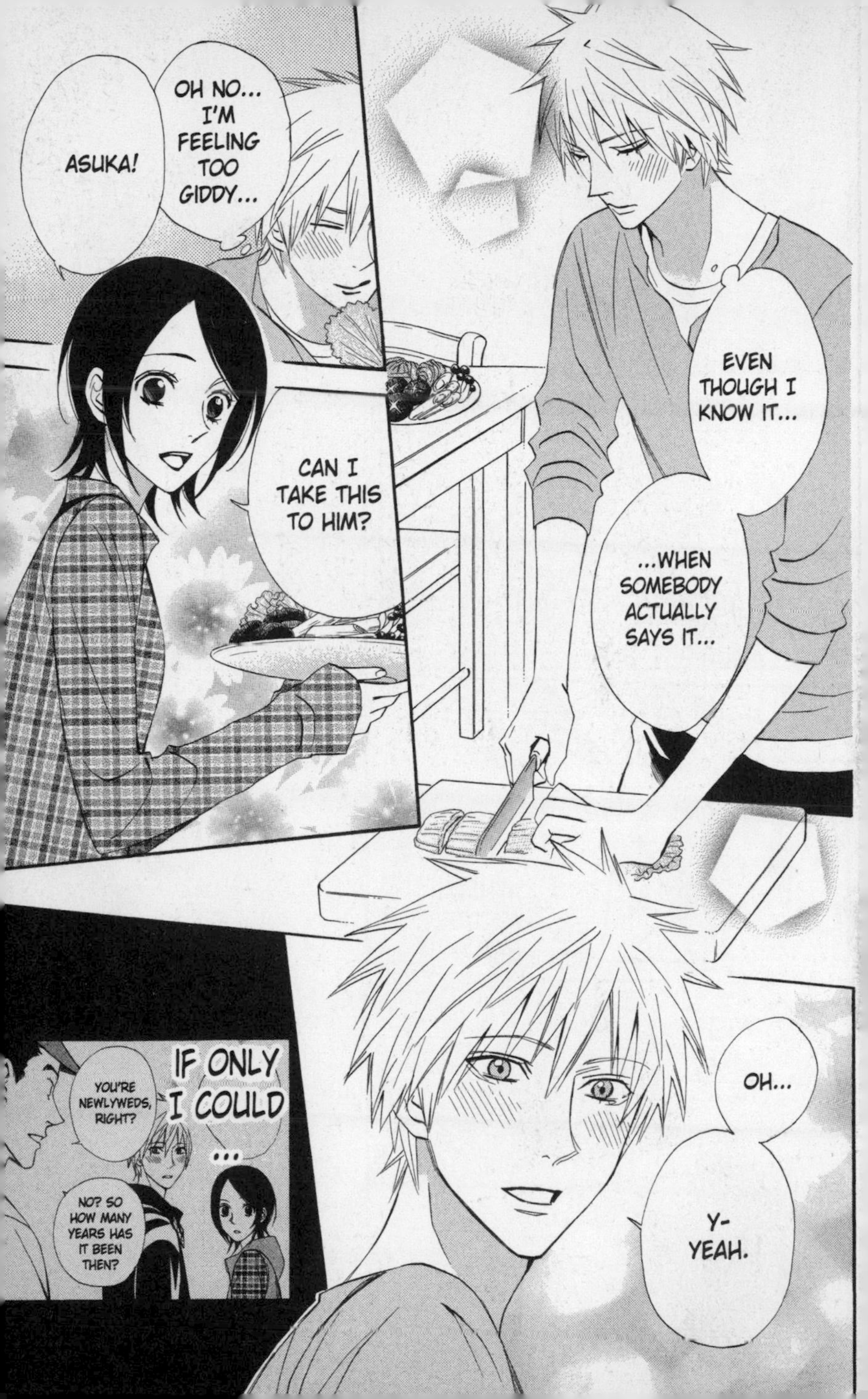
EVEN THOUGH I KNOW IT...
...WHEN SOMEBODY ACTUALLY SAYS IT...
OH NO... I'M FEELING TOO GIDDY...
ASUKA!
CAN I TAKE THIS TO HIM?
OH...
Y-YEAH.
YOU'RE NEWLYWEDS, RIGHT?
IF ONLY I COULD
...
NO? SO HOW MANY YEARS HAS IT BEEN THEN?

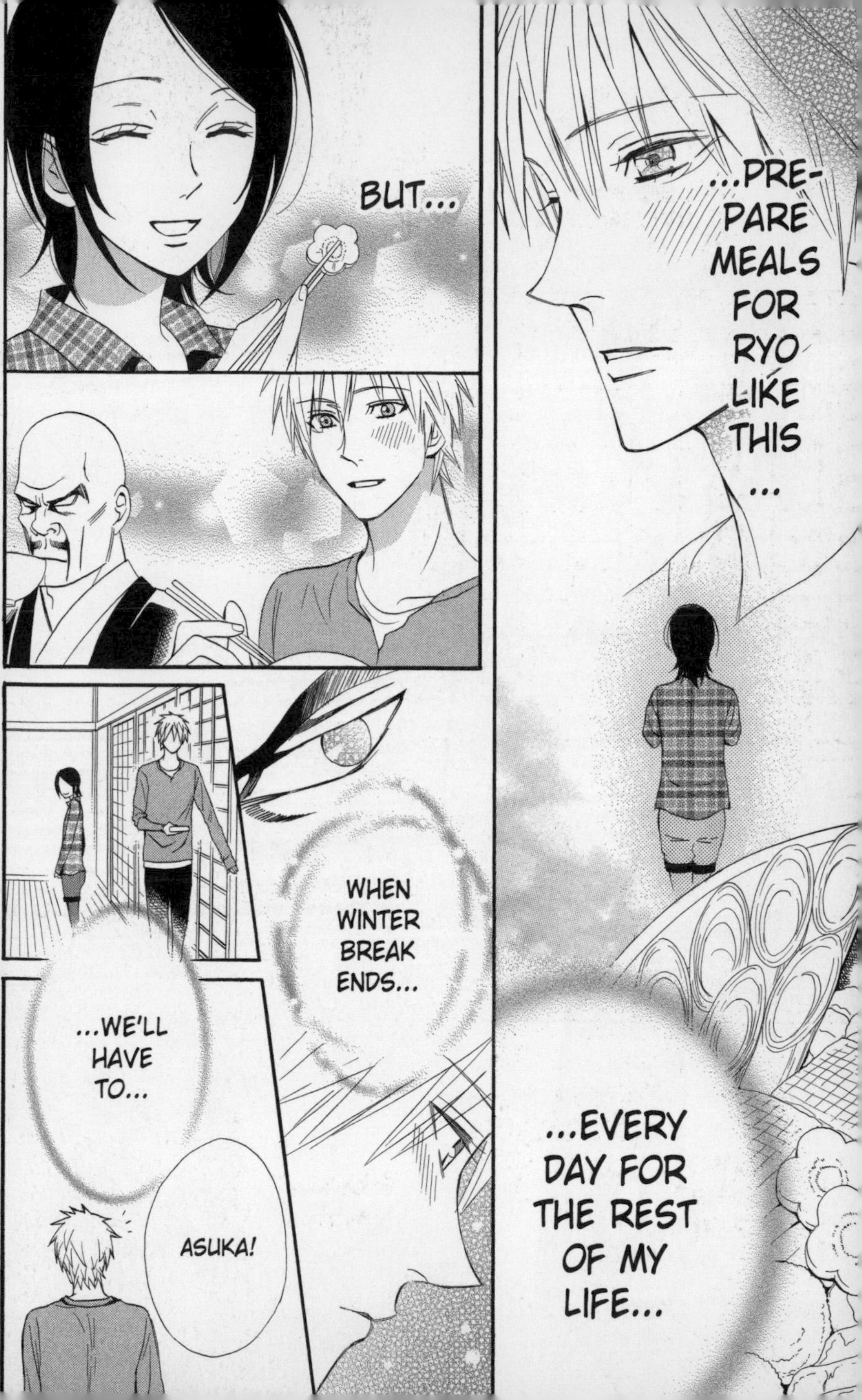
...PRE-PARE MEALS FOR RYO LIKE THIS...
...EVERY DAY FOR THE REST OF MY LIFE...
BUT...
WHEN WINTER BREAK ENDS...
...WE'LL HAVE TO...
ASUKA!

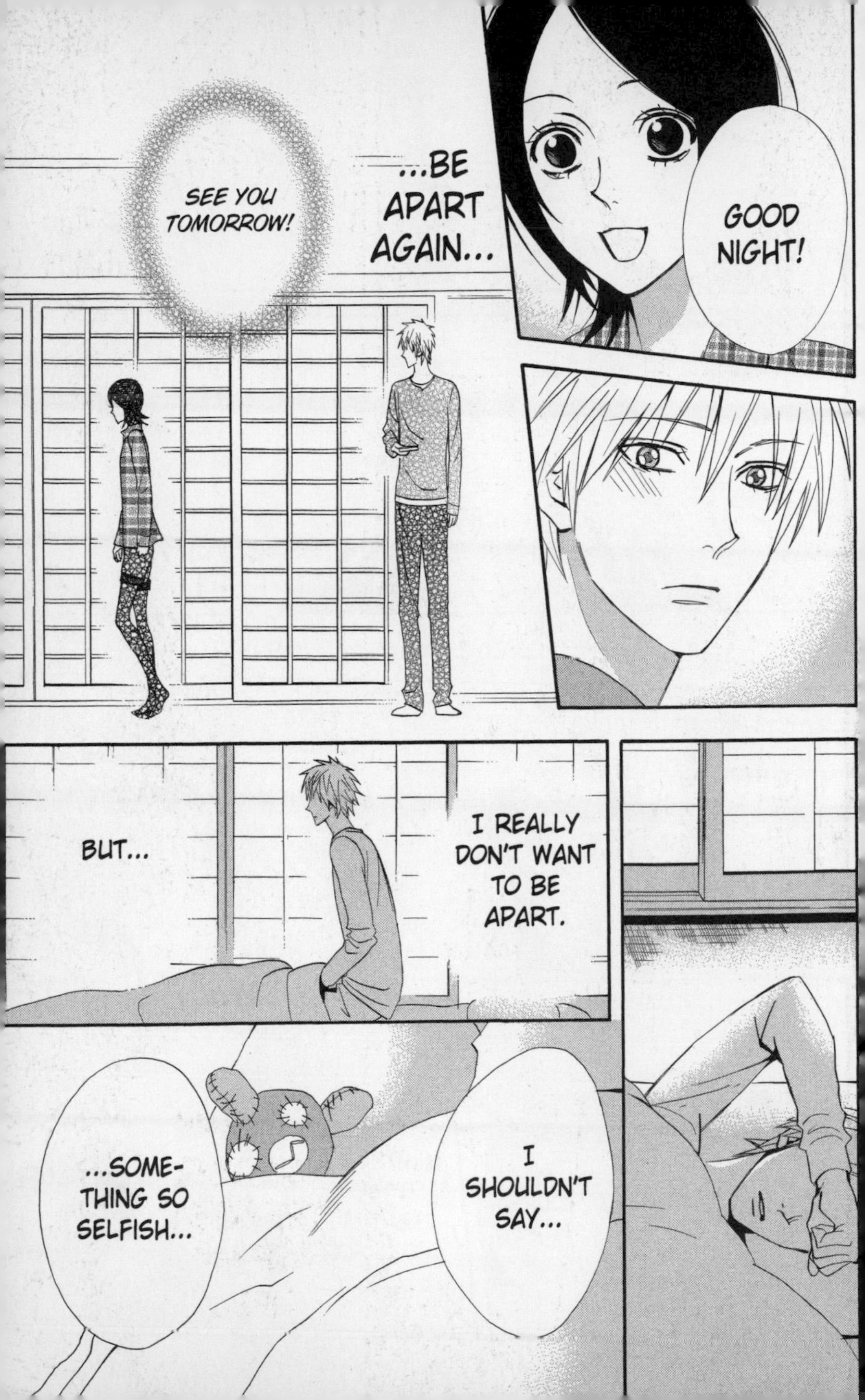
GOOD NIGHT!
...BE APART AGAIN...
SEE YOU TOMORROW!
I REALLY DON'T WANT TO BE APART.
BUT...
I SHOULDN'T SAY...
...SOME-THING SO SELFISH...

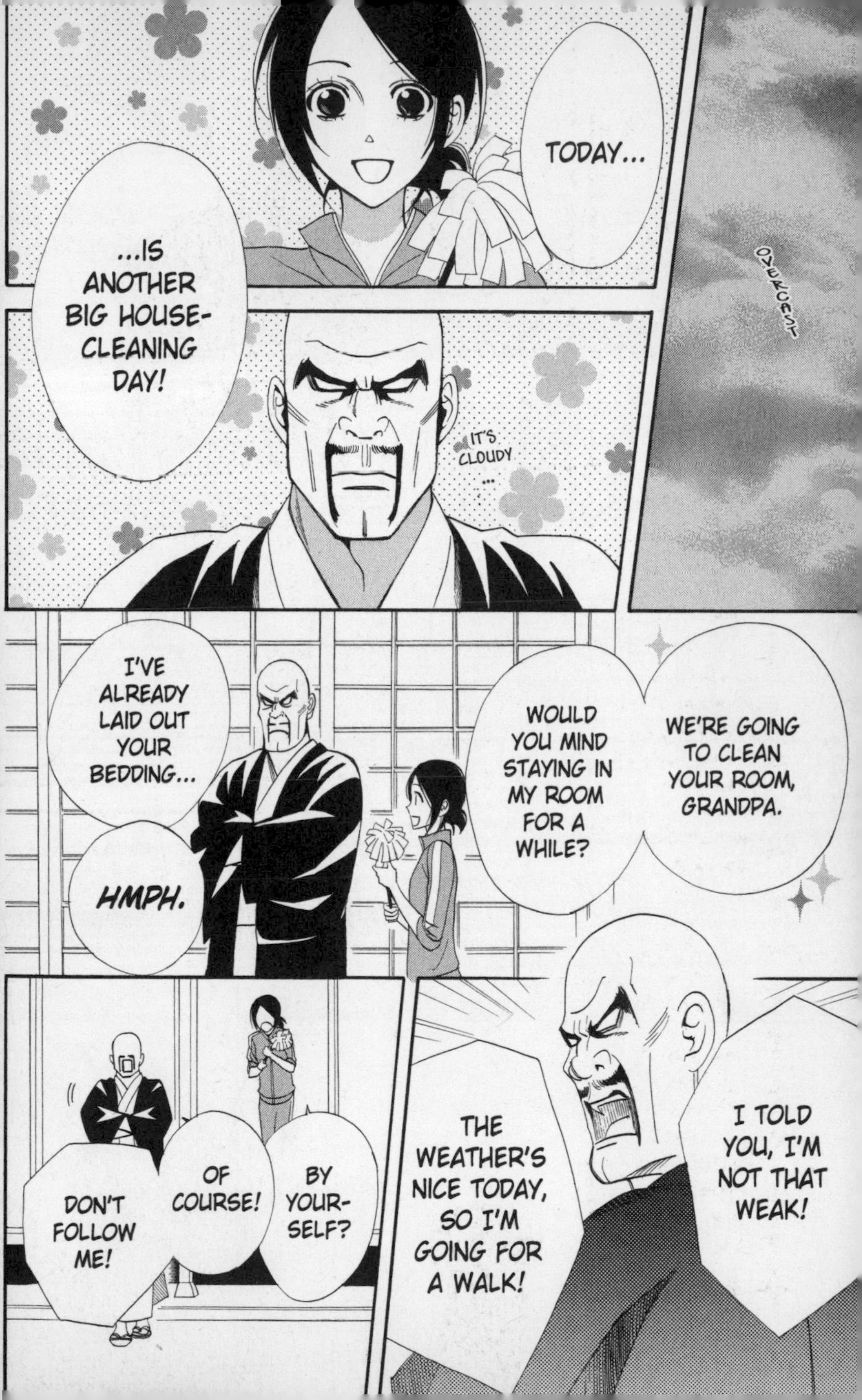
OVERCAST
TODAY...
...IS ANOTHER BIG HOUSE-CLEANING DAY!
IT'S CLOUDY...
WE'RE GOING TO CLEAN YOUR ROOM, GRANDPA.
WOULD YOU MIND STAYING IN MY ROOM FOR A WHILE?
I'VE ALREADY LAID OUT YOUR BEDDING...
HMPH.
I TOLD YOU, I'M NOT THAT WEAK!
THE WEATHER'S NICE TODAY, SO I'M GOING FOR A WALK!
BY YOURSELF?
OF COURSE!
DON'T FOLLOW ME!

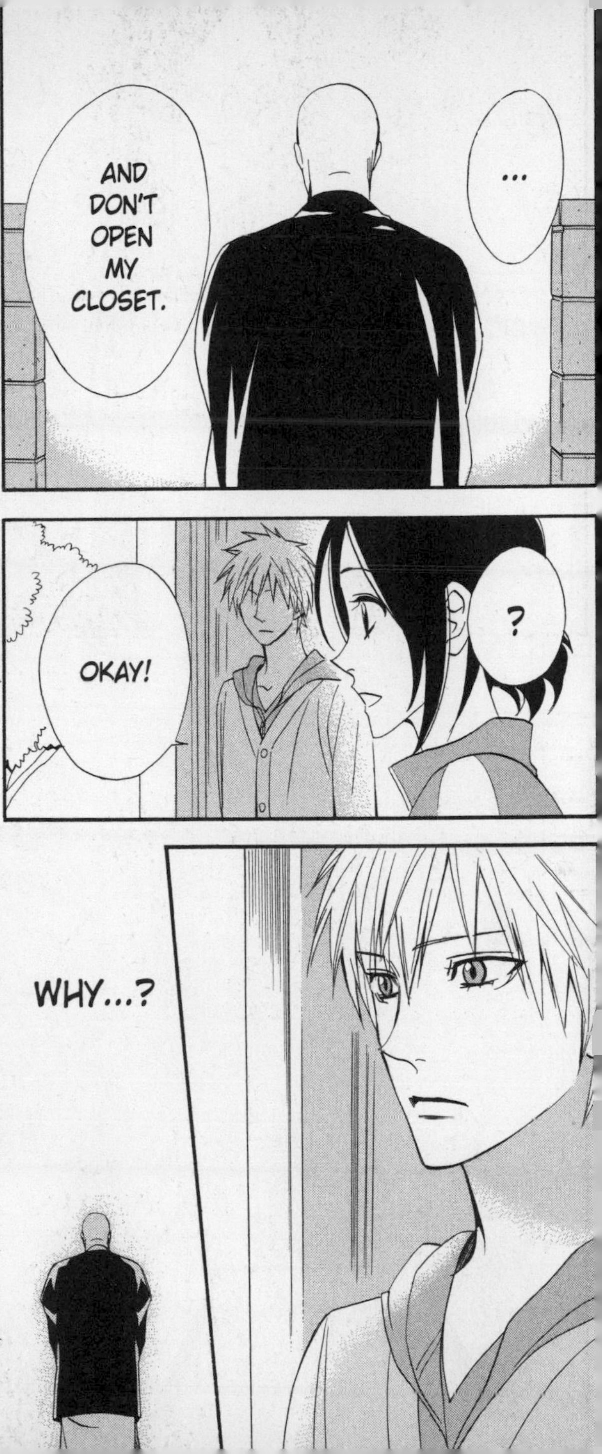
...
AND DON'T OPEN MY CLOSET.
?
OKAY!
WHY...?

Kitora Kurokawa

Ginyuri Academy High School
Second-year, Class E
Born June 20
Gemini,
Blood Type AB
Height: 193 cm
Favorite flower: Tulip

Hajime Tonomine

Kinbara High School
Second-year, Class 1
Born November 11
Scorpio, Blood Type A
Height: 177 cm
Takes care of his skin every day. (He has beautiful skin.)

Yamato Ariake

Ginyuri Academy High School
First-year, Class C
Born August 3
Leo, Blood Type B
Height: 156 cm
Favorite karaoke song: "Love Crazed"

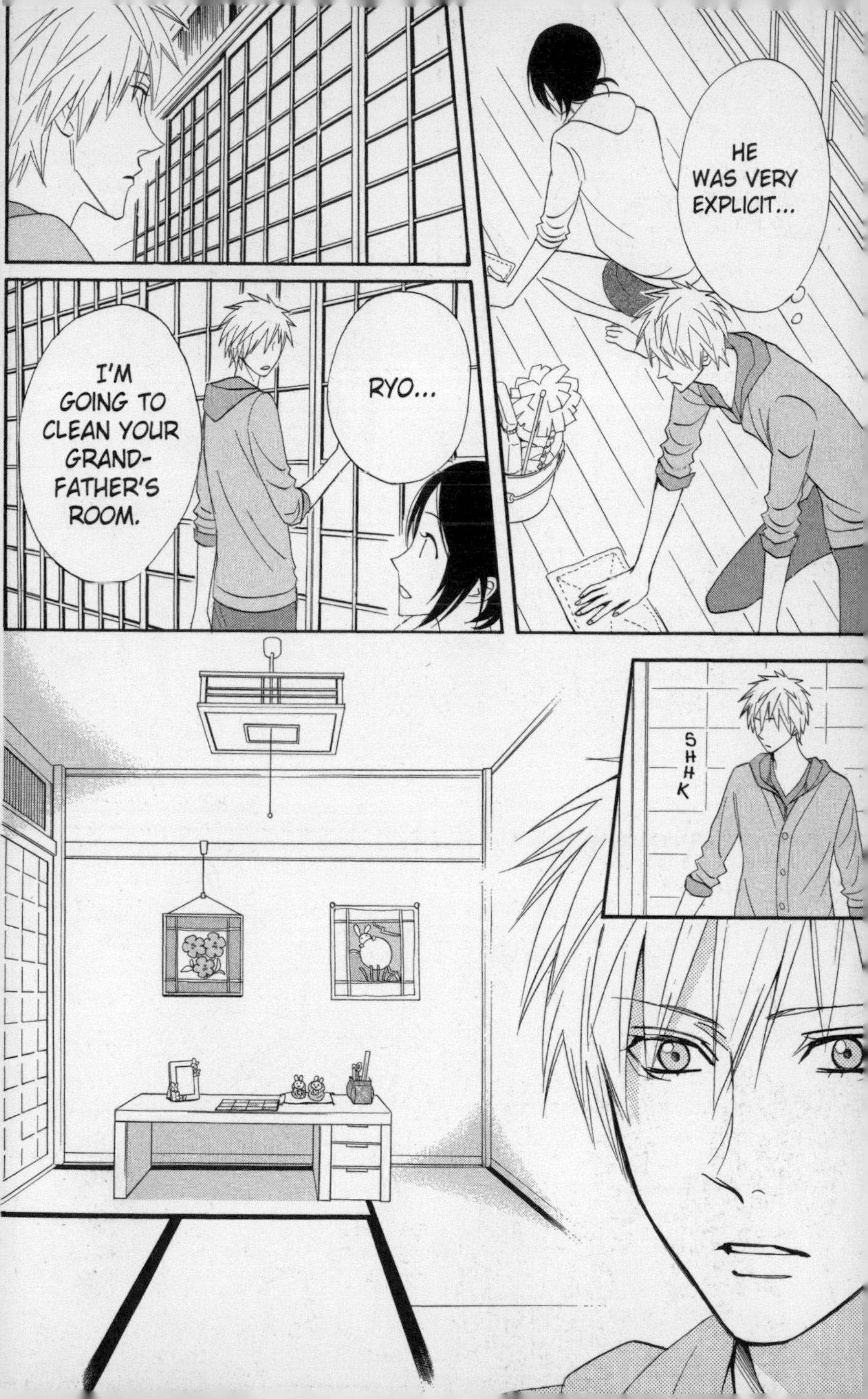
HE WAS VERY EXPLICIT...
RYO...
I'M GOING TO CLEAN YOUR GRAND-FATHER'S ROOM.
SHHK

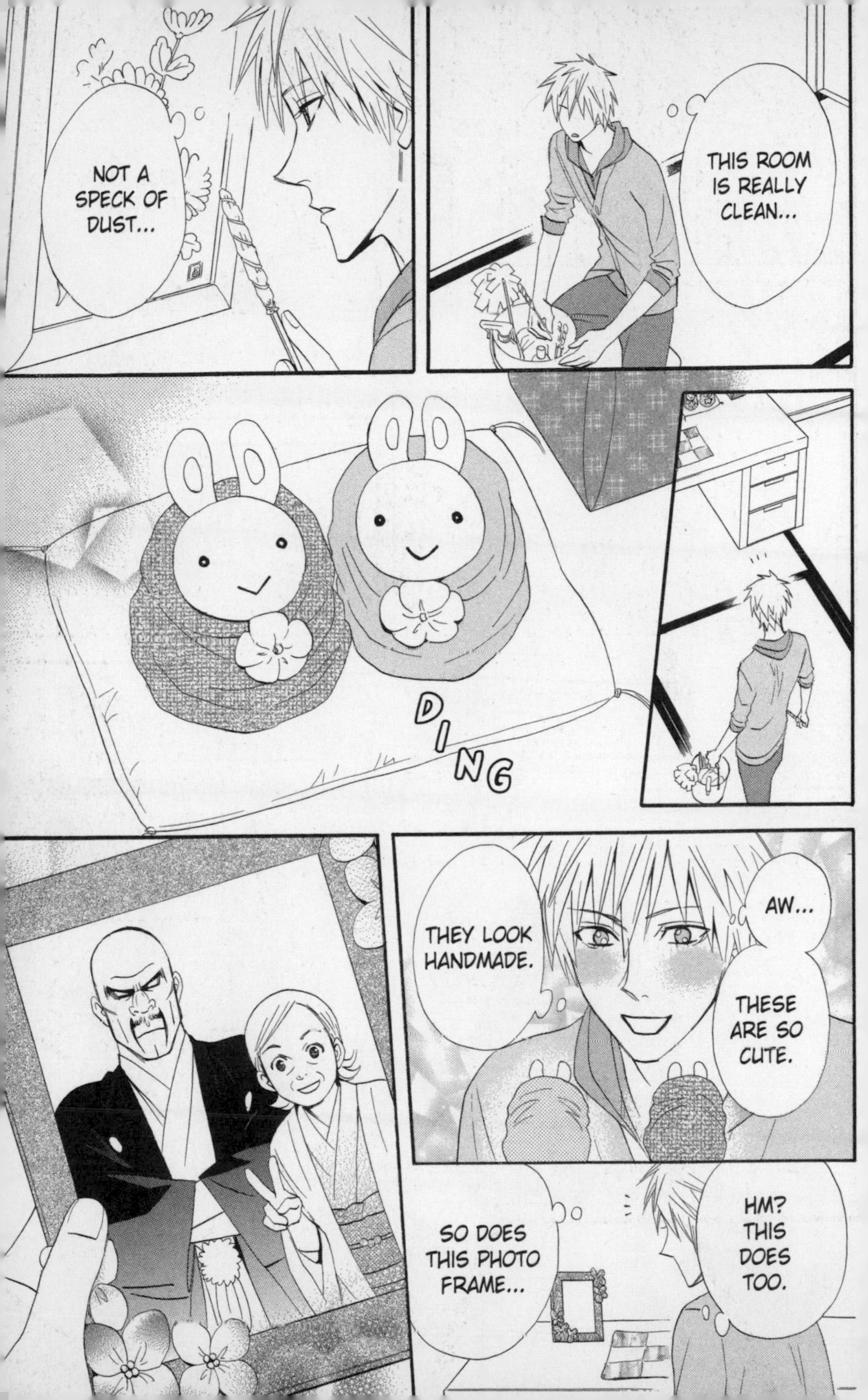
THIS ROOM IS REALLY CLEAN...
NOT A SPECK OF DUST...
DING
AW...
THESE ARE SO CUTE.
THEY LOOK HANDMADE.
HM? THIS DOES TOO.
SO DOES THIS PHOTO FRAME...

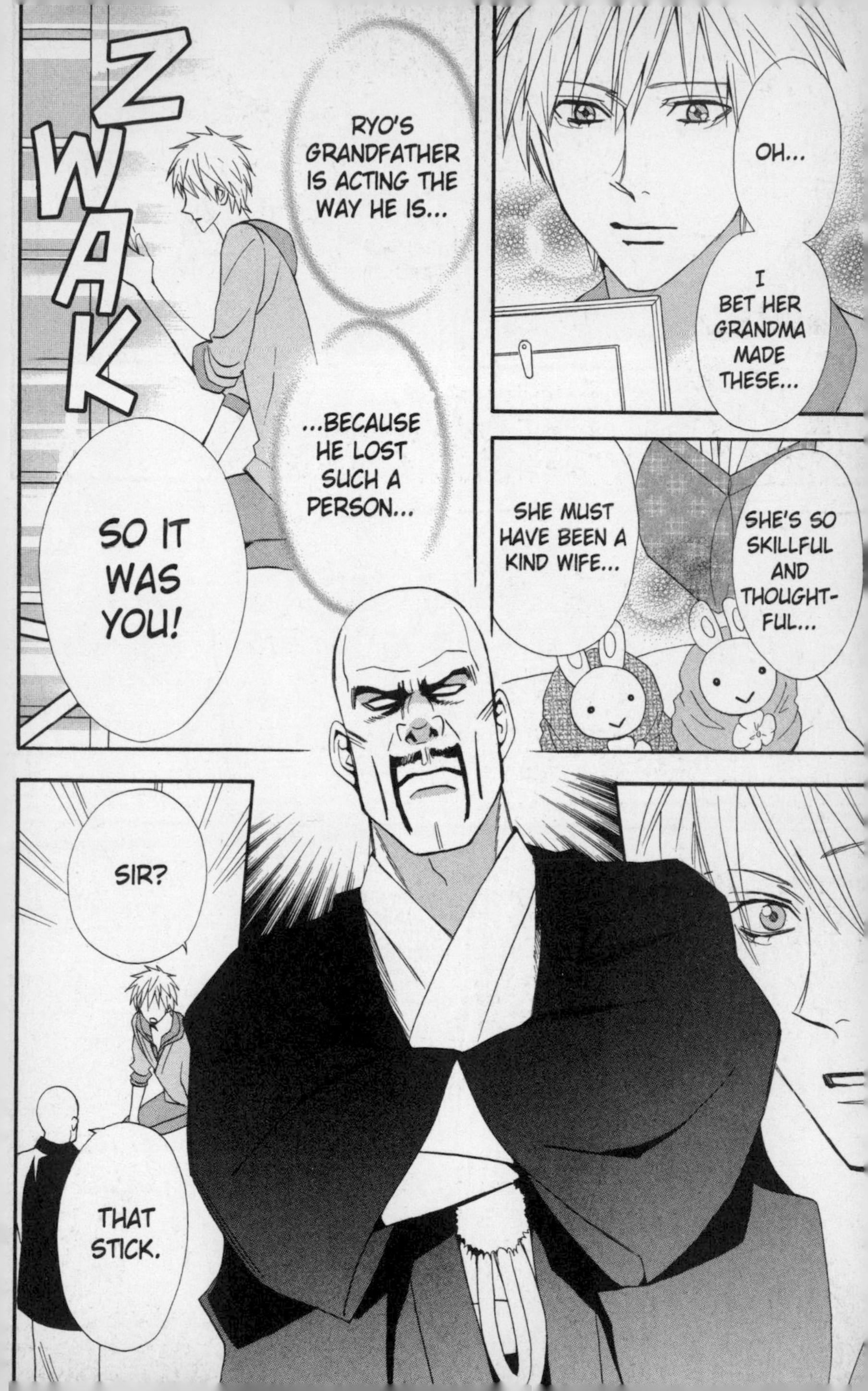
OH...
I BET HER GRANDMA MADE THESE...
SHE'S SO SKILLFUL AND THOUGHTFUL...
SHE MUST HAVE BEEN A KIND WIFE...
RYO'S GRANDFATHER IS ACTING THE WAY HE IS...
...BECAUSE HE LOST SUCH A PERSON...
ZWAK
SO IT WAS YOU!
SIR?
THAT STICK.

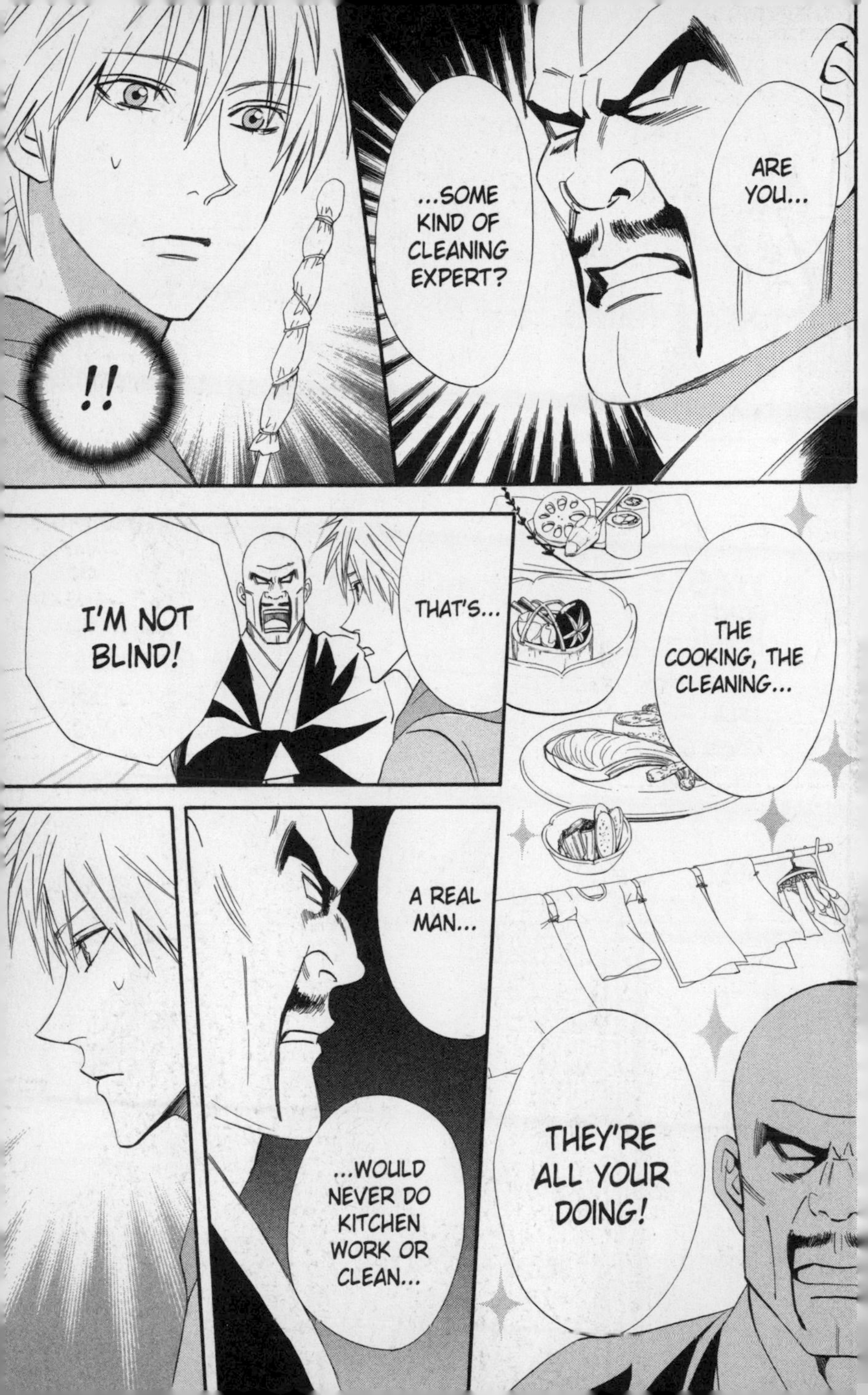
ARE YOU...
...SOME KIND OF CLEANING EXPERT?
!!
THE COOKING, THE CLEANING...
THEY'RE ALL YOUR DOING!
THAT'S...
I'M NOT BLIND!
A REAL MAN...
...WOULD NEVER DO KITCHEN WORK OR CLEAN...

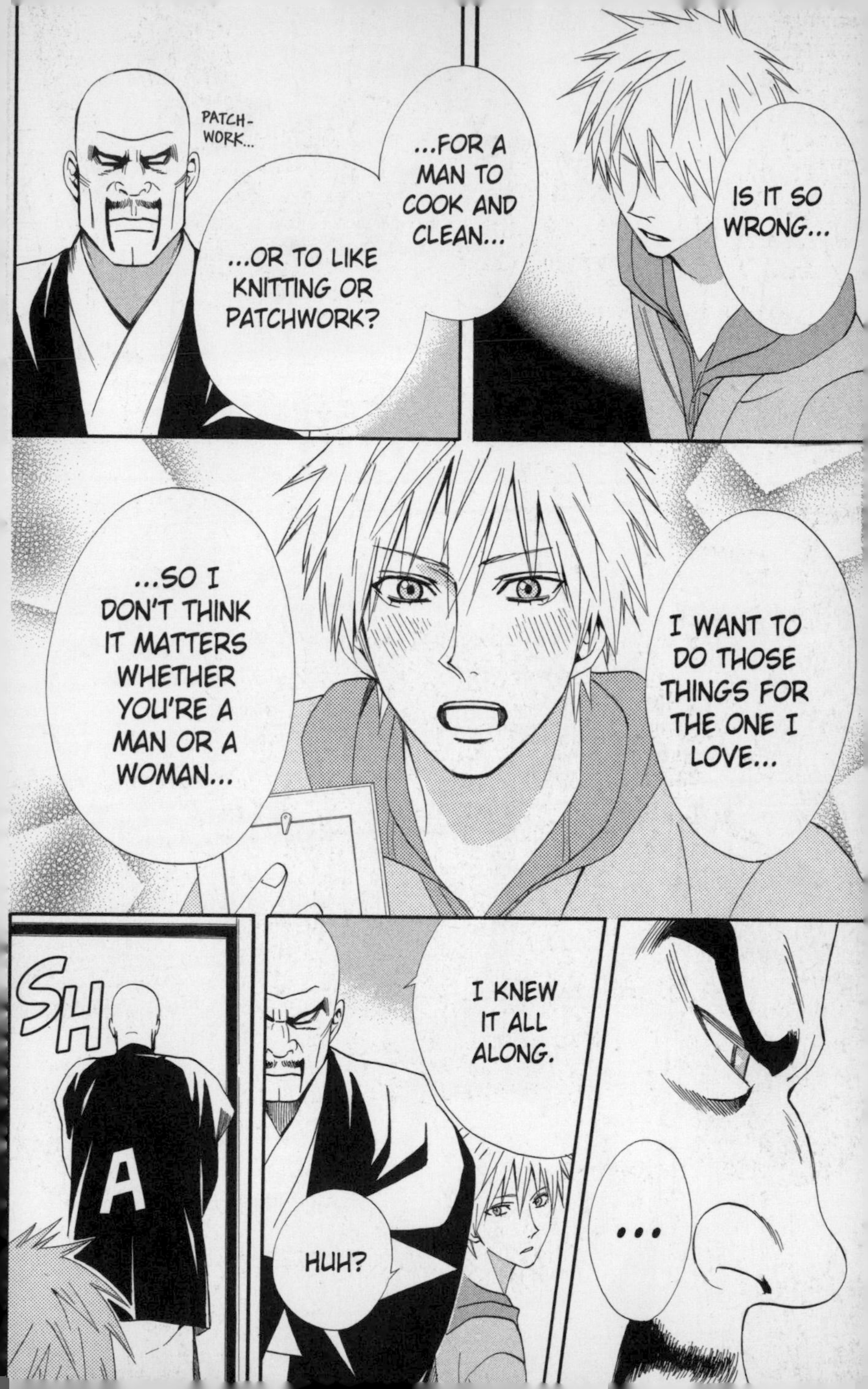
IS IT SO WRONG...
...FOR A MAN TO COOK AND CLEAN...
...OR TO LIKE KNITTING OR PATCHWORK?
PATCH-WORK...
I WANT TO DO THOSE THINGS FOR THE ONE I LOVE...
...SO I DON'T THINK IT MATTERS WHETHER YOU'RE A MAN OR A WOMAN...
...
I KNEW IT ALL ALONG.
HUH?
SHA

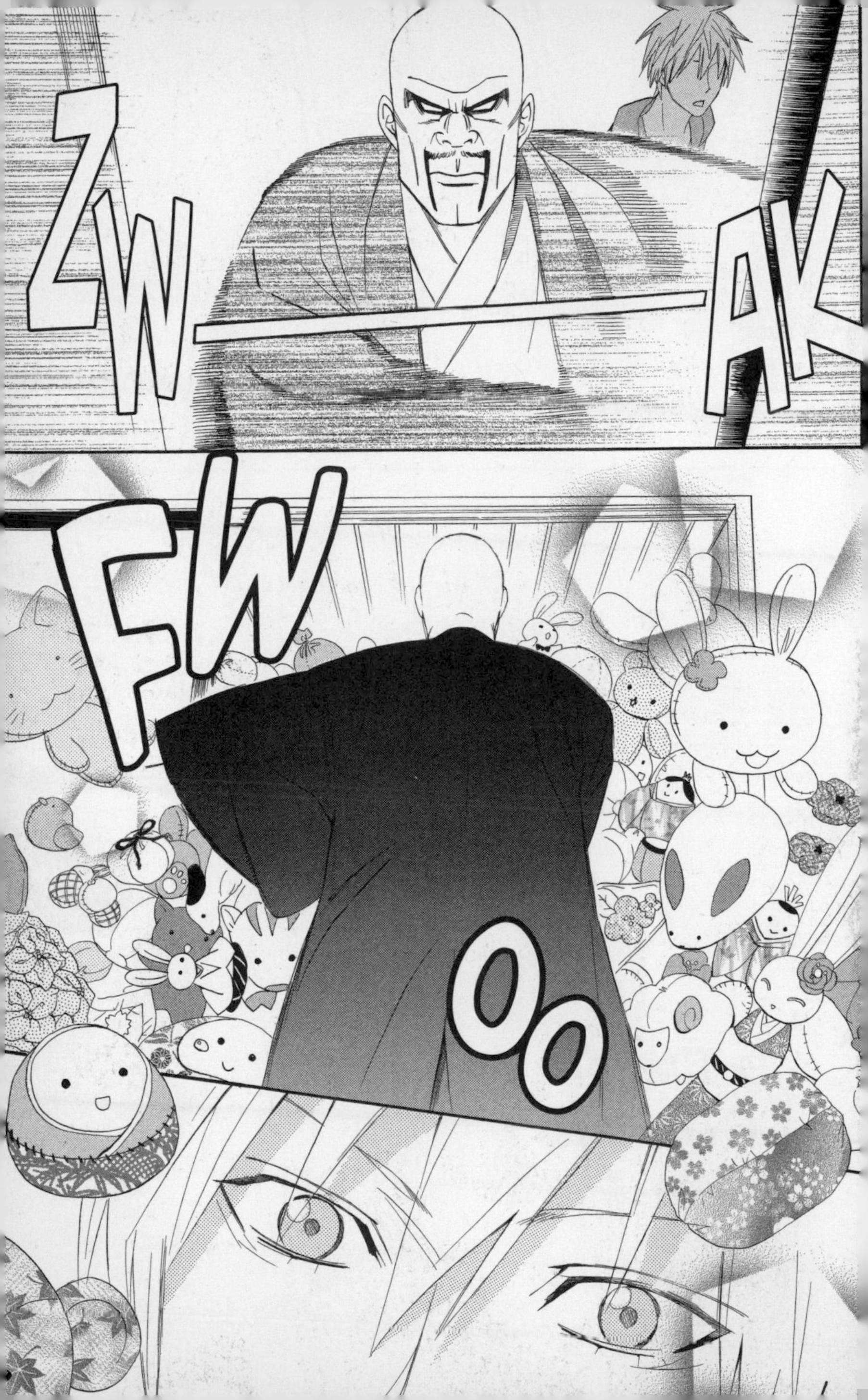

ZWAK
FW
OO

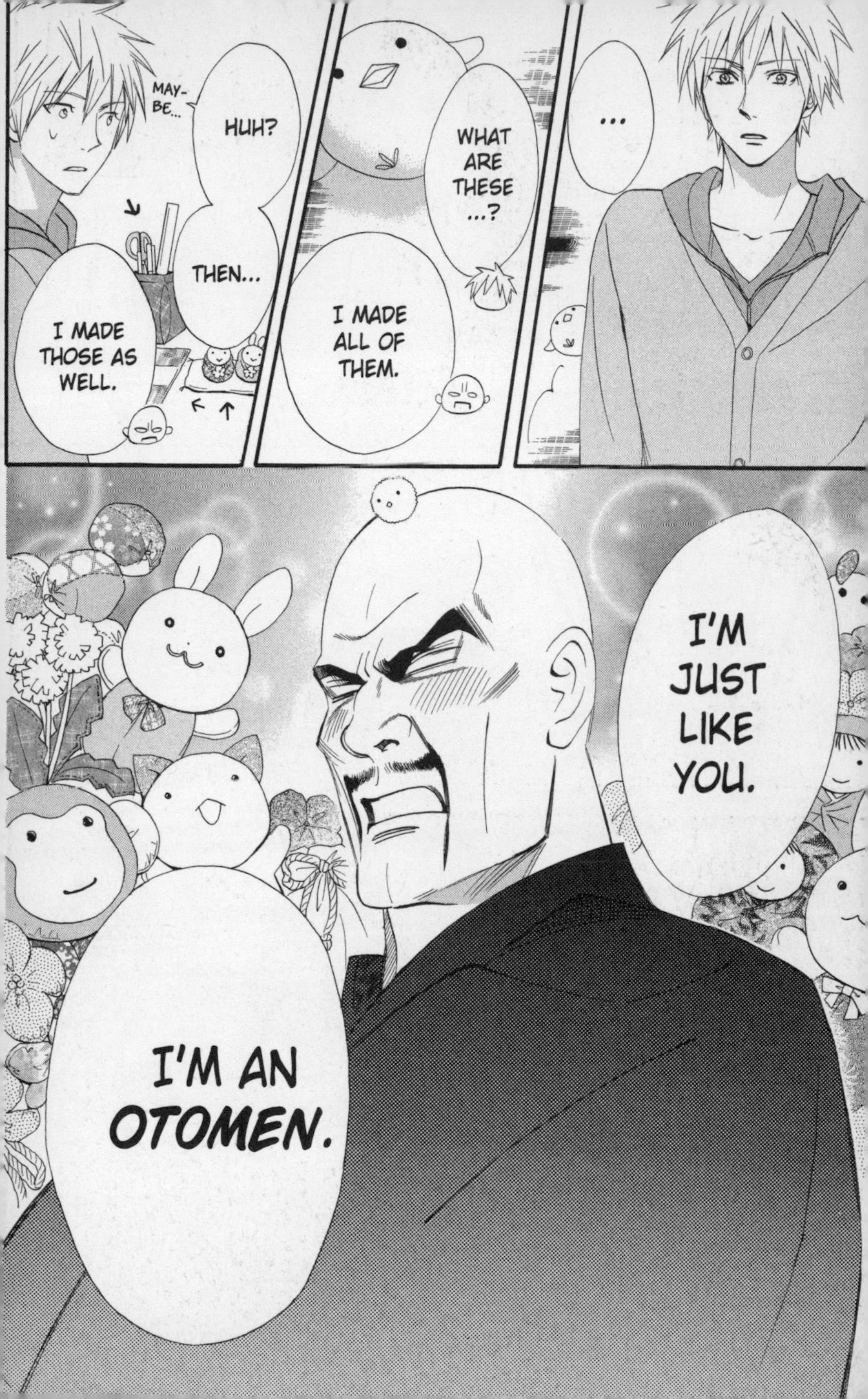

...
WHAT ARE THESE ...?
I MADE ALL OF THEM.
HUH?
MAY-BE...
THEN...
I MADE THOSE AS WELL.
I'M JUST LIKE YOU.
I'M AN OTOMEN.

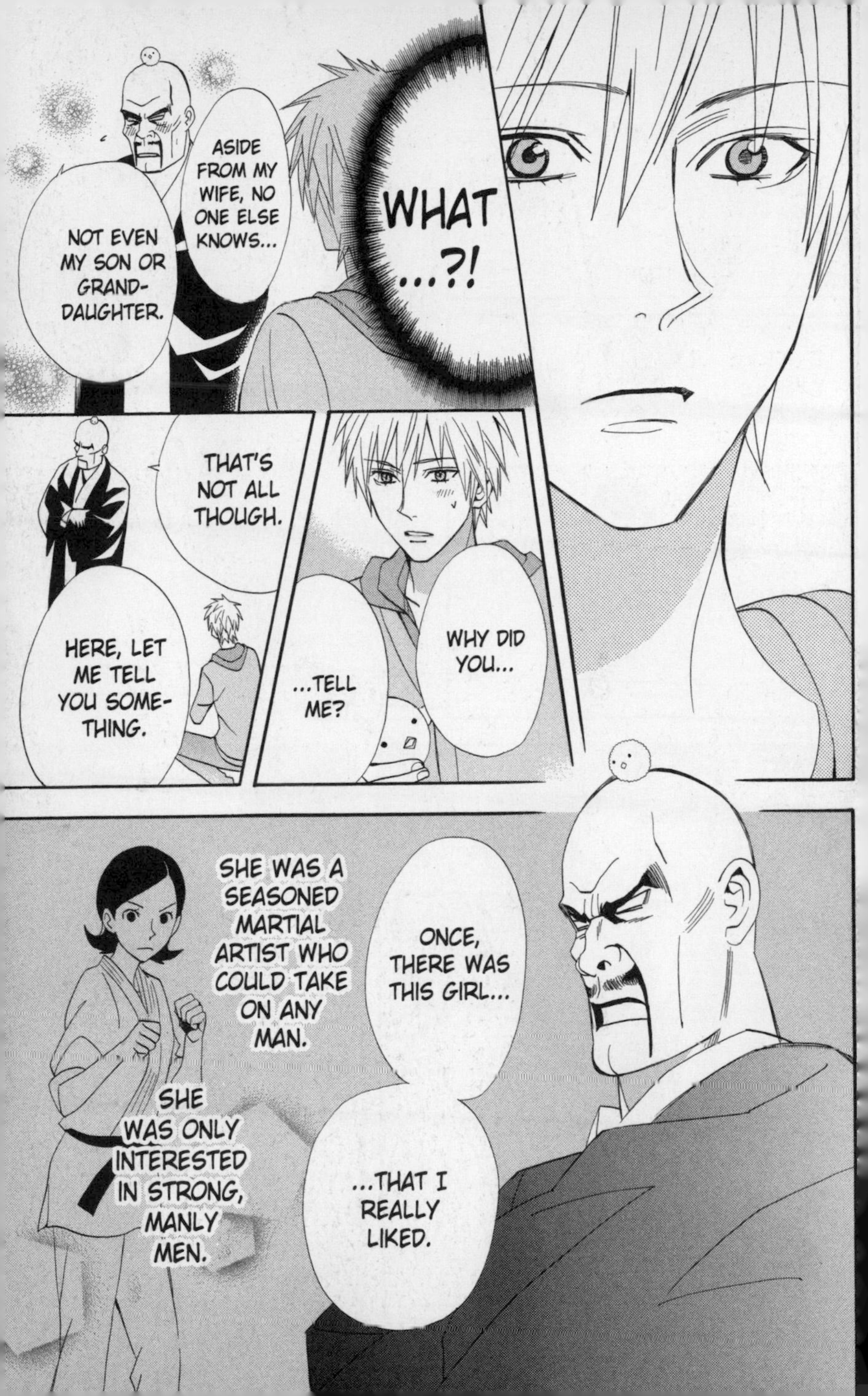
ASIDE FROM MY WIFE, NO ONE ELSE KNOWS...
NOT EVEN MY SON OR GRAND-DAUGHTER.
WHAT ...?!
WHY DID YOU...
...TELL ME?
THAT'S NOT ALL THOUGH.
HERE, LET ME TELL YOU SOME-THING.
ONCE, THERE WAS THIS GIRL...
...THAT I REALLY LIKED.
SHE WAS A SEASONED MARTIAL ARTIST WHO COULD TAKE ON ANY MAN.
SHE WAS ONLY INTERESTED IN STRONG, MANLY MEN.

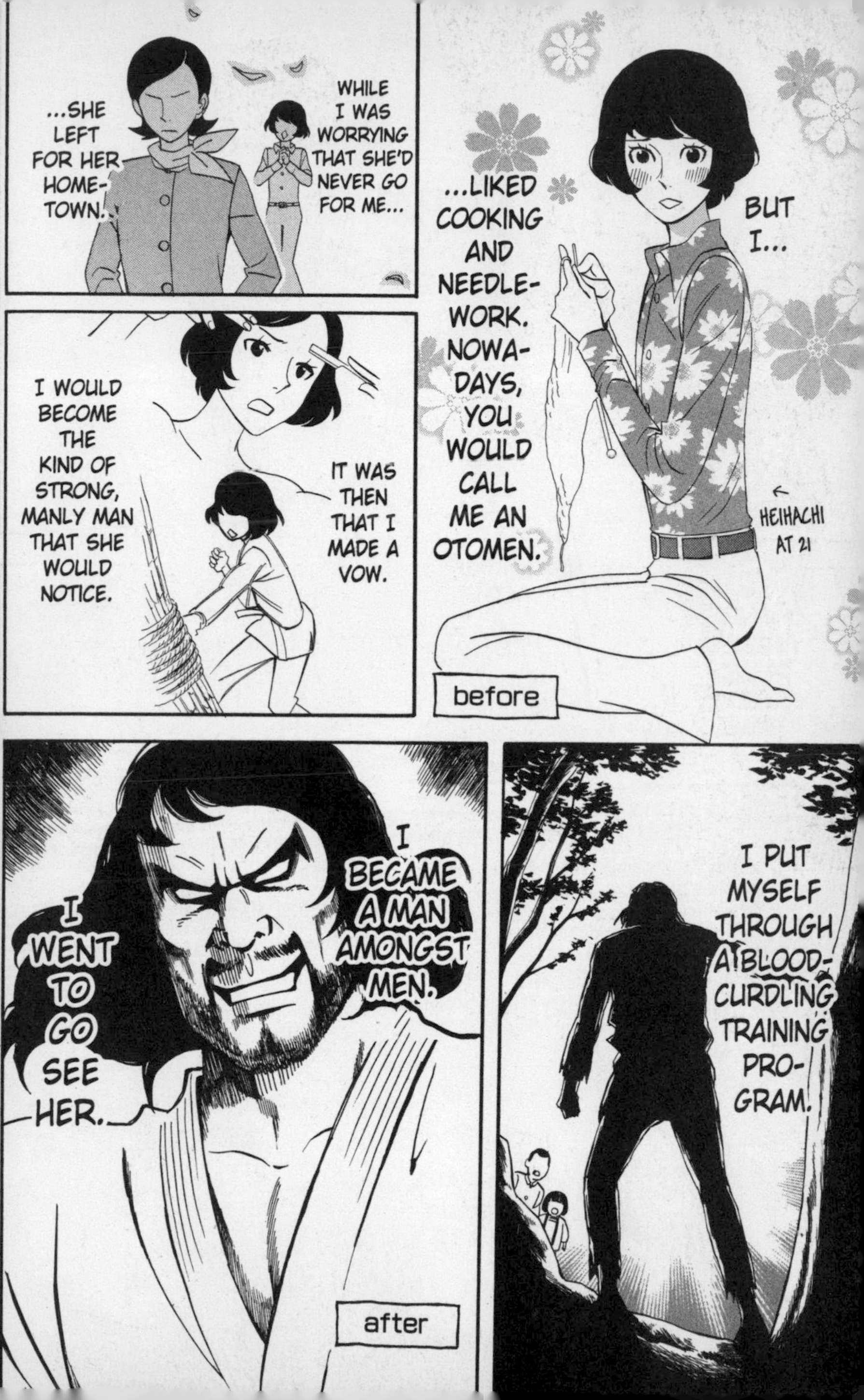
BUT I...
...LIKED COOKING AND NEEDLE-WORK. NOWA-DAYS, YOU WOULD CALL ME AN OTOMEN.
← HEIHACHI AT 21
before
WHILE I WAS WORRYING THAT SHE'D NEVER GO FOR ME...
...SHE LEFT FOR HER HOME-TOWN.
IT WAS THEN THAT I MADE A VOW.
I WOULD BECOME THE KIND OF STRONG, MANLY MAN THAT SHE WOULD NOTICE.
I PUT MYSELF THROUGH A BLOOD-CURDLING TRAINING PRO-GRAM.
I BECAME A MAN AMONGST MEN.
I WENT TO GO SEE HER.
after

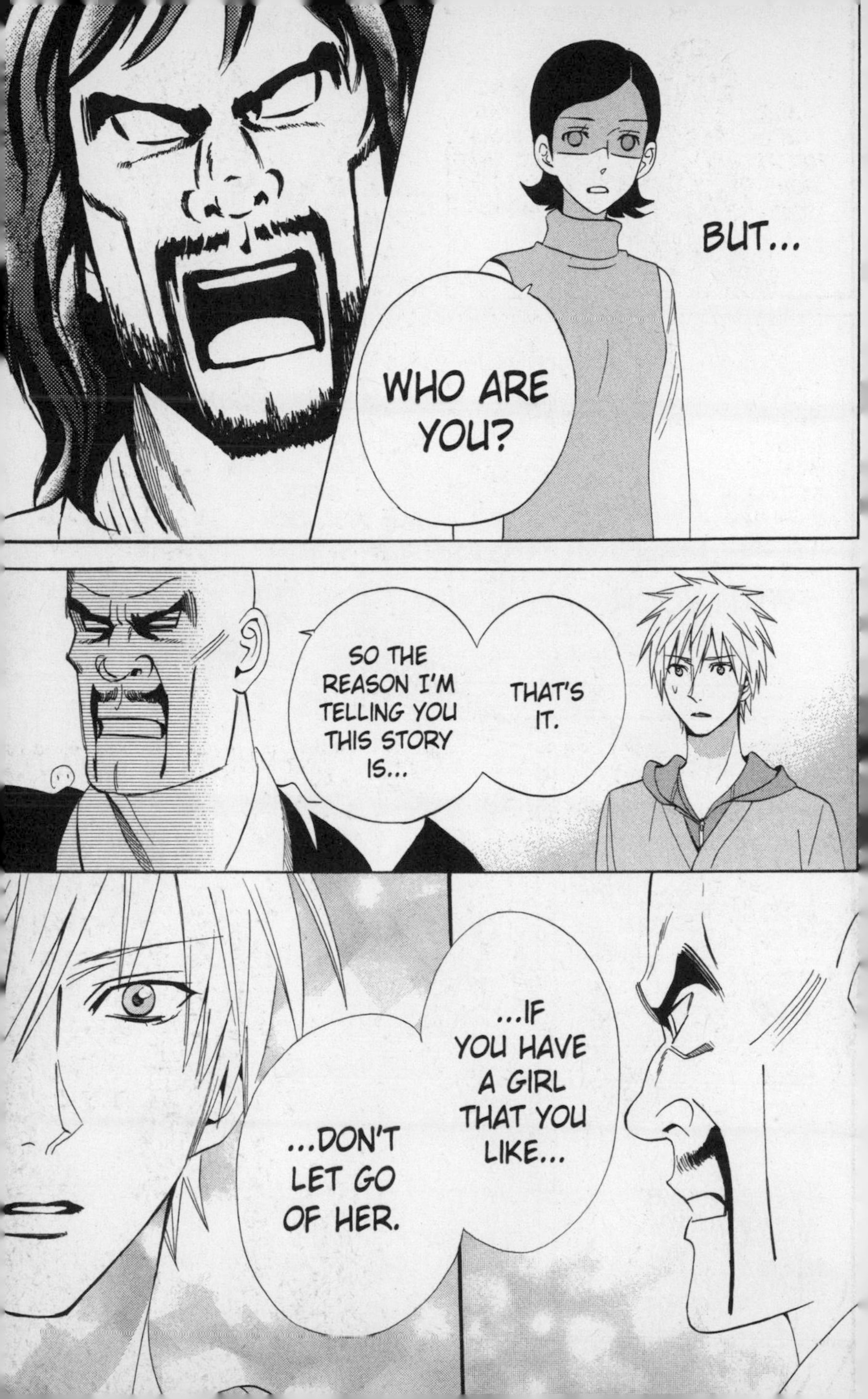
BUT...
WHO ARE YOU?
THAT'S IT.
SO THE REASON I'M TELLING YOU THIS STORY IS...
...IF YOU HAVE A GIRL THAT YOU LIKE...
...DON'T LET GO OF HER.

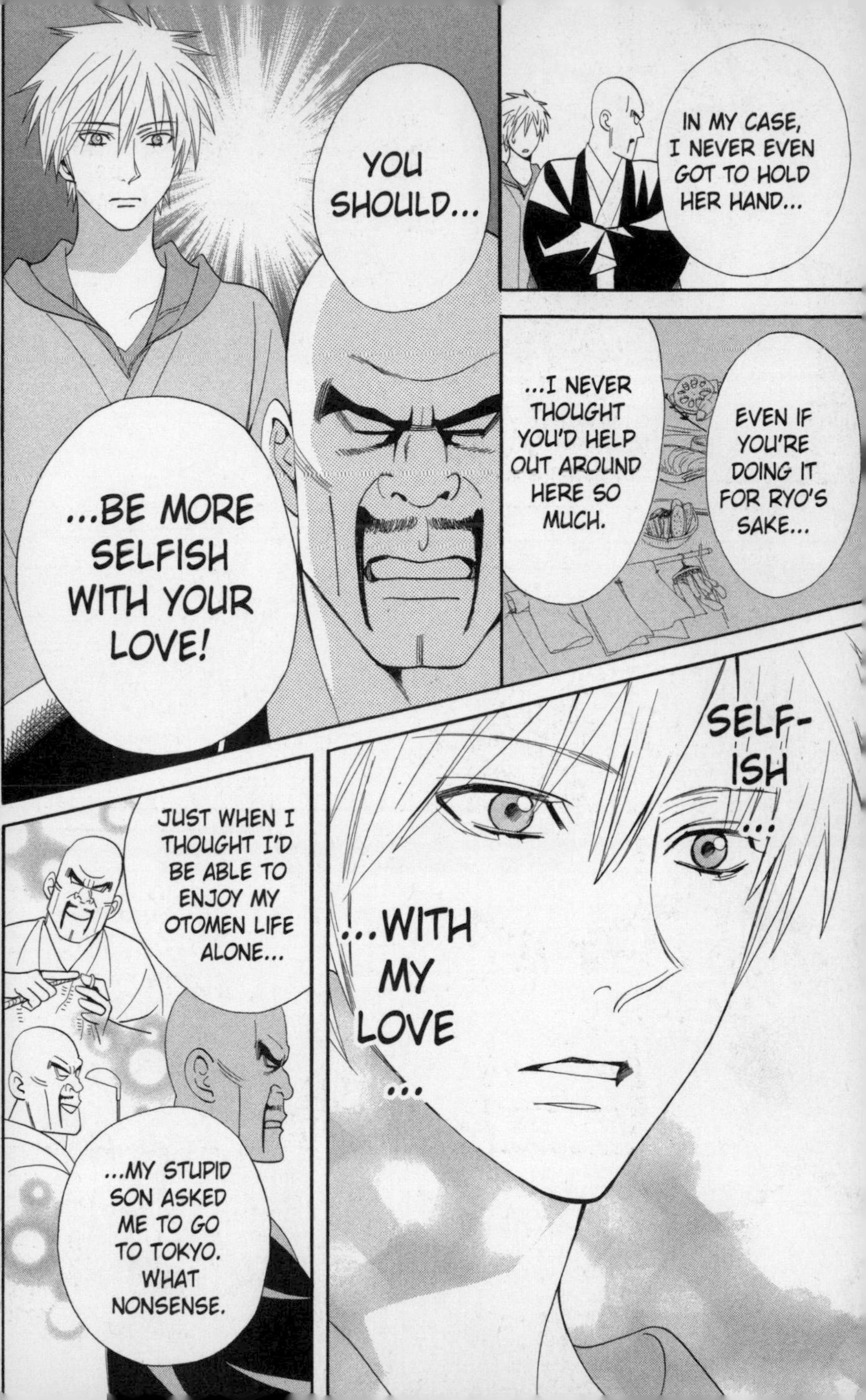
IN MY CASE, I NEVER EVEN GOT TO HOLD HER HAND...
EVEN IF YOU'RE DOING IT FOR RYO'S SAKE...
...I NEVER THOUGHT YOU'D HELP OUT AROUND HERE SO MUCH.
YOU SHOULD...
...BE MORE SELFISH WITH YOUR LOVE!
SELF-ISH...
...WITH MY LOVE...
JUST WHEN I THOUGHT I'D BE ABLE TO ENJOY MY OTOMEN LIFE ALONE...
...MY STUPID SON ASKED ME TO GO TO TOKYO. WHAT NONSENSE.

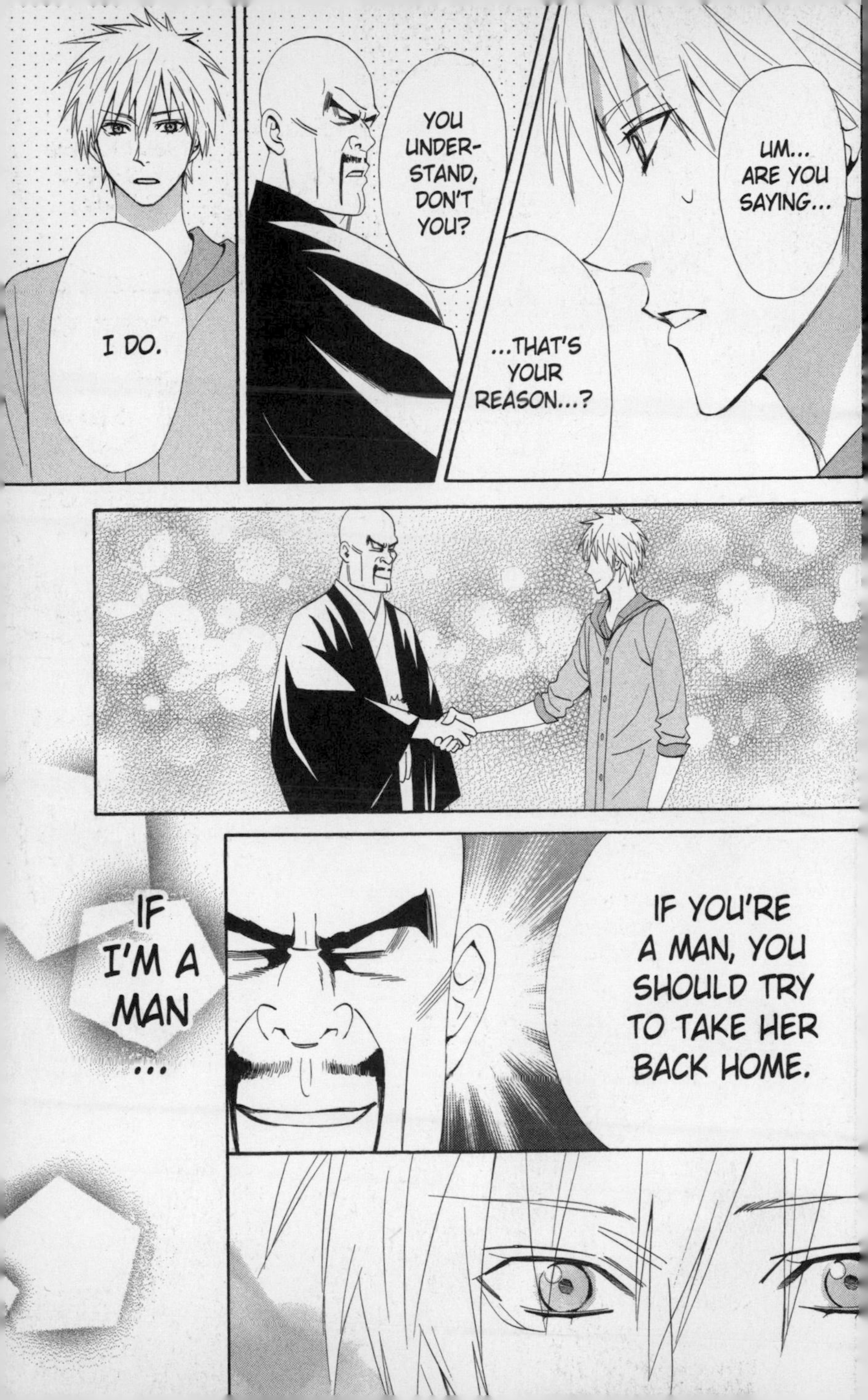
UM... ARE YOU SAYING...
...THAT'S YOUR REASON...?
YOU UNDER-STAND, DON'T YOU?
I DO.
IF YOU'RE A MAN, YOU SHOULD TRY TO TAKE HER BACK HOME.
IF I'M A MAN ...

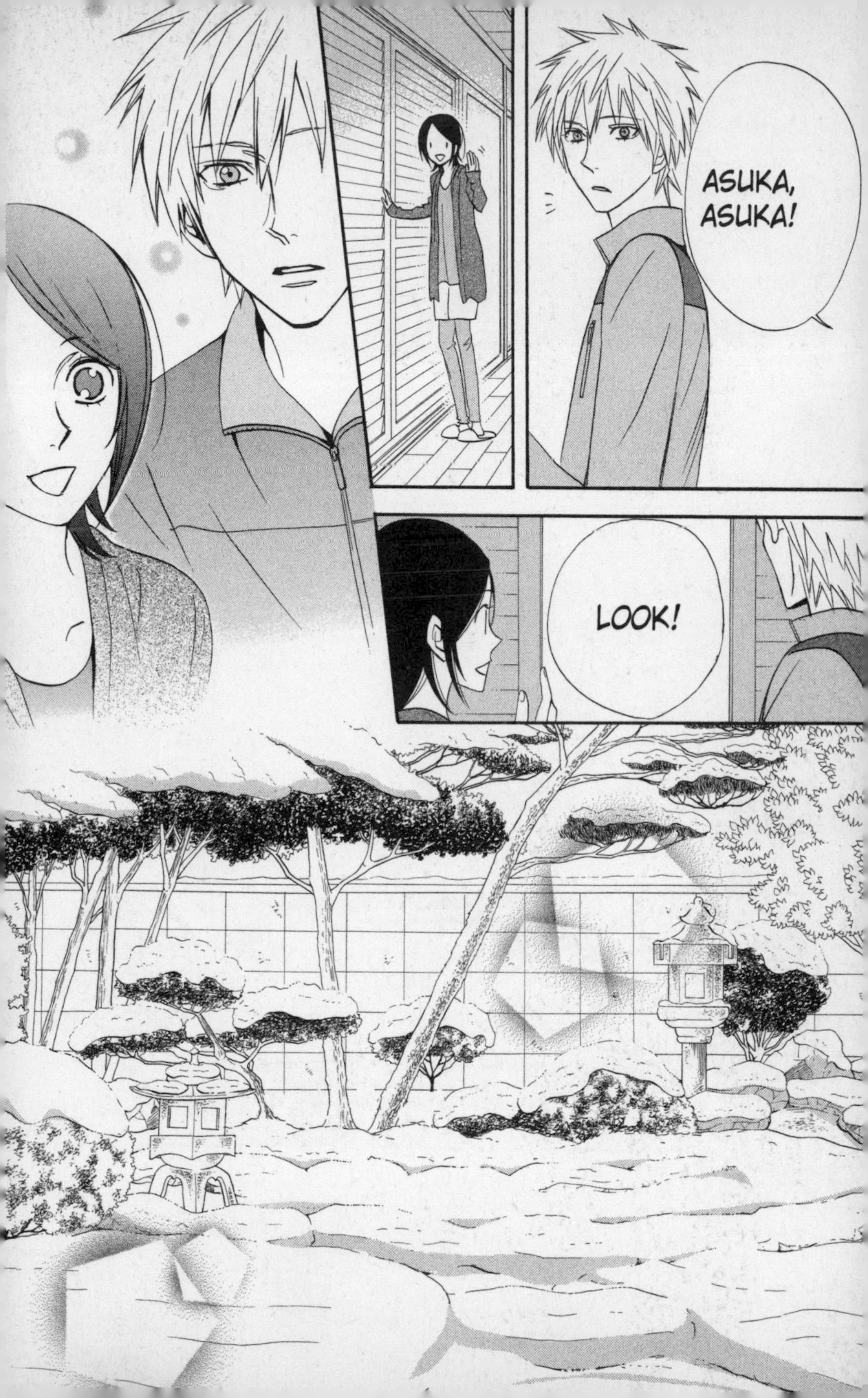
ASUKA, ASUKA!
LOOK!

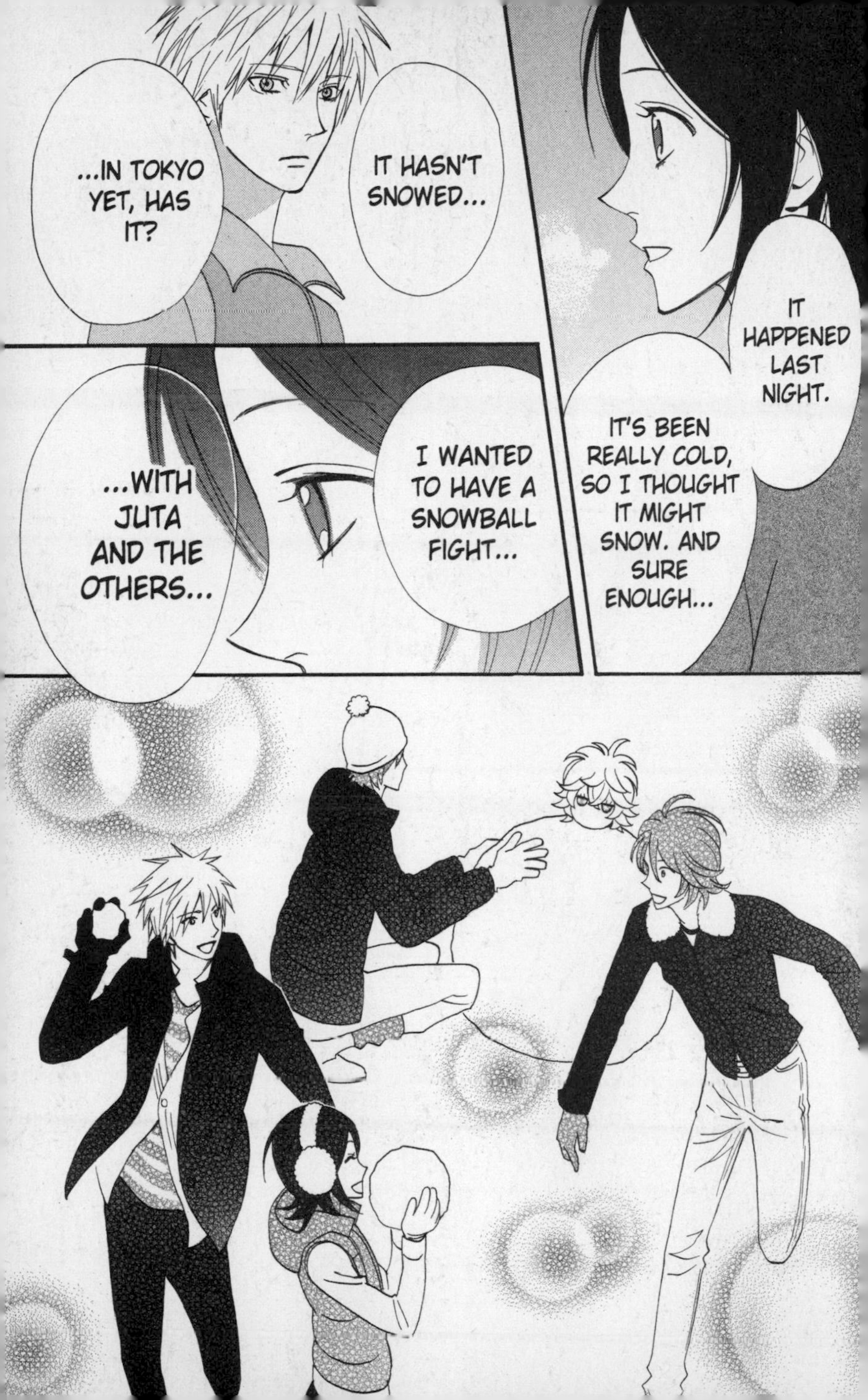
IT HAPPENED LAST NIGHT.
IT'S BEEN REALLY COLD, SO I THOUGHT IT MIGHT SNOW. AND SURE ENOUGH...
IT HASN'T SNOWED...
...IN TOKYO YET, HAS IT?
I WANTED TO HAVE A SNOWBALL FIGHT...
...WITH JUTA AND THE OTHERS...

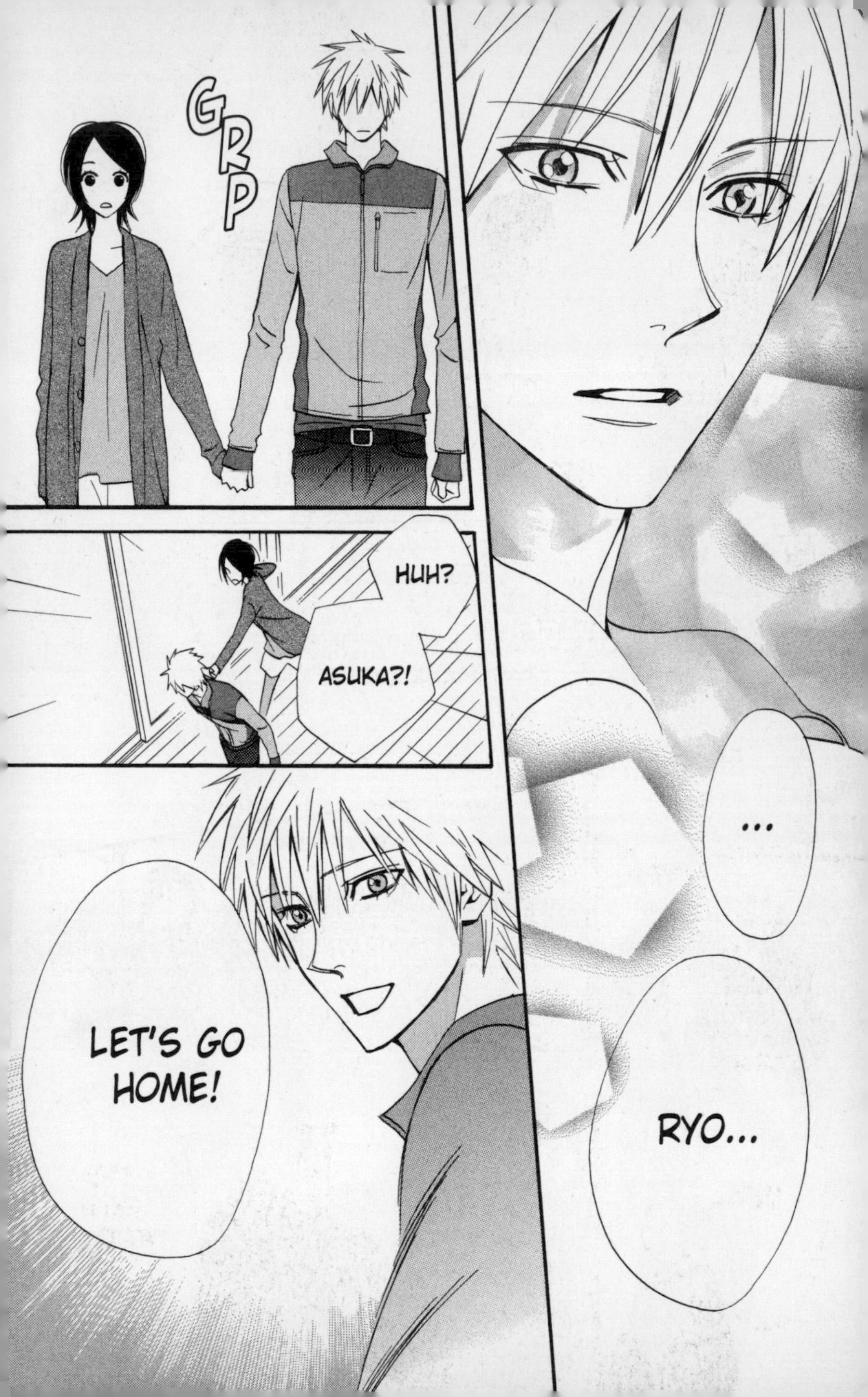
...
RYO...
GRP
HUH?
ASUKA?!
LET'S GO HOME!

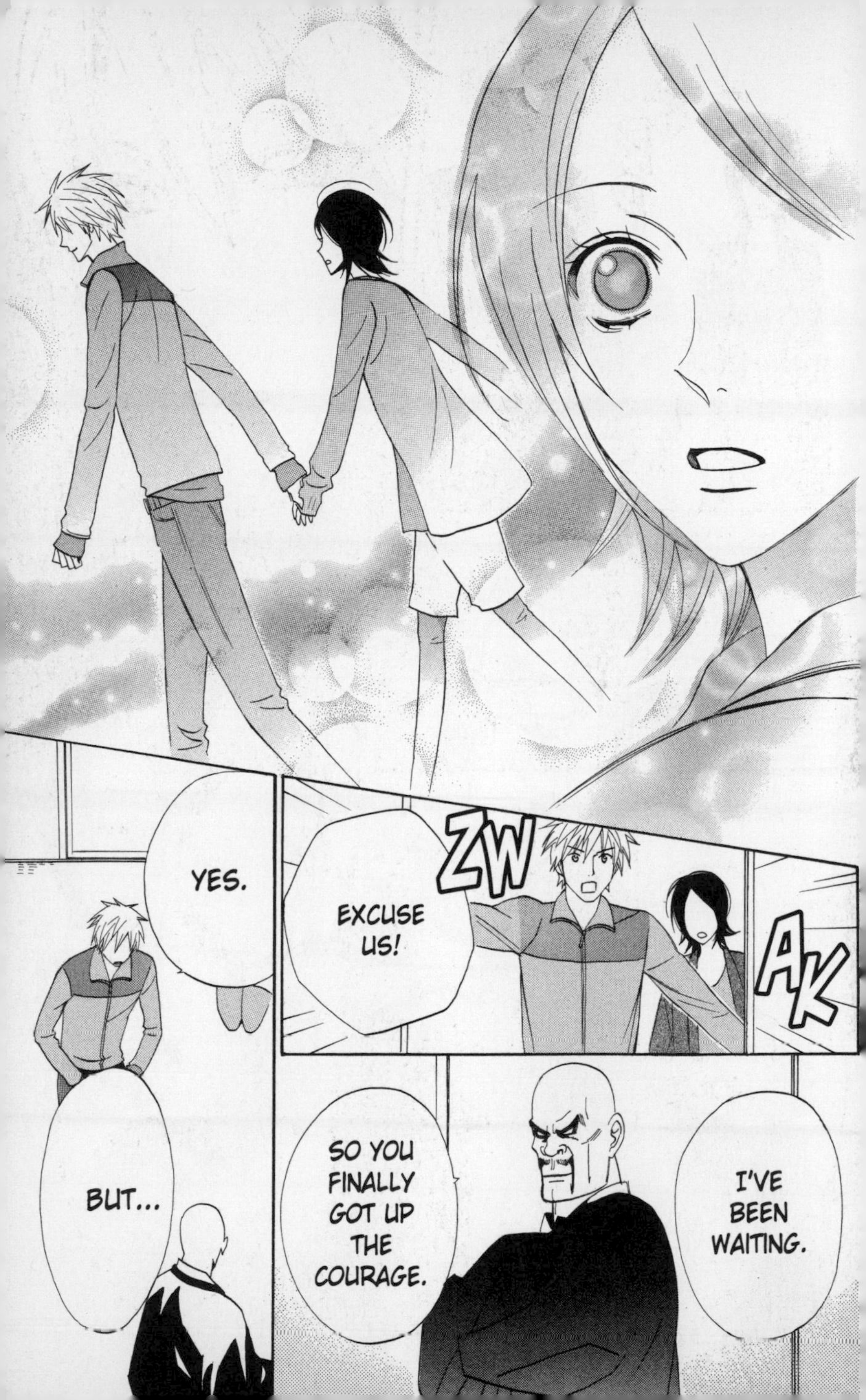
ZW
AK
EXCUSE US!
I'VE BEEN WAITING.
SO YOU FINALLY GOT UP THE COURAGE.
YES.
BUT...

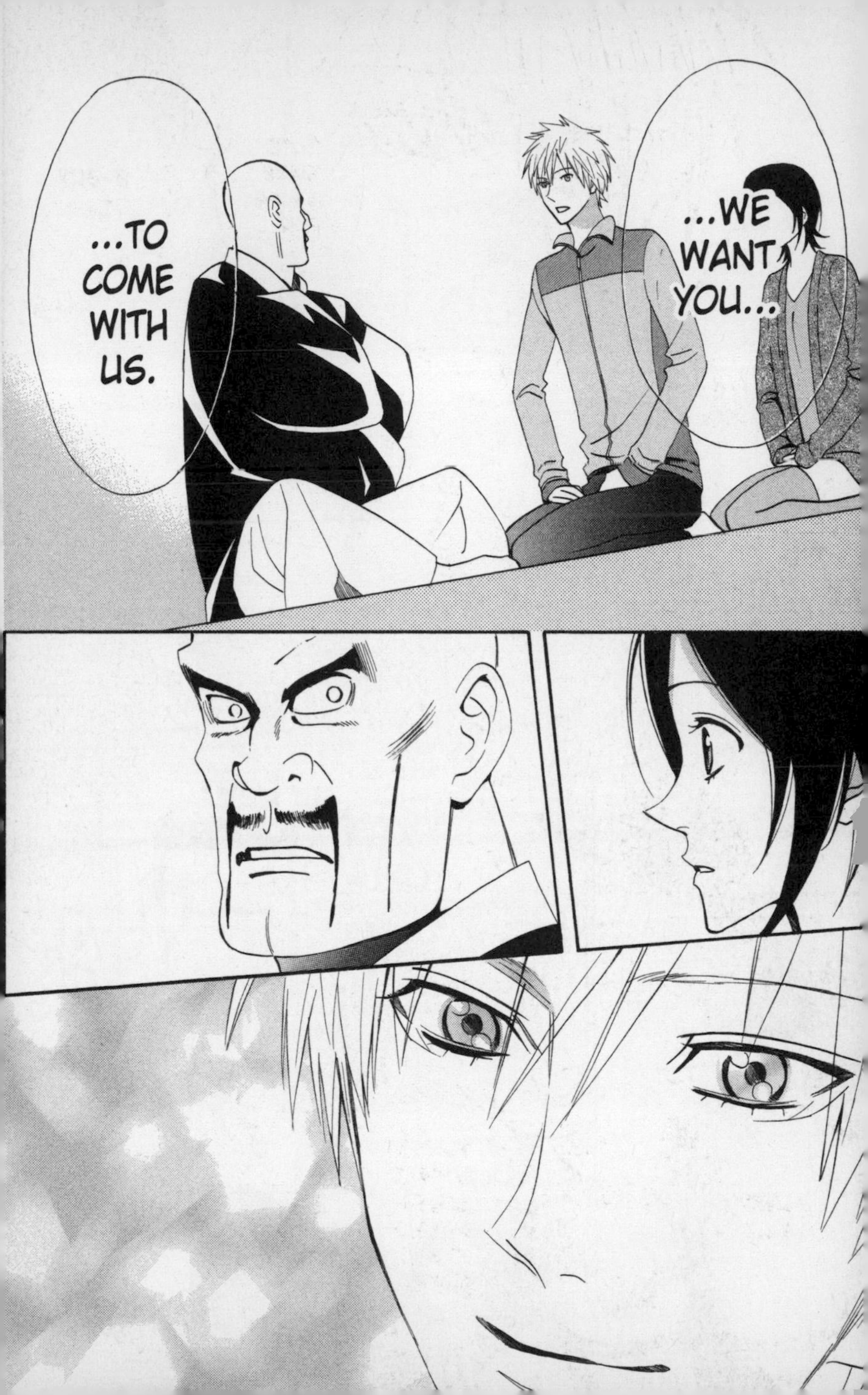
...WE WANT YOU...
...TO COME WITH US.

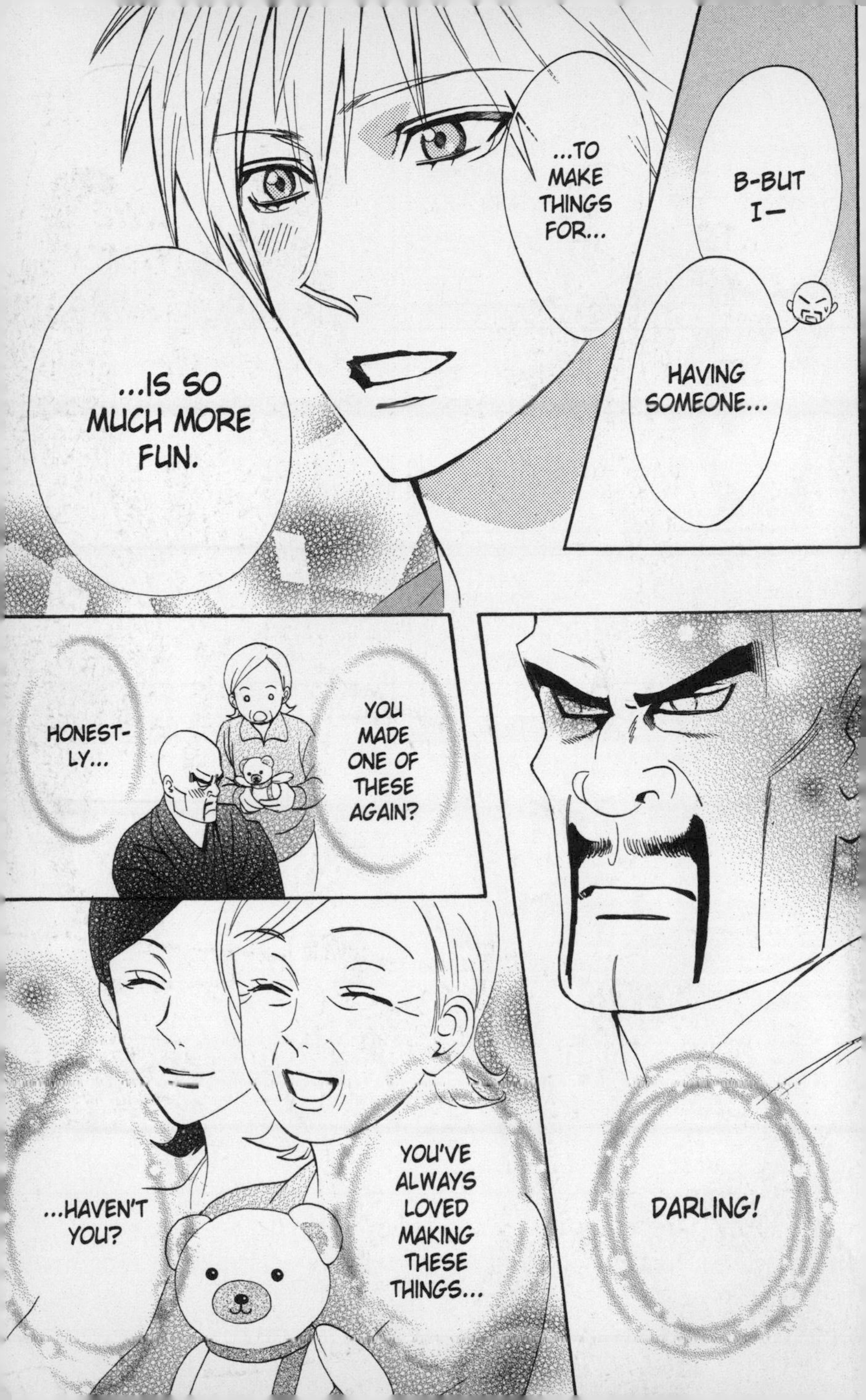
B-BUT I—
HAVING SOMEONE...
...TO MAKE THINGS FOR...
...IS SO MUCH MORE FUN.
DARLING!
YOU MADE ONE OF THESE AGAIN?
HONESTLY...
YOU'VE ALWAYS LOVED MAKING THESE THINGS...
...HAVEN'T YOU?

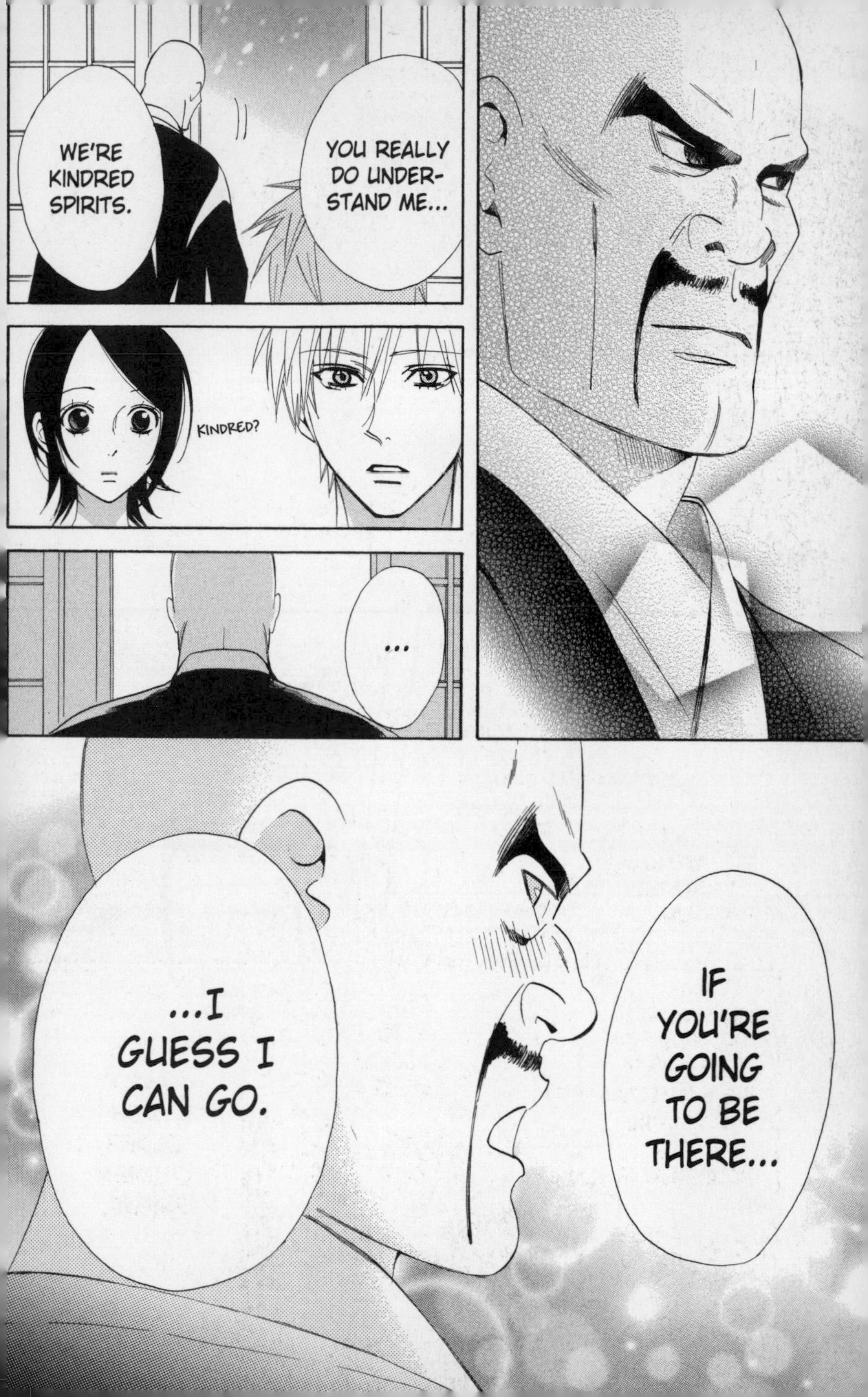
YOU REALLY DO UNDER-STAND ME...
WE'RE KINDRED SPIRITS.
KINDRED?
...
IF YOU'RE GOING TO BE THERE...
...I GUESS I CAN GO.

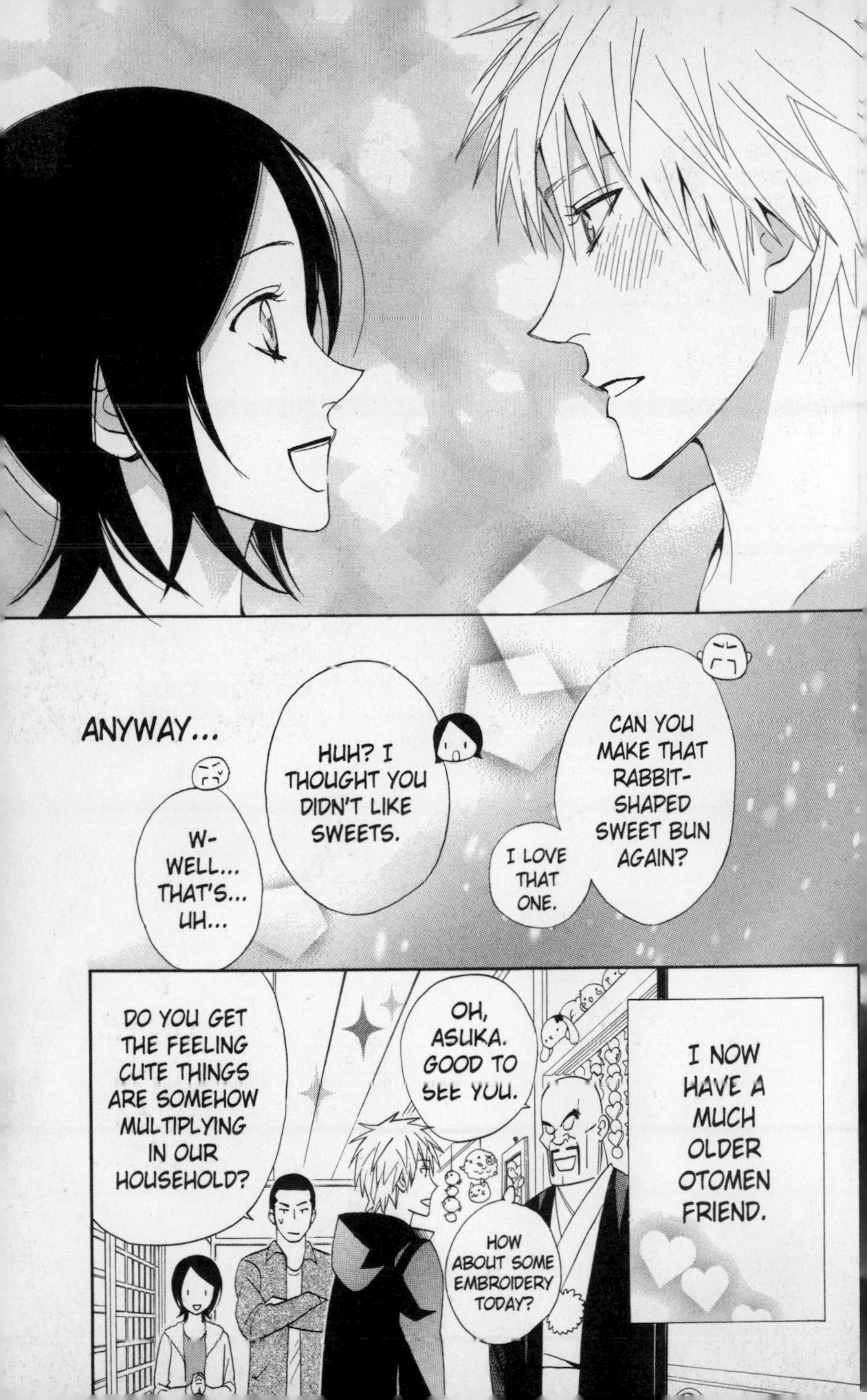
CAN YOU MAKE THAT RABBIT-SHAPED SWEET BUN AGAIN?
I LOVE THAT ONE.
HUH? I THOUGHT YOU DIDN'T LIKE SWEETS.
W-WELL... THAT'S... UH...
ANYWAY...
I NOW HAVE A MUCH OLDER OTOMEN FRIEND.
OH, ASUKA. GOOD TO SEE YOU.
HOW ABOUT SOME EMBROIDERY TODAY?
DO YOU GET THE FEELING CUTE THINGS ARE SOMEHOW MULTIPLYING IN OUR HOUSEHOLD?

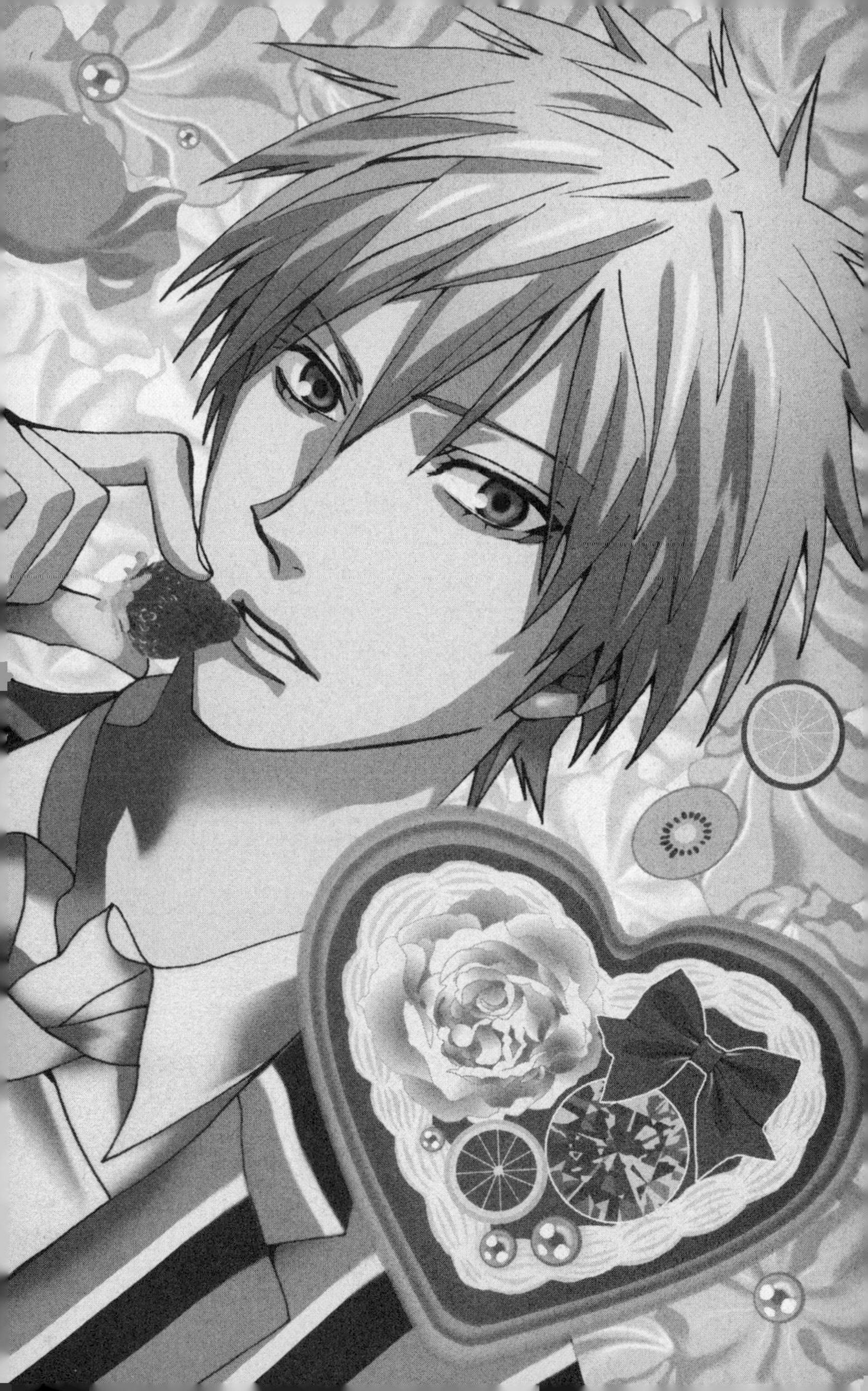

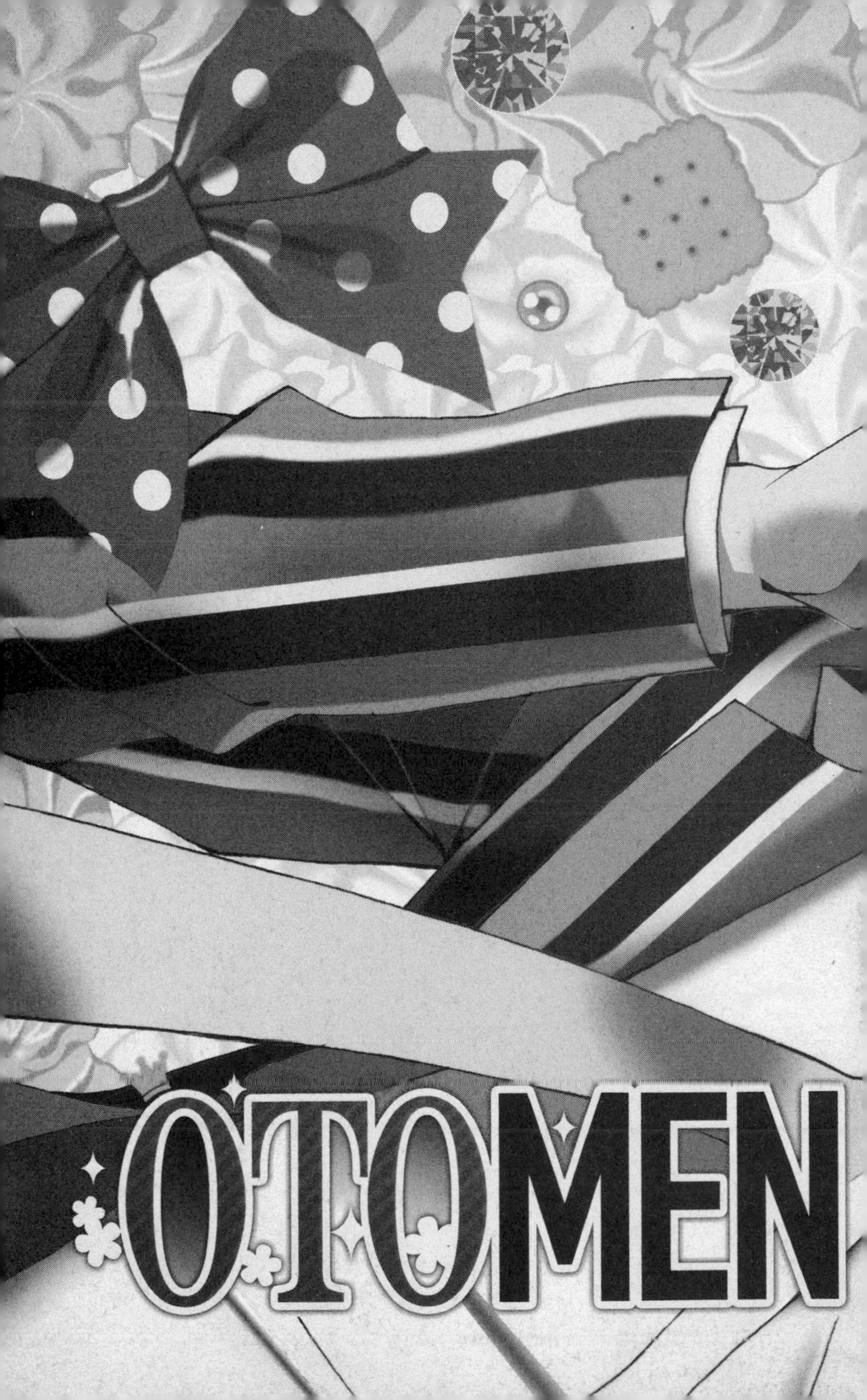
OTOMEN

OTOMEN

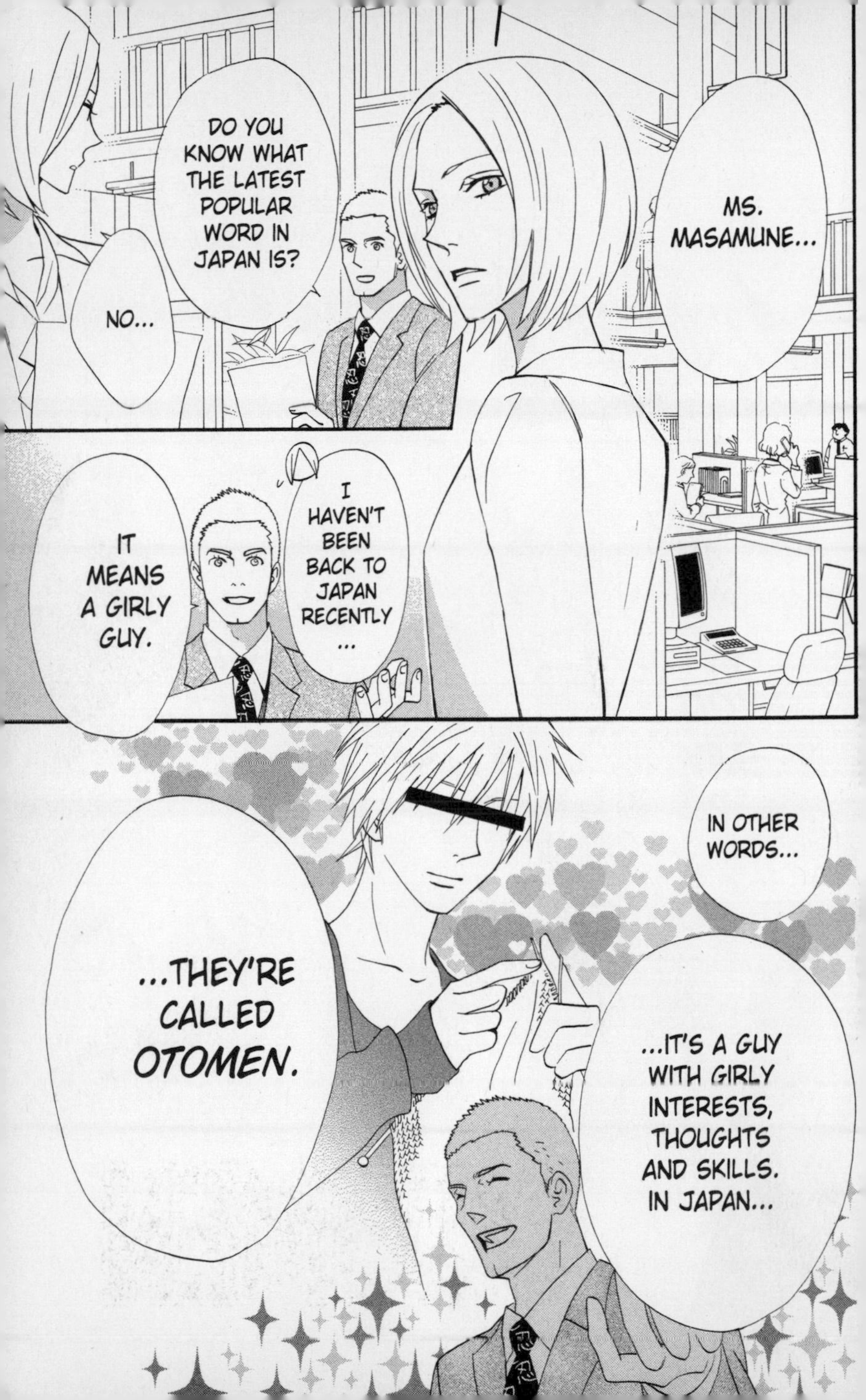
MS. MASAMUNE...
DO YOU KNOW WHAT THE LATEST POPULAR WORD IN JAPAN IS?
NO...
I HAVEN'T BEEN BACK TO JAPAN RECENTLY ...
IT MEANS A GIRLY GUY.
IN OTHER WORDS...
...IT'S A GUY WITH GIRLY INTERESTS, THOUGHTS AND SKILLS. IN JAPAN...
...THEY'RE CALLED OTOMEN.

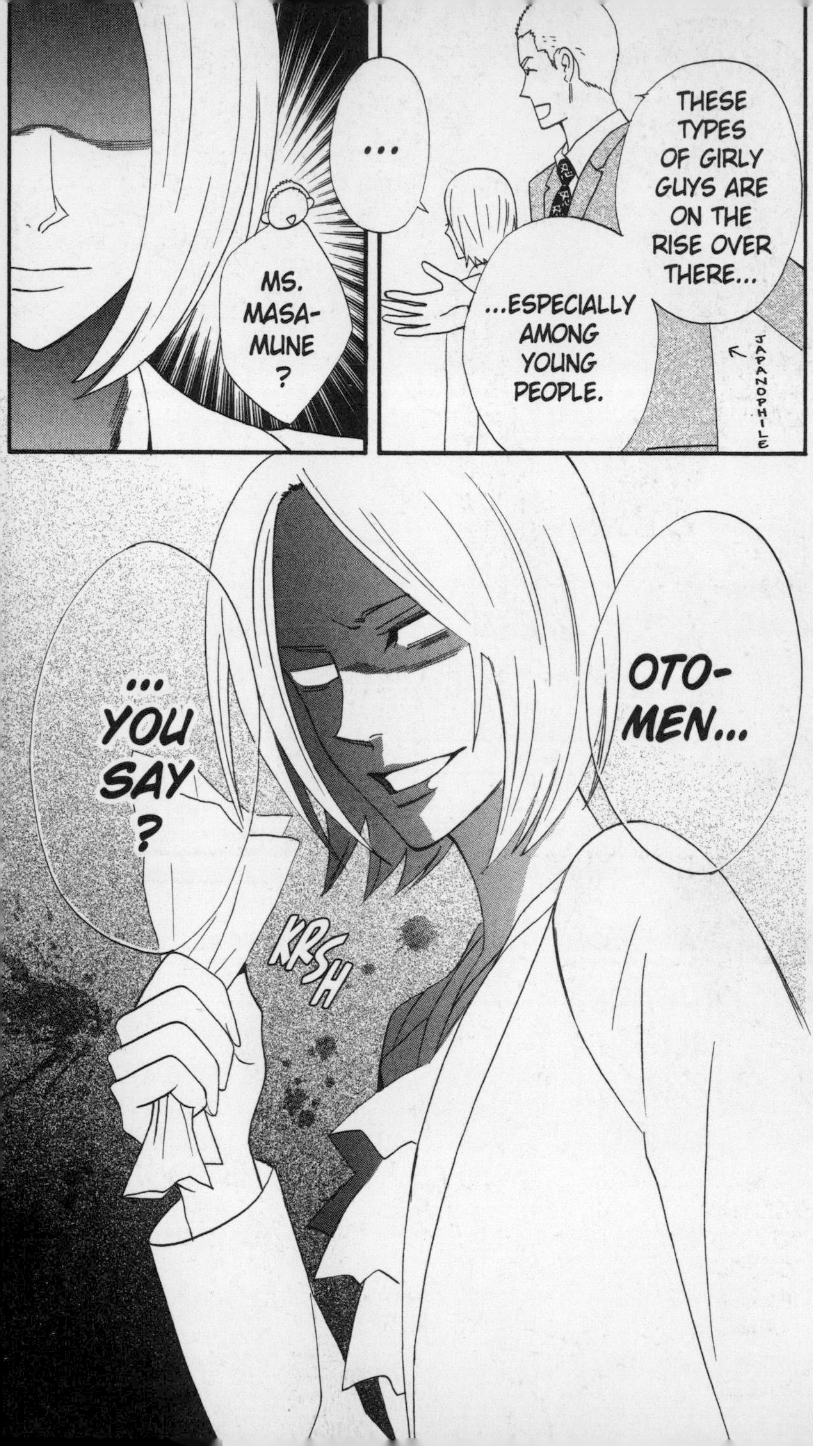
THESE TYPES OF GIRLY GUYS ARE ON THE RISE OVER THERE...
...ESPECIALLY AMONG YOUNG PEOPLE.
JAPANOPHILE
...
MS. MASAMUNE?
OTO-MEN...
...YOU SAY?
KRSH

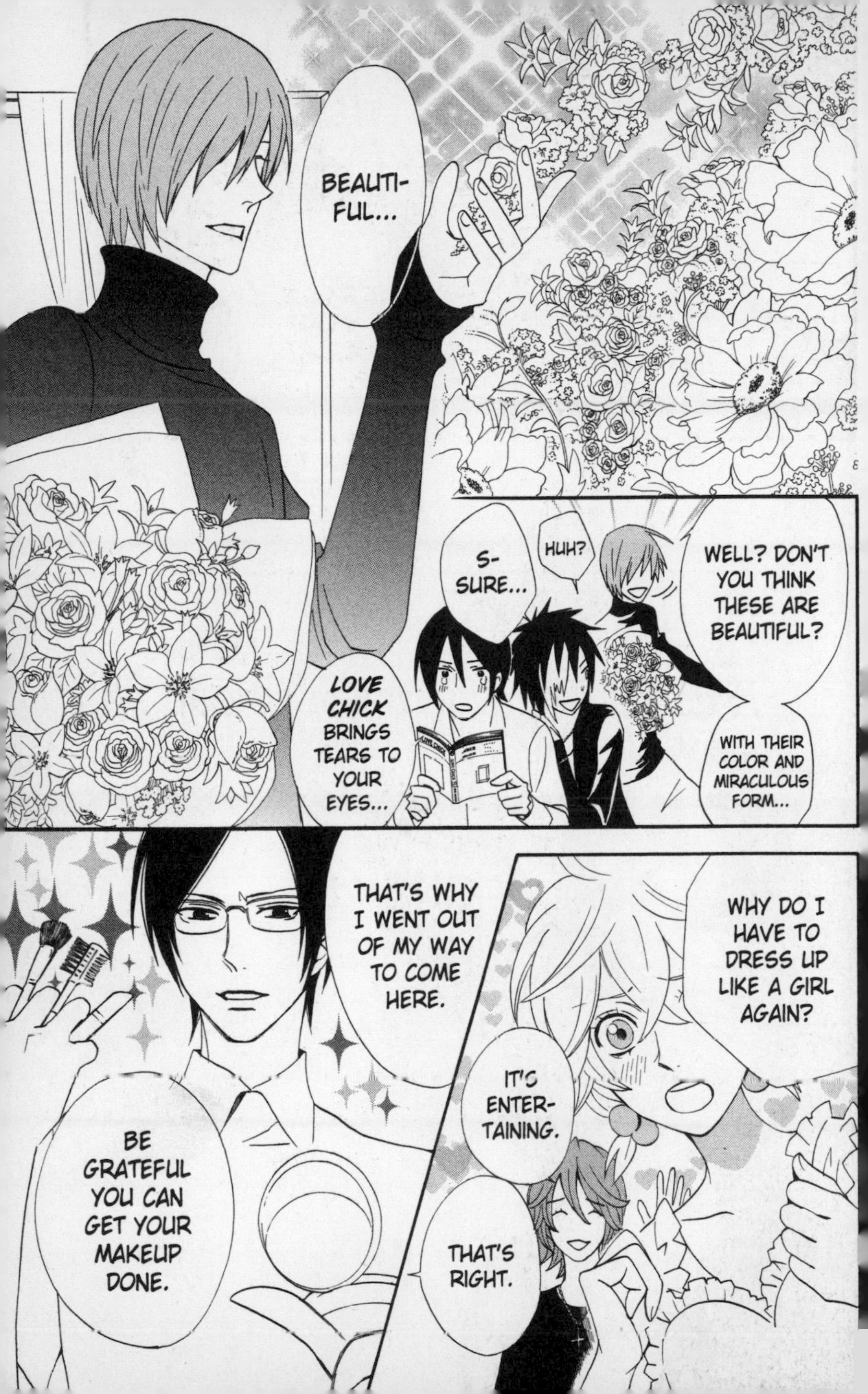
BEAUTIFUL...
WELL? DON'T YOU THINK THESE ARE BEAUTIFUL?
WITH THEIR COLOR AND MIRACULOUS FORM...
HUH?
S-SURE...
LOVE CHICK BRINGS TEARS TO YOUR EYES...
WHY DO I HAVE TO DRESS UP LIKE A GIRL AGAIN?
IT'S ENTERTAINING.
THAT'S RIGHT.
THAT'S WHY I WENT OUT OF MY WAY TO COME HERE.
BE GRATEFUL YOU CAN GET YOUR MAKEUP DONE.

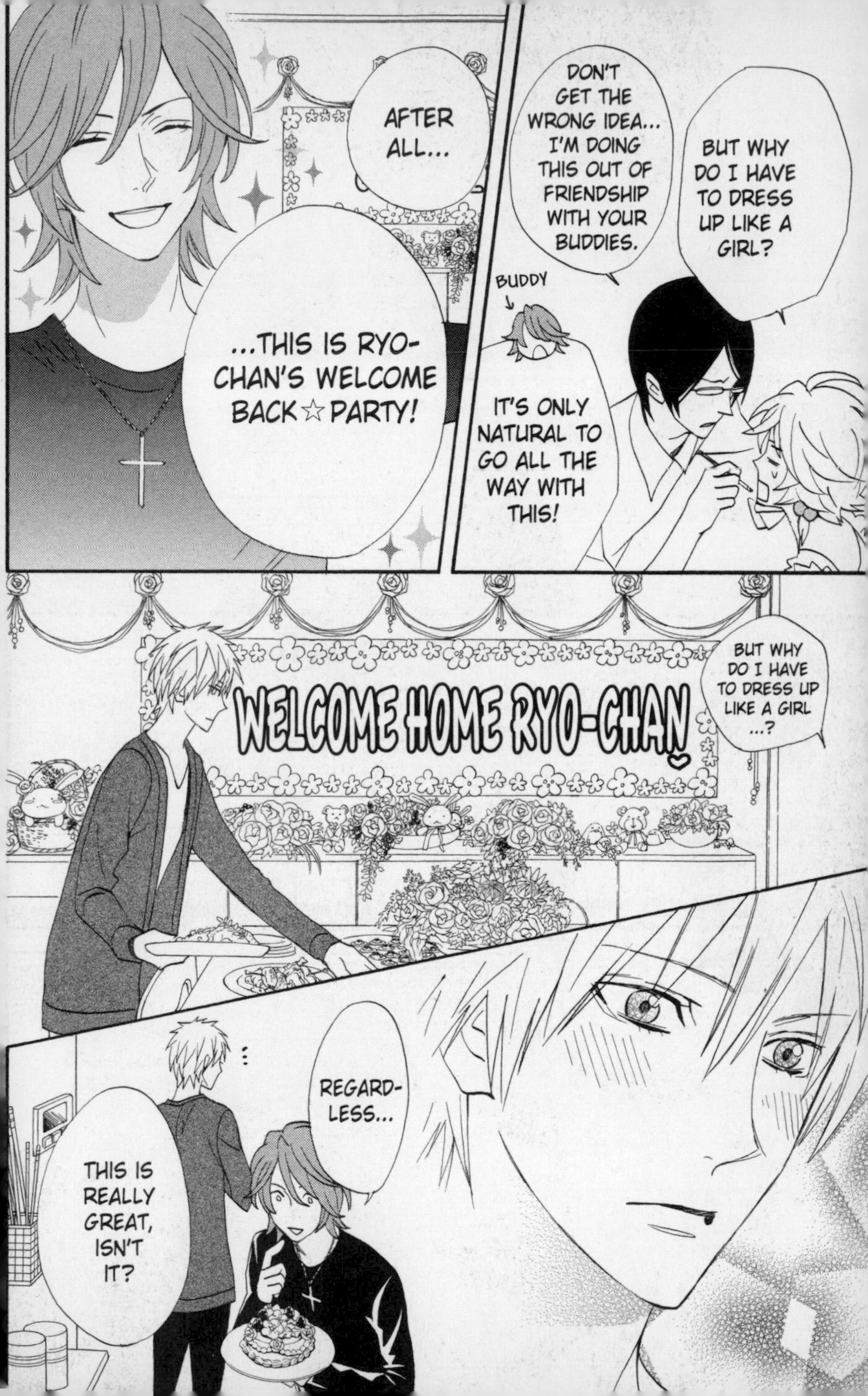
BUT WHY DO I HAVE TO DRESS UP LIKE A GIRL?
DON'T GET THE WRONG IDEA... I'M DOING THIS OUT OF FRIENDSHIP WITH YOUR BUDDIES.
BUDDY
IT'S ONLY NATURAL TO GO ALL THE WAY WITH THIS!
AFTER ALL...
...THIS IS RYO-CHAN'S WELCOME BACK☆PARTY!
BUT WHY DO I HAVE TO DRESS UP LIKE A GIRL ...?
WELCOME HOME RYO-CHAN
...
REGARDLESS...
THIS IS REALLY GREAT, ISN'T IT?

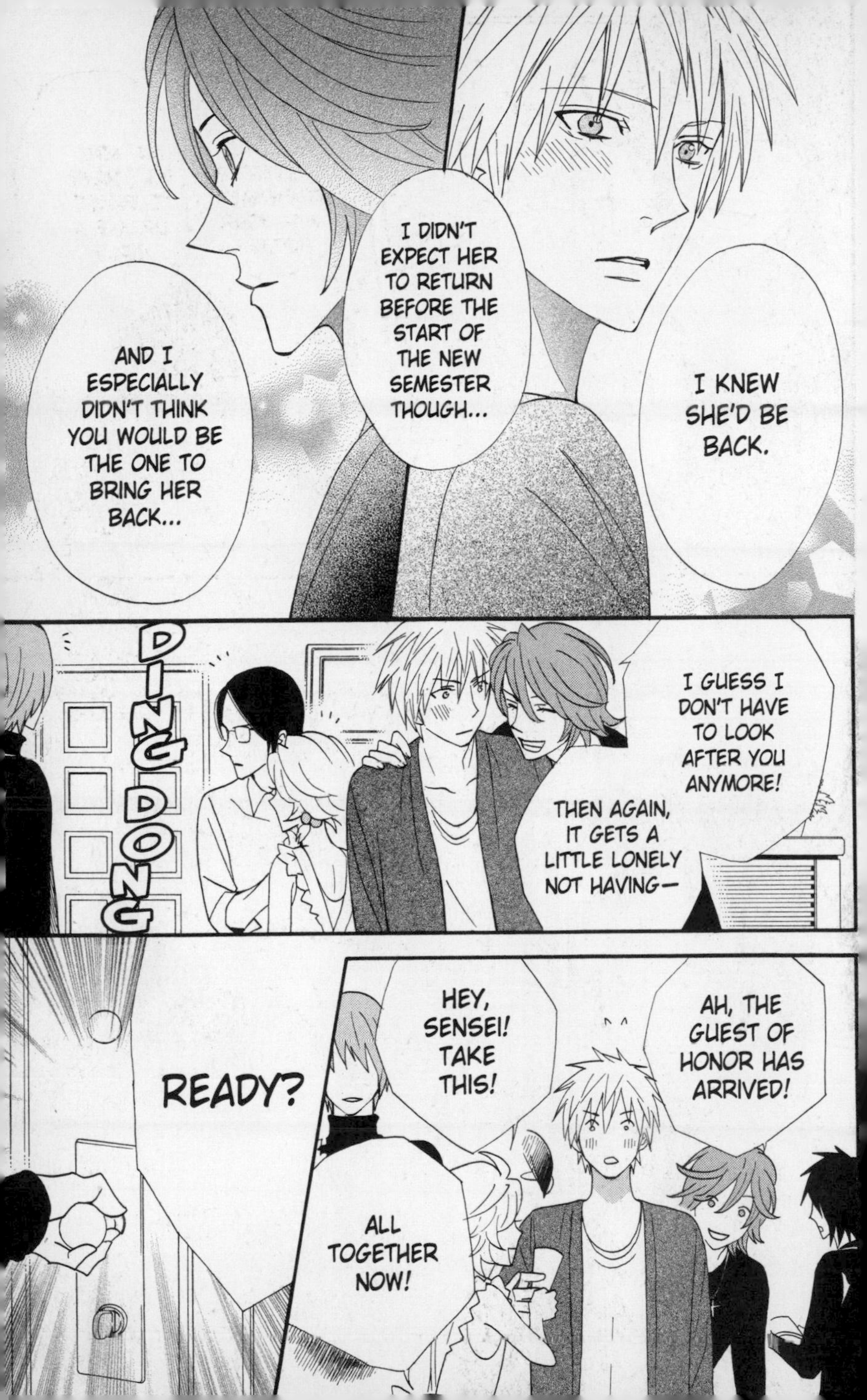
I KNEW SHE'D BE BACK.
I DIDN'T EXPECT HER TO RETURN BEFORE THE START OF THE NEW SEMESTER THOUGH...
AND I ESPECIALLY DIDN'T THINK YOU WOULD BE THE ONE TO BRING HER BACK...
I GUESS I DON'T HAVE TO LOOK AFTER YOU ANYMORE!
THEN AGAIN, IT GETS A LITTLE LONELY NOT HAVING—
DING DONG
AH, THE GUEST OF HONOR HAS ARRIVED!
HEY, SENSEI! TAKE THIS!
ALL TOGETHER NOW!
READY?

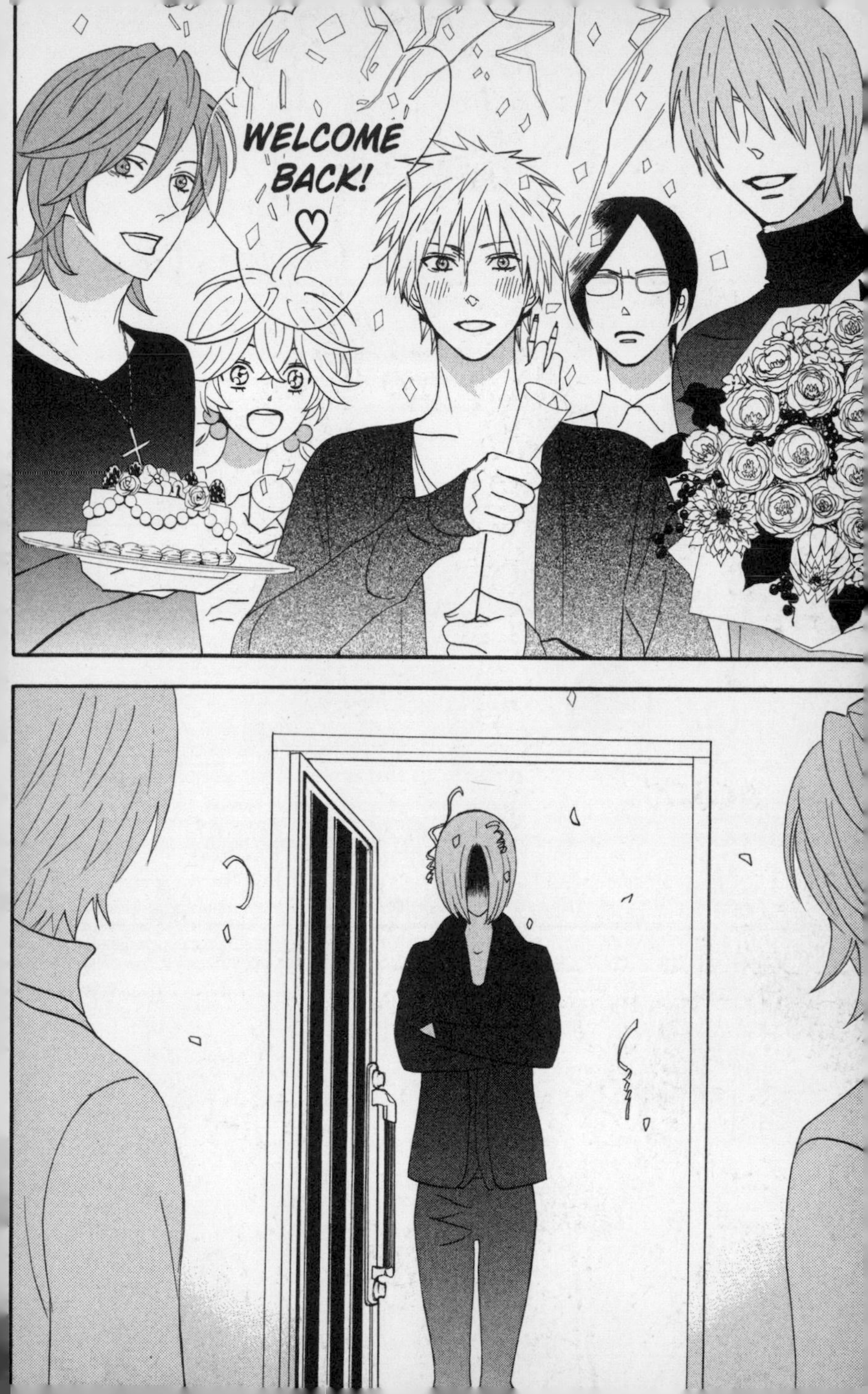
WELCOME BACK!
♡

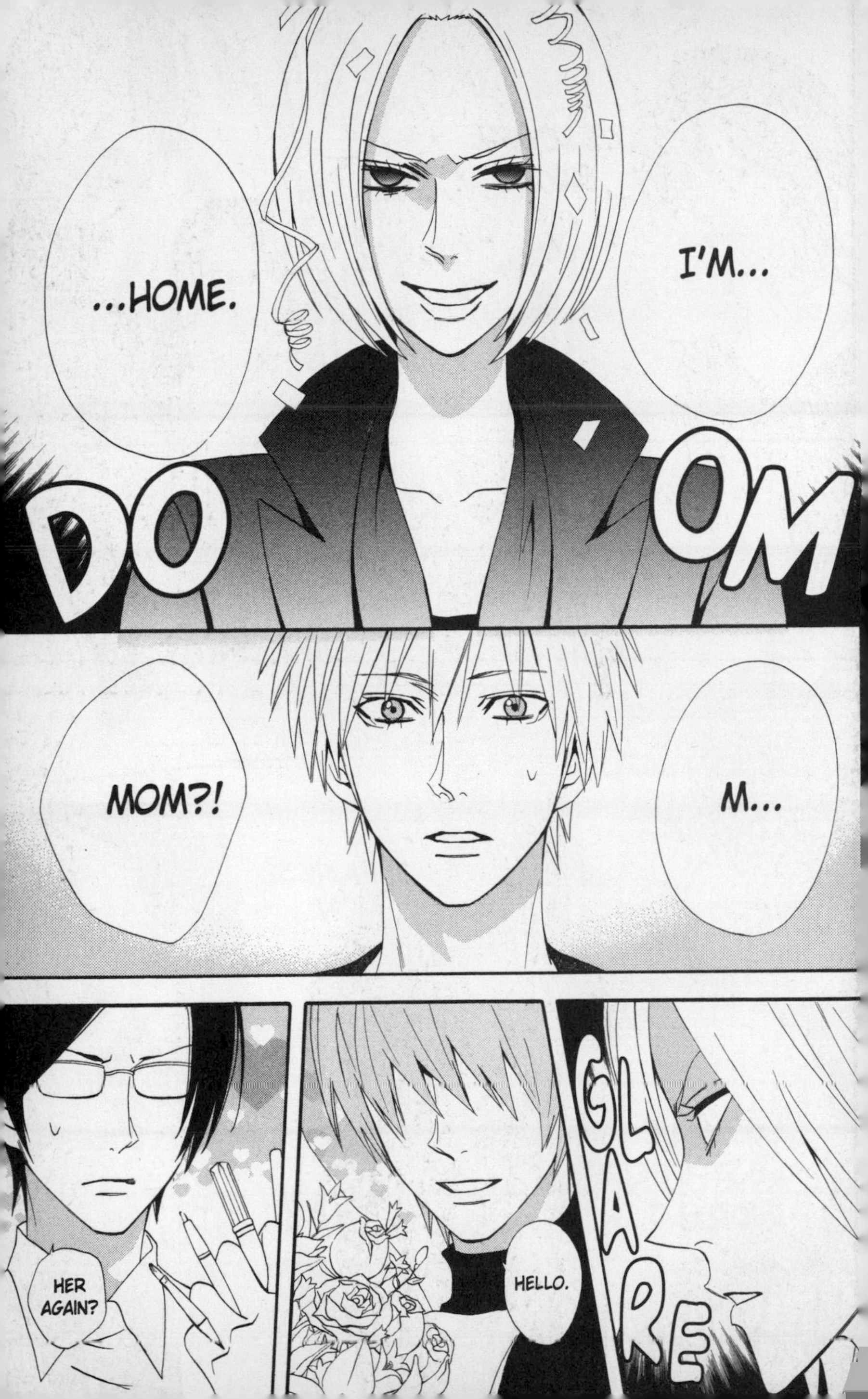
I'M...
...HOME.
DO OM
M...
MOM?!
GLARE
HELLO.
HER AGAIN?

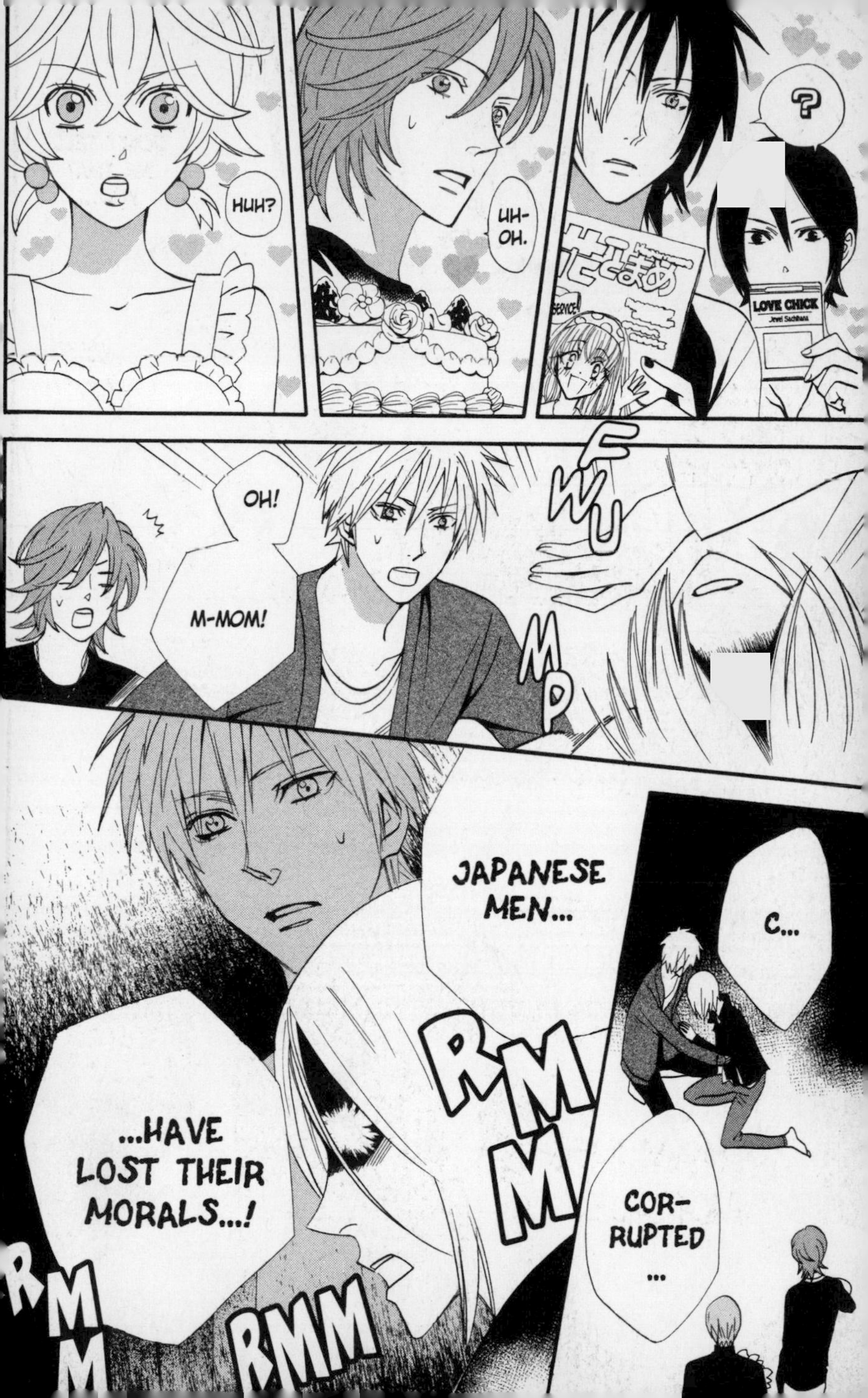
?
LOVE CHICK
Jewel Sachihana
SERVICE!
UH-OH.
HUH?
FWU
MMP
OH!
M-MOM!
C...
COR-RUPTED ...
JAPANESE MEN...
RMMM
...HAVE LOST THEIR MORALS...!
RMM
RMM

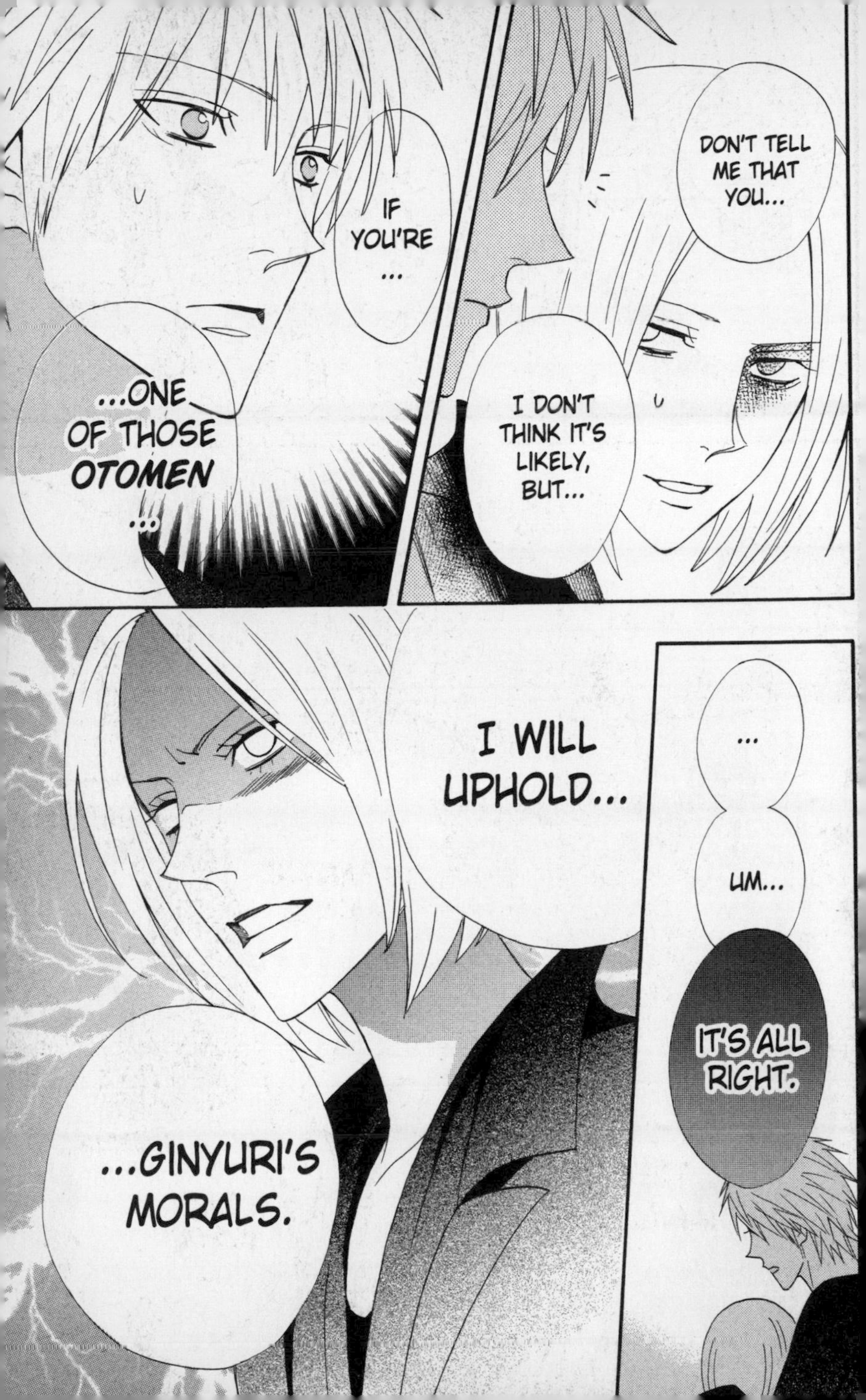
DON'T TELL ME THAT YOU...
I DON'T THINK IT'S LIKELY, BUT...
IF YOU'RE ...
...ONE OF THOSE OTOMEN ...
...
UM...
IT'S ALL RIGHT.
I WILL UPHOLD...
...GINYURI'S MORALS.

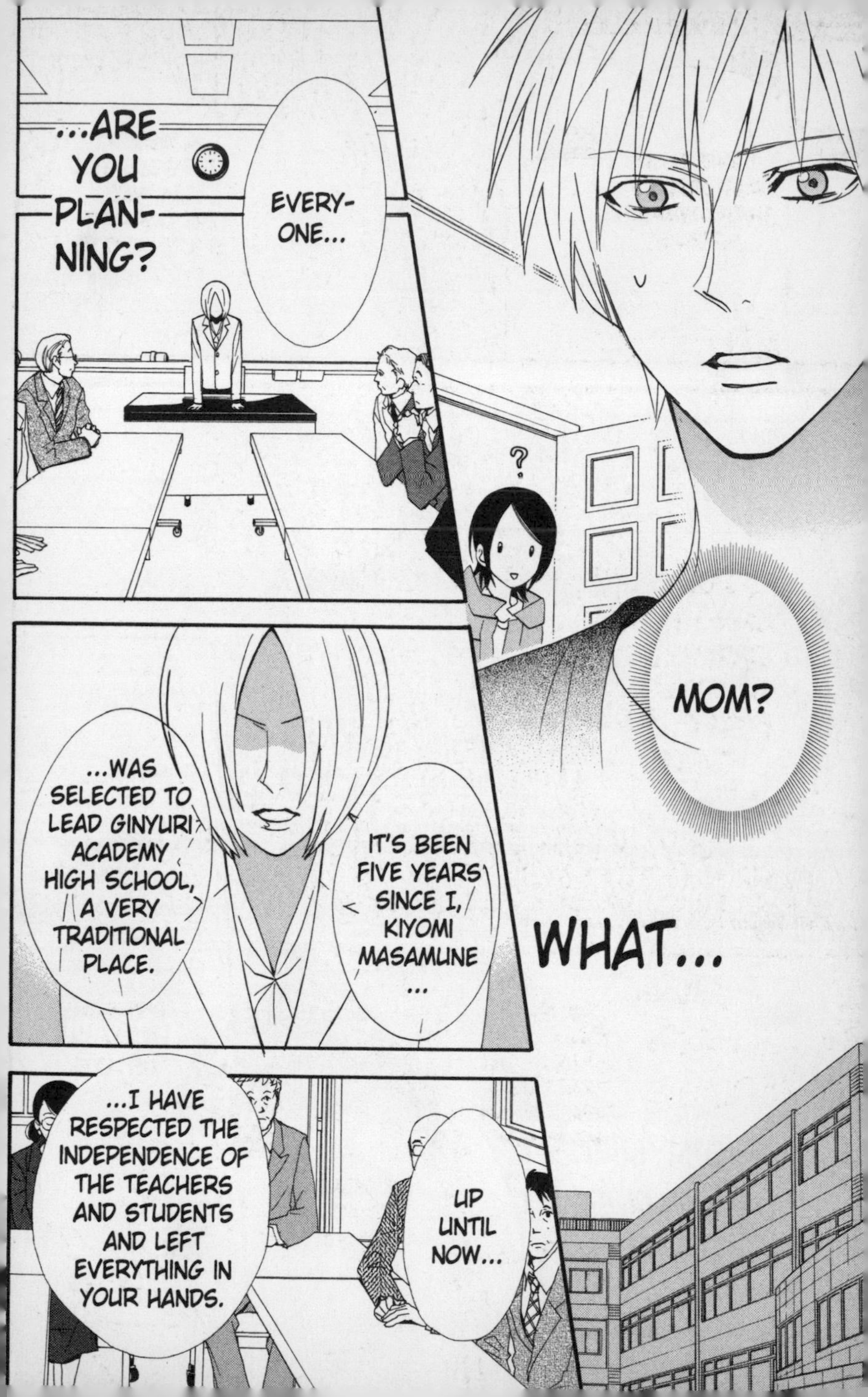
MOM?
WHAT...
...ARE YOU PLAN-NING?
EVERY-ONE...
IT'S BEEN FIVE YEARS SINCE I, KIYOMI MASAMUNE ...
...WAS SELECTED TO LEAD GINYURI ACADEMY HIGH SCHOOL, A VERY TRADITIONAL PLACE.
UP UNTIL NOW...
...I HAVE RESPECTED THE INDEPENDENCE OF THE TEACHERS AND STUDENTS AND LEFT EVERYTHING IN YOUR HANDS.

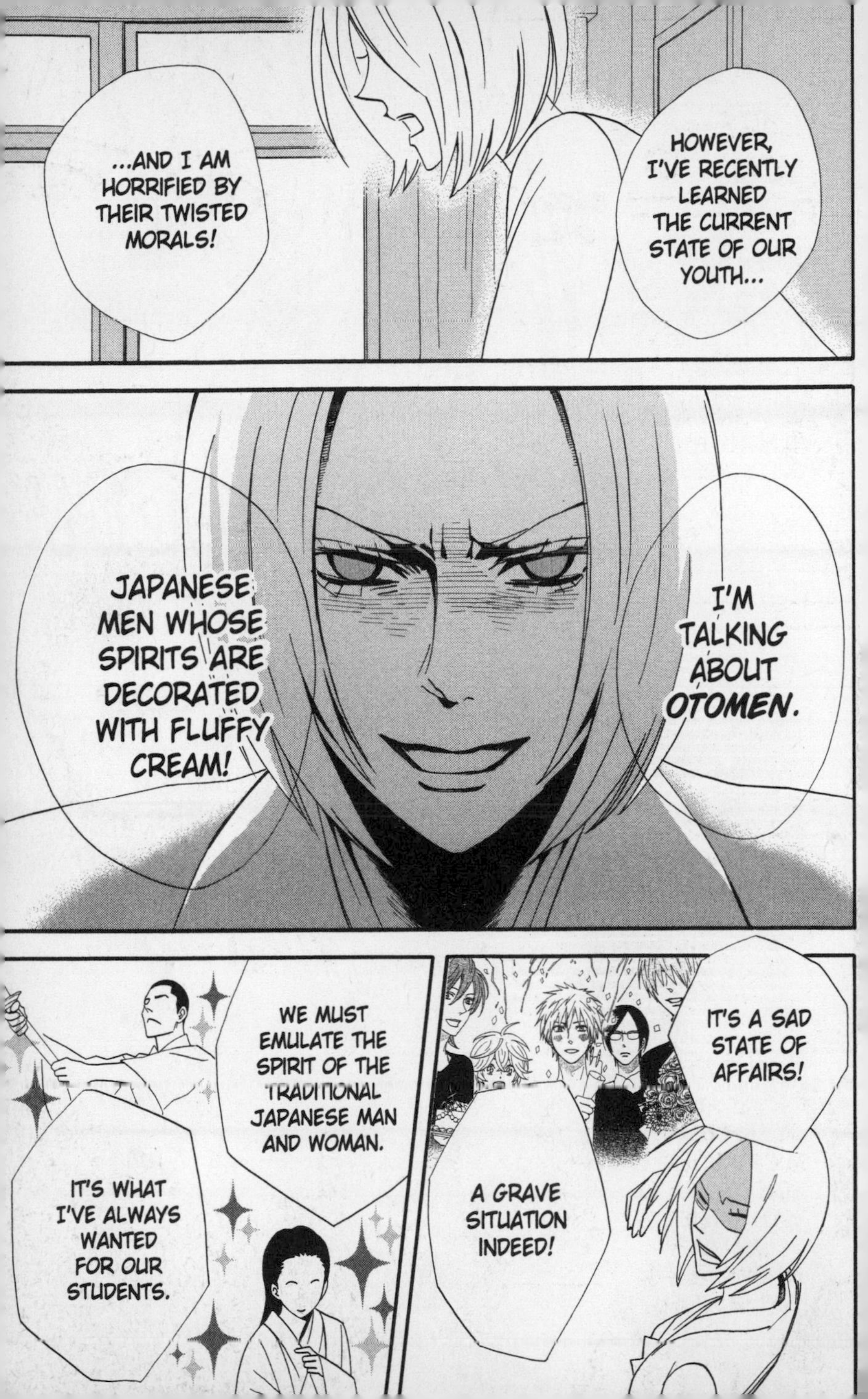
HOWEVER, I'VE RECENTLY LEARNED THE CURRENT STATE OF OUR YOUTH...
...AND I AM HORRIFIED BY THEIR TWISTED MORALS!
I'M TALKING ABOUT OTOMEN.
JAPANESE MEN WHOSE SPIRITS ARE DECORATED WITH FLUFFY CREAM!
IT'S A SAD STATE OF AFFAIRS!
A GRAVE SITUATION INDEED!
WE MUST EMULATE THE SPIRIT OF THE TRADITIONAL JAPANESE MAN AND WOMAN.
IT'S WHAT I'VE ALWAYS WANTED FOR OUR STUDENTS.

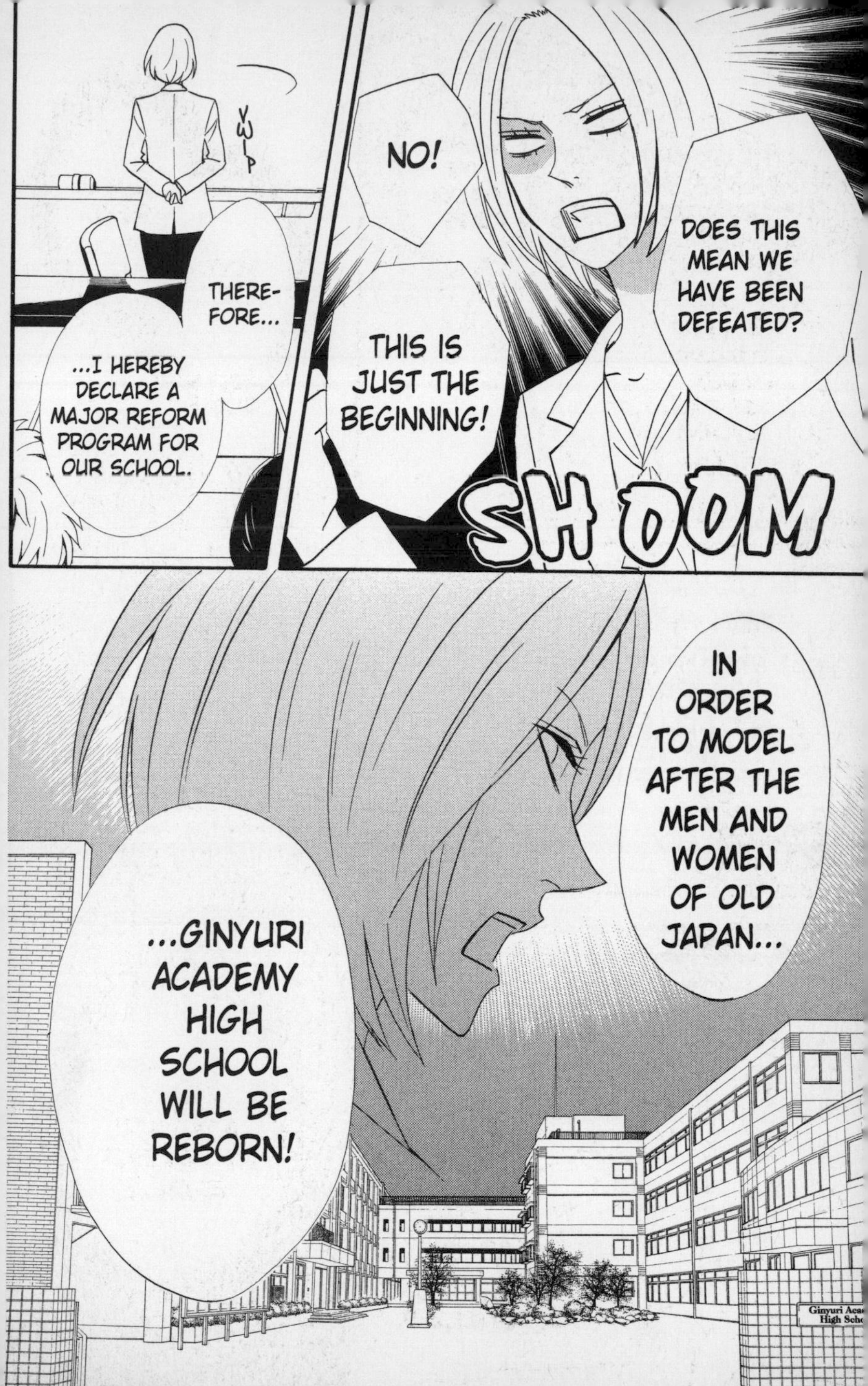
DOES THIS MEAN WE HAVE BEEN DEFEATED?
NO!
THIS IS JUST THE BEGINNING!
SHOOM
VWIP
THERE-FORE...
...I HEREBY DECLARE A MAJOR REFORM PROGRAM FOR OUR SCHOOL.
IN ORDER TO MODEL AFTER THE MEN AND WOMEN OF OLD JAPAN...
...GINYURI ACADEMY HIGH SCHOOL WILL BE REBORN!

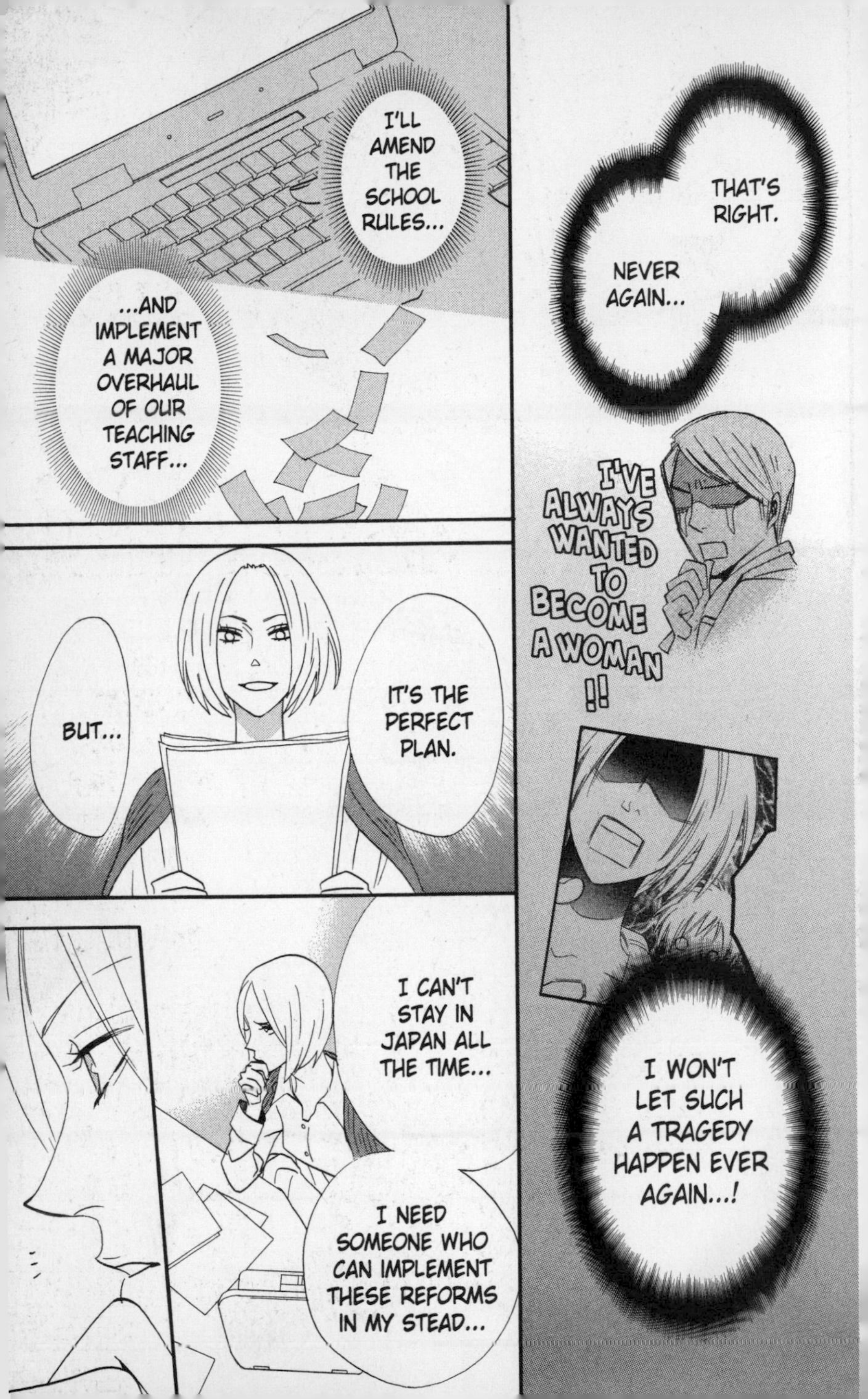
THAT'S RIGHT.
NEVER AGAIN...
I'VE ALWAYS WANTED TO BECOME A WOMAN!!
I WON'T LET SUCH A TRAGEDY HAPPEN EVER AGAIN...!
I'LL AMEND THE SCHOOL RULES...
...AND IMPLEMENT A MAJOR OVERHAUL OF OUR TEACHING STAFF...
IT'S THE PERFECT PLAN.
BUT...
I CAN'T STAY IN JAPAN ALL THE TIME...
I NEED SOMEONE WHO CAN IMPLEMENT THESE REFORMS IN MY STEAD...

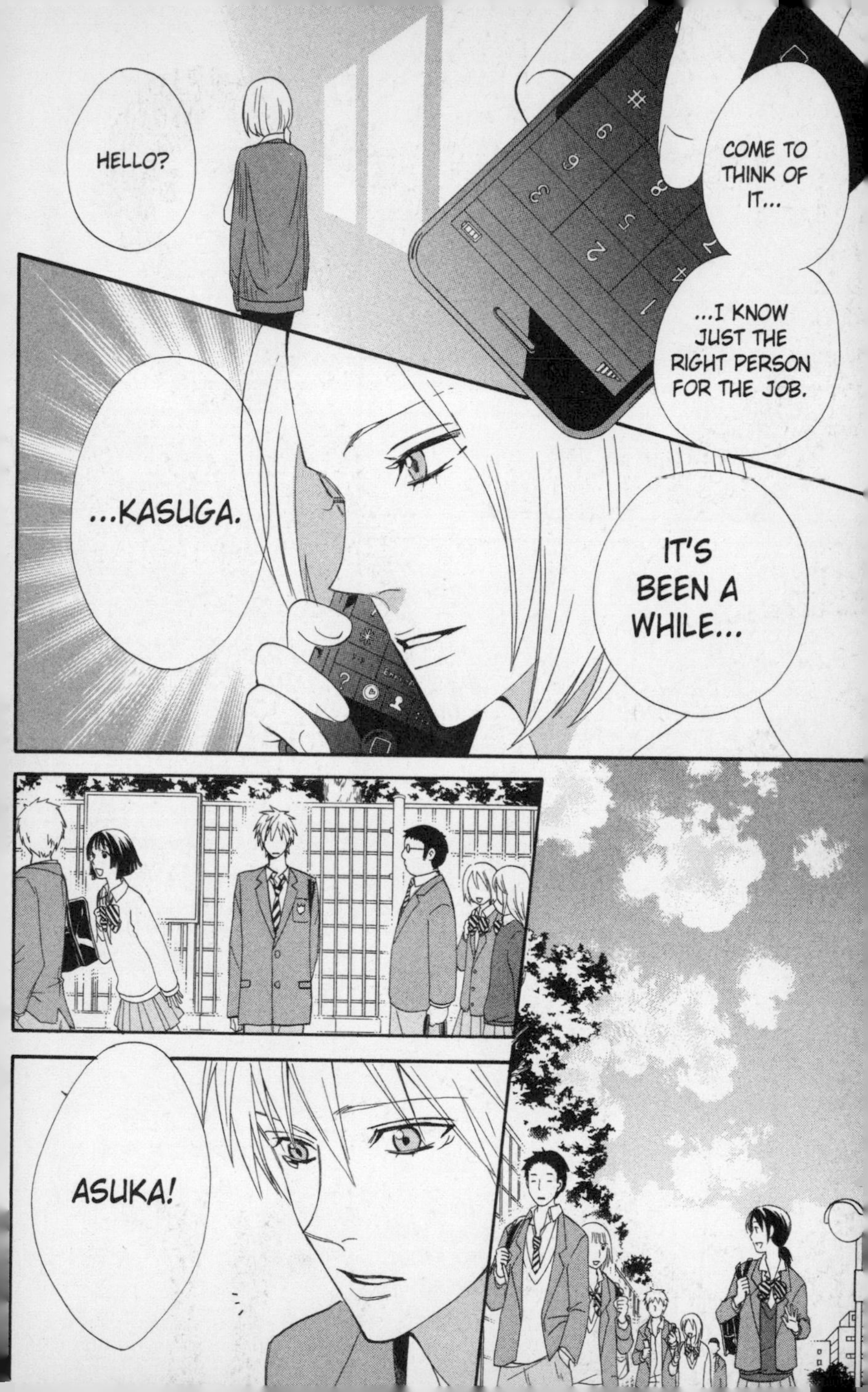
COME TO THINK OF IT...
...I KNOW JUST THE RIGHT PERSON FOR THE JOB.
HELLO?
IT'S BEEN A WHILE...
...KASUGA.
ASUKA!

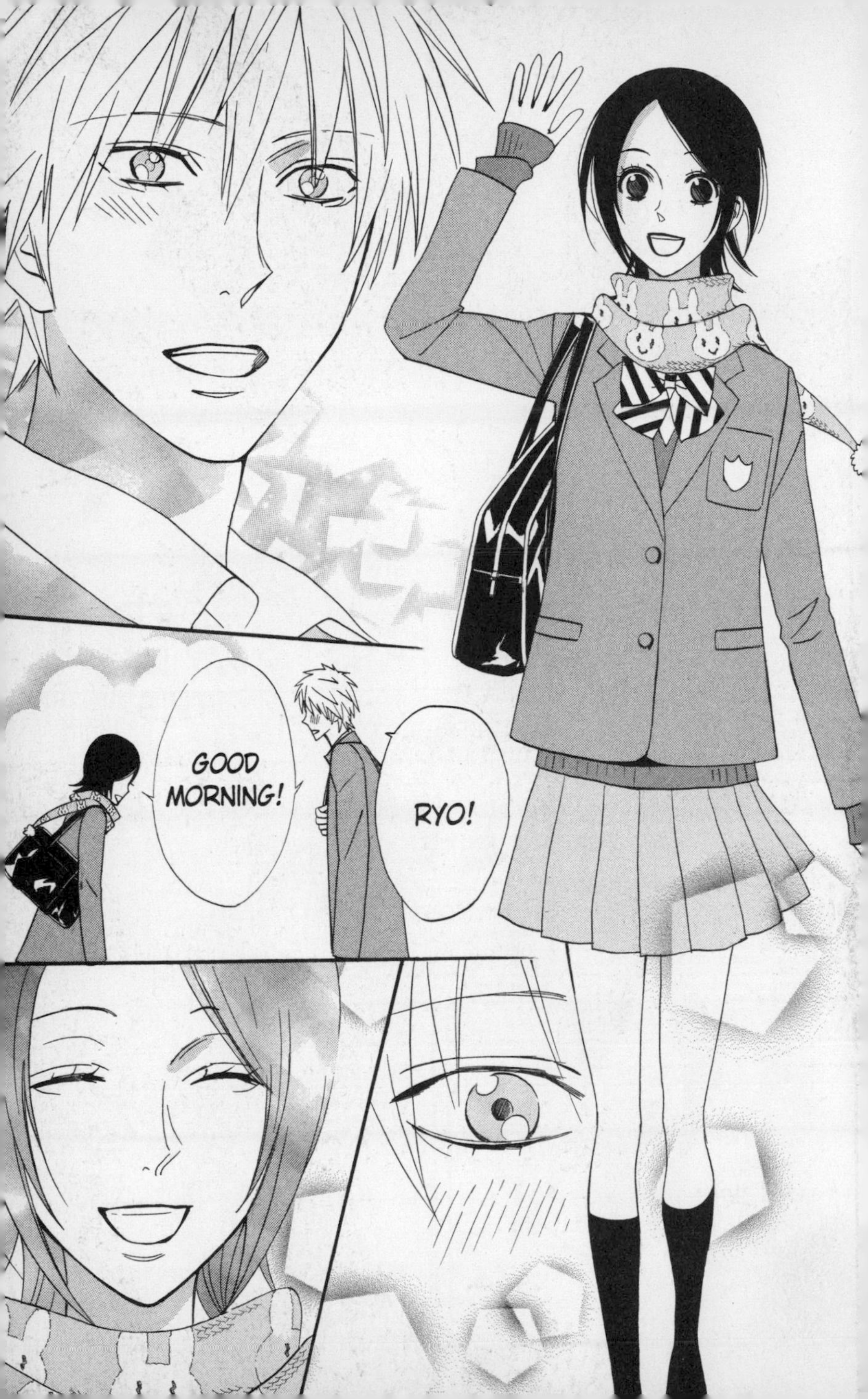
RYO!
GOOD MORNING!

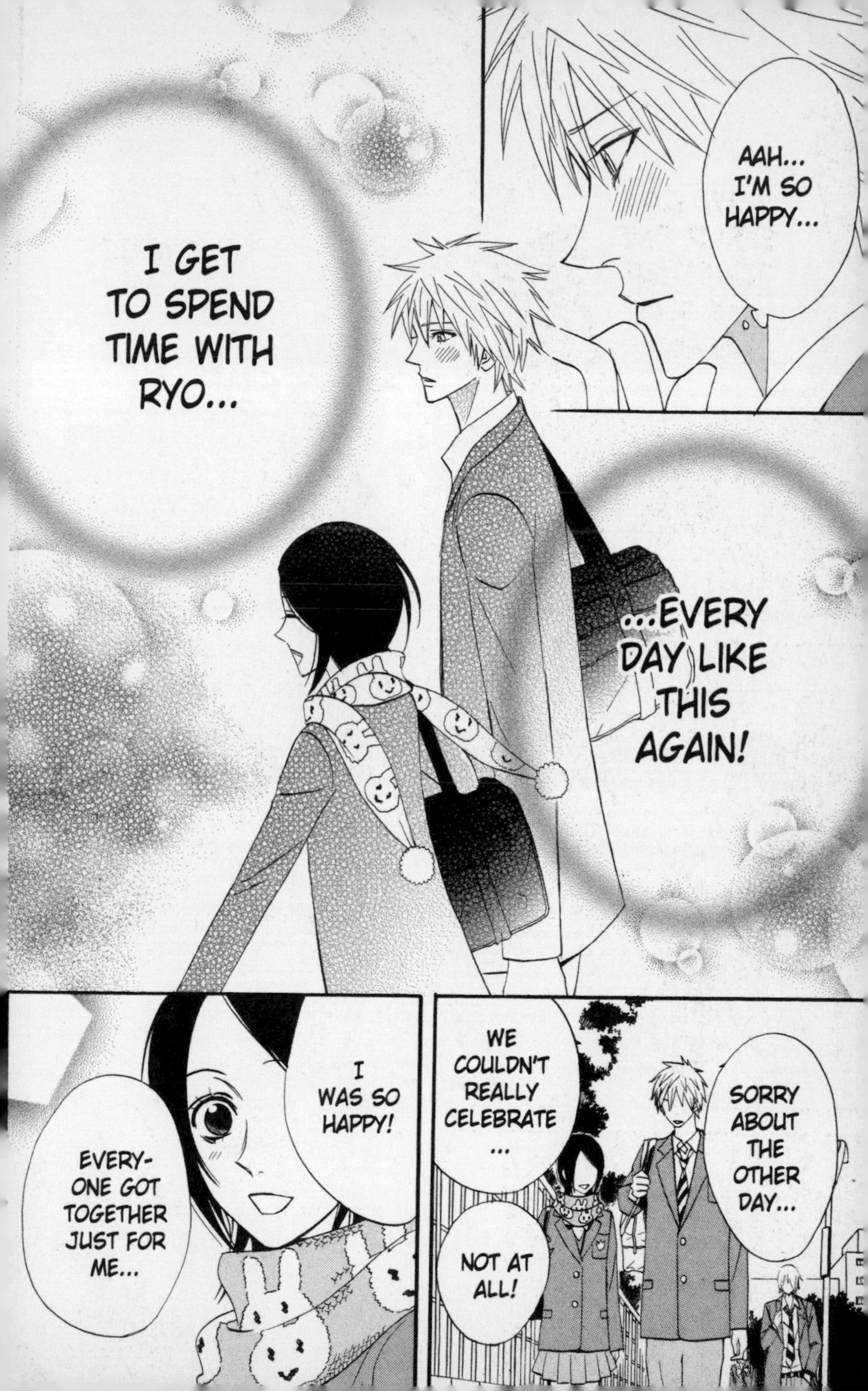
AAH... I'M SO HAPPY...
I GET TO SPEND TIME WITH RYO...
...EVERY DAY LIKE THIS AGAIN!
SORRY ABOUT THE OTHER DAY...
WE COULDN'T REALLY CELEBRATE...
NOT AT ALL!
I WAS SO HAPPY!
EVERY-ONE GOT TOGETHER JUST FOR ME...

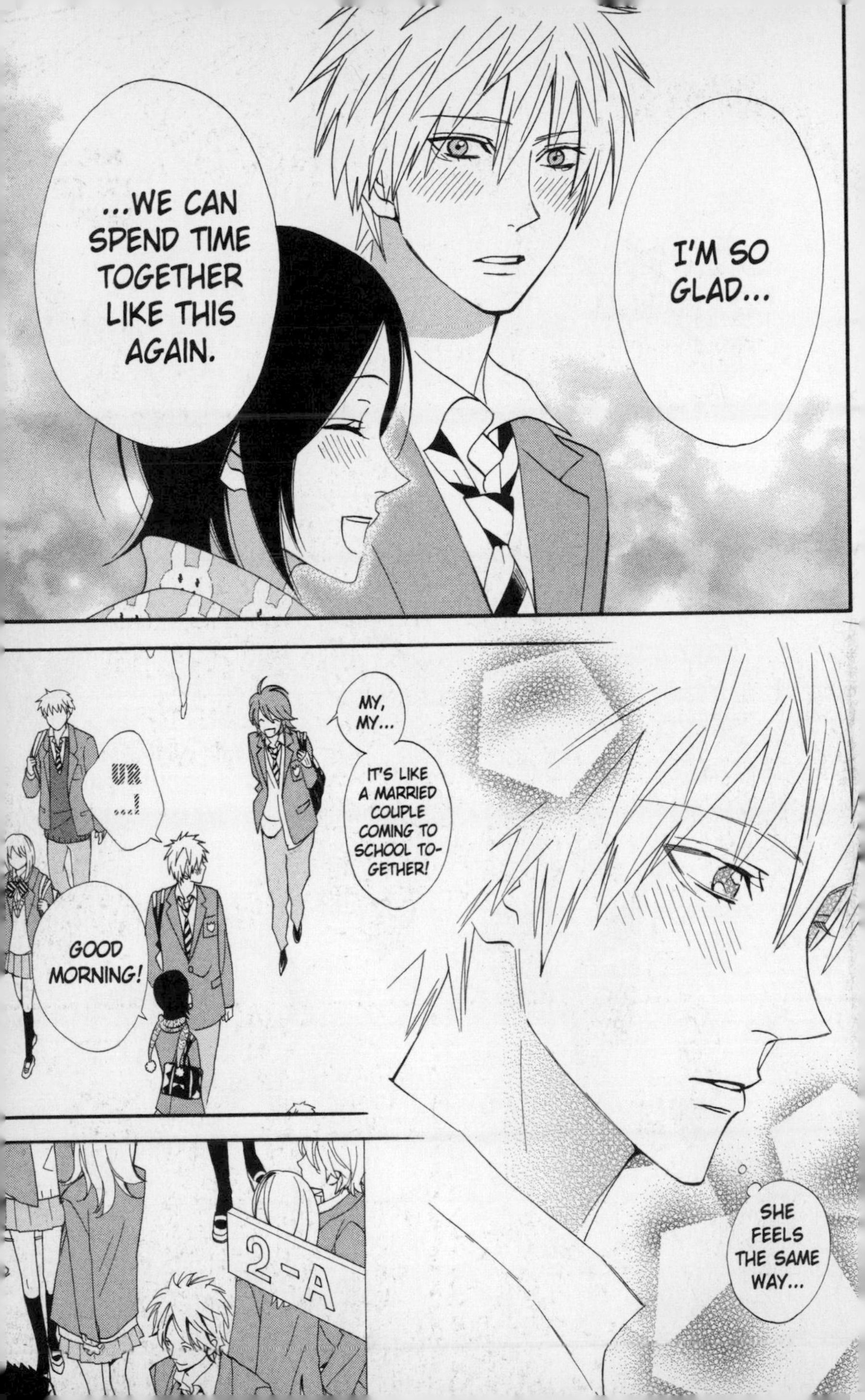
I'M SO GLAD...
...WE CAN SPEND TIME TOGETHER LIKE THIS AGAIN.
SHE FEELS THE SAME WAY...
MY, MY...
IT'S LIKE A MARRIED COUPLE COMING TO SCHOOL TO-GETHER!
UR ...!
GOOD MORNING!
2-A

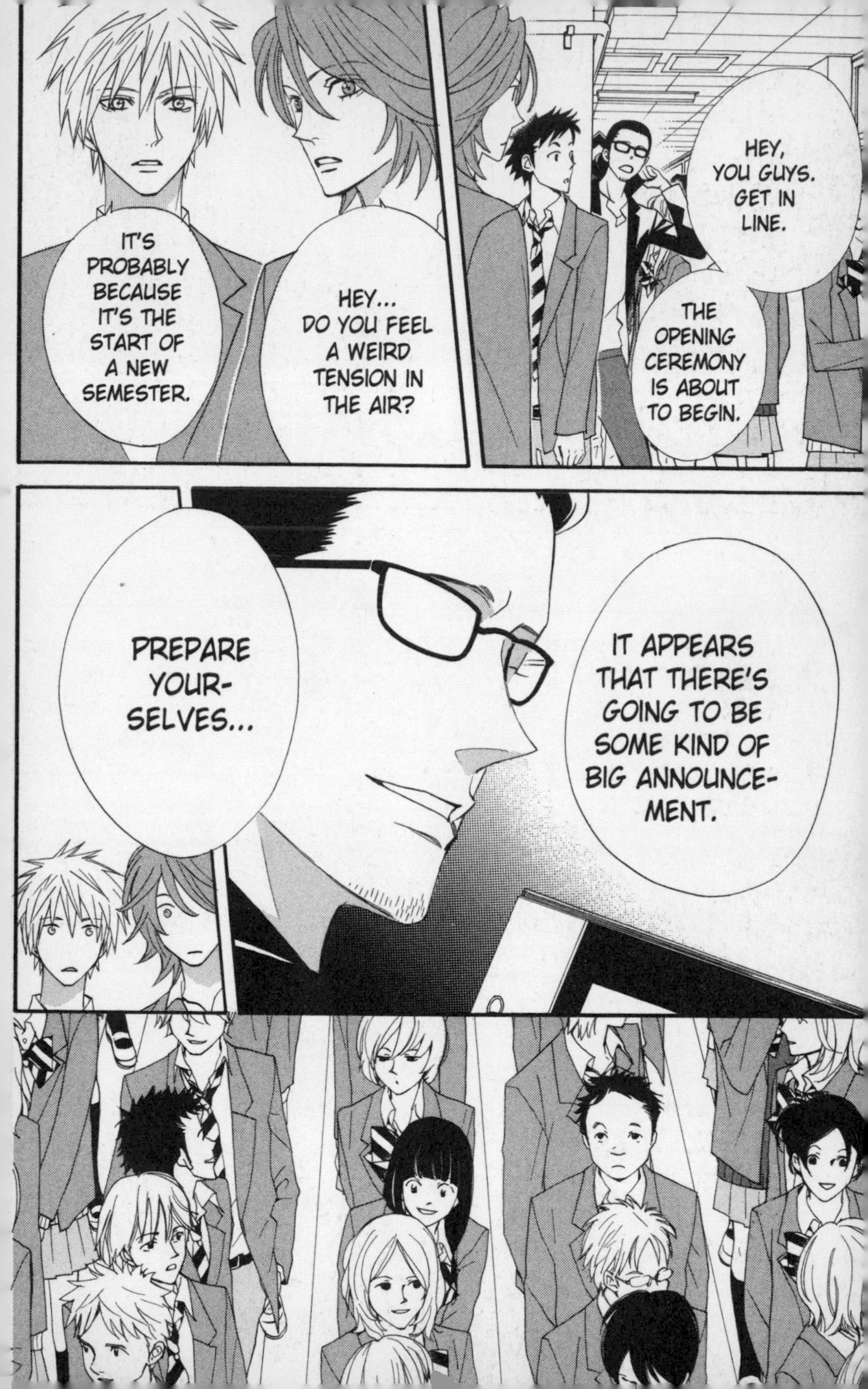
HEY, YOU GUYS. GET IN LINE.
THE OPENING CEREMONY IS ABOUT TO BEGIN.
HEY... DO YOU FEEL A WEIRD TENSION IN THE AIR?
IT'S PROBABLY BECAUSE IT'S THE START OF A NEW SEMESTER.
IT APPEARS THAT THERE'S GOING TO BE SOME KIND OF BIG ANNOUNCE-MENT.
PREPARE YOUR-SELVES...

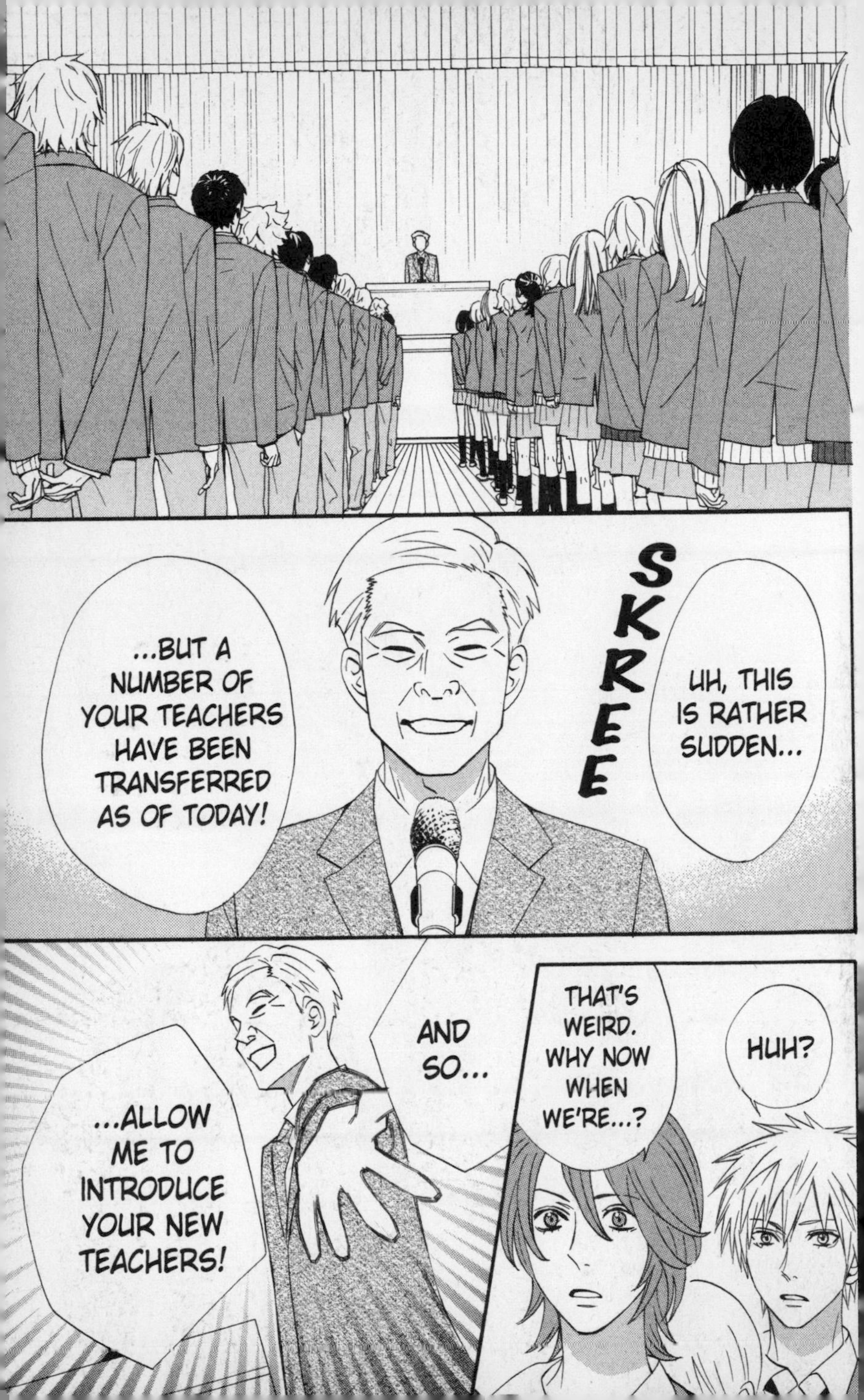
UH, THIS IS RATHER SUDDEN...
SKREE
...BUT A NUMBER OF YOUR TEACHERS HAVE BEEN TRANSFERRED AS OF TODAY!
HUH?
THAT'S WEIRD. WHY NOW WHEN WE'RE...?
AND SO...
...ALLOW ME TO INTRODUCE YOUR NEW TEACHERS!

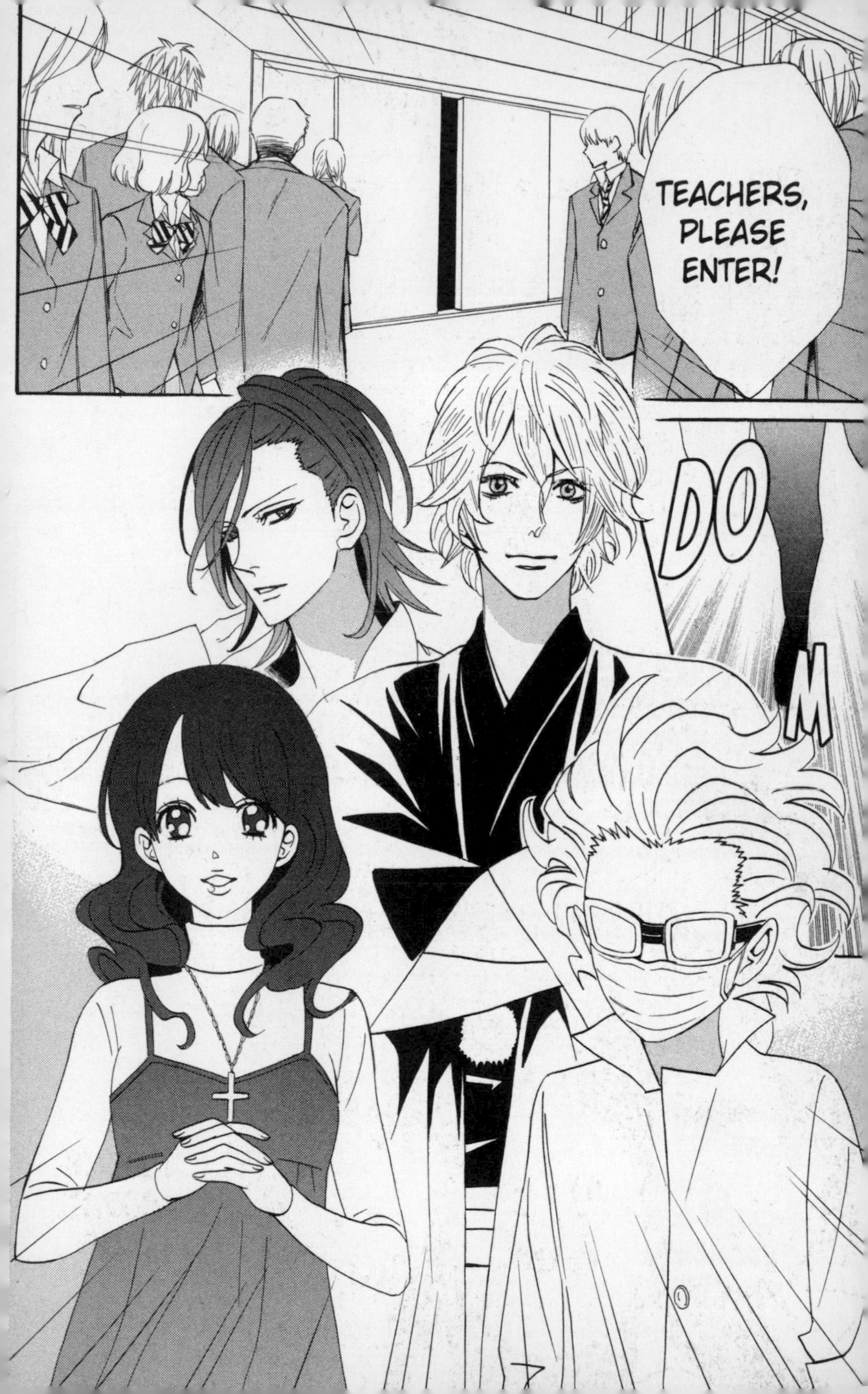
TEACHERS, PLEASE ENTER!
DOOM

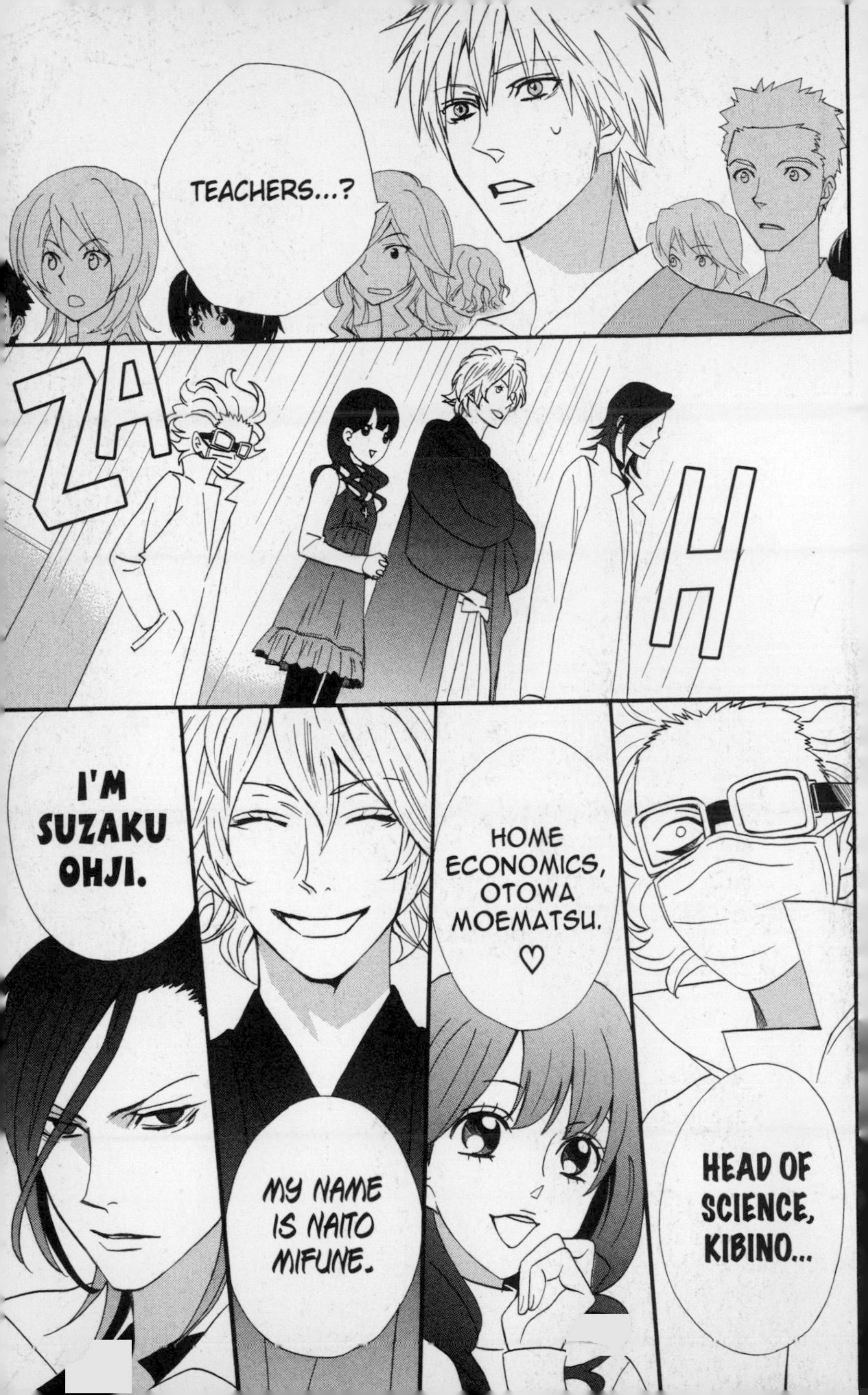
TEACHERS...?
ZA
H
HEAD OF SCIENCE, KIBINO...
HOME ECONOMICS, OTOWA MOEMATSU. ♡
MY NAME IS NAITO MIFUNE.
I'M SUZAKU OHJI.

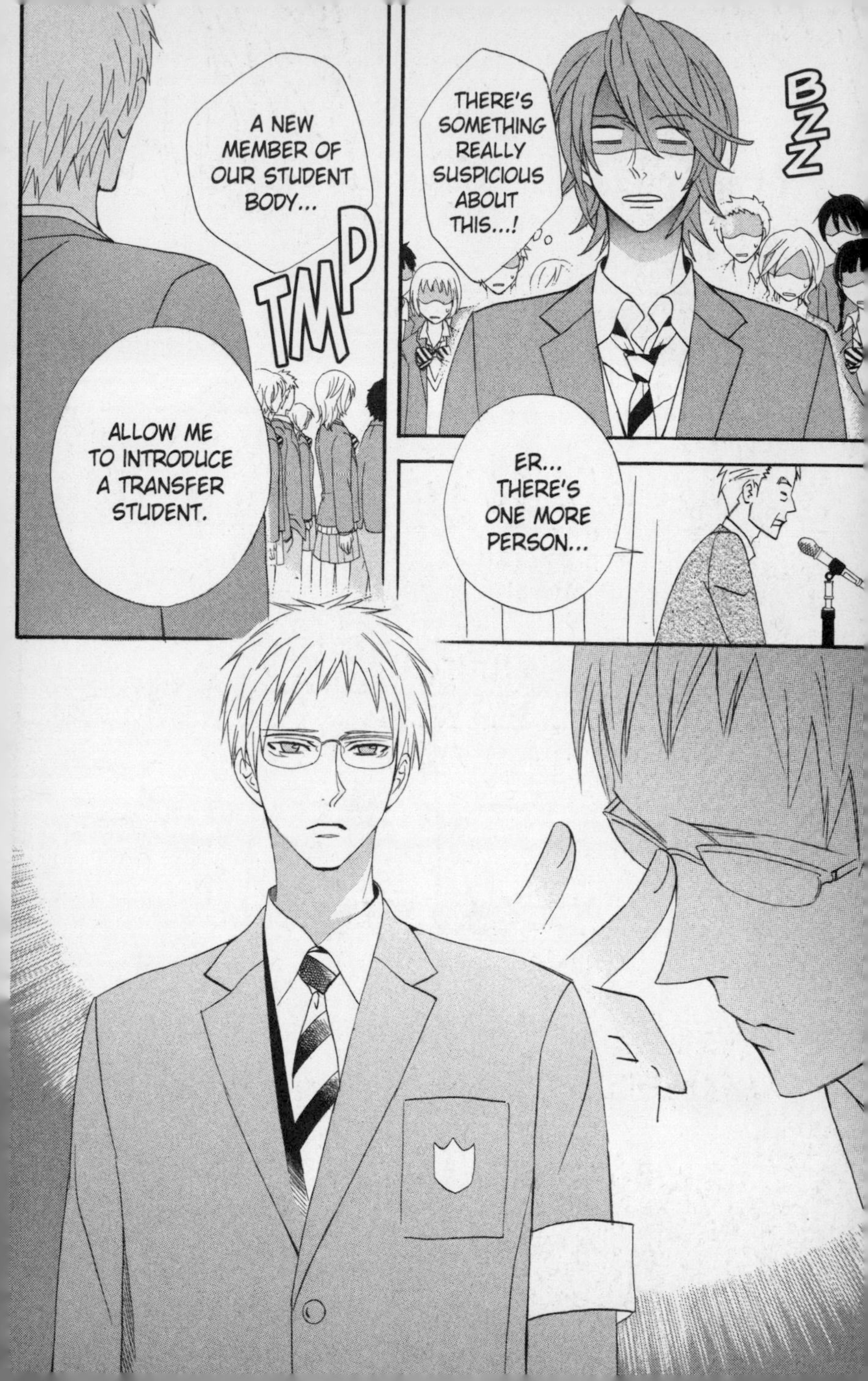
BZZ
THERE'S SOMETHING REALLY SUSPICIOUS ABOUT THIS...!
ER... THERE'S ONE MORE PERSON...
A NEW MEMBER OF OUR STUDENT BODY...
TMP
ALLOW ME TO INTRODUCE A TRANSFER STUDENT.

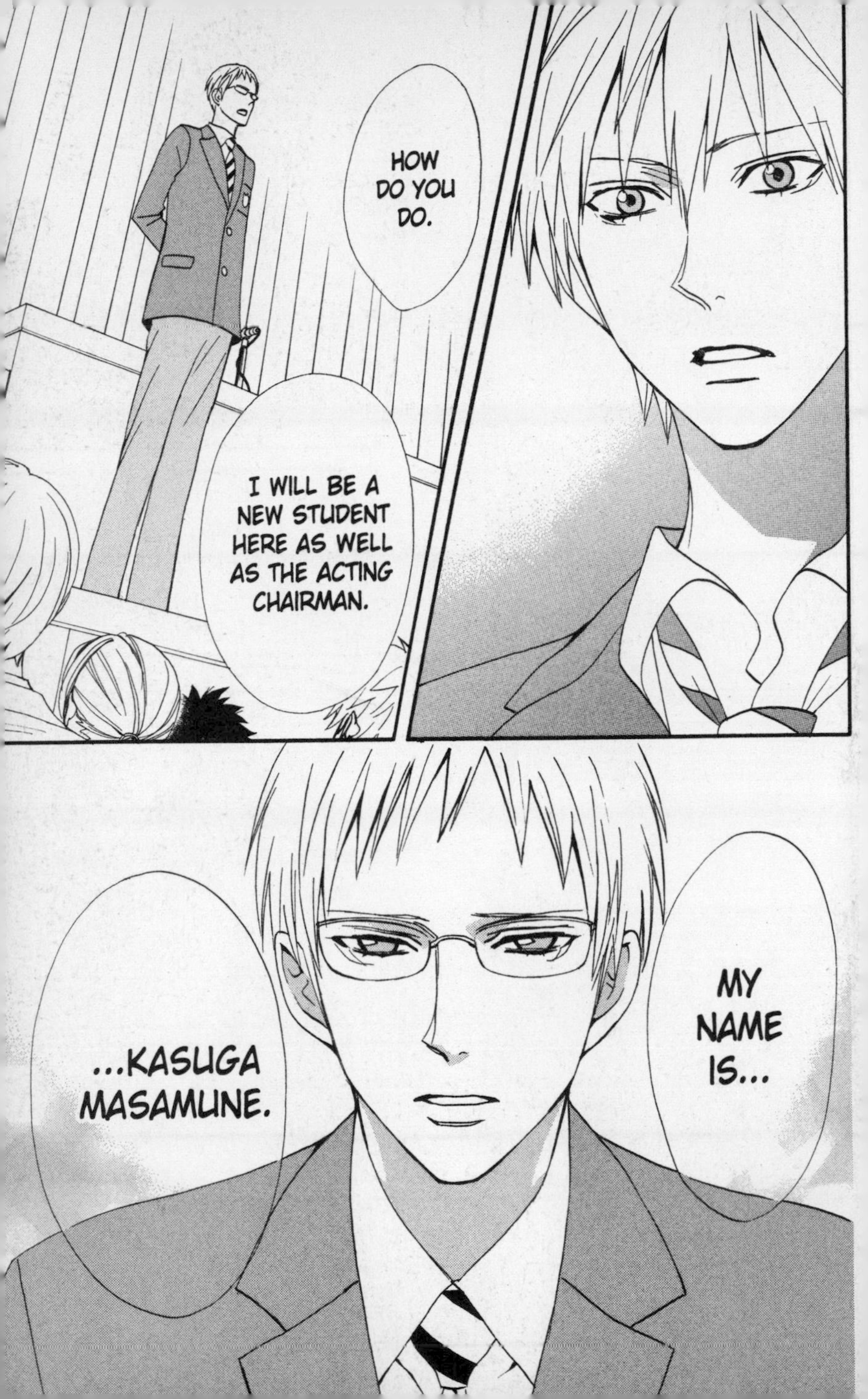
HOW DO YOU DO.
I WILL BE A NEW STUDENT HERE AS WELL AS THE ACTING CHAIRMAN.
MY NAME IS...
...KASUGA MASAMUNE.

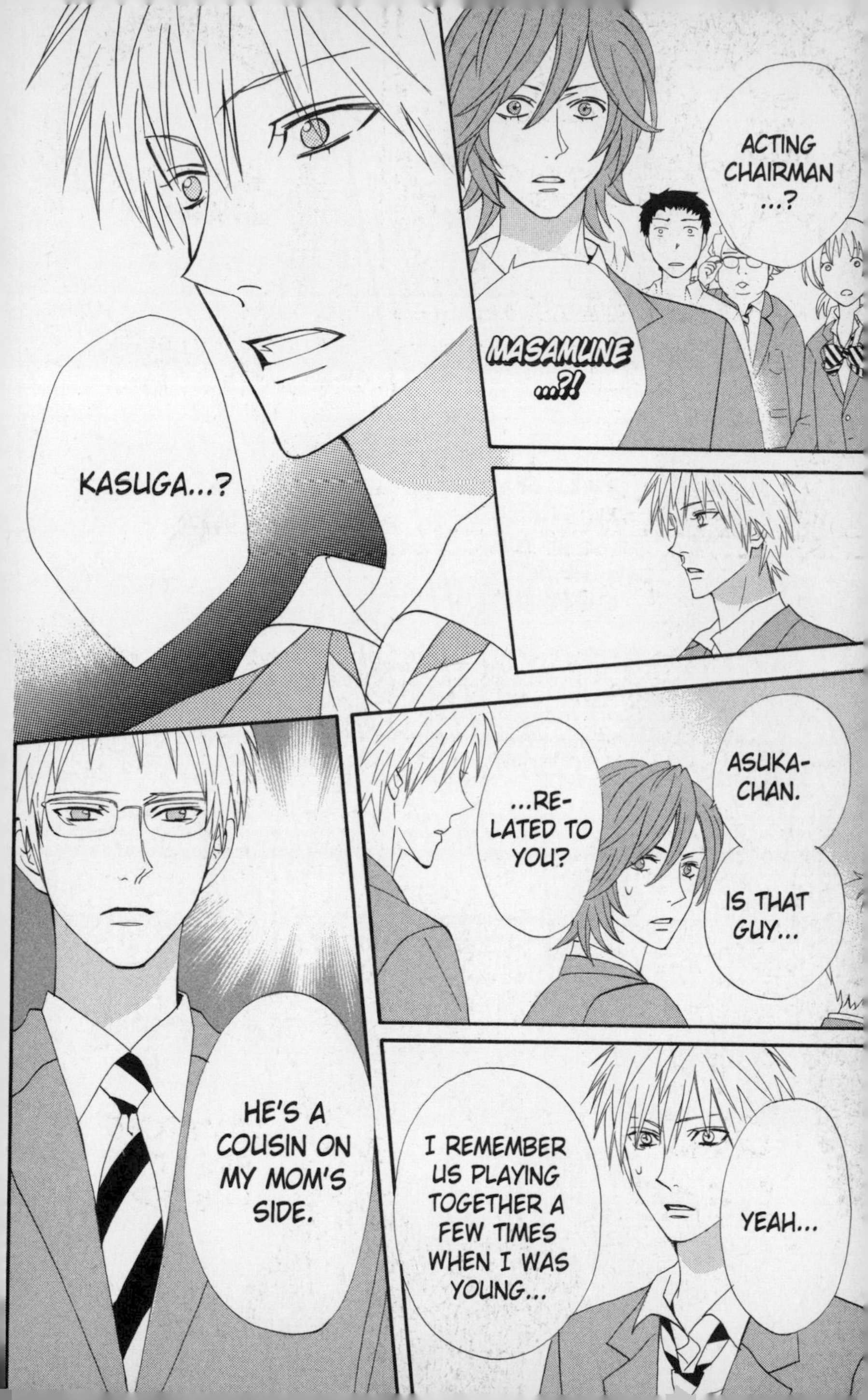
ACTING CHAIRMAN ...?
MASAMUNE ...?!
KASUGA...?
ASUKA-CHAN.
IS THAT GUY...
...RE-LATED TO YOU?
YEAH...
I REMEMBER US PLAYING TOGETHER A FEW TIMES WHEN I WAS YOUNG...
HE'S A COUSIN ON MY MOM'S SIDE.

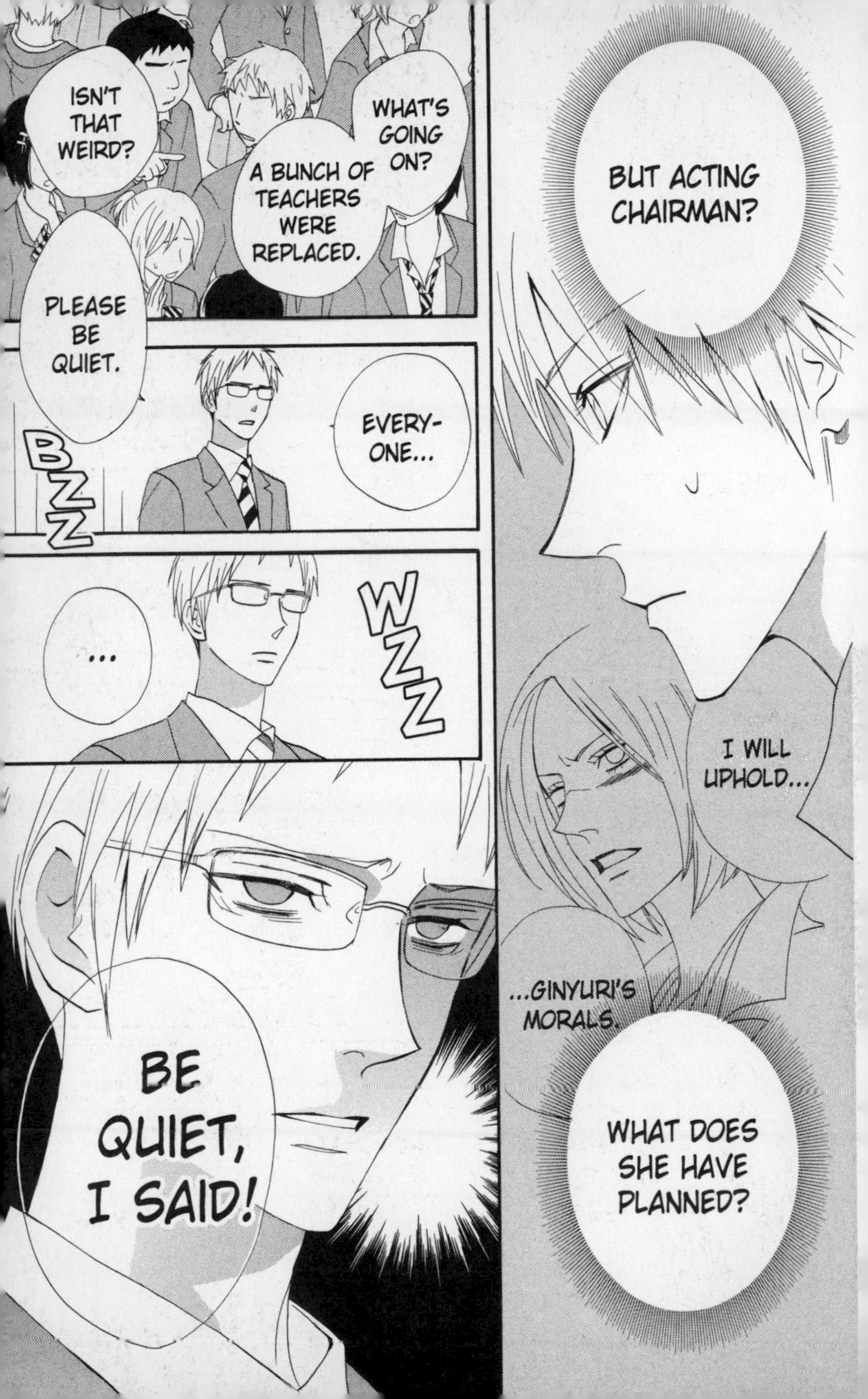
BUT ACTING CHAIRMAN?
I WILL UPHOLD...
...GINYURI'S MORALS.
WHAT DOES SHE HAVE PLANNED?
WHAT'S GOING ON?
A BUNCH OF TEACHERS WERE REPLACED.
ISN'T THAT WEIRD?
PLEASE BE QUIET.
EVERY-ONE...
BZZ
WZZ
...
BE QUIET, I SAID!

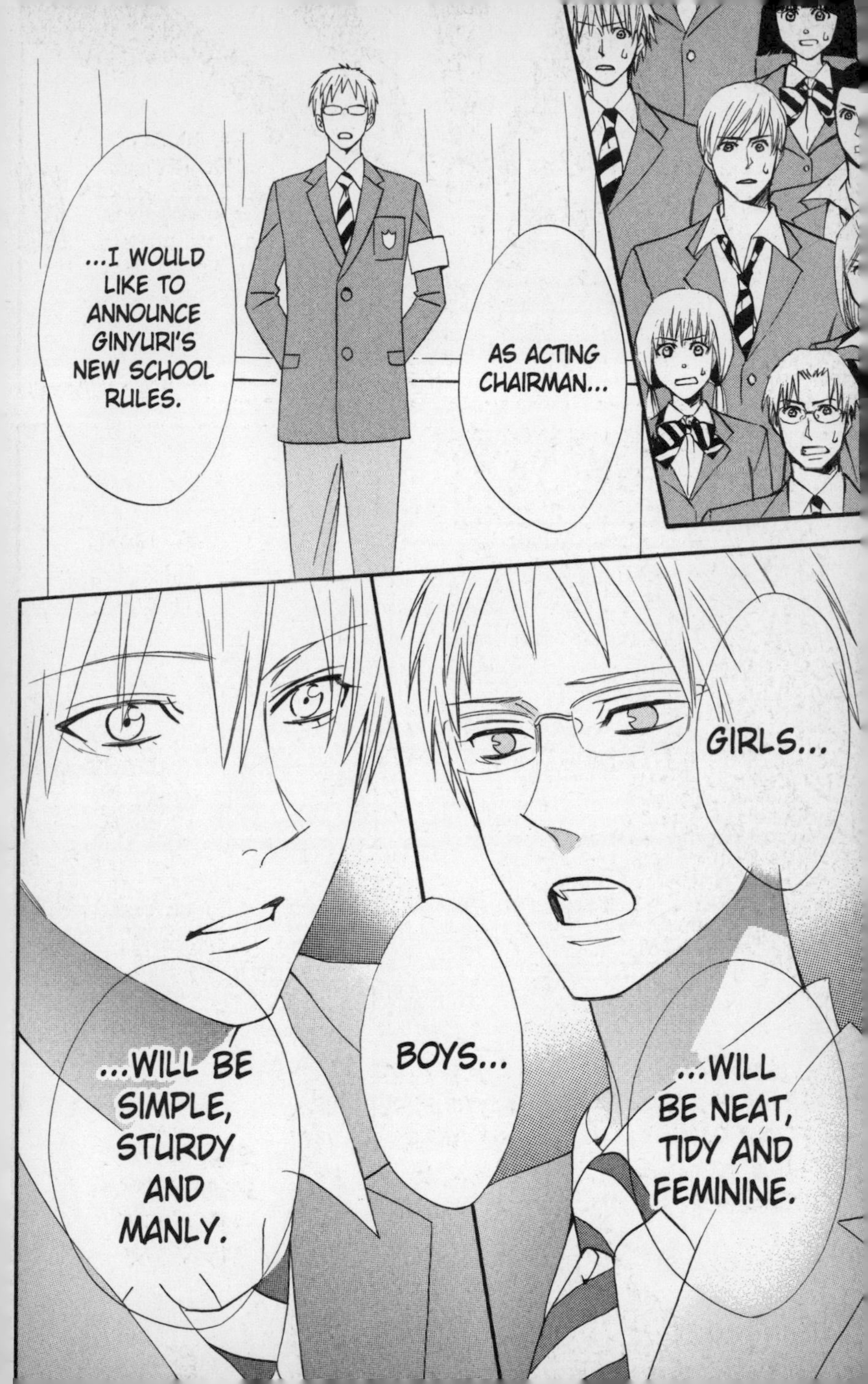
AS ACTING CHAIRMAN...
...I WOULD LIKE TO ANNOUNCE GINYURI'S NEW SCHOOL RULES.
GIRLS...
...WILL BE NEAT, TIDY AND FEMININE.
BOYS...
...WILL BE SIMPLE, STURDY AND MANLY.

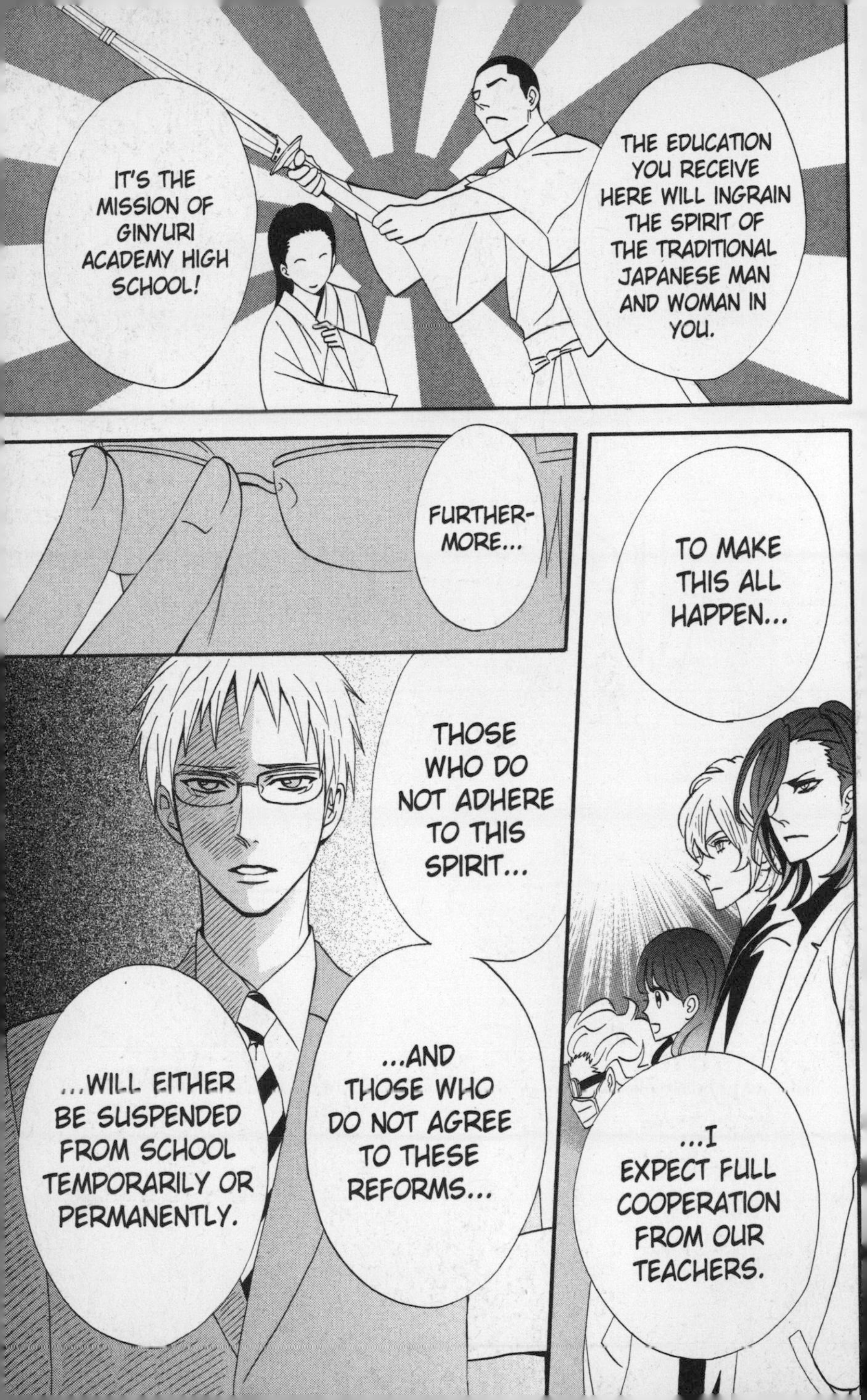
THE EDUCATION YOU RECEIVE HERE WILL INGRAIN THE SPIRIT OF THE TRADITIONAL JAPANESE MAN AND WOMAN IN YOU.
IT'S THE MISSION OF GINYURI ACADEMY HIGH SCHOOL!
TO MAKE THIS ALL HAPPEN...
...I EXPECT FULL COOPERATION FROM OUR TEACHERS.
FURTHER-MORE...
THOSE WHO DO NOT ADHERE TO THIS SPIRIT...
...AND THOSE WHO DO NOT AGREE TO THESE REFORMS...
...WILL EITHER BE SUSPENDED FROM SCHOOL TEMPORARILY OR PERMANENTLY.

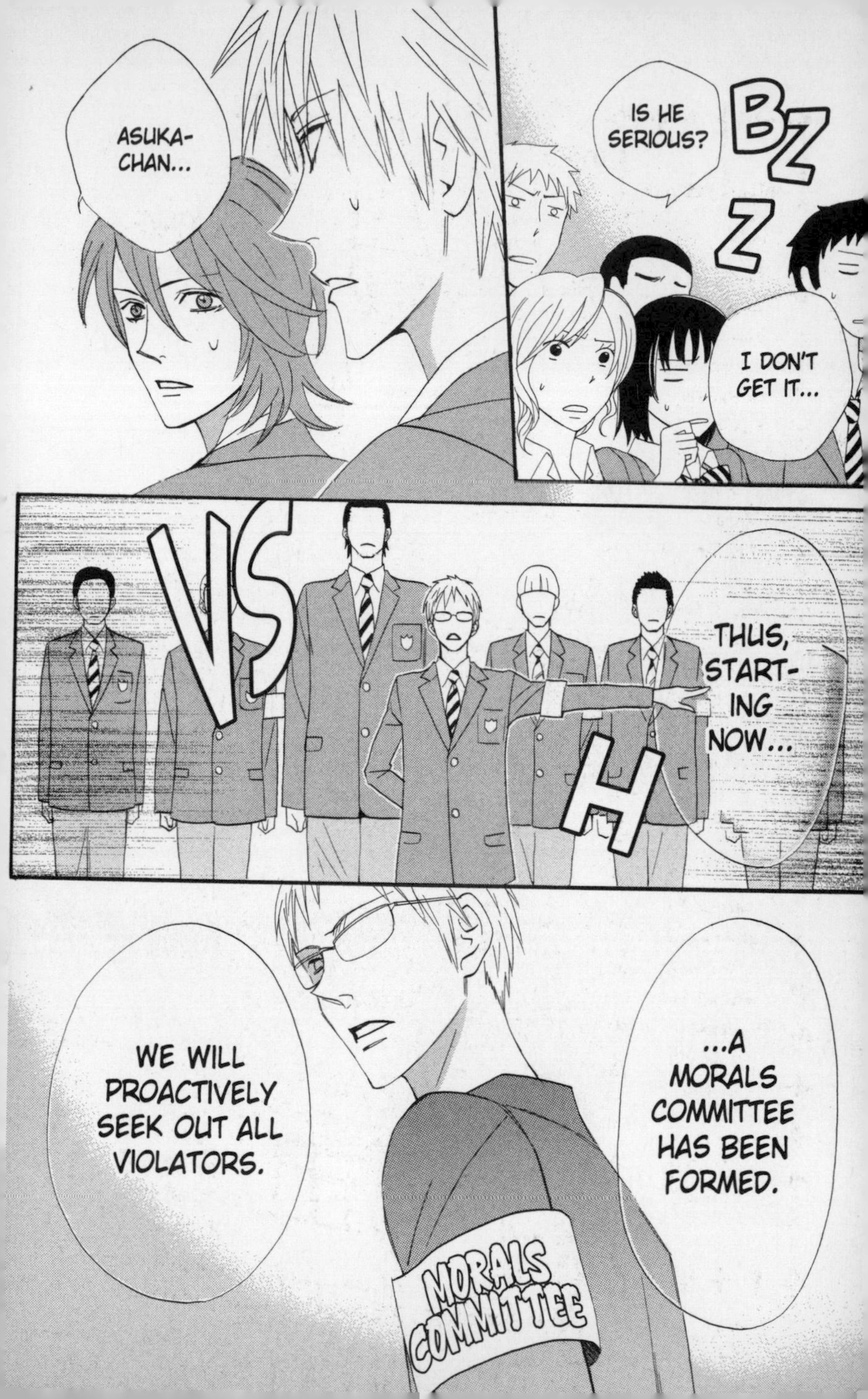
BZZ
IS HE SERIOUS?
I DON'T GET IT...
ASUKA-CHAN...
THUS, STARTING NOW...
H
VS
...A MORALS COMMITTEE HAS BEEN FORMED.
WE WILL PROACTIVELY SEEK OUT ALL VIOLATORS.
MORALS COMMITTEE

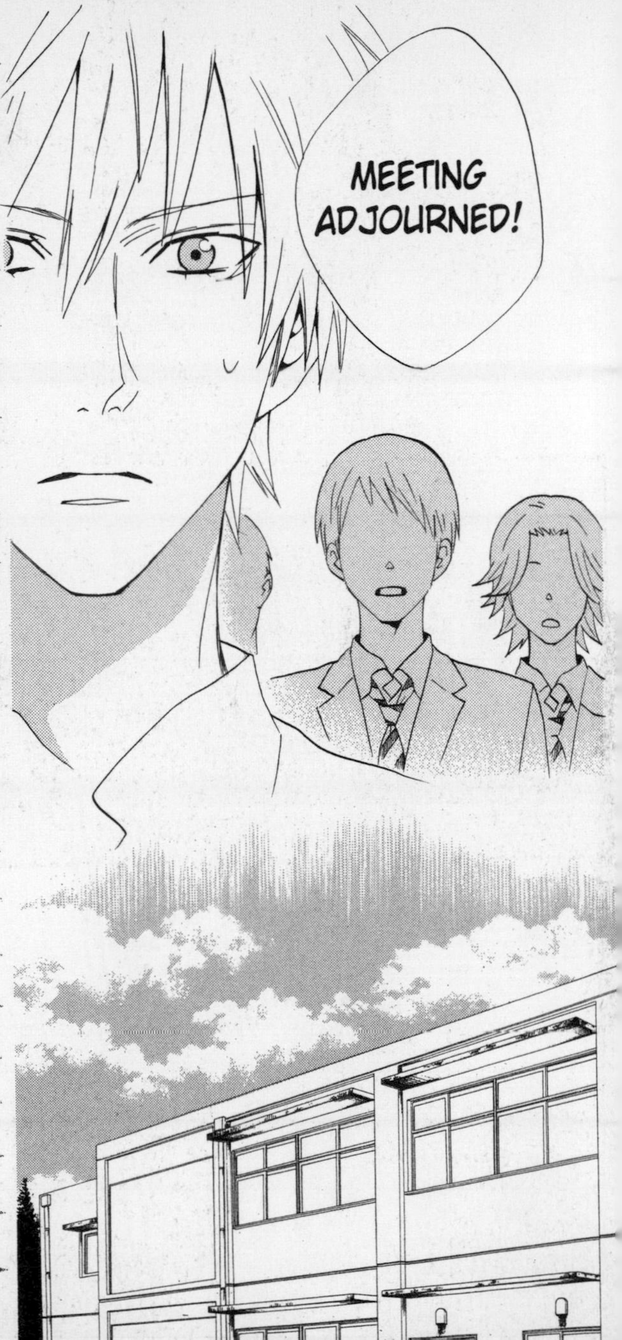
MEETING ADJOURNED!

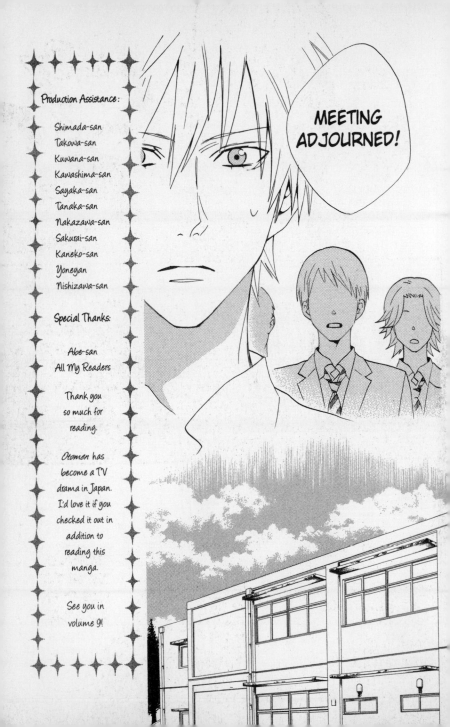

Production Assistance:

Shimada-san
Takowa-san
Kuwana-san
Kawashima-san
Sayaka-san
Tanaka-san
Nakazawa-san
Sakurai-san
Kaneko-san
Yoneyan
Nishizawa-san

Special Thanks:

Abe-san
All My Readers

Thank you so much for reading.

Otomen has become a TV drama in Japan. I'd love it if you checked it out in addition to reading this manga.

See you in volume 9!

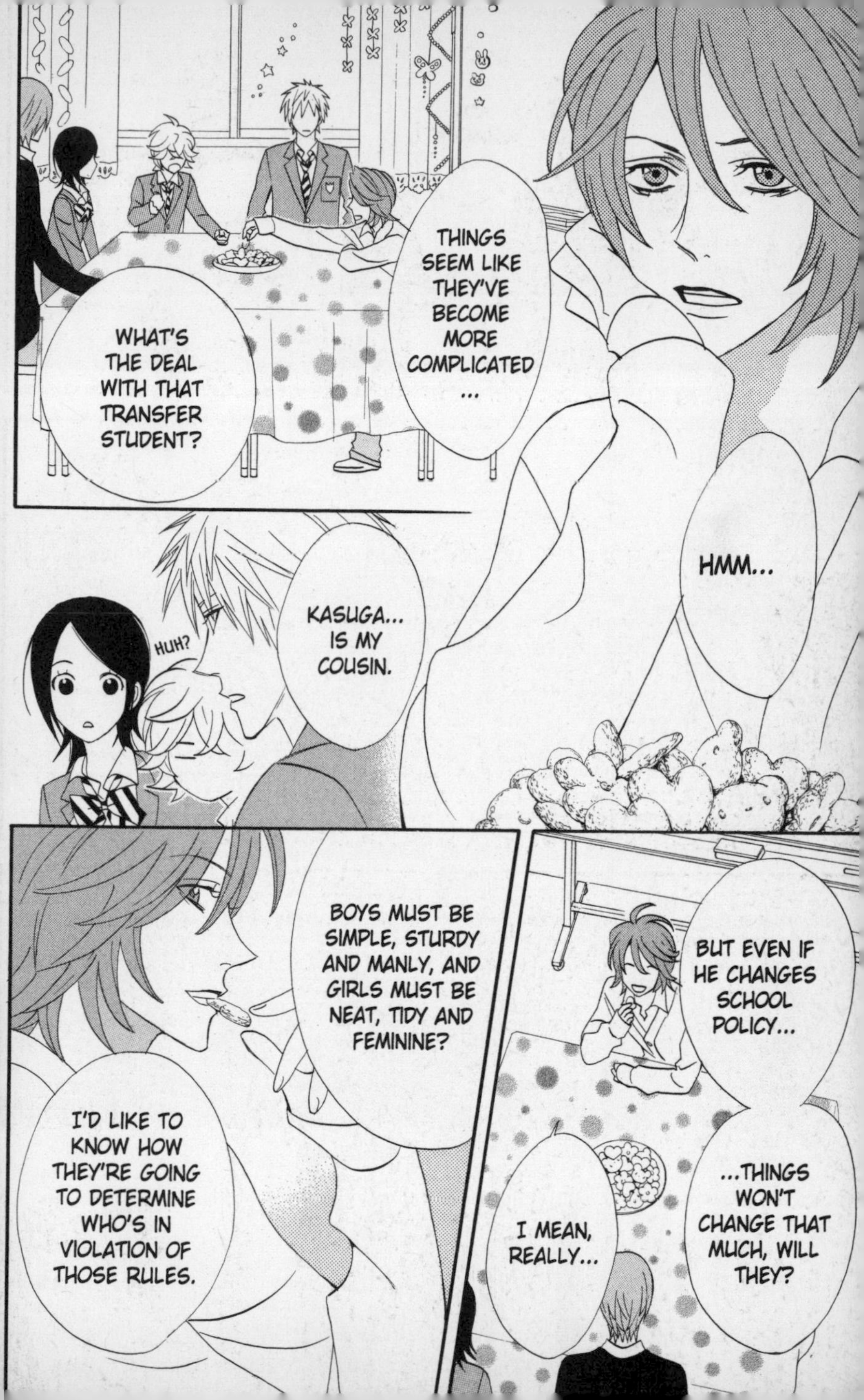
THINGS SEEM LIKE THEY'VE BECOME MORE COMPLICATED...
HMM...
WHAT'S THE DEAL WITH THAT TRANSFER STUDENT?
HUH?
KASUGA... IS MY COUSIN.
BUT EVEN IF HE CHANGES SCHOOL POLICY...
...THINGS WON'T CHANGE THAT MUCH, WILL THEY?
I MEAN, REALLY...
BOYS MUST BE SIMPLE, STURDY AND MANLY, AND GIRLS MUST BE NEAT, TIDY AND FEMININE?
I'D LIKE TO KNOW HOW THEY'RE GOING TO DETERMINE WHO'S IN VIOLATION OF THOSE RULES.

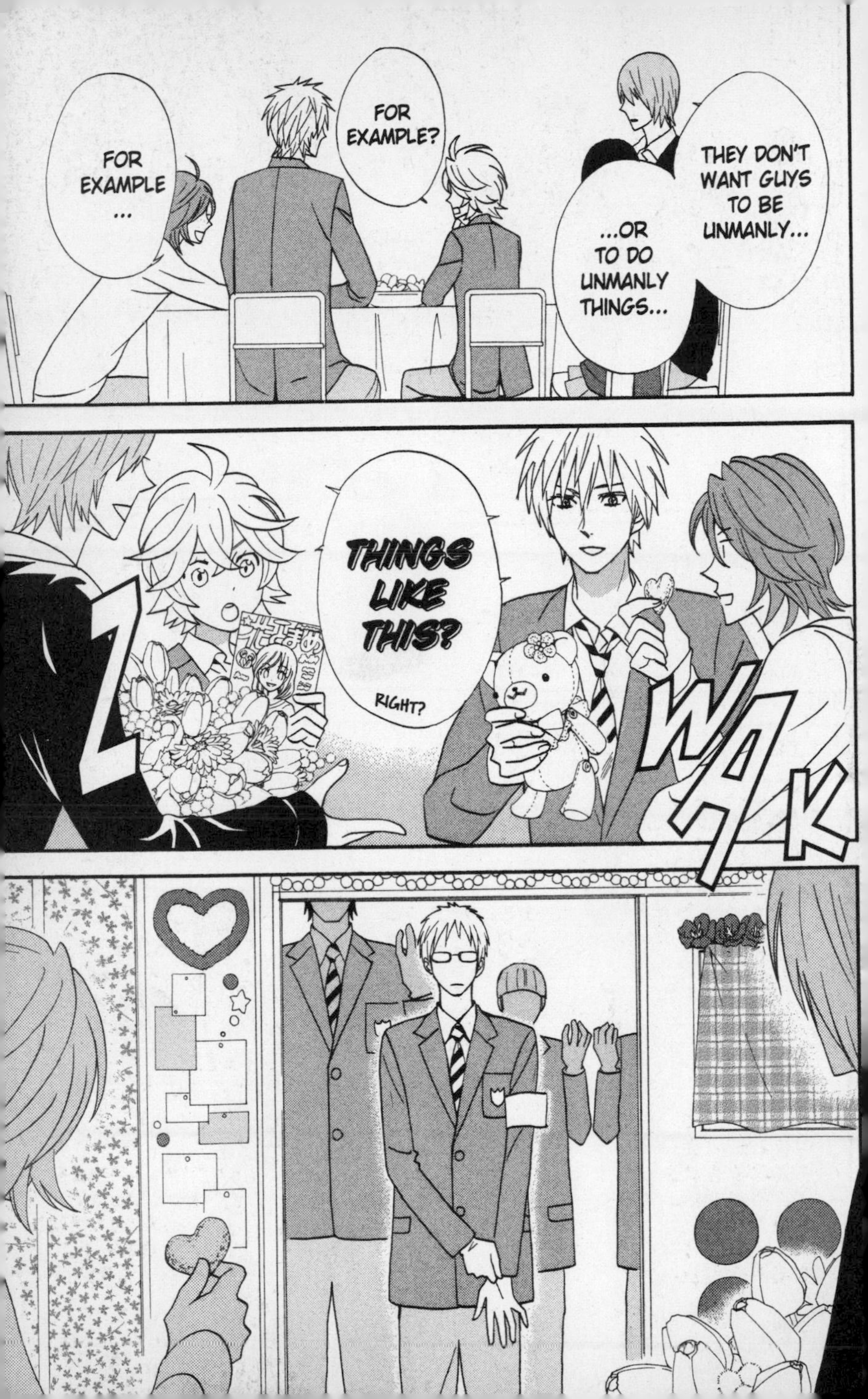
THEY DON'T WANT GUYS TO BE UNMANLY...
...OR TO DO UNMANLY THINGS...
FOR EXAMPLE?
FOR EXAMPLE ...
WAK
THINGS LIKE THIS?
RIGHT?

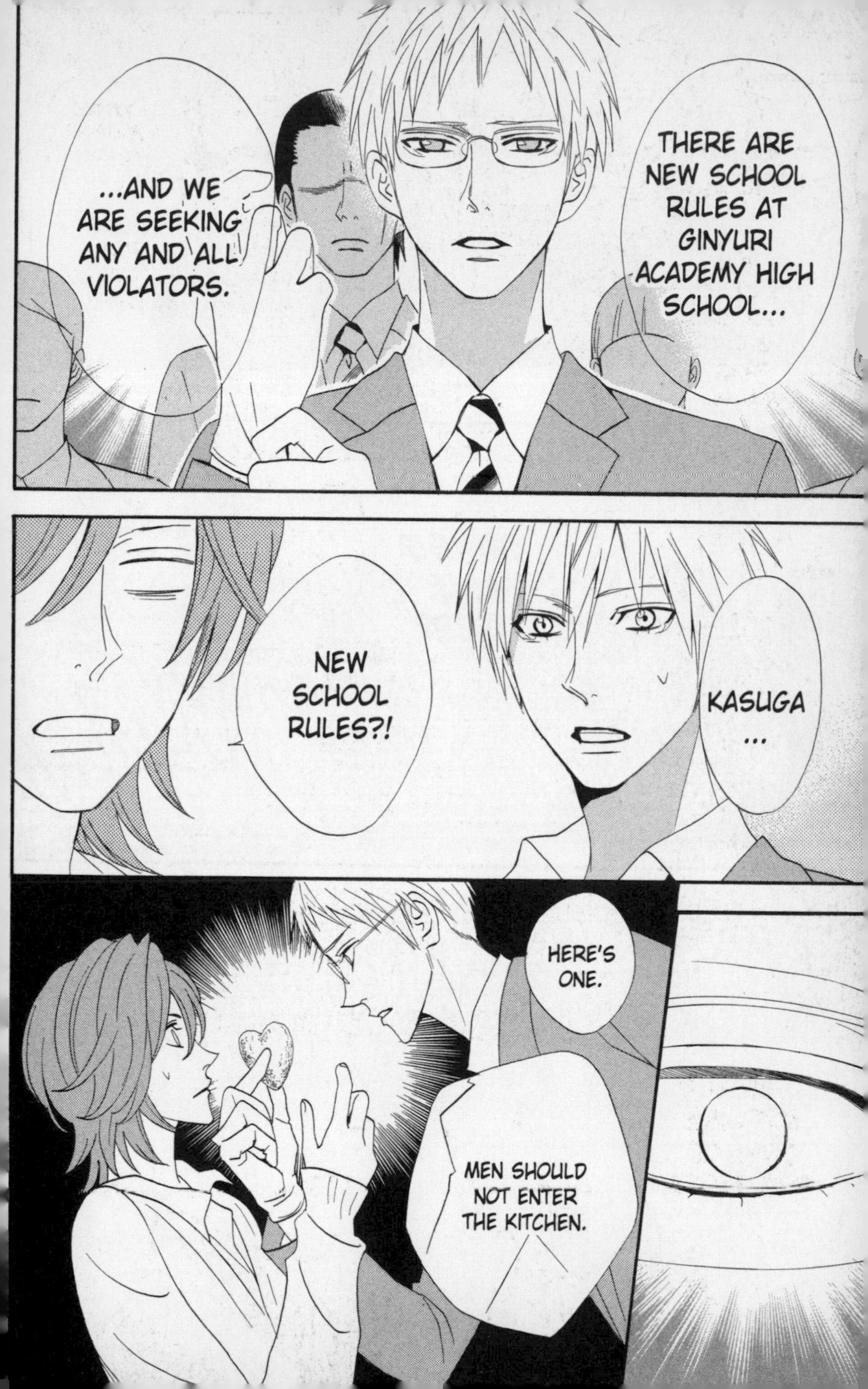
THERE ARE NEW SCHOOL RULES AT GINYURI ACADEMY HIGH SCHOOL...
...AND WE ARE SEEKING ANY AND ALL VIOLATORS.
KASUGA ...
NEW SCHOOL RULES?!
HERE'S ONE.
MEN SHOULD NOT ENTER THE KITCHEN.

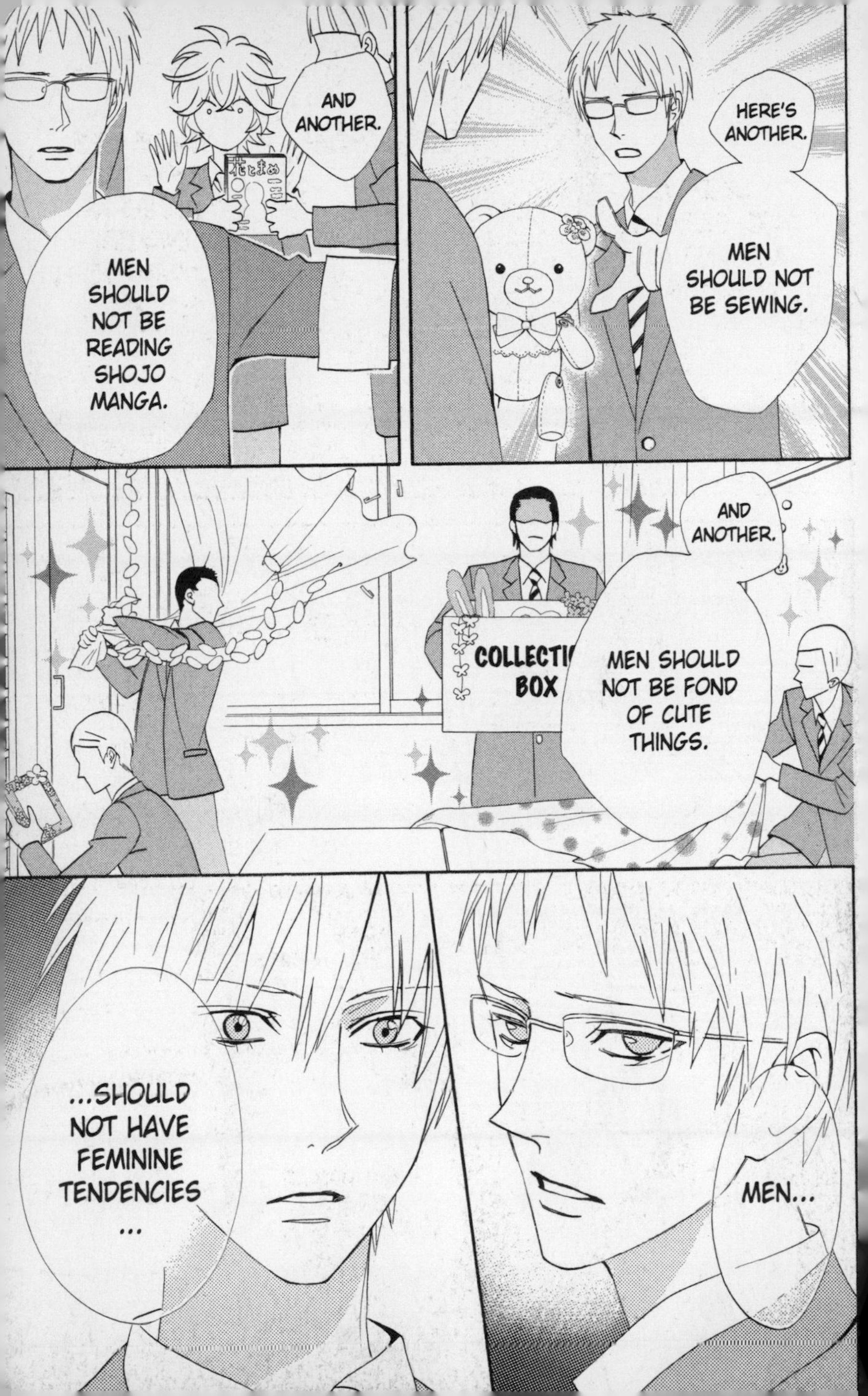
HERE'S ANOTHER.
MEN SHOULD NOT BE SEWING.
AND ANOTHER.
MEN SHOULD NOT BE READING SHOJO MANGA.
AND ANOTHER.
MEN SHOULD NOT BE FOND OF CUTE THINGS.
COLLECTI BOX
MEN...
...SHOULD NOT HAVE FEMININE TENDENCIES ...

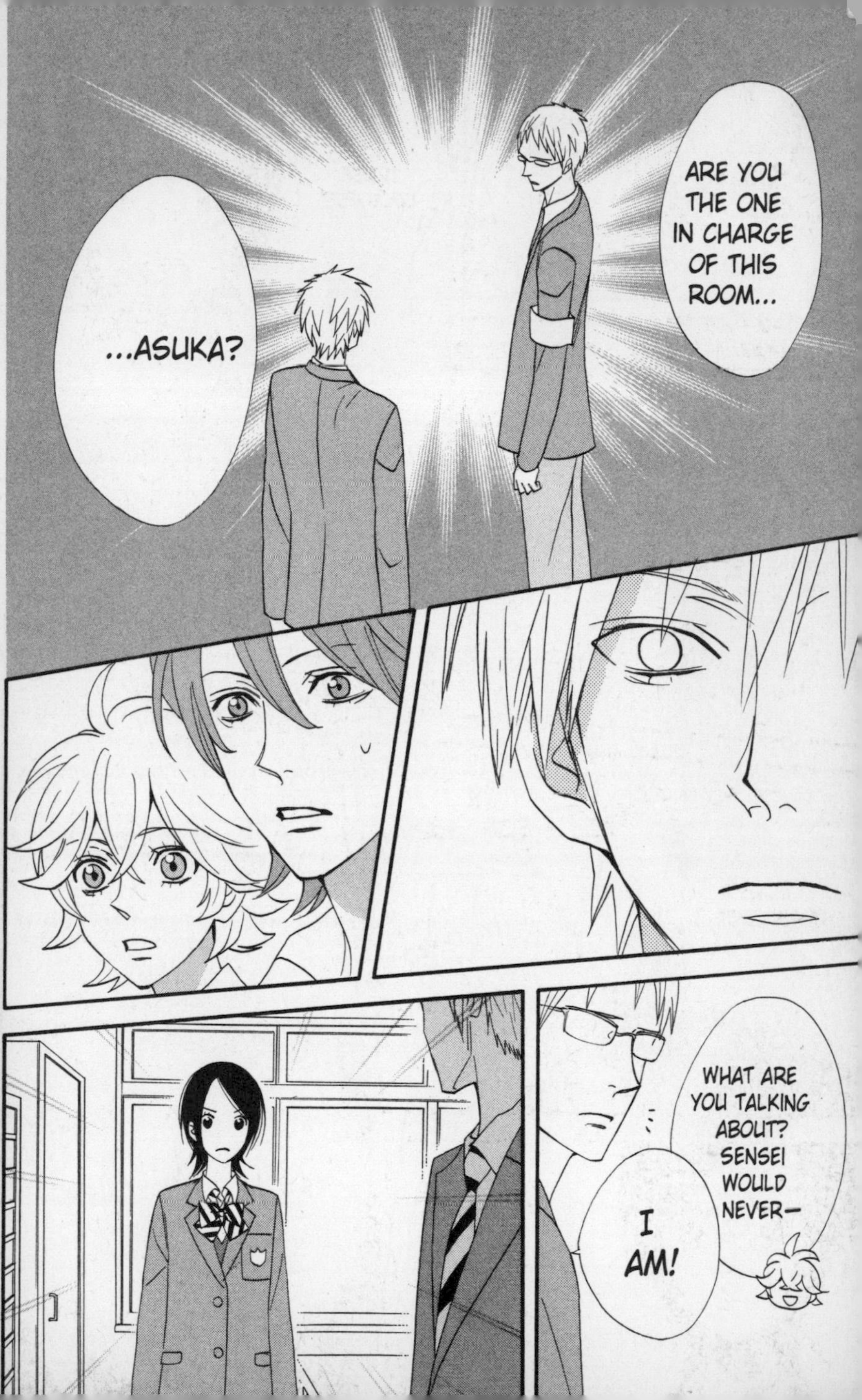
ARE YOU THE ONE IN CHARGE OF THIS ROOM...
...ASUKA?
WHAT ARE YOU TALKING ABOUT? SENSEI WOULD NEVER—
I AM!

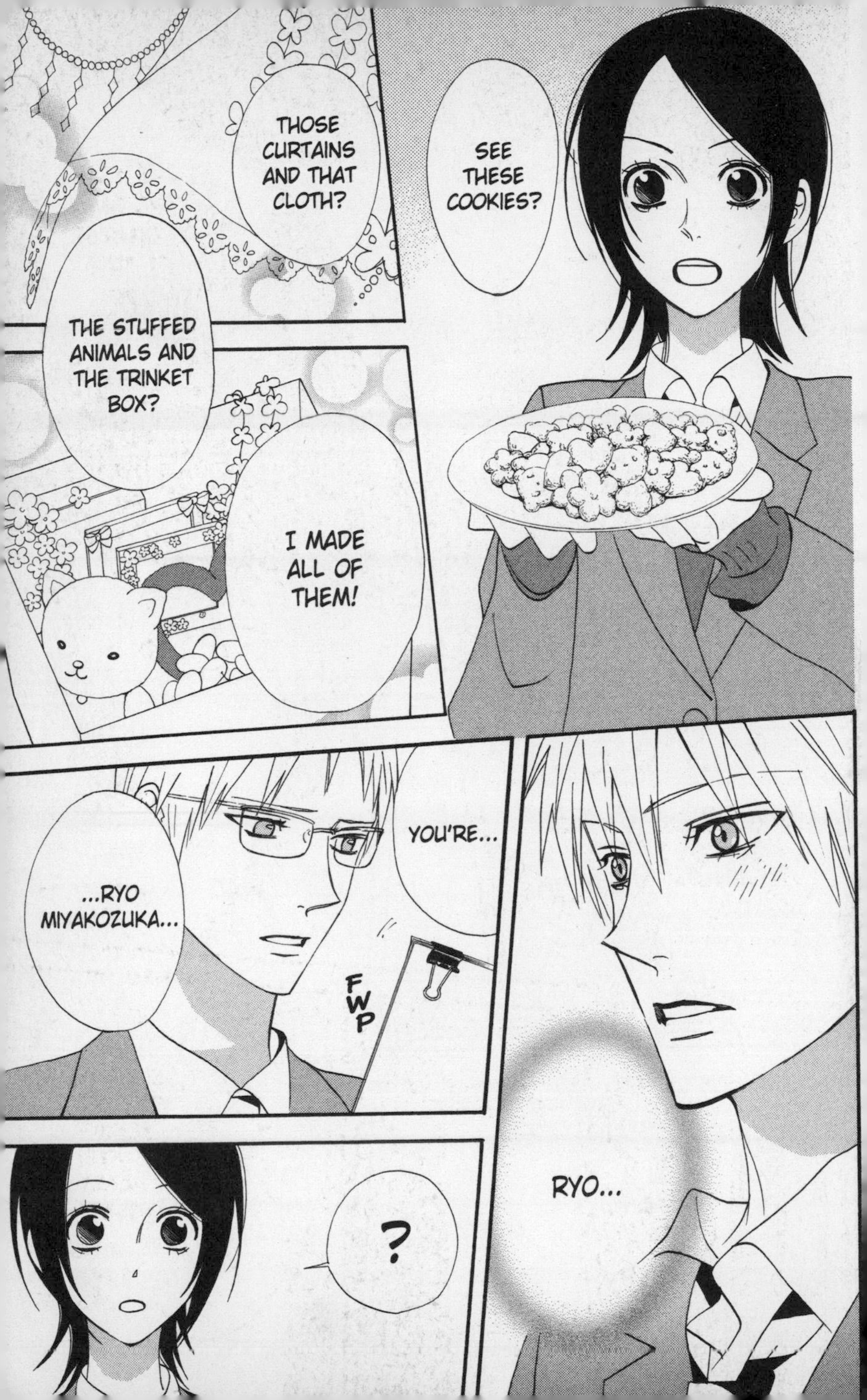
SEE THESE COOKIES?
THOSE CURTAINS AND THAT CLOTH?
THE STUFFED ANIMALS AND THE TRINKET BOX?
I MADE ALL OF THEM!
RYO...
YOU'RE...
...RYO MIYAKOZUKA...
FWP
?

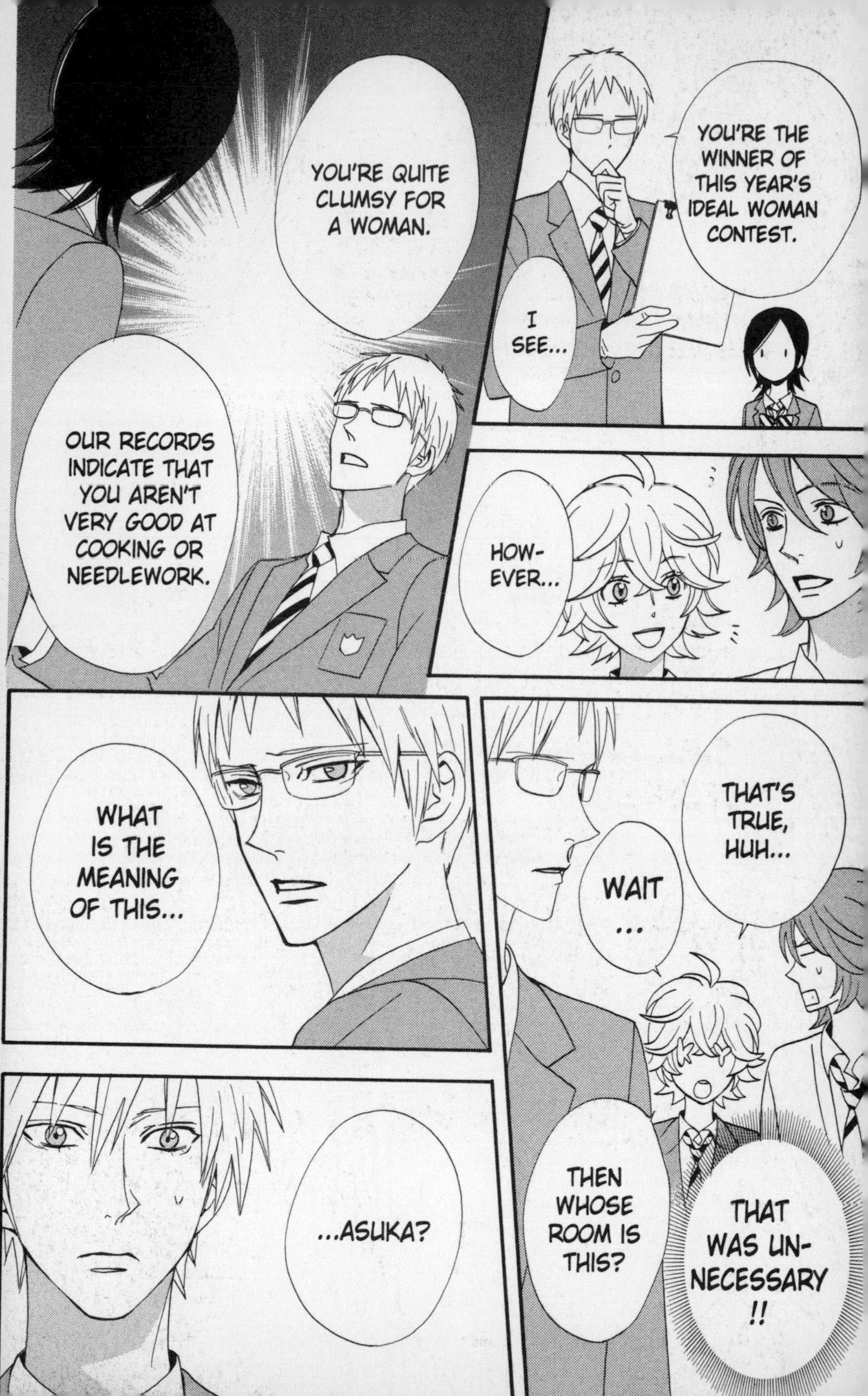
YOU'RE THE WINNER OF THIS YEAR'S IDEAL WOMAN CONTEST.
I SEE...
HOW-EVER...
YOU'RE QUITE CLUMSY FOR A WOMAN.
OUR RECORDS INDICATE THAT YOU AREN'T VERY GOOD AT COOKING OR NEEDLEWORK.
THAT'S TRUE, HUH...
WAIT...
THAT WAS UN-NECESSARY!!
THEN WHOSE ROOM IS THIS?
WHAT IS THE MEANING OF THIS...
...ASUKA?

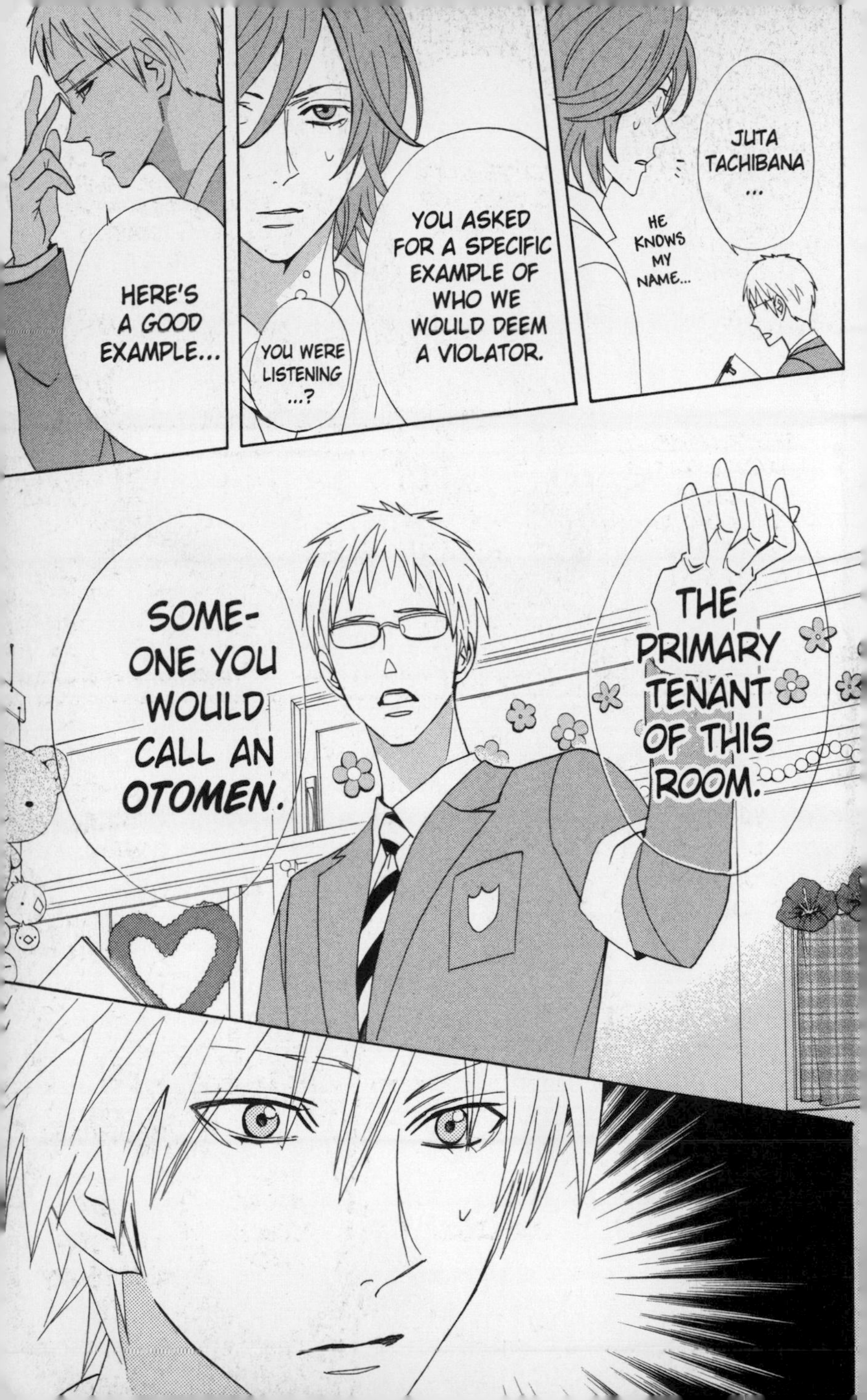
JUTA TACHIBANA ...
HE KNOWS MY NAME...
YOU ASKED FOR A SPECIFIC EXAMPLE OF WHO WE WOULD DEEM A VIOLATOR.
YOU WERE LISTENING ...?
HERE'S A GOOD EXAMPLE...
THE PRIMARY TENANT OF THIS ROOM.
SOME-ONE YOU WOULD CALL AN OTOMEN.

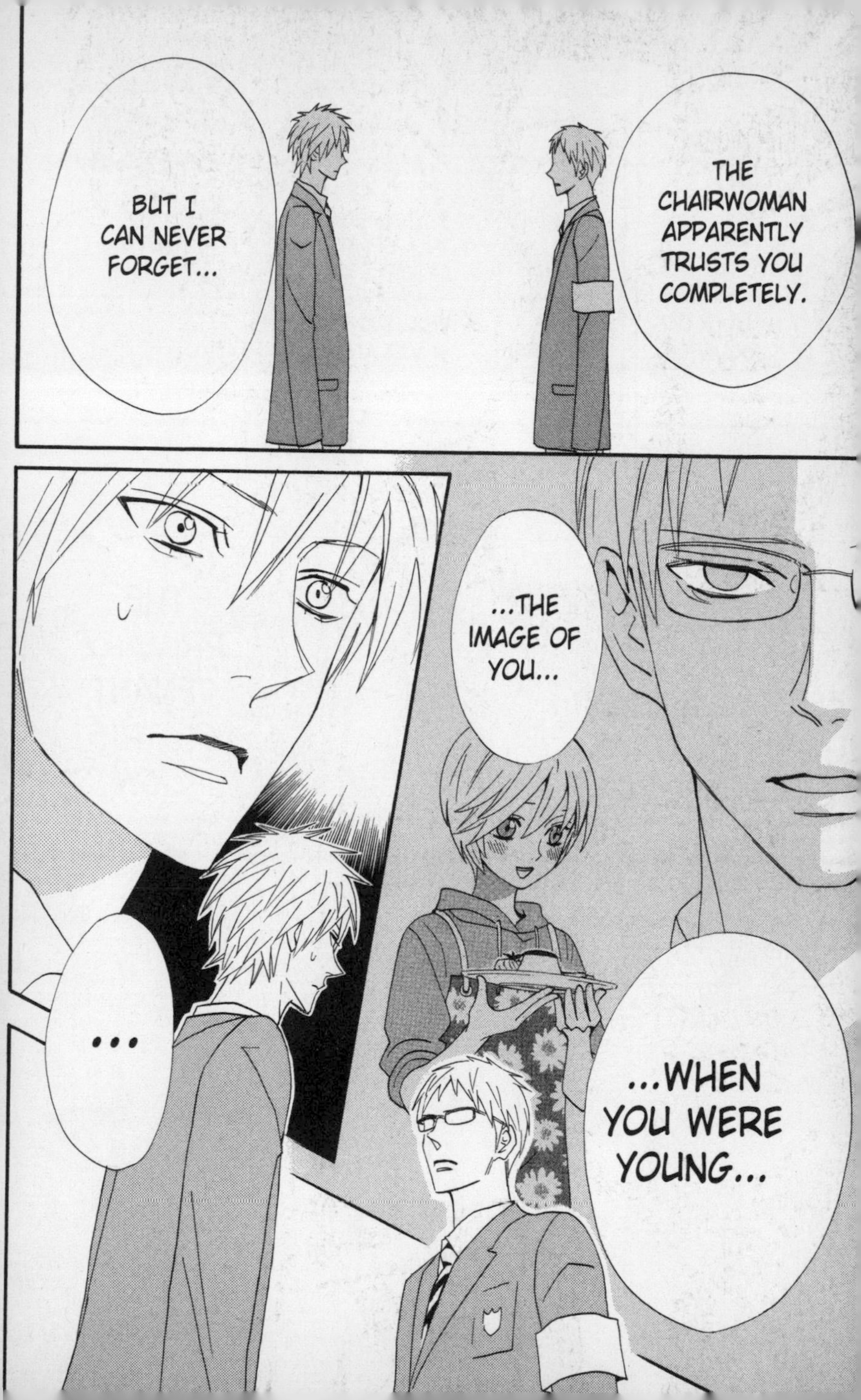
THE CHAIRWOMAN APPARENTLY TRUSTS YOU COMPLETELY.
BUT I CAN NEVER FORGET...
...THE IMAGE OF YOU...
...WHEN YOU WERE YOUNG...
...

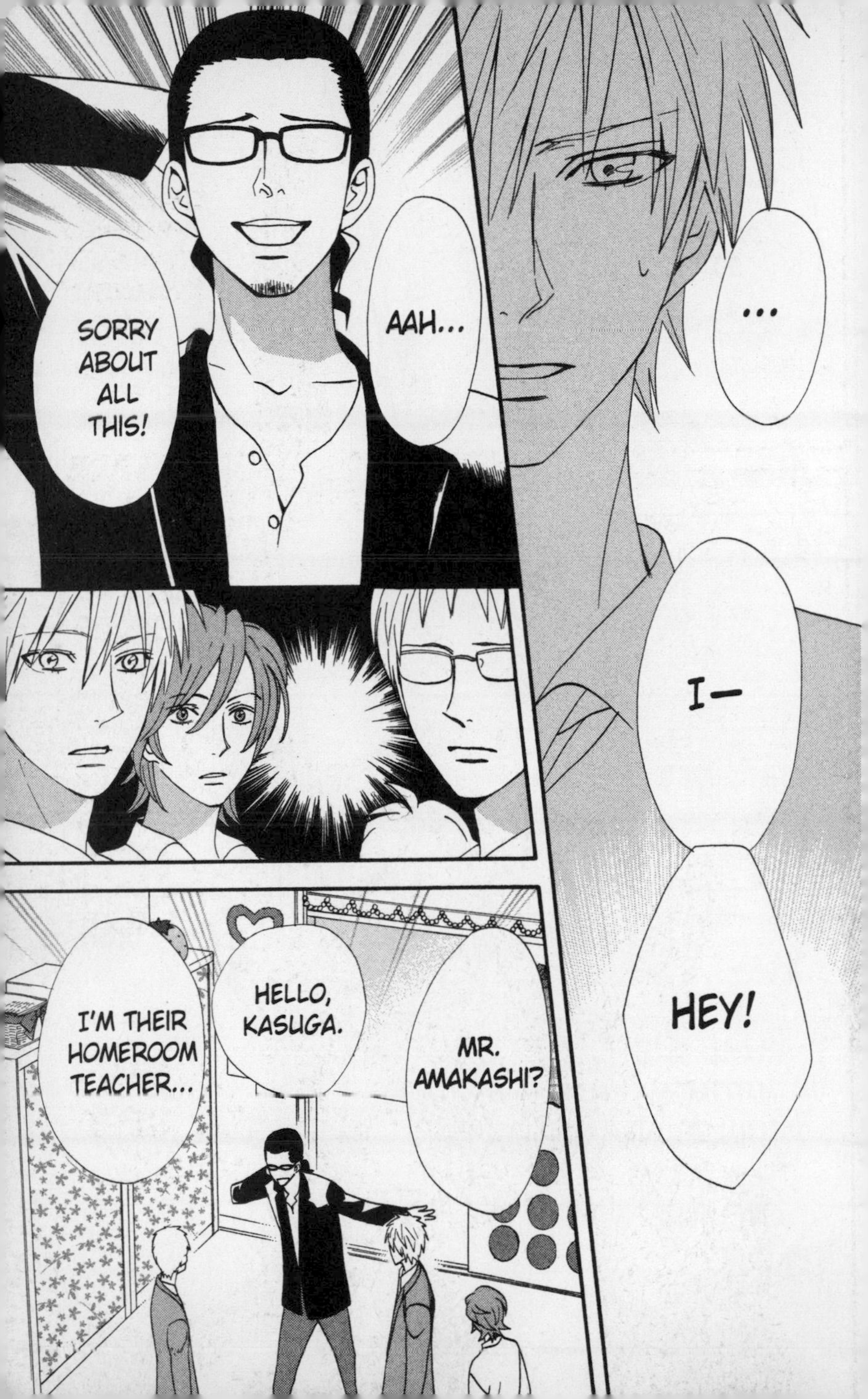
...
I—
HEY!
AAH...
SORRY ABOUT ALL THIS!
MR. AMAKASHI?
HELLO, KASUGA.
I'M THEIR HOMEROOM TEACHER...

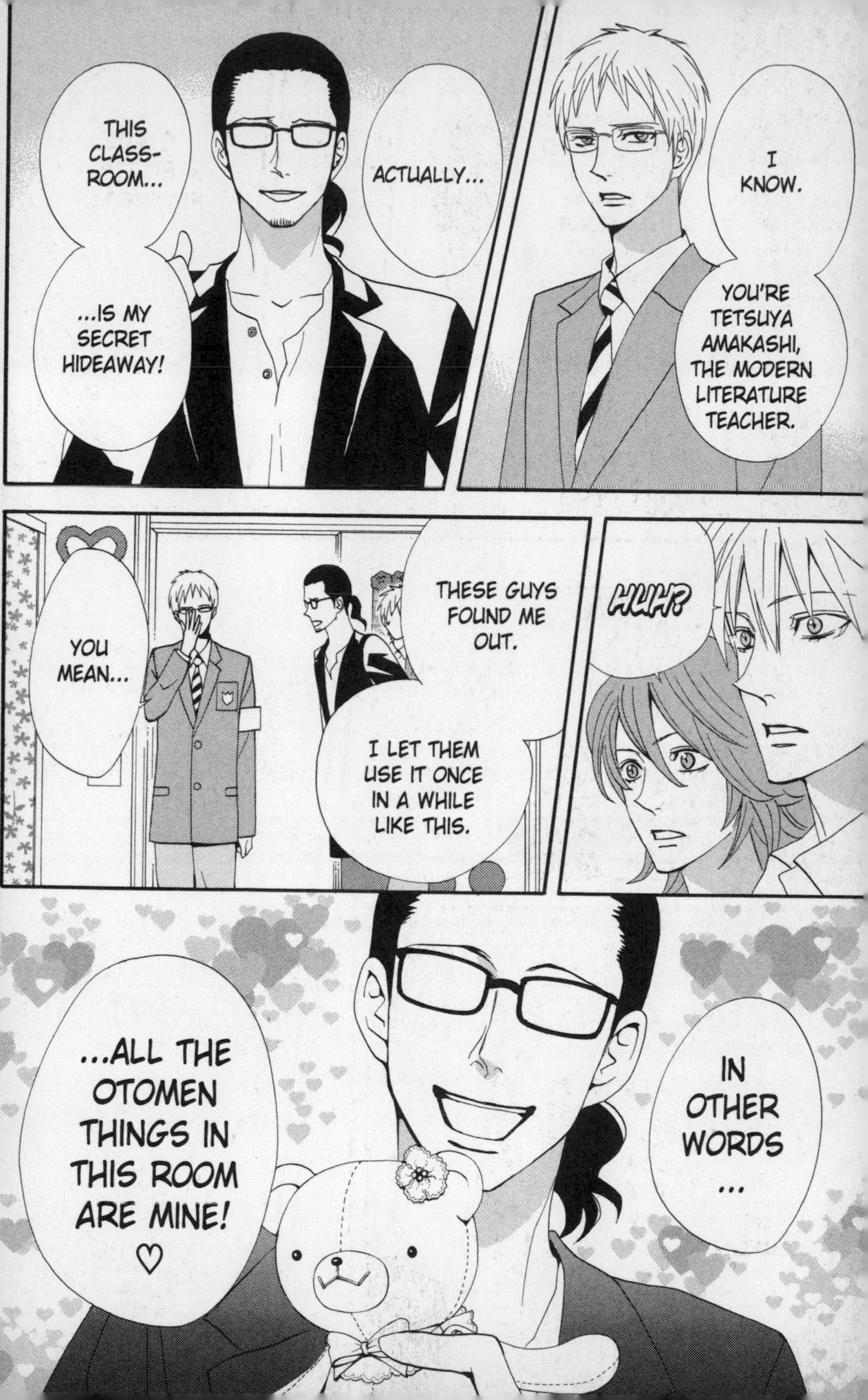
I KNOW.
YOU'RE TETSUYA AMAKASHI, THE MODERN LITERATURE TEACHER.
ACTUALLY...
THIS CLASS-ROOM...
...IS MY SECRET HIDEAWAY!
HUH?
THESE GUYS FOUND ME OUT.
YOU MEAN...
I LET THEM USE IT ONCE IN A WHILE LIKE THIS.
IN OTHER WORDS...
...ALL THE OTOMEN THINGS IN THIS ROOM ARE MINE! ♡

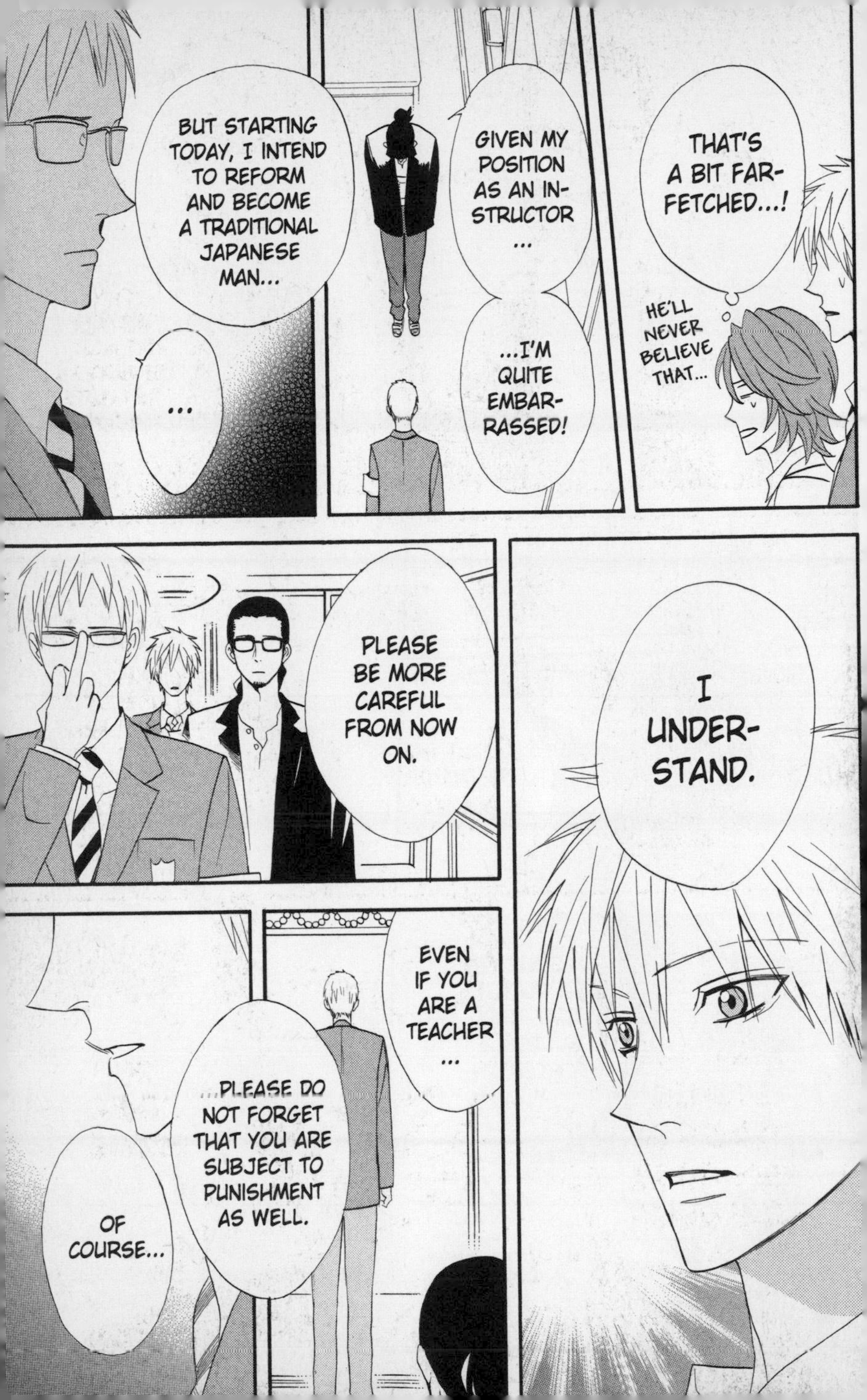
THAT'S A BIT FAR-FETCHED...!
HE'LL NEVER BELIEVE THAT...
GIVEN MY POSITION AS AN IN-STRUCTOR...
...I'M QUITE EMBAR-RASSED!
BUT STARTING TODAY, I INTEND TO REFORM AND BECOME A TRADITIONAL JAPANESE MAN...
...
I UNDER-STAND.
PLEASE BE MORE CAREFUL FROM NOW ON.
EVEN IF YOU ARE A TEACHER...
...PLEASE DO NOT FORGET THAT YOU ARE SUBJECT TO PUNISHMENT AS WELL.
OF COURSE...

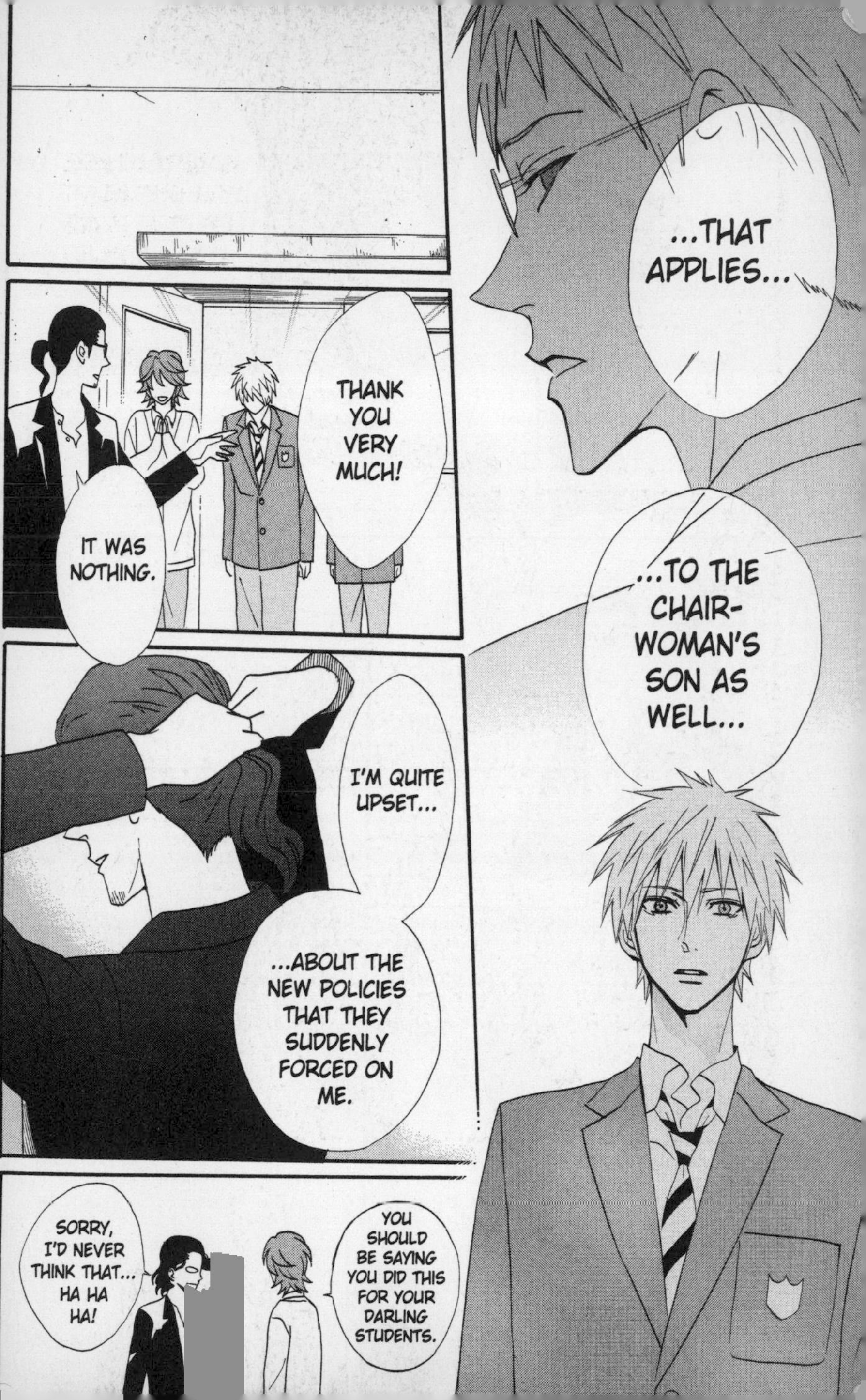
...THAT APPLIES...
...TO THE CHAIR-WOMAN'S SON AS WELL...
THANK YOU VERY MUCH!
IT WAS NOTHING.
I'M QUITE UPSET...
...ABOUT THE NEW POLICIES THAT THEY SUDDENLY FORCED ON ME.
YOU SHOULD BE SAYING YOU DID THIS FOR YOUR DARLING STUDENTS.
SORRY, I'D NEVER THINK THAT... HA HA HA!

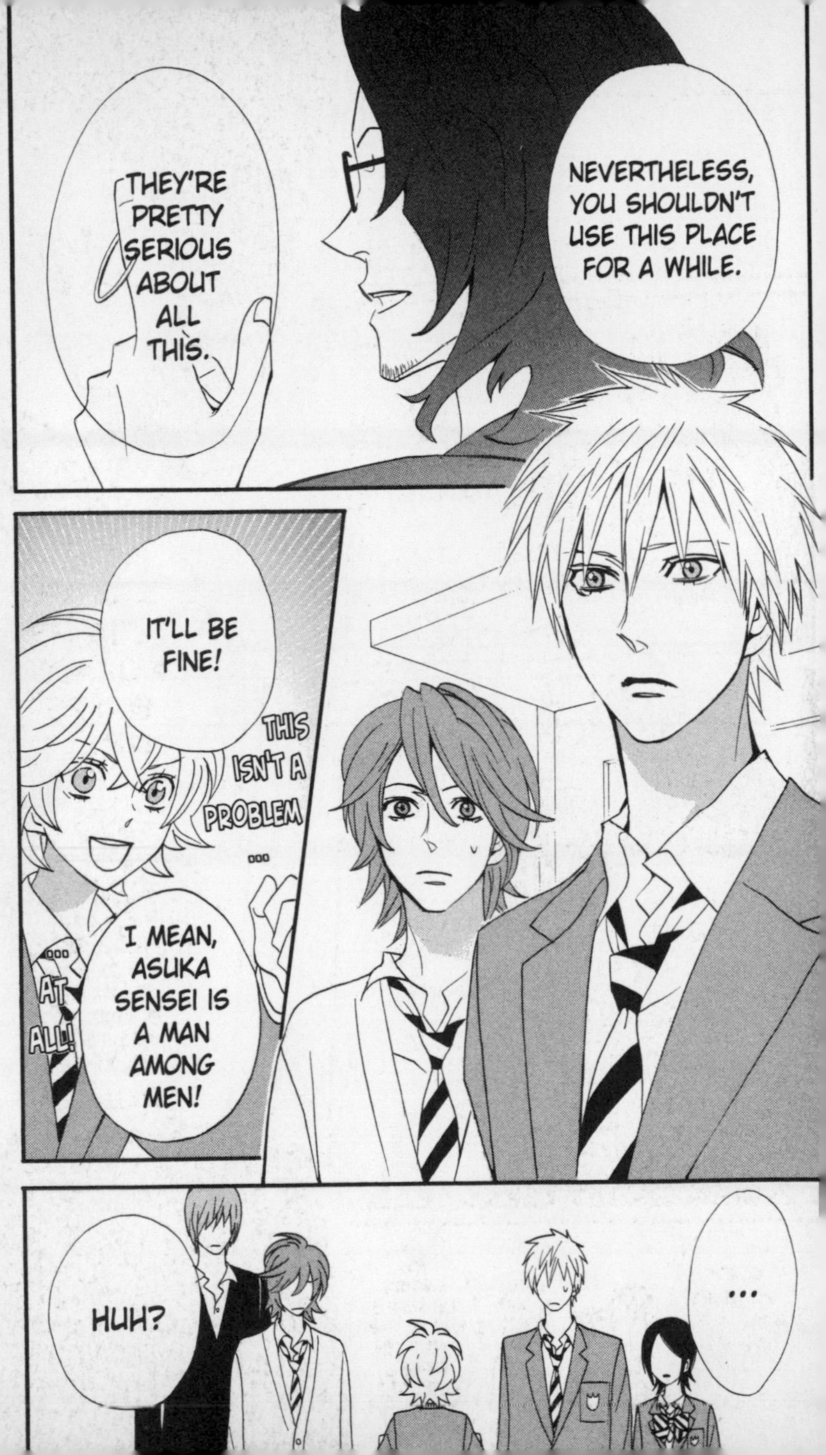
NEVERTHELESS, YOU SHOULDN'T USE THIS PLACE FOR A WHILE.
THEY'RE PRETTY SERIOUS ABOUT ALL THIS.
IT'LL BE FINE!
THIS ISN'T A PROBLEM ...
I MEAN, ASUKA SENSEI IS A MAN AMONG MEN!
... AT ALL!
...
HUH?

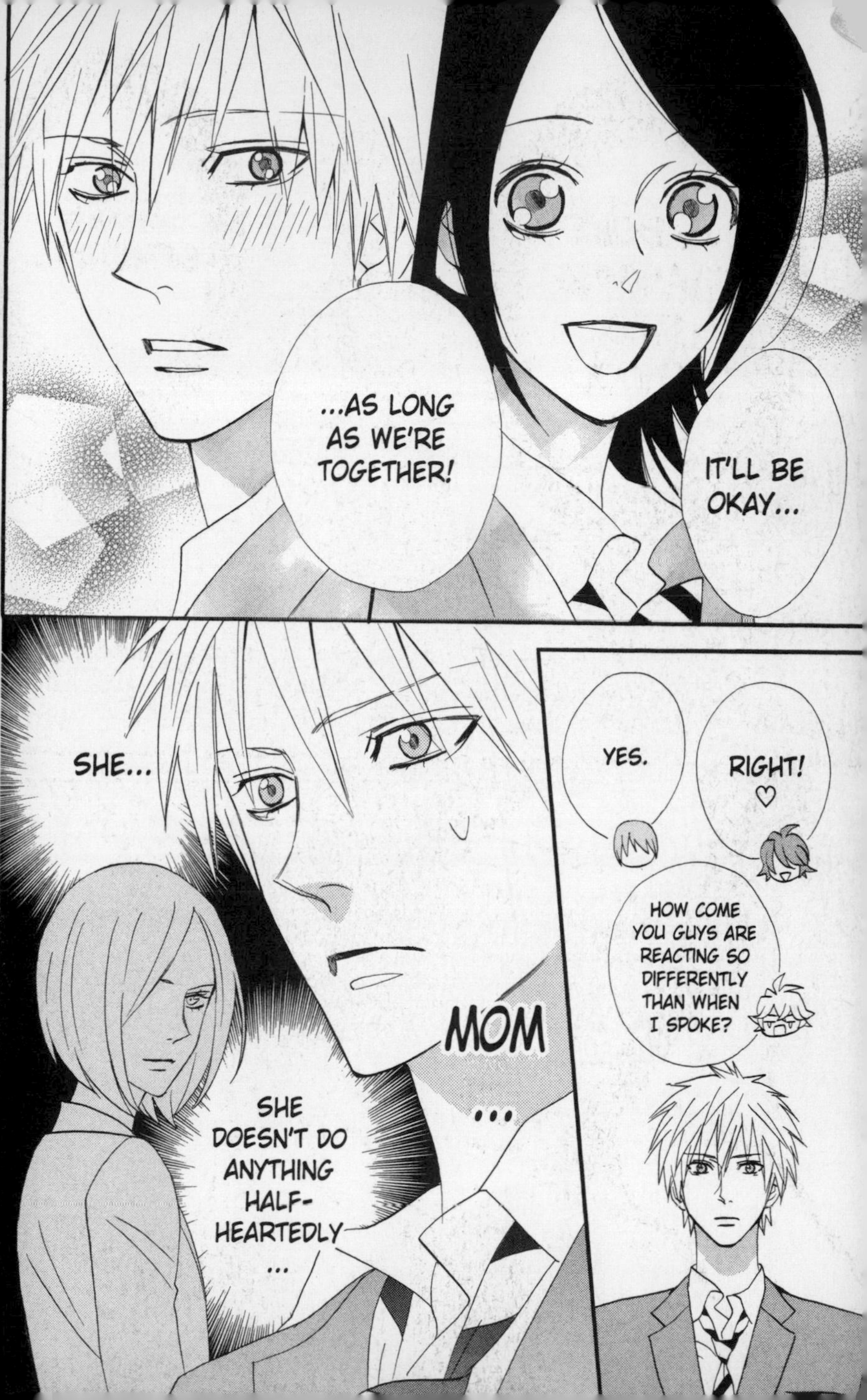
IT'LL BE OKAY...
...AS LONG AS WE'RE TOGETHER!
RIGHT! ♡
YES.
HOW COME YOU GUYS ARE REACTING SO DIFFERENTLY THAN WHEN I SPOKE?
SHE...
MOM
...
SHE DOESN'T DO ANYTHING HALF-HEARTEDLY
...

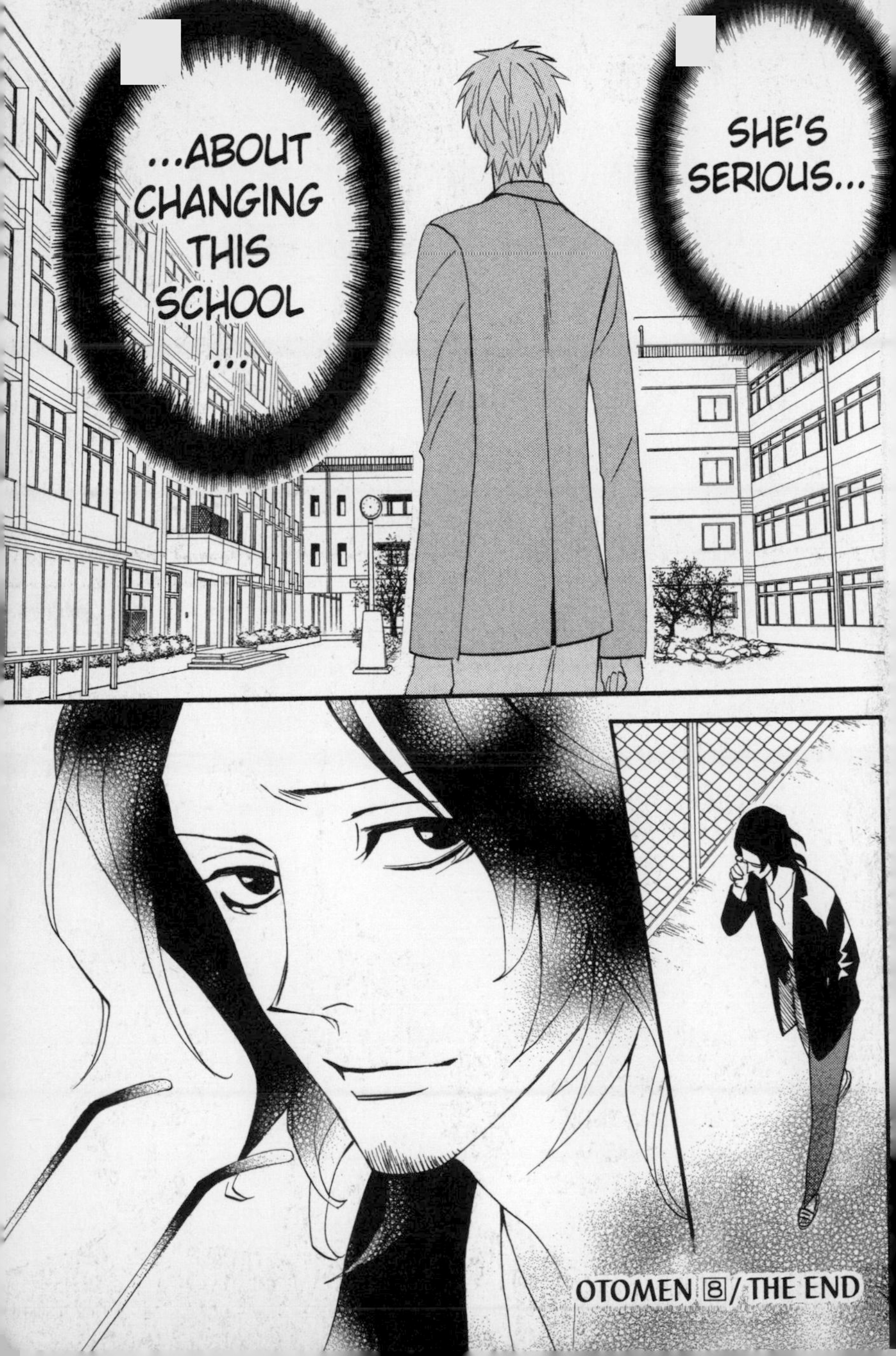
SHE'S SERIOUS...
...ABOUT CHANGING THIS SCHOOL
...
OTOMEN 8 / THE END

Confused by some of the terms, but too MANLY to ask for help?

Here are some **cultural notes** to assist you!

HONORIFICS

Chan – an informal honorific used to address children and females. *Chan* can also be used toward animals, lovers, intimate friends and people whom one has known since childhood.

San – the most common honorific title. It is used to address people outside one's immediate family and close circle of friends.

Sensei – honorific title used to address teachers as well as professionals such as doctors, lawyers and artists.

Sama – honorific used to address persons much higher in rank than oneself.

NOTES

Page 3 | Hana to Mame
The name *Hana to Mame* (Flowers and Beans) is a play on the real shojo manga magazine *Hana to Yume* (Flowers and Dreams) published by Hakusensha, Inc.

Page 3 | Tsun-sama
Juta makes this word up by combining *tsundere* and *ore-sama*. *Tsundere* describes a character who is *tsuntsun* (cold or irritable) and later becomes *deredere* (affectionate or sentimental). *Ore-sama* describes a pompous and arrogant person, as it combines *ore* (me) with the honorific *sama*.

Page 8, panel 3 | Fukuoka
Located on the island of Kyushu in Japan, Fukuoka City is about 686 miles away from Tokyo. On page 49, there is a train bound for Hakata, one of the wards in Fukuoka.

Page 21, panel 3 | Sayonalovers
In Japanese, the "ra" in *sayonara* (goodbye) sounds like the "lo" part of "lovers." Yamato drops the "ra" part when he combines these two words to create the word "sayonalovers."

Page 26, panel 1 | Okaeri
The characters on the ground spell out *okaeri*, which means "welcome back."

Page 79, panel 4 | Mas Oyama
Masutatsu Oyama, also known as Mas Oyama, was a famous karate master/instructor who founded an extremely influential style of full-contact karate.

Page 96, panel 4 | Soba and Mochi
In Japan, it's traditional to eat *toshikoshi soba* (buckwheat noodles) on New Year's Eve and to eat *mochi* (pounded sticky rice) on New Year's Day.

Aya Kanno was born in Tokyo, Japan.
She is the creator of *Soul Rescue* and *Blank Slate*
(originally published as *Akusaga* in Japan's
BetsuHana magazine). Her latest work, *Otomen*,
is currently being serialized in *BetsuHana*.

OTOMEN
Vol. 8
Shojo Beat Edition

Story and Art by | **AYA KANNO**

Translation & Adaptation | **JN Productions**
Touch-up Art & Lettering | **Mark McMurray**
Design | **Fawn Lau**
Editor | **Amy Yu**

VP, Production | **Alvin Lu**
VP, Sales & Product Marketing | **Gonzalo Ferreyra**
VP, Creative | **Linda Espinosa**
Publisher | **Hyoe Narita**

Otomen by Aya Kanno © Aya Kanno 2009
All rights reserved. First published in Japan in 2009 by HAKUSENSHA, Inc., Tokyo.
English language translation rights arranged with HAKUSENSHA, Inc., Tokyo.

The rights of the author(s) of the work(s) in this publication to be so identified
have been asserted in accordance with the Copyright, Designs and Patents Act 1988.
A CIP catalogue record for this book is available from the British Library.

Printed in the U.S.A.

Published by VIZ Media, LLC
P.O. Box 77010
San Francisco, CA 94107

10 9 8 7 6 5 4 3 2 1
First printing, November 2010

PARENTAL ADVISORY
OTOMEN is rated T for Teen and is recommended
for ages 13 and up. This volume contains
suggestive themes.
ratings.viz.com

www.viz.com

www.shojobeat.com

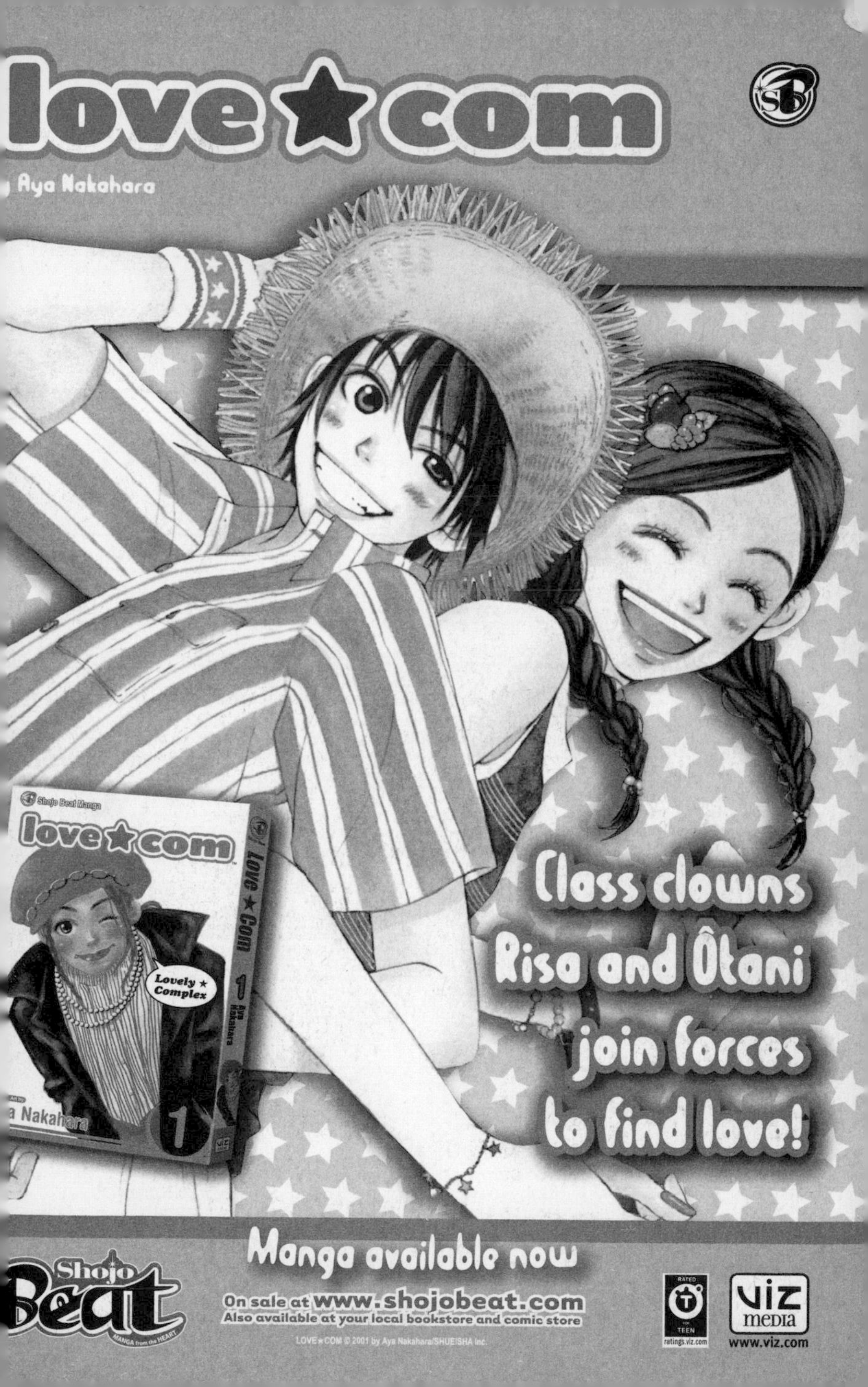

love★com
Aya Nakahara
Shojo Beat Manga
love★com
Love★Com
1
Aya Nakahara
Lovely★ Complex
a Nakahara
1
Class clowns Risa and Ôtani join forces to find love!
Manga available now
Shojo Beat
MANGA from the HEART
On sale at www.shojobeat.com
Also available at your local bookstore and comic store
LOVE★COM © 2001 by Aya Nakahara/SHUEISHA Inc.
RATED
T
TEEN
ratings.viz.com
VIZ media
www.viz.com